KEEPING QUIET

Also by Julian Dutton:

Shakespeare's Journey Home:
A Traveller's Guide Through Elizabethan England

The Bumper Book of Curious Clubs:
A Miscellany of the World's Oddest Organisations & Strangest Societies

KEEPING QUIET

Visual Comedy in the Age of Sound

Julian Dutton

CHAPLIN BOOKS

www.chaplinbooks.co.uk

First published in 2015 by Chaplin Books

ISBN 978-1-909183-77-3

A CIP catalogue record for this book is available from The British Library

Design by Michael Walsh at The Better Book Company

Printed by Imprint Digital

Chaplin Books
1 Eliza Place
Gosport PO12 4UN
Tel: 023 9252 9020
www.chaplinbooks.co.uk

For Jack & Florence – my inspirations

CONTENTS

FOREWORD

Ah! Julian, I completely misunderstood. I had thought when agreeing on the phone to write a Foreword to this brand new (and admittedly impressively definitive) history of visual comedy that I merely had to come up with *four words*. In which case I was deliberating between 'Hello I am Matt' and 'Arsenal 5 Spurs 0'.

Now you tell me more is expected. I feel a bit of a fraud, though. *Pompidou*, the series that you, me and Ashley Blaker have co-created and co-written is far from silent. The eponymous Pompidou jabbers away a good deal more than the characters in most sitcoms. However, the words that come from his big fat mouth are in a gibberish language hitherto unspoken, which is why you are crowbarring *Pompidou* into this book. After all, we've always thought of the show as a visual comedy, a 'live-action cartoon' if you will, and it was certainly created with the intention of being something that audiences from all nations could despise equally.

Nonetheless I do think it's a bit rich that I'm expected not only to read this bloody book but write a so-called Foreword about it. In asking me to give up my precious time to write this, did you not stop to consider for one moment all the other things a man of my importance actually has to do in a day? There are beds to lie in until 3pm, crisps to eat, reality shows on Five to watch, and abusive tweets to read.

And though it pains me to say it, surely this Foreword would have been better written by popular entertainer David Walliams? After all, isn't he now the best-selling author in the bloody world or something? Or was he too busy swimming across another puddle?

No I will not write a Foreword to this (pretty flipping authoritative) brand new history of visual comedy since sound arrived in the late 1920s. Not a word, do you hear? Nothing! And if you dare print this I will sue you. In fact I won't just stop there. I'll sue your wife, your kids, your cousins, your friends. Hell, I'll even sue myself, just for the association.

Go write your own Foreword, you lazy git.

Matt Lucas

INTRODUCTION

On Easter Day in 1956 ageing comic Buster Keaton was cruising through the Hollywood hills in his dark blue Cadillac. He passed Charlie Chaplin's old estate, wound his way along the dry hot avenue by Harold Lloyd's mansion 'Greenacres', and headed along Summit Drive in San Ysidro Canyon towards Mary Pickford's decaying manor, 'Pickfair.' Pickford had been one of the greatest stars of the silent era and, now in her mid-sixties, was throwing a reunion party for everyone she'd known, on and off-screen, from those lost decades.

According to Keaton the gathering was a melancholy affair – a reunion of phantoms, a regrouping of the old guard whose careers had been brought to a juddering halt when Al Jolson first squeaked out 'you ain't heard nothin' yet!' in *The Jazz Singer*. Pickford's mansion was full of shadows and memories, drifting butlers, a sense of lost time. But one thing Mary said to Keaton that day stuck in his mind. He recalls her saying, *'It would have been more logical if silent pictures had grown out of the talkie instead of the other way round.'*

It is a commonly held belief that on October 6 1927 when Jolson belted out those pioneering songs in *The Jazz Singer* he was sounding the death knell of silent film – and with it, visual comedy.

This is a myth. Certainly the careers of many silent comedians were damaged, if not ruined, by the microphone, and many had completed their best work anyway by the end of the 1920s and had already hung up their comedy hats, such as Harry Langdon. But just as many continued to make films throughout the 1930s and beyond, including the Big Four – Charlie Chaplin, Laurel & Hardy, Buster Keaton, and Harold Lloyd – all of whom released pictures throughout the first decade of the sound era but whose principal laughs still came from purely visual routines. In addition, new film comedians were appearing on the scene who were making talkies but whose schtick was nevertheless firmly rooted in the visual tradition of clowning, mime, routine-building, sight-gag and facial reaction – supreme comics like the Marx Brothers, W C Fields and Will Hay. These comedians didn't abandon visual comedy with the arrival of talkies; they simply bent the sound picture to their will. Later – in the 1940s and beyond – they would be joined by Jacques Tati, Norman Wisdom, Jerry Lewis, Ernie Kovacs, Eric Sykes and many more.

This book, then, is a history and celebration of visual comedy from *after* the appearance of sound in 1927 to the present day – a chronicle of non-verbal humour in the age of dialogue. Its primary *raison d'être* is

Voted by TV viewers as 'Britain's Funniest Ever Television Moment,' David Jason's stunt from John Sullivan's sitcom Only Fools and Horses *is more than mere pratfall. The toppling of the South London market trader as he attempts to impress a woman with his 'cool' is a joke that stretches back centuries, right to Ancient Rome via Shakespeare's Malvolio in* Twelfth Night *with his yellow cross-gartering – and is a sublime demonstration of the perennial puncturing of the male ego.*

to tell the stories of the lives and work of the great pantomimic clowns of the last eighty years, but it also aims to argue that visual comedy is a genre in its own right. Of course, there is one genre of TV and film that never abandoned visual comedy at all, and that is animation. Because of the wealth of existing books and studies on cartoon history, however, I have chosen in this book to focus solely on live-action humour.

Pickford's observation that *'It would have been more logical if silent pictures had grown out of the talkie instead of the other way round,'* was not simply that of an unemployed actress bitter at having been cast aside by her industry after a seismic technological innovation – it was an astute assessment of the aesthetic of film. Sound technology was, despite what we may think, *not* an advance in the cinematic art – it was actually a setback. It is only because silent comedy predates verbal comedy in the history of film technology that we view spoken comedy as a progression. The coming of sound occurred at the point where cinema was approaching a peak of artistic excellence: just as the aesthetic of free-flowing cinematic drama and comedy was exploding onscreen in the mid to late 20s, along came dialogue – and suddenly both camera and actor were bolted

As any parent will know through playing the ancient game of 'peekaboo', a perennial visual comedy device is the sudden appearance or disappearance of an object or human. Here Dawn French proves that someone falling down a hole will always be funny – as she plummets into a puddle in The Vicar of Dibley.

ruthlessly to the floor. Comedy became the static fast-talking two-shot, and the endlessly inventive long-shot visual routines of the silent decades – made possible by not having to record any actor's dialogue – became suddenly 'old-fashioned'.

Ever since, visual comedy has been perceived as an act of nostalgia, looked down on as a childish, almost idiot cousin to its more refined and literate elders, satire and observational humour. Indeed, the very word 'slapstick' conjures up images of crude violence, the comedy of the unsophisticated: the Three Stooges, the Chuckle Brothers, *Futtock's End, The Plank*. We may have laughed at that kind of stuff when were kids, but well, we've grown out of it now …

Yet in one of those recent ubiquitous TV chart-shows, *The Greatest TV Comedy Moments of all Time*, many of the top clips turned out to be sight-gags: Cleese's silly walks, Fawlty's goose-step, Dawn French collapsing into a puddle in *The Vicar of Dibley*, and – the winner – David Jason's Del Boy falling through the bar in the sitcom *Only Fools and Horses.* The latter formed the target of a sustained lampooning attack by Stewart Lee in his BBC2 series *Stewart Lee's Comedy Vehicle*: 'Is this what we really think is the funniest TV moment? Del Boy falling through a bar, and Trigger making a face? Is that really what we've come to, Britain?'

Lee's scorn for this comedy visual moment is not surprising, occupying as he does the position of comedy's *enfant-terrible*, an intellectual stand-up with a persistent distrust of the mainstream. Lee is one of the few original rebel artists working in comedy today, occupying a position at the end of a long line of Oxbridge satirists from Peter Cook to Armando Iannucci whose humour is verbal, intellectual, satirical and reflective. Visual comedy, slapstick – that's what our grandfathers laughed at: it belongs to the old days.

But does it?

Certainly through the 1930s and 40s, fast-talking comedy ousted pantomime and threatened to bury it for good – though Laurel & Hardy and Chaplin valiantly continued to produce visual music-hall material. But in 1949 James Agee wrote an article for *Life* magazine, 'Comedy's Greatest Era', a hymn to the glories of silent comedy and a lament for its side-lining. In this landmark piece Agee recognised visual comedy as a genre in its own right. Co-incidentally, around the same time as Agee's article appeared, across the Atlantic in France novelist Colette was penning a paean to an obscure vaudevillian named Jacques Tati.

Tati was a pantomimist who had been performing on the European cabaret circuit for nearly a decade. He knew visual comedy had never gone away (a view shared by Buster Keaton who, though demoted to the position of a hack gag-writer for M-G-M, was given standing ovations in Paris theatres after the war where he performed his old silent routines).

Tati went on to make a sequence of four comic, near-silent masterpieces between 1949 and 1967 – *Jour de Fête, Monsieur Hulot's Holiday, Mon Oncle* and *Playtime* – films which reinvented visual comedy and which set the bar of wordless humour so high that it has been scarcely reached since. The richness of Tati's gags – a traffic roundabout behaving like a fairground carousel; an inner tube gathering leaves as it rolls into a cemetery where, now covered in foliage, it becomes a funeral wreath – proved that purely visual comedy was far from being 'childish'. This was comedy of poetry and metaphor: a surreal playing with planes of vision.

Since Tati's revival of silent film comedy there have been periodic flowerings of wonderfully inventive pantomime – Norman Wisdom; Ernie Kovacs exploding onto American TV in the 50s with his surreal and largely visual conceits, including sketches containing only household objects; Jerry Lewis; Benny Hill's early innovative work; Pierre Etaix; Richard Hearne; Eric Sykes; Ronnie Barker; Marty Feldman's brilliant work in the late 60s and early 70s including his classic 'Long Distance Golfer' and 'Coach Tour'; The Goodies; Reeves & Mortimer; Harry Hill; Rowan Atkinson.

This book chronicles and celebrates this continuous but hitherto neglected tradition. In so doing, it sets out the argument that far from being the unsophisticated cousin of verbal comedy, slapstick has often achieved a greater level of satire and humanity than linguistic humour; and that it persists as a dynamic creative force, ripe for reinvention by anyone with the creative will to do so.

*

My love affair with silent comedy began as a small boy when I watched Bob Monkhouse's series *Mad Movies* on ITV between 1966 and 1967, and *The Golden Silents*, the BBC's slightly more upmarket version filmed at the National Film Theatre and presented by Michael Bentine, in 1969. The black-and-white antics of the clowns presented in these clip-shows were a revelation to me: the wild physical adventures of the Keystone Cops, Fatty Arbuckle, Chaplin, Keaton, Langdon, Snub Pollard and Ben Turpin, with their violence, chases, unrelenting pace, and unfailing championing of the underdog, had a powerful and long-lasting effect. They were my first taste of cinema comedy, and although the clips were of films made more than fifty years before I was born, the style and nature of these films formed a template in my brain which still acts today as a standard by which I measure all other film comedy.

For several years I sourced my love for visual humour from these black-and-white pioneers from the silent decades, and from the middle-aged lunacy of Richard Hearne's *Mr Pastry* or the stunts of Charlie Drake. Then I discovered the films of Norman Wisdom, and his 1950s British version of the brow-beaten underdog filled me with equal admiration. At some period in the 60s and 70s, the films of Laurel & Hardy were shown on BBC2 on Saturday mornings; their TV popularity waned in the 80s and 90s but their routines had by then worked into the deepest recesses of my mind as the most perfect demonstrations of the slow build, and an exquisite portrait of the benign loser in the harsh world of the adult.

In the late 60s and 70s, TV series like Marty Feldman's *Marty* with their wonderful examples of the clown as outsider; the occasional but memorable visual routines from Morecambe & Wise; the best visual sketches of Benny Hill; the fish-slapping dance in Monty Python, and the wonderful physical routines in sitcoms like *Dad's Army* and *Some Mothers Do 'Ave 'Em*, – plus big movies like *It's a Mad, Mad, Mad, Mad World,*

Those Magnificent Men in their Flying Machines, *The Great Race*, and *Monte Carlo or Bust* – all nourished in me an abiding love for wordless comedy.

Then, in my twenties, I discovered Jacques Tati, and once again experienced that same frisson of excitement I'd felt all those years before when first seeing the Keystone Cops. What Tati proved to me was that purely visual humour could not only sustain a full-length feature, it could be modern, sophisticated, experimental, and creative – in a word, *new*. The great silent comedians of the early twentieth century *hadn't* used up every sight gag and every routine; silent comedy wasn't an exhausted seam of inspiration. And when I came across the work of people like Ernie Kovacs – a now almost-forgotten pioneer of early American TV in the 1950s whose shows reflect some of the most advanced visual comedy ever made – it strengthened my belief that visual comedy was still able to prove itself radical and innovative. I ended up writing and performing in TV comedy, and even when I was writing shows like *The Big Impression* I often steered the humour towards the visual and made sure that many of the big laughs came from sight gags – quite a feat for a show based on celebrity impressions. And when I was offered a chance to write and perform in children's television I jumped at it, knowing that children's networks are one of the last homes of physical comedy. I wrote three series for the double-act Paul and Barry Chuckle and co-created and wrote three seasons of *Scoop* for CBBC, once again attempting new slapstick variations each week.

Remarkably, *Pompidou*, the BBC series I created with Matt Lucas and Ashley Blaker, screened in 2015, was the first dialogue-free TV comedy series for nearly twenty years (the last TV episode of *Mr Bean* was made in 1997). Since Bean, a new global internet audience of billions has arisen, hungry for language-less humour – only now is mainstream TV catching up. We live in a world saturated with dumb-show – on our CCTVs, our iPhones, on Youtube – which is why there could be an argument for calling visual comedy avant-garde. Ours is a global age, and though much divides us, humour still acts as a unifying force – and it is visual comedy above all else that by its very definition transcends cultural boundaries. Who was the chief comic performer at the 2012 Olympic Opening Ceremony, viewed by audiences around the world? Pantomimist Rowan Atkinson.

During my lifetime the old silent pioneers have fallen off our TV screens, banished to niche art-house showings in obscure provincial cinemas; to the Cinema Museum in Kennington, South London (in the very workhouse in which the young Chaplin lived as an inmate); or to occasional seasons at the NFT. Chaplin, in particular, fell out of favour with mainstream broadcasters, mistakenly viewed as excessively sentimental compared with the steely stoic gaze of Keaton.

Then, in 2009, Paul Merton made the ground-breaking series *Silent Clowns* for BBC Four, and once again the genius of those early cinema comics was on display, introduced with the affection that only a true aficionado like Merton can convey. Merton's admiration for Buster Keaton is, of course, well known but one of the major achievements of his series is, I believe, the restoration of Chaplin to his rightful supremacy in the hierarchy – if there is such a thing – of the comedy world.

Merton's book version of the series, *Silent Comedy*, ended with the coming of sound, and the traditional 'tailing off' of visual comedy in the early 30s. This book attempts to take up the story where Paul Merton left off. Some of the comedians in these pages will be familiar to the reader, others less so. It is a remarkable story – full of innovation, struggle, a consciousness of and a connectedness with a comic tradition that goes back way beyond the beginnings of cinema – and, most importantly, full of a lot of laughs.

Julian Dutton
March 2015

CHAPTER 1

Origins: From Ritual to Film

Is visual comedy more than someone simply falling over?

Del Boy's famous collapse through the open bar in John Sullivan's classic TV sitcom *Only Fools and Horses*, if one cares to deconstruct it (and I am not one of those who feels that to study comedy is to diminish it) is actually one of the most complex and richly persistent jokes in Western culture. Del Boy (David Jason) is attempting to signal his 'coolness' to a couple of women on the other side of the pub, and the humour stems from the collapse of the male peacock, the crumpling of male vanity, the puncturing of the deluded ego – in short, a perfect example of the perennial comedy of the mating game. As such, the joke is profoundly sophisticated: a lens directed powerfully at two thousand years of human cultural history. It is Britain's Funniest TV Moment because it is a huge, ambitious joke; not small, local and culturally specific like the material of most stand-ups and satirists working today. And because it is dumb-show, it will be understood and laughed at in a thousand years' time, all over the world, while every gag of every stand-up working today will be meaningless gibberish.

Can there be a unified theory of laughter? Many philosophers and psychologists, from Aristotle to Hazlitt and from Bergson to Freud, have attempted to reduce this odd biological response to one single cause – yet if there is no single cause for crying, why should there be one for laughter? Arthur Koestler believed laughter separates us from the animals; Freud believed it demonstrates our fundamental connection with them. I shall confine myself to observing visual comedy, which you might think would lead to a simplistic appraisal and therefore a unified theory, but even when a joke is stripped of all language and confined to a single human sense – sight – one still finds a multitude of sources for the odd and delightful reaction we call the laugh.

By definition, visual comedy predates language itself. The oldest joke in the world was probably someone falling over – that is to say, slapstick. Much of visual comedy is rooted in slapstick: when Fatty Arbuckle throws a brick at Mack Sennett, we laugh partly from a sense of *schadenfreude* – relief that is not us that is the target of the brick. But when the group of tourists in Tati's film *Playtime* are sitting in a coach and we view them through a window about to be cleaned, and the cleaner tilts the window and in his tilting makes the occupants of the coach themselves sway backwards in their seats, it is clear that something very different to slapstick is going on. It is a surreal gag which plays with reality and which elevates visual comedy to a status superior to the wittiest of one-liners.

The French philosopher Henri Bergson asserts that physical comedy reduces human beings to the status of objects and that when they behave as such, we find it funny. In Laurel & Hardy's *Busy Bodies*, for example, Ollie is reduced to the status of a barrel when he gets sucked into a tunnel which drags him along behind the other barrels, then expels him from the opening like a bullet. If we saw this happen in real life we would certainly not laugh – indeed, we'd probably be traumatised. And yet when we see that exact same scene acted out on screen, it fills us with joy. Why is this?

The answer lies in the words 'acted out.' The reduction of an awful accident to pantomime distances us from any emotional impact the event could have on us: its closeness to reality, however, still instils a state of anxiety within us – after all, we are still witnessing the image of man experiencing suffering. When Ollie is dragged into the tunnel, we are so glad it's not us, and (hopefully) also glad to see him emerge unscathed. We release the pent-up anxiety in a laugh. Perhaps we enjoy the spectacle because it is also satisfies our primitive evolutionary need to rehearse danger. An additional factor, of course, is the extent to which laughter is triggered by our sense of expectation that comes from knowing what genre we are watching: in a thriller, seeing a character being sucked into a barrel-chute would create tension; in a horror film, we know the outcome will probably be death, so the consequent emotion would be terror; but in a comedy, we know that the character is likely to emerge unscathed, so it's safe to laugh. In conversation with the author, leading comedy writer Peter Baynham – the creative mind behind such comic characters as Alan Partridge and Borat – went further, telling me that a closeness to death is a fundamental attribute of all great visual comic characters. 'Sacha (Baron Cohen) and I agree that all the silent comedy characters, if they lived in the real world, would die very quickly,' adding 'that's the key to them – their suffering.'

Social conditioning also infuses the laugh. In a TV interview, comedian Tony Hancock said that someone stumbling off a kerb into the gutter is funny – but that the wealthier the person, the bigger the laugh. A subversion of the pecking order is happening here. Our laugh is a secret relish, a dark delight at seeing the mighty fallen.

The silent comics take this subversion, magnify it and build on it. When Chaplin, the down-on-his-luck hobo, knocks the top hat from the head of an aristocrat, the laugh is triggered by something one would have never seen in real life without an arrest. Society in the early part of the twentieth century was far more rigid than it is today, the class structure fossilised and defined, so to see a tramp knock the hat off a gentleman was, for the Edwardian cinema audience, an incredible subversion of the norm; their laugh one of shock, a sudden animal bark of delight born from a deep, repressed desire to see those above them in the social pecking order brought down to their level. It is the same gag as the Court Jester knocking the crown off the head of the King.

But comedy is not simply an attack on success – it is also an attack on the ubiquitous pretence of success. As comedy writer and actor Larry David has said, we all pretend to be able to operate successfully in the adult social world, but inside, none of us are actually doing so. The great comedians do not pretend – they show us, time and time again, their own failure; they are acting out the truth in front of us and that's why we love them. And visual comedians display their failure in its most basic form – by falling over. So I would venture to assert that the dominant instinct invoked by the greatest visual comedy is not *schadenfreude* at all, but empathy.

At bottom, then, perhaps visual comedy *is* just falling over. But, of course, there are many ways of falling.

*

If tragedy was born from the ritual attempt to restore spring to the world, then early comedy was a celebration of that spring. For four thousand years, to 400 AD, the Egyptians enacted the *Abydos Passion Play* which dramatised the death and rebirth of the god Osiris. In earliest times, participants in these ceremonies were mimes – *mimetics* – dialogue always being subservient to the action. When Greek Old Comedy first appeared around 500 BC, its principal ingredient was a celebration of vernal fertility, mainly involving people prancing about dressed up as animals: with a dash of Sicilian mime and native Greek burlesque, the first comedy dumb-shows were born. These rituals, far from being ancient phenomena, are still seen today, with the Padstow horse ceremony in Cornwall being staged every May Day. Our own era's silent comedy – from Chaplin to Mr Bean – is an echo of those ancestral passions.

An academic analysis might focus on the evolution of cultural forms, identifying the 'sudden appearance' of visual comedy in, say, 500 BC, as a

Since ancient times comedy has subverted solemnity. Here Stan Laurel cocks-a-snook at the bravery of a matador in one of his early solo parodies, Mud and Sand *(1922) – an anarchic flipside, of course, of Rudolph Valentino's* Blood and Sand, *released earlier the same year. Two thousand years earlier the first Greek Comedies were parodies of existing heroic plays.*

result of Sicilian mimes performing a show in a Greek amphitheatre. A more sensible approach would be to presume an innate sense of humour in human beings that stretches back to the age of the primates, and to conclude that this instinct was bound to manifest itself no matter what the evolutionary state of a particular performance genre at any one time. When American Plains Indians enacted their rain dance, if one participant performed a mis-step or a mistake the entire ritual had to begin again – tiresome for some, no doubt, but conducive I would surmise to surreptitious social laughter. These mistakes may even have become an eagerly-looked-forward-to element. If a certain participant became a regular committer of mistakes he would gain an inevitable reputation – and the first comedian (and outsider) was born.

Religious ritual and the theatrical forms that grew out of it didn't create visual comedy, but did become the social outlet for a pre-existing love of laughter; and that laughter, once manifested, was encouraged and formalised in developing genres such as the Satyr play, usually performed after a trilogy of tragedies. This dumb-show masquerade was the comic flipside of what had just been witnessed – the sight of gods and heroes tripping up, falling over, bumping into furniture and getting drunk being a cathartic release from the seriousness of the previous entertainment (Satyr being the origin, of course, of *satire*).

Just as two-and-a-half thousand years later Chaplin would get huge laughs from knocking off a policeman's helmet, so too the early Greek comics would extract humour from removing Zeus's helmet or tripping up Achilles. The comic actor would wear a short gown and a trademark big red leather phallus – just as modern-day Liverpudlian jester Ken Dodd would wave a symbolic phallus before an audience at the Palladium.

By the third century BC, mime was a well-established genre of performance in Rome and many of its most celebrated practitioners were women. Once again these shows were vulgarised comic versions of contemporary tragedies, just as Stan Laurel's early shorts were send-ups of serious movies – such as his *Mud and Sand* being a comic cock-a-snook at Rudolph Valentino's *Blood and Sand.* In the glorious years of Imperial Rome these *pantomimi* – dumb-shows and dances with a chorus telling the story being enacted – had reached such heights of popularity that they were a favourite of Augustus himself, and the leading performer of such entertainments became known as a *Pantomimus,* described by Lucian of Samosata in the second century AD as 'the imitator of all.'

With the crumbling of the empires of Greece and Rome and the rise of the theocratic Holy Roman Empire, classical forms of performance fragmented into less formalised shows, with individual *jongleurs* traipsing from court to court and, in England, the Mummers presenting their dialogue-free versions of the death and rebirth of St George. In these 'Dark Ages', visual comedy didn't die out but simply continued to be performed in every type of place other than a public theatre. Even the so-called Barbarians kept slapstick live – Attila the Hun is recorded as presenting a show in Constantinople in 448 AD consisting of a Scythian Clown and a Moorish Buffoon. Although the Church frowned on the bawdy of theatre, and sought to close them all down, pantomime persisted in private. Mystery Plays – despite possessing high religious themes – were also, of course, full of slapstick, and perhaps gave rise to the development and persistence of the dumb-show that figured hugely in Elizabethan dramas and masques.

But it was in humanist Italy in the sixteenth century that the flame of visual comedy performance was truly re-lit, and the more recognisable modern comic characters were born. Onto a ramshackle stage in the middle of an Italian marketplace there stepped on-stage for the very first time two archetypal figures of comical history, Arlecchino and Pantalone, whose characters established many of the tropes of what was to become 'modern visual comedy.' The Commedia dell'arte, the world's first professional theatre, synthesised the individual medieval tradition of the solo jester, jongleur and clown with the farcical matter of Ancient Greece and Rome. It wasn't just Arlecchino and Pantalone (think Chaplin and Eric Campbell – the Tramp's huge-framed foil with the gigantic whiskers) that proved enduring types – the Commedia also included madcap servants as a regular fixture of the cast, known as *Zanni* (origin of 'zany') whose horseplay, mime and acrobatics would form a template for everyone from the Marx Brothers and the Three Stooges to the Keystone Kops and the Chuckle Brothers. Additional characters included the violent hook-nosed Pulcinella and the wan, pale peasant boy Pedrolino – ancestors respectively of Mr Punch and Pierrot – and with touring companies such as the Gelosi (a company that heavily influenced Molière and gave rise to the Comédie-Italienne) the Commedia dell'arte became a huge cultural force, spawning Shakespearian comedy, circus and pantomime.

The Shakespearian connection is more than speculative, for it is thought the eleven-year-old future playwright was present at the theatrical revels staged at Kenilworth Castle in 1575 for Queen Elizabeth during her two-week sojourn. Robert Dudley, the Earl of Leicester, is said to have lavished an extraordinary £1,700 on the spectacles, including an Italian Commedia company that a spectator afterwards was to describe as exhibiting '... such feats of agility, in goings, turnings, tumblings, castings, hops, jumps, leaps, skips, springs, gambols, somersaults, caprettiez, and slights; forward, backward, sideways, downward, upward, and with such sundry windings, gyrings and circumflexions; also lightly and with such easiness as by me in a few words it is not expressible by pen or speech, I tell you plain,' an eyewitness account that reads like a Tudor review of a Chaplin picture. That the fledgling Bard of Avon was in the audience for this display of the new European slapstick is evinced by his later making Oberon in *A Midsummer Night's Dream* say – 'Once I sat upon a promontory, and heard a mermaid on a dolphin's back, uttering such dulcet and harmonious breath, that the rude sea grew civil at her song, and certain stars shot madly from their spheres, to hear the sea-maid's music' – an almost blow-by-blow account of the firework display above the aquatic entertainments that were on display in that high summer of the 1570s.

The other silent traditions that form the bedrock of our story comprise the dumb-show, the masque, and the pantomime.

A distinct part of a play performed between acts and derived from either the Italian *Intermedii* or the English Morality Play, dumb-show was a performance genre that developed alongside the Commedia, and appears famously in *Hamlet* and in *The Duchess of Malfi.* That these 'silent interludes' were quaint even by the time of the Elizabethan Renaissance is indicated by Ophelia's reaction to the Players' pantomime: 'What is this, my lord?' True, dumb-show gradually became an object of satire, so by the late seventeenth century, Henry Fielding was promising comically that an epilogue to one of his plays would be performed in dumb-show 'by a cat.'

Masques were courtly, unspeaking and ceremonial, and despite some of the finest examples of the genre being written by the great Ben Jonson, as a genre they too fell out of favour. It was perhaps the high seriousness and pomposity of the themes that sowed the seeds of the increasing risibility of these forms: in short, if a performance was to be wholly visual, it needed to be comical. At least that's what audiences preferred, and as a new middle-class theatre-going public emerged after the Restoration, it was the slapstick element of wordless performance that they clamoured to see.

John Weaver, Dancing Master at Drury Lane Theatre in the eighteenth century, bears witness to the survival of the slapstick tradition – his book *History of the Mimes and Pantomimes* published in 1728 is a sublime chronicle of this rich heritage. He waxes lyrical about the visual comedians whose 'chief art lay in ... silently demonstrating all sorts of manners and passions ... carried on by Dancing, Action and Motion only.' Weaver's dialogue-free productions were a roaring success, attracting lavish praise from Colley Cibber who described them thus: 'A connected presentation of dancers in character, wherein the passions were so happily expressed, and the whole story so intelligently told, by a mute narration of gesture only, that even thinking spectators allowed it both a pleasing and rational entertainment.'

Weaver's book extends beyond mere dry chronicle – it lays out the vocabulary of pantomimic technique: 'Admiration is expressed by the raising of the right hand, the palm turned upwards, the fingers closed; and in one motion the wrist turned round and the fingers spread; the body reclining, and the eyes fixed on the object'; he goes on to describe how a threat is expressed by 'raising the hand and shaking the bended fist, knitting the brow, biting the nails, and catching back the breath'; and impatience by the 'smiting of the thigh or breast with the hand.'

His successor at Drury Lane, actor-manager John Rich, expanded on Weaver's rediscovery of ancient slapstick by inventing the English Pantomime, and these two men can be accurately described as the link between Commedia dell'arte and the silent comedy of the early twentieth century, for they brought back 'capering and tumbling' to the English stage, establishing it as a popular art that continued to the nineteenth century. Key protagonist in this continuation of slapstick into the modern age was Joseph Grimaldi, who made the role of the Clown in the Harlequinade part of English Pantomime his own. Not only did he expand the role of the Clown, but he drew on the more knockabout style of the baser English circus and fed it into the mainstream theatrical pieces that so dazzled audiences first at Sadler's Wells, then from 1806 at the Theatre Royal Covent Garden.

He did not spring out of a vacuum: Delpini, Dubois, and his own father Giuseppe were all stars of the English stage, but Joseph Grimaldi is rightly heralded as the Chaplin of his day, revered by the poor, the cultured middle-class and by the King. Dickens was perhaps his greatest fan, attending many of his performances and editing Grimaldi's memoirs after his death.

By all accounts he was as self-punishing a comic as Buster Keaton; indeed, a review from the *Times* of 1813 of one his performances might have been of the great stone-face himself: 'Grimaldi is the most assiduous of all imaginable buffoons and it is absolutely surprising that any human head or hide can resist the rough trials he volunteers. Serious tumbles from serious heights, innumerable kicks, and incessant beatings come on him as matters of common occurrence, and leave him every night fresh and free for the next night's flagellation.'

Like Keaton he began as a child performer, learning at a tender age not to care about pain. Aged six he played a monkey and was led onto the stage by his father, who had attached a chain to Grimaldi's waist. Giuseppe swung his young son around his head 'with the utmost velocity', when the chain snapped, causing young Grimaldi to land in the orchestra pit. From 1789 Grimaldi would appear alongside his siblings in an act entitled 'The Three Young Grimaldis'. If ever one was to seek proof of the veracity of reincarnation one would be do worse than proffer Grimaldi and Keaton as examples: from the age of three Buster was hurled around the stage by his performer father as part of a quartet of visual vaudevillians 'The Four Keatons.'

What was the kind of comedy Grimaldi was performing, and did it influence the later age of silent film comedians? Theatre is the most transient and gossamer of the arts, but Grimaldi's comedy is not completely lost to us, for the reviews of the time give us intriguing glimpses of the fare on offer to audiences a century and a half ago before the advent of film. The critic Leigh Hunt described the pleasures of English Pantomime thus: 'The stage is never empty or still. Either Pantaloon is hobbling about or somebody falling flat, or somebody else is receiving an ingenious thump on the face, or the Clown is jolting himself with jaunty dislocations, or Columbine is skimming across like a frightened pigeon, or Harlequin is quivering hither and thither, or gliding out a window.'

The great clown Joseph Grimaldi (1778-1837), whose antics enthralled Charles Dickens and whose comic onstage business forged a direct link between nineteenth century pantomime and the slapstick of early cinema.

This reads like the review of an early Fatty

Arbuckle or Chaplin picture; indeed, one can imagine Chaplin appearing in the production of *Mirth's Motley: or Harlequin at Home,* the bill for which promises 'A Leap through a Hogshead of Water, a flight across the stage from Balcony to Balcony; an escape through a cask of fire; and an astonishing Leap through a Hoop of Daggers'. This is precisely the same fare offered by a Keaton or a Lloyd less than a century later: thrill comedy, in which the comic hero is unfeasibly indestructible and an acrobat. Another review of a Drury Lane show describes the lead comedian being 'Crammed down a pump, pumped out into a pail, rolled flat, and fired out of a cannon.' In 1932 cinema audiences were laughing at exactly the same thing when Oliver Hardy was sucked into a pumping system at a saw-mill and ejected onto a woodpile in *Busy Bodies.*

The stage slapstick of the nineteenth century was, then, just as violent and spectacular as that practised in the golden era of silent movies. A stage direction by Tom Dibdin for one of his Theatre Royal Shows in 1814 reads thus: 'Harlequin is carried on the tail of a kite to the very top of the theatre and is then dropped back onto the stage, falls through an open trap door, and is shot out of it again enveloped in flames as if blown from the crater of a volcano ... In order to meet Columbine at the street door, he throws himself out of a three pair of stairs window, and is caught with his head in a lamp-iron.'

The continuity between stage and film slapstick is further brought home by the fact that Grimaldi seldom spoke onstage, apart from the odd monosyllable, much like Monsieur Hulot or Mr Bean. Driven by an insatiable desire for food (another Chaplinesque trope) Grimaldi would consume a slap-up feast, smack his lips and mutter *'Nice!'* One reviewer wrote: 'Whether he was robbing a pieman, opening an oyster, grasping a red-hot poker, devouring a pudding, picking a pocket, beating a watchman, sneezing, snuffing, courting, or nursing a child, he was always so extravagantly natural.' This litany of antics could, in all honesty, be offered as a summation of the contents of every single one of Chaplin's films. And Dickens' eye-witness description of a Grimaldi performance deserves to be reproduced in its entirety, so close a resemblance does it bear to a scene from a Mack Sennett, Hal Roach or Chaplin picture:

> I see him now. His amazement and awe of Harlequin, his amorous glances at Columbine, and his winks at the imbecility and dandyism of that doting pair. He watches them intently, his nose screwed to one side, his eyes nearly closed, though twinkling forth his rapture, and his tongue vibrating in his capacious mouth in the very fullness of his enjoyment. He

watches. The lovers leave. The coast is clear! He sees on the table the dinner that was laid for Harlequin and his mistress. He will eat a Sussex dumpling or two. Down he sits, inviting himself with as many ceremonies as if he had the whole day ahead of him. But when once he begins to eat – it seems as if he has not a moment to lose. The dumplings vanish at a cram: the sausages are abolished: down go a dozen yards of macaroni: and he is in the act of paying his duty to a gallon of rum – when in come Pantaloon and one of the Inn Servants, at opposite doors, looking for the glutton.

But they've not seen him. For the moment, he's safe. And away goes the monstrous booty into that leviathan pocket of his, that receptacle of all sorts of edibles and occasionally of kettles of boiling water and even of lighted candles.

But Pantaloon and the Inn servant now spot him, and resolve to pounce on him headlong. They rush forward – and he slips from between them. And the two poor devils dash their heads against one another, like rams, and fall back fainting to the sides of the stage!

The Clown, laughing with all his shoulders, nods a health to each, and finishes his rum. He then holds a great cask of a snuff box to each of their noses, to bring them to; and while they are sneezing and tearing their souls out, jogs off at his leisure.

This account above all others surely proves that the great clowns of the silent film era were simply continuing a tradition. And great stage clowning didn't die with Grimaldi – others equally adventurous followed: there was Tom Matthews, whose speciality was knocking on the doors of shops and immediately lying prostrate to trip up the owner; Robert Bradbury, who would jump from the flies to the stage; Paulo Redige who died onstage after a pratfall went wrong; and Harry Payne, who invented all sorts of enduring comic business with strings of sausages and red hot pokers. Most of them remained dumb – while some attempted to endow the Clown with speech, each effort was met with criticism. As far back as 1759 Garrick had invoked the ire of critics when he was the first actor in history to make Harlequin speak – and even in 1820 a revival of the piece, entitled *Harlequin Invasion*, brought on the vitriol of eminent critic William Hazlitt, who castigated the writer and producer for 'giving the fool a tongue.' 'It is called a speaking pantomime. We had rather it said nothing. The essence of a pantomime is practical absurdity in keeping the wits in constant chase, coming upon one with surprise, and starting off again before you can arrest the fleeting phantom … A speaking pantomime like this one is not unlike a flying waggon.' And when Jefferini spoke in 1843 he was berated in the newspapers: 'He talks too much,' said *The Times*, bluntly.

Across the channel in France, pantomime flourished as strongly throughout the nineteenth century as in England, with several theatres in the Boulevard de Crime (the nickname for the Boulevard de Temple) devoted to acrobatics, mime and variety. The most famous of these was the Théâtre de Funambules, home of Jean-Gaspard Deburau, inventor of Pierrot, and a theatre whose glory years were immortalised in Jean Louis-Barrault's masterpiece *Les Enfants du Paradis*. Like its English counterpart, French clowning built on the stereotypes of the Commedia dell'arte, and Deburau's Pierrot was as just as such a mercenary, cunning glutton as Grimaldi's Clown. Although French pantomimes differed in style from the English – they fell into strict categories such as realistic pantomime, fairy pantomime etc – the penchant of audiences for slapstick and knockabout routines were identical on both sides of the channel. Out of this rich tradition of the Théâtre des Funambules came an outstanding artist whose work in the 1940s would represent the second supreme flowering of visual comedy in the twentieth century – Jacques Tati, whose style was a fusion of Deburau and the corporeal mime of Etienne Decroux.

There is another link, of course, between these pantomime clowns of the theatrical stage and the first film comedians – and that is the music-hall.

From the 1840s onwards there had been an organic growth of 'entertainment' rooms, usually behind pubs and inns – places where shows could be put on that were not plays. Why not plays? Very simply, only two theatres in the country were permitted to stage plays – Covent Garden Theatre, and the Theatre Royal. Thus music-hall and variety was born. Monologues, songs and ballets were permitted, but any piece consisting of dialogue between two or more people was strictly forbidden until 1907: hence the invention of the dumb-show sketch.

Proto-stars of the silent screen who achieved great fame on the stage in the latter part of the nineteenth century include Paul Martinetti who, with his brother Alfred, formed a pantomime troupe and whose mimed sketches included 'A Terrible Night', 'After the Ball', 'Duel in the Snow' – the titles of which could so easily have been the titles of early film comedies. Alongside the music-hall as the flowerbed of visual comedy was the circus, giving birth to acts like the Ravels, and the Hanlon-Lees, the latter touring Britain, France and the USA from the 1860s to the 1880s.

Once again, a description of their show *Voyage en Suisse* at the Gaiety Theatre, London in March 1880 sounds like a scenario for an early Mack Sennett two-reeler: '... a bus smash, an exploding Pullman car, a banquet transformed into a wholesale juggling party after one of the Hanlons had crashed through the ceiling onto the table, and one of the cleverest drunk scenes ever presented onstage.'

By 1900 the 'silent' sketch was the staple of theatrical entertainment, with stage shows becoming as famous as the later movies would become: Harry Tate's 'Motoring, Golfing, Flying, Billiards, and Fishing'; Joe Boganny's 'Lunatic Bakers', Charlie Baldwin's 'Bank Clerks', the Six Brothers Luck, the Boisset and Manon troupes, and the most celebrated mime company of all, of course, Fred Karno's Speechless Comedians.

Karno was ideally suited to ride the crest of the wave of this craze for silent onstage comedy. He straddled all three traditions of pantomime, circus and music-hall – beginning as an acrobat for Manley's Circus, moving his act to the music-halls, then forming his own company and recruiting stars of the Drury Lane pantomimes like Fred Kitchen, an eminent Harlequin of the 1890s. His eye for talent was seemingly unmatched, and he legendarily hired both Stan Laurel and Charlie Chaplin – in so doing forging the link between English theatrical dumb-show and two of the greatest early stars of visual film comedy. Sketches like 'The Football Match', 'Hilarity', and most famously, 'Mumming Birds', were the training ground of the future stars of the silent screen.

Comedy impresario Fred Karno (1866-1941), mentor of both Chaplin and Laurel, whose popularising of stage dumb-show trained a generation of performers for the new medium of film comedy.

Chaplin himself sums up the continuity from stage dumb-show to screen in his memoirs thus:

> Christmas in London in the old days when it was hard scratching for me to get sixpence so that I might see the Christmas pantomime spectacle at Drury Lane, *Jack and the Beanstalk, Puss in Boots, or Cinderella.* I used to watch the Clowns in the

> pantomime breathlessly. They were clever fellows. There were Montgomery, Laffin, Brough, Feefe, Cameron – all high-class performers. Every move they made registered on my young brain like a photograph. I used to try it all over when I got home. But what I think of now is the rapt attention with which six or seven thousand boys and girls would watch the clowns work. It was slapstick stuff. Everybody said that sort of thing would be dead in another ten years. What has happened is that pantomime, through motion picture developments, has taken the lead in the world's entertainment.

This glance at the theatrical origins of twentieth century dumb-show shows us how silent comedy was actually invented centuries before the advent of film, which is why as a genre of performance it was destined to survive after the invention of sound technology. The great visual clowns of the twentieth century can be directly traced back to ancient and early modern types, and their careers derive from genres of performance with deep-rooted traditions; Chaplin and Harpo are Scaramouches, Keaton is Arlecchino, W C Fields and Oliver Hardy are Pantalones. And with the traditions of Commedia dell'arte, pantomime and clowning still flourishing in England and France right through the nineteenth century it is no accident that when the film pioneers first began to make comedies to satisfy audiences at the Kinema theatres and the sideshows, it was France that first established a lead, and it was to English performers to whom American directors turned when casting their pictures. Silent film comedy was a glorious explosion of talent, innovation and experimentation, but it had a brief flowering. In 1927 it came to a juddering halt.

CHAPTER 2

Keeping Still: the Coming of Sound

November 19 1927. A long queue shuffles and stamps in the cold outside the Hippodrome Cinema, Sheffield, England. Dusk falls over the factories and the smoke-stacks; the cigarette ends of the patient cinema-goers glow orange in the autumn evening.

In our age of multiplexes the long cinema queue, apart from at blockbuster premieres, is now largely a thing of the past. But in the 20s and 30s in towns and cities up and down Britain a regular sight on most nights of the week would be a coated and scarved line of folk, collars turned up, winding its slow way like a patient snake past brightly coloured posters proclaiming 'What's on this week!'

And what were they there to see at the Sheffield Hippodrome that week? Well, they were there to see George Bernard Shaw being interviewed on Movietone News. Such was the incredible novel appeal of the arrival of the Talking Picture that hundreds of blue-collar workers in the north of England were willing to queue to spend their hard-earned pay on watching an Irish playwright discuss the finer points of didactic drama. It is the equivalent of half the population of Newcastle-on-Tyne today pouring out of the estates and the back-streets to crowd into a cinema to watch the philosopher Roger Scruton being interviewed by Andrew Graham-Dixon on BBC2's *The Culture Show.* Hundreds of people formed queues simply to watch and listen to the noise of the football crowds as the matches were reported on the big screen. '100 per cent All Talking Pictures!' screamed the posters. It didn't matter what the picture was, so long as it was audible.

The story of the coming of sound in films is very familiar to us, its emotional and personal impact having been immortalised and mythologised in Hollywood's typically self-referential way in movies such as *Singing in the Rain, Sunset Boulevard* and *The Artist.* Moreover, its technical story has also been told many times, so I will not go over already well-trodden ground – instead concentrating on its effect on comedy.

*

Over dinner in downtown Hollywood, Wallace Beery joined Chaplin at his table after watching Jolson's *The Singing Fool.* 'Not so hot,' said Beery as he tucked in his napkin. 'Too many people go into motion pictures to sleep. They don't want to be annoyed by a lot of conversation.'

Some critics were indeed annoyed by the conversation. Buster Keaton's first talkie, a picture he co-starred in with Anita Page and Trixie Friganza, *Free and Easy,* in 1930, was the subject of a perceptive and not entirely unsympathetic appraisal by a reviewer in *Bioscope:* 'It will be generally admitted that Mr. Keaton's funniest scenes are those in which he does not speak … with the use of his voice (he) definitely leaves the rank of those supreme fun makers, including, besides himself, Charlie Chaplin, whose misfortunes rouse laughter un-hampered by human sympathy. (By talking) he becomes a human being, and therefore has to abandon a form of entertainment in which he was supreme, and enter into competition with many already well-established in the same line.'

The screen speaks with a magic voice: sound comes to the Capitol Theater, Jasper Avenue, Edmonton, March 1929.

It is an exaggeration to assert that Keaton was a victim of the revolution, and his work in the early era of sound will be appraised in a subsequent chapter: but there were certainly casualties of the upheaval, especially among those with with heavy accents or disagreeable voices. What is less frequently observed is that the biggest victim was film itself. Indeed, it is not an exaggeration to say that movie-making was crippled by the advent of the talkie. Historian

Kevin Brownlow goes so far as to state that 'Film-making techniques are as little developed today than they were at the end of the silent era ... Startling innovations excite critics, but any capable historian can point to the introduction of hand-held cameras, wild cutting, and abbreviated narration: it was all being done in the twenties.' Not all film historians agree with this thesis: eminent film critic André Bazin's assessment of the impact of sound on the aesthetic of film was more nuanced – in his essay *The Evolution of the Language of Cinema* he praises the addition of dialogue because '... reality and everything that can support it such as sound, deep focus, and invisible editing, define what film should be.' Although Bazin admits that 'it was montage (silent image) that gave birth to film as an art', he is apprehensive of anything that supports 'the creation of a sense or meaning not proper to the images themselves but derived entirely from their juxtaposition' – in other words Bazin welcomed the new realism that talking injected into film, displacing the stylising expression and dominance of image that had characterised the work of Eisenstein and indeed all the great comic cinematic artists too, like Chaplin, Keaton and Lloyd.

Whatever one thinks of the progress of cinematic art prior to the advent of sound, all such innovation was stopped dead in its tracks by the Vitaphone and its ascent to supremacy. On the level of simple practicalities, the day-to-day process of shooting was hampered to the point of stasis: Warner Brothers even had to fly 'Silence!' balloons above their studios to warn passing aeroplanes. Acting styles altered overnight because performers had to remain as rigid as statues. Only those with voices verging on the bass became employable, for the early microphones recorded the human voice a complete register higher than it was. Chaplin, fighting a rear-guard action against the new phenomenon, declared his intention to make a series of silent pictures using all those performers discarded by the studios – but sadly nothing came of it.

Two of the biggest victims of the seismic shift that sound technology affected were the smaller independent studios, and the *aesthetic* of film comedy itself.

The 'cottage industry' ethos of the golden era of silent comedy had been apparent from the very outset. A budding director could gather together a handful of his vaudeville comedian friends, drive out into the California desert, unload his camera, and shoot a two-reeler in a single afternoon. Graduating from location shoots to stages, the small studios in the US were born: Mack Sennett, Joe Rock, Hal Roach, Essanay, Vitagraph and Universal City. In the UK the early film industry followed a similar pattern. It was a 'mighty oaks from little acorns grow' process:

the music-hall comedian Will Evans set up a camera in Shoreham-by-Sea, Sussex, and shot a successful series of short comedies under the umbrella of his company Sunny South Films. The British Oak Film Company set up shop at 115a Ebury Street, Victoria, London, and in their 90ft by 25ft studio shot movies adapted from the works of Rider Haggard, Jerome K Jerome, and the Baroness Orczy. There were film studios on Champion Hill, Dulwich – essentially just a field; Lucky Cat Films at Kew Bridge; a proto-Ealing Studios built by Will Barker in 1907, where in 1908 he shot probably the first talking films in Britain – an actor miming to a gramophone disc. The Leyton Studio at 588 Lea Bridge Road was converted from an old horse tram shed, while another studio at Tuilerie Street, Hackney, had originally been a gas retort house. The Cricks and Martin Studio in Waddon, near Croydon, South London, became a centre for comedy film production, and it was here that they made the very successful 'Charley Smiler' comedies, including *Charley Smiler joins the Boy Scouts*.

Meanwhile in the US, enterprising young businessmen were leaving the trades they had learned as youngsters and were setting up movie studios. Adolph Zukor left the fur industry to found Famous Players Film Company in 1912, which was to evolve into Paramount. William Fox turned also turned his back on the clothes business to found first, the Greater New Yorker Film Rental Company, then Fox Office Attractions – merging both in 1915 to form Fox Pictures.

Hal Roach – whose encounter with Mark Twain as a boy when the great humourist made a presentation at Roach's school led to a lifelong passion for comedy – came into a bit of money in 1915, so started shooting pictures with his friend and fellow film extra, Harold Lloyd. And Canadian-born Irish ex-boiler-maker Mikall Sinnott exchanged steam-plumbing for slapstick, to become – as Mack Sennett – the most famous of the early pioneers in forming his Keystone Studios.

By the late 1920s, however, this 'cottage industry' ethos was changing, the big studios growing bigger and rapidly swallowing up the smaller ones. Some had even taken over the distribution network, like M-G-M. And when sound took over, the sheer cost of production – together with the construction of sound-stages and all the technology attendant on making a talking picture – all served to hasten the decline of these 'Mom & Pop' studios. Some small studios struggled on, such as Educational Pictures, a Poverty Row studio that stubbornly continued to make comedy two- and three-reelers throughout the decade of emergent sound and became the refuge of neglected visual comedy stars such as Charlie Chase, Harry Langdon and even Buster Keaton.

If the economics of movie making were changed forever by sound, the aesthetic revolution was just as far-reaching. The look and feel of movies were never to be the same again. One charge levelled at silent movies is that they are 'theatrical' – yet the first talking pictures couldn't have been more so: scenes became static, and the long-shot was virtually abandoned for the mid-shot and close-up. With this loss of the long-shot, the screen ceased to be a broad canvas upon which the director could paint in broad strokes and instead became a virtual stage, upon which actors stood immobile and delivered lines in staccato monotone. The reputation of the 'stiltedness' of movies had begun.

When, in 1949, James Agee published his famous article in *Life* magazine, 'Comedy's Greatest Era', what precisely was Agee praising in the silent comedian? He stated that '... anyone who has watched screen comedy over the past ten or fifteen years is bound to realise that it has quietly but steadily deteriorated... To put it unkindly, the only thing wrong with screen comedy today is that it takes place on a screen that talks ... Because there is a screen, talking comedians are trapped into a continual exhibition of their inadequacy as screen comedians on a surface as big as the side of a barn.' Agee surveyed the whole range of greater and lesser silent comics, and extolled their use of a universally understood pantomimic language: in their exaggeration lay their poetic beauty.

No greater pantomimists existed in movies – alongside Chaplin and Keaton – than Laurel & Hardy. After two long solo careers characterised by struggle, hardship and occasional minor success, they had found a natural chemistry together when they were paired in *Duck Soup* in 1927. Under the perceptive directorial tutelage of Leo McCarey, who although only officially directing the team's pictures from *We Faw Down* (1928) onwards was already acting as a supervisory director at the Roach Studios, so had much input into their early development, the double-act flourished, and in a matter of eighteen months they had become world famous. Their comedy was slapstick, acrobatic and clownish, to be sure, but it was nevertheless underpinned by a sophisticated character relationship. They bridged the abstract, ethereal world of the silent clown as exemplified by Keaton, and the real, socially recognisable world of Harold Lloyd.

Yet it seemed that no sooner had two new stars been added to the pantheon than their very existence was threatened by the appearance of a new technology: sound. How would the two finest exponents of pantomime react to this seismic shift in movie making? Their solution was not to treat it as a threat at all – but as a challenge.

CHAPTER 3

Slowing Down: Laurel and Hardy

On March 25 1929 two comedians arrived on set to begin work on their first sound picture. The atmosphere, usually so happy and carefree (the nickname for the Hal Roach studio was the 'Lot of Fun') was, on this day, peculiarly tense. Strange new signs had appeared on walls and on the door leading into the studio: 'Do Not Enter When Red Light is On'. Four film cameras – all encased in huge soundproof boxes to prevent the whirr of the machinery being picked up by the recording device – stood on the sound stage, obscuring the set.

No one was more anxious than Stan Laurel. Concerned about his voice and apprehensive about a lisp that had dogged him since his teenage years, Laurel's demeanour that day was more than usually agitated, as Randy Skretvedt related in his book *Laurel & Hardy: the Magic Behind the Movies.* 'Stan was worried sick before sound came in,' recalled Roach Studio construction chief Thomas Benton Roberts. 'He was afraid he wouldn't be able to talk. And every take we'd make, he wanted to hear a playback on it.'

Laurel need not have worried. 'You lost a lot of comedians when sound came in,' recalled Hal Roach, 'but with Laurel and Hardy, almost from their first picture in sound, they were good.' (ibid).

The press agreed: reviews of their first talkie declared that 'their voices sound funnier than the two clowns look!' Laurel's English accent with its deadpan comic flatness provided a perfect foil to Hardy's high-flown, optimistic southern extravagance.

From the outset Laurel & Hardy and the film crew treated the momentous event comedically, entitling their movie *Unaccustomed As We Are.* It is noteworthy that the first sound movies of both Laurel & Hardy and Chaplin were, in part, satires on the role of sound in comedy. In *Modern Times* – strictly not a sound picture but Chaplin's first to utilise synchronised audio – the first words spoken onscreen are 'Actions speak louder than words!' when the inventor proposes to demonstrate his new fast-eating device for factory workers. And in *Unaccustomed As We Are,* Laurel & Hardy present a studied lampooning of the over-written and over-expositional dialogue of early sound pictures when they engage in a lengthy conversation with a Mrs Kennedy (Thelma Todd) in the hallway of Ollie's apartment block:

> 'Hello, Mrs Kennedy.'
> 'Hello, Mr Hardy.'
> 'How are you, Mrs Kennedy?'
> 'I'm very well, Mr Hardy.'
> 'How is Mr Kennedy, Mrs Kennedy?'

and so on – the tag of which is Ollie turning to Stan and unnecessarily explaining 'That was Mrs Kennedy,' to which Stan responds for the benefit of the already dialogue-weary cinema spectator, 'I was wondering who it was.' The fact that this gag was retained in the movie after a preview – all Laurel & Hardy movies were shown to an audience prior to the final edit – indicates that it had got a big laugh, meaning that onscreen dialogue was a legitimate target for satire even at its inception.

The ease with which they adapted to sound was remarkable, the transition being made easier by two things – Hal Roach's foresight, and Laurel's convictions and understanding about the nature of their comedy. 'We had decided we weren't talking comedians, and of course preferred to do pantomime, like in our silents,' Laurel recalled in 1960. 'So we said as little as possible – only what was necessary to motivate the things we were doing. If there was any plot to be told, we generally would have somebody else tell it ... as time went on, we became a little more accustomed, and did more talking than we first intended.'

From the outset their producer Hal Roach – with a businessman's prescience – had envisaged challenges in adapting his stable of performers to the new medium. On October 4 1928 he made an agreement with the Victor Talking Machine Company for 'synchronizing certain pictures and installation of sound equipment at the studio.' Victor were based in Camden, New Jersey, and were gramophone record producers – they resisted the move into pictures. But Roach persuaded them: in early October 1928 he sent Richard Currier, the head of his film editing department, to Camden, where he learned sound recording. Music and sound effects were then added in the Roach Studio to a backlog of silent films that had already been shot.

So Laurel & Hardy stole a march on other silent comics by instigating a transitional phase in their movie careers – the half-sound picture. Hal Roach's foresight combined with the gag-writing skills of Laurel, Leo McCarey and Charley Rogers, created films with extraordinarily fresh and inventive jokes: sound jokes that are now the staple of film comedy grammar. A classic example is the off-screen pratfall accompanied by a comedy sound effect – a Laurel & Hardy invention. In *Unaccustomed as We Are*, the final shot is of Stan disappearing headlong down the stairs. We don't see this – he simply flies out of frame, while Ollie stares after him, crumpling his face in a wince. Silent, this is funny: with an accompanying 'crash!' it is doubly so.

The conversion of the Hal Roach Studio to sound took place in the winter and spring of 1929: by March every sound stage had been installed. Instead of hiring specialist architects to design the complex new studio layouts, Roach saved money by using his own on-the-spot construction guy, Thomas Benton Roberts. Skretvedt, who interviewed Roberts, quotes him thus: 'I was the only guy in the middle ranks who had class A construction experience – instead of hiring an architect and construction engineer, they could get me for a dollar an hour. Nobody gave us any advice on acoustics or anything – at the Roach Studio we didn't have the money to pay for the help. All I had were a few sketches from the Victor Recording Company, like floor plans which showed where to place the projection machines and so on. I had to design all the structural stuff around it.'

Even with the sound stages in place, Laurel & Hardy shot three more silent pictures: *Double Whoopee*, *Bacon Grabbers*, and their last soundless comedy, *Angora Love* – although the last two were released with synchronised music and effects soundtracks. *Angora Love* was not released until December 14 1929: by then they had made seven talking pictures.

Roach appointed a Head of Sound, Elmer Raguse. The way Raguse was perceived by the other members of the Hal Roach Studio is interesting evidence of the initial awe in which sound was held. From his arrival in the studio, his word was law. Whereas previously the director or star dominated the logistics of film-making, in these early stages the sound man was briefly king. As Skretvedt notes, editor Richard Currier had many confrontations with the new technical overlord.

So how did Laurel & Hardy respond to the new medium they were working in? Far from rejecting visual comedy, they deepened it. As Walter Kerr put it, 'Sound-film, with its naturalistic rate and consequently subdued deportment, couldn't slow them down. They had got there first.' That is to say, in their late silents the team had invented pantomime of character and inter-reaction which perfectly suited the introduction of dialogue. So when speech entered their world, the change was seamless. The role of Leo McCarey in the creation of the slower Laurel character cannot be overestimated: in conversation with the author in December

2014 comedian and silent comedy aficionado Paul Merton told me: 'It was Leo McCarey who influenced Stan most – before he met Leo his onscreen persona was a cheekie chappie, a rascal like Chaplin. He kept jumping up in the air, for example. But after he started working with Leo McCarey, he slowed down. In fact, one of the common pieces of direction McCarey would call out during rehearals was 'slow down, boys!''

If Chaplin was the comedian of late Victorian England, then Laurel & Hardy were the supreme comics of the Great Depression. The police that chase Chaplin are clearly London constables: the streets they pursue him down are South London streets. Indeed, the set for one of his greatest shorts, *Easy Street*, bears a remarkable resemblance in both name and appearance to the rough market street in Kennington where he grew up – East Street. But the authorities that harass the hapless Stan and Ollie in their efforts to make their way in the Battle of Life are cops in the era of Prohibition and beyond. Laurel & Hardy are just as much victims as Chaplin was – they are arrested as vagrants and thrown into prison, reduced to begging from door to door or busking. We know they are never going to make it in life – and deep down they know it too. Sometimes it's all too much for them, and they attempt suicide. But something always pulls them through. They struggle to make a go of it, in particular the Hardy character. They marry, they join the Freemasons, they set up their own businesses. They're desperate to join in the normal social world. There is almost a chronological path one can trace in their movies – in the early shorts, they are young and thrusting go-getters: they woo girls in soda cafés, they try to sell Christmas trees to the citizens of Los Angles in midsummer and they are dogged by failure. But as the years pass, the doom that constantly hovers over their endeavours crashes down with tragic regularity. They are constantly falling on hard times. We find them living in dingy rented rooms owned by psychotic landlords. They busk in the frozen streets for pennies. They find wallets in the snow that turn out to belong to the cop they have – out of their generosity – bought lunch for.

If the entire canon of Laurel & Hardy films were a novel then it would constitute a Russian epic of the lower orders, akin to the work of Gogol or Dostoyevsky. Despite their jobs (when they have them) being traditionally working-class and manual, they continually aspire – or more accurately the Hardy character does – to become middle class. But despite Ollie's constant optimism, they keep descending into a twilight, violent world of hardship, back-street bars, dosshouses, prisons and rough hotel kitchens where they are forced to do the washing up.

Even when they do struggle out of this world of destitution and make semi-successful forays into the normal world of society they find themselves trapped in awful marriages. The childlike spirit of their characters, exploited and abused by the world outside the home, is also exploited and abused inside the home: their harridan wives control them like gaolers, give them pocket money, refuse to 'allow' them to go out, hit them with plates, frying pans, gramophone records, and their fists. Feminist critics have pointed to the misogyny of the portrayal of women in their films – but in truth the dominance of their women over them and their inability to function in the adult world of 'the household' is simply the writers and performers being absolutely truthful to the characters. The theatrical matriarchies that are the Laurel and Hardy homes are natural consequences of their inner story, not fake constructs imposed from without. Indeed, there are several occasions in their movies where mutual affection is displayed between man and wife: in short, the domestic comedies were quite probably highly accurate and searingly honest portrayals of married life for most couples in the early part of the twentieth century – which is why they achieved such success with audiences.

Taking sound technology in their stride, Laurel & Hardy refused to abandon their pantomimic roots, and in so doing became the biggest comedy double-act of the 1930s and beyond – showcased here in M-G-M's Pick a Star *(1937).*

The Stan character is so far removed from normality that we know he will never make it on his own. He faithfully follows in Ollie's optimistic wake, clinging to his coat-tails both literally and metaphorically. It is for this reason that Ollie, ultimately, is the more tragic of the two: for it is he who persists in retaining one foot in the normal social world. He is surely the most generous character in the history of comedy, for he alone has taken Stan under his wing and is carrying him for what he knows in his heart will be his whole life. In the opening scene of one of their finest features, *Sons of the Desert*, they sit listening to a speech by the Grand Master of their Masonic Lodge, and when he reaches the dictum 'The strong shall look after the weak,' Ollie casts a stoic look at Stan that sums up their entire relationship.

Ollie will never stop believing that he can make it, which makes his innumerable falls, both literal and social, all the more tragic – and funny. It is always Ollie who falls in love, attempts to get married; Ollie who sets up the business, whether it's fishing, greetings card selling or Christmas tree delivery. And it is always Ollie who ends face down in the mud, staring out at us in acknowledgement of his failure.

Stan has no such self-knowledge – he is beyond redemption: he doesn't even know that he's failed, for he has nothing but minimal awareness of the concepts of success or failure. He is the Holy Fool who wanders with his human companion through thick and thin, occasionally creating what Laurel later described as 'white magic' – fire with his hands, the manipulation of shadows. When, in *Their Purple Moment*, Ollie declares that 'We are completely broke,' Stan replies 'Yeah. It sure is going to be a hard winter.' The reply comes without despair, without anxiety, for he seems to dwell in a virtual spiritual realm beyond physical survival – a Buddhist *nirvana* divested of all attachments.

The essential schtick of Laurel & Hardy was slapstick and pantomime, to be sure, but slapstick and pantomime *with character*. Their routines and jokes are not imposed from without but emanate from the personalities themselves. As Chaplin said, 'nothing transcends character,' and just as his own acrobatics derive from the impishness of the Little Tramp's desire to play (the roller-skating routine in *Modern Times*), or to escape (the rolling under the fence routine in *A Dog's Life*) so too Laurel & Hardy's pantomime is not 'an act', but what those two characters would do in those circumstances. I would venture to suggest that their slapstick was, at times, more dramatically truthful than Chaplin's: for example, when Chaplin crosses the tightrope in *The Circus* we gasp at his dexterity: he is *almost* not the Tramp. When the monkeys appear on the tightrope with him, and nearly topple him off – *then* he becomes the Tramp again.

With Laurel & Hardy, the mask of their characters never falls: when they struggle to maintain their grip on the iron girders atop a skyscraper in *Liberty*, they are the same incompetent, fearful, bumbling no-hopers tested to their limits by a hostile environment and a malevolent world as they are when, on firm ground, they launch into their classic 'never-ending hat' routine. Despite the huge success of Harold Lloyd's 'thrill' pictures, I have never been fully convinced that the bespectacled and happy-go-lucky character he portrayed was ever socially disadvantaged enough to get himself into such jeopardy-ridden situations.

Even though, in their silent films, Laurel & Hardy had employed some of the familiar knockabout and chase routines of the Mack Sennett style of comedy, they had – from the time of their first wordless comedies – begun to present a more studied, slower and thoughtful pantomime. This was undoubtedly one of the reasons for their success in the sound era. They still made their 'thrill pictures', like *Liberty*, but they also made slower, smaller, comedies like *They Go Boom*, and *Angora Love* where the pantomime takes place almost entirely indoors, in one room. Gone are the frantic chases, the surreal Keystone violence and the Harold Lloyd stunt jeopardy. Here are two men stuck in a dingy boarding-house, with the camera practically in an unmoving two-shot lock-off. The plot of *They Go Boom* is that one man has a cold, and the other is trying to help him. The story is Beckettian in its simplicity. So even in their silent films Laurel & Hardy had progressed to a deeper, more theatrical performance than their peers, producing a sort of 'chamber comedy' – meaning that when sound came and the technology dictated the necessity to restrict a scene to one place, the boys were ready for it: they had the routines, they had the relationship.

Further evidence of the relative ease with which they made the transition from silence to sound was the fact that quite a few of their sound shorts were actually straightforward adaptations of their silent films: *Angora Love* became *Laughing Gravy* and *The Chimp*; *Duck Soup* became *Another Fine Mess*; *Love em and Weep* became *Chickens come Home*, and – most significantly – *Hats Off* (a film that has been lost for 80 years) became the Oscar-winning *The Music Box*.

The team's first sound film did employ dialogue routines, mostly in the set-ups, but the bulk of the comedy is derived from extended physical routines. In fact, ironically, the only film of theirs which perhaps relied overly on speech was their very first, *Unaccustomed As We Are*. Their next, *Berth Marks*, reverts to being almost totally visual: as two vaudevillians travelling on board an express train to Pottsville, the pair spend the entire movie getting ready for bed in an upper berth, only to find that once they've finally settled down, they've arrived at their destination.

Although mostly pantomimic, the opening of *Berth Marks* has a wonderful sound gag in the scene at the railway station, where the two men stand silent and bemused in an attempt to understand the muffled and garbled announcement from the platform announcer; a gag that was perhaps the inspiration for Jacques Tati's opening sequence in *Monsieur Hulot's Holiday*, where crowds of holidaymakers are sent repeatedly to what they think is the correct platform, only to all surge into the pedestrian tunnel, heaving their suitcases with them, to the opposite platform – while the train moves slowly into frame ... at the first, now comically empty, platform ...

The filming of *Berth Marks* provided the team's first major technical difficulties in shooting a sound picture: not so much the challenge of shooting on board a train, though this was tricky enough, but the more problematic challenge of corpsing. The boys making the film crew laugh was a perennial feature of a Laurel & Hardy shoot, but in the silent days it hadn't presented a problem – in fact, the performers were perhaps inspired to further heights by the encouraging laughter. And more – the director, of course, could give instructions from behind the camera. In fact, when previewing an early sound short, Hal Roach's voice could clearly be heard saying 'That's good, that's good.'

With sound, corpsing meant a cut. Every inadvertent titter or belly-laugh would be captured on the soundtrack, so utter silence had to be enforced. The extended routine of Laurel & Hardy getting ready for bed in the upper berth led to so much corpsing that the scene took an unprecedented three days to shoot.

Some critics found these extended routines a source of frustration. Laurel spoke about them in an interview with Boyd Verb in 1959: 'We'd do what you call a milking routine ... If, from the audience reaction ... (in a preview) ... we felt they could stand more, we'd go back and add more and more to it ... Sometimes these early pictures were what you call over-milked' (quoted in Randy Skretvedt's book Laurel and Hardy: *the Magic Behind the Movies*). One prime example of the extended milking routine was in their 1931 three-reeler *Be Big*, the entire plot of which consists of Stan attempting to help Ollie get his boots on. Some critics found this comedy to be frustration heaped on frustration, with no end in sight, and no tag.

I personally find these extended routines evidence of their originality and sheer genius. They display that rarest of things, utter comic bravery. For it is the instinct of every comedian to get to the tag as quickly as possible, to race to the laugh in order to expiate anxiety. Each of Groucho's wisecracks was a moment of relaxation for him: he'd quickly set up and reach the guaranteed laugh a mere few seconds later. Not so Laurel & Hardy. Their slower, lengthier routines had no guaranteed laugh – there were laughs along the way, to be sure, but because they were consistently true to their characters there was not a single gratuitous joke in their movies. This kind of comedy, I would argue, had never before been seen in film history.

It was doubly remarkable in the nascent era of sound, when almost every other comic was chatting away and re-inventing cross-talk music-hall and vaudeville routines for the camera. Laurel & Hardy refused to be obsequious to the microphone, and stubbornly and rightly played to their strengths: pantomime. There were several exceptions in their very earliest talkies – for example, in *Men O'War* they presented their own version of a theatrical standard, the 'Glass of Beer Routine'. *Men O'War* is only their third talkie: playing young sailors, they escort two young flappers to a soda café, where the soda jerk is played by Jimmy Finlayson. Finding they only possess fifteen cents, Ollie instructs Stan to refuse a drink – which of course he doesn't. Each time he is asked, increasingly pointedly by Ollie, 'and what will you have, Stanley?' the hapless Stan replies 'Soda.' This original take on a vaudeville routine first performed twenty-five years previously by the double-act Weber and Fields proved they excelled in spoken-word comedy – but the last section of the film reverts to glorious visual slapstick and one of their classic building routines when they take the girls out onto the boating lake.

Men O'War was Jimmy Finlayson's first talking picture and so moviegoers heard the debut of his now-famous 'D'oh!' as he double-takes at Stan's shenanigans. Once again, in the café routine a creative and original use of soundtrack is evident where Stan – who has been presented by Ollie with the bill of thirty cents – resorts to playing the fruit machine in order to get his hands on some cash. The camera stays on the faces of Stan and Jimmy as the click and whirr of the machine punctuates the tense silence. It is one of the first examples of the use of diegetic sound in movies – specifically, sound from objects not seen onscreen – a technique that, later, Jacques Tati was to elevate into an art. When the fruit machine finally clicks to a stop and we hear the rush and tumble of dozens of jangling coins, the broadness of Stan's smile must have been matched by the cinema audiences – for they were hearing these sound-gags for the very first time, fresh and without precedent. Like all their early sound films, *Men O'War* seems to alternate between being dialogue heavy, and being pure pantomime. It was almost as if there was a conscious policy on the part of the creative team behind the films to switch back and forth so as to settle on a firm aesthetic.

By the time they shot their next movie, *A Perfect Day*, in June 1929, that goal had been reached. Laurel, in particular, hardly has a line of dialogue in the whole picture, apart from 'Goodbye!' as he waves to the neighbours as they attempt to drive off on a summer picnic.

A Perfect Day is, for me, their first truly great sound picture. It has everything – a central funny premise (a family attempting to have a good time) providing a constant backdrop of amusement to the whole story; superb visual gags; several creative running jokes that are repeated exactly the correct number of times; a perfectly formed comic relationship between the two main characters; good supporting performances by Edgar Kennedy, Kay Deslys and Isobel Keith – and a peerless tag, or closing joke, that rounds the comedy off in a way that is both hilarious and existential at the same time

A Perfect Day is a social comedy, sending up the perennial human dilemma of what to do with ourselves on our 'days off.' It is akin to Tony Hancock's 1950s radio comedy *Sunday Afternoon at Home*, where he and Sid James, Bill Kerr and Hattie Jacques, struggle to fill an empty Sunday. Laurel & Hardy and their family are struggling too, but they think they've found a solution – a picnic. The film mines the territory of that terrible truth that whenever one tries consciously and deliberately to have a good time, things never quite work out well: happiness can never be contrived – it comes upon us in moments of unbidden surprise.

In *A Perfect Day* Laurel & Hardy are both now married: it's as if they have courted and won the girls from *Men O'War* and are now settled in domestic bliss. But from the outset they cannot operate in this grown-up world – of running a household, behaving normally, undertaking simple acts like preparing sandwiches for an outing. Such things are completely beyond them. They end up squabbling, fighting and throwing the food around: they are, truly, infants in an adult world.

The bulk of the comedy in *A Perfect Day* is visual but once again none of the visual gags are gratuitous – they grow naturally and believably from their characters. No other comedian could have performed these gags: the mixed-up jacket routine where Stan threads his arm through Ollie's sleeve, and vice-versa; the antics with the car's puncture, when Stan cannot understand how to get the tyre out from underneath the jack. There's a lovely gag with the local priest, whose sudden presence in the street makes the picnickers rush back inside so as not to offend him by being seen to be embarking on a pleasurable day out on the Sabbath.

Laurel's ability to perform 'white magic' – produce fire from his thumb, manipulate shadows at will, eat bowler hats – stems from the performer's theory of comedy that roots it in youthful imagination: 'Slapstick closely approximates the daydreams of childhood,' said Laurel in an interview. Picasso asserted that it had 'taken him a lifetime to learn how to paint like a child,' and it took twenty years in the film industry before Laurel discovered the Talmudic Holy Innocent within him.

With *A Perfect Day* the creative team – Stan Laurel, director Leo McCarey, Hal Roach and the gag-writers Charley Rogers and Charley Chase – found their feet in the new sound era. It is both a social comedy and a broader human 'existential' comedy – but for all that subtlety, it is primarily still a purely visual picture. They'd only been making talking pictures for about a year but already they had reached the conclusion that pantomime was perennial; it would never be defeated by sound, but rather augmented by it.

So by the time they were shooting *Night Owls,* in October 1929, Laurel was reporting to the press that they would be telling their stories chiefly through visual comedy. He told Los Angeles critic Philip K Scheuer: 'We did talk too much at first. (But) if you have seen us in our latest, *Night Owls,* you will have observed that most of our talk is limited to 'shushes'.' For biographer Simon Louvish it was in the film *Hog Wild* that the team reached the zenith of their aesthetic in terms of what might be termed modern pantomime. '... *Hog Wild* is an excellent example of the maturity reached by Stan and Ollie's comedy within just one year of their initiation into the talkie world. Although dialogue is central to the opening sequence of Ollie and his vanishing hat, the rest of the film relies almost solely on visual gags, give or take the inevitable crashes, crunches and cries as Ollie goes off the roof yet again.' Louvish goes on to make the perceptive observation that, 'although slapstick – and slapstick of the thrill kind given the comics location atop a roof – it was nevertheless an advance on the slapstick of earlier years as practised by a pure thrill-seeker like Harold Lloyd. This was slapstick of character: the pratfalls caused by the people themselves, not simply by their situation: (... in *Hog Wild*) the balancing act on the slanted roof of the Hardy home is a comedy of everyday manners.'

Sticking with pantomime was extraordinarily brave, given that most other comedians were moving in the opposite direction, but this resolution was not purely creative but also economic. Laurel & Hardy pictures were popular and lucrative abroad – from the outset, their silents had sold all over the world. Hal Roach had a dilemma. Did he make his comedies dialogue-heavy and therefore endanger this profitable income stream from foreign movie distributors? Or did he work with his leading comics to continue making predominantly visual pictures and maintain international high sales? Ultimately, the studios hit upon a very successful synthesis: the movies remained mostly visual, but the dialogue scenes were shot in several foreign language versions – German, Spanish, Portuguese, Italian and French.

It was a shrewd move. Within a short time Laurel & Hardy became international stars, though they hardly knew it: their modus operandi was so insular as they toiled away inside the Hal Roach Studios month after month that they were strangely unaware of their burgeoning fame. They were making seven shorts a year. Classic after classic rolled out of the Lot of Fun – *Brats, Below Zero, Hog Wild, Another Fine Mess, Laughing Gravy, Beau Hunks,* their Oscar-winning *The Music Box, Helpmates, Scram* – until by the time they emerged, blinking, into the sunlight for what was intended to be a vacation in Britain, they discovered to their surprise that they were the biggest comedy stars in the world.

One ingredient of this success was their innovative use of music: in their 1931 short *Be Big* this is used to masterly effect when Marvin Hatley's score so perfectly complements the extended pantomime that the music almost becomes a third character in the scene.

Another unique visual signature of their films was surrealism. As the chief creative thinker, Laurel always had a penchant for the bizarre. He shared this with neglected comic Larry Semon, whose premature death in 1929 prevented him from making any headway in the new

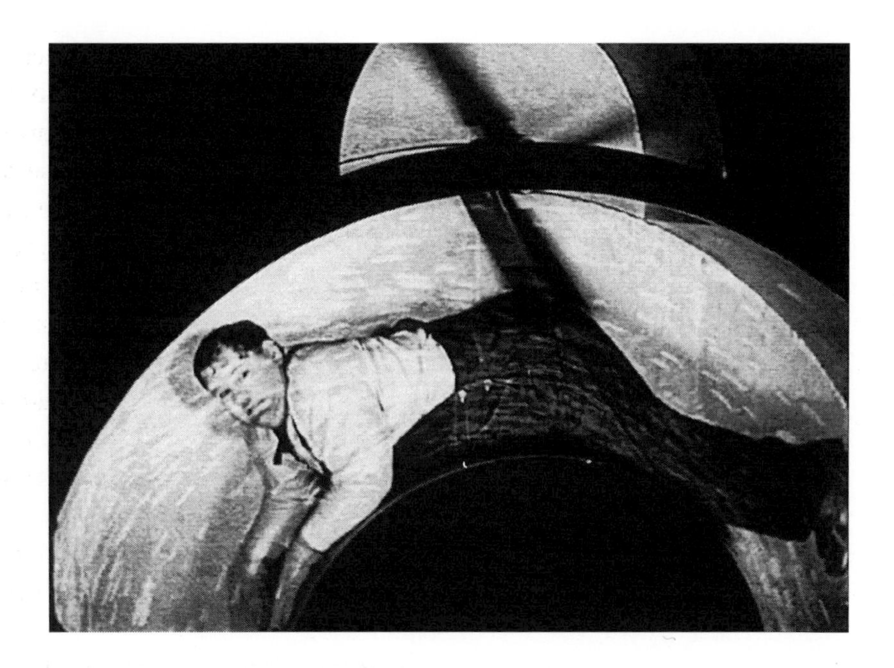

Oliver Hardy fulfilling philosopher Henri Bergson's dictum in his book Laughter: an Essay on the Meaning of the Comic *(1900) that when the human body acts in a mechanical way it becomes funny. In* Busy Bodies *(1933), Ollie adopts the nature and behaviour of a wooden barrel as he is sucked into a chute while working in a sawmill. The tag of the joke is that he is expelled from the tunnel and falls fifty feet to the ground – an event which, in reality, would result in his instant death. For Bergson it is our detachment from the reality that makes slapstick amusing.*

Laurel & Hardy are descendants of Commedia dell'arte Zanni – incompetent servants. While most of their films are set in the 1930s, in Fra Diavolo *(1933) they revert to their historical roots and play medieval servants. One major trope of the comedy of the Zanni was to 'look after something valuable for a Master', – in* Below Zero *(1930) Stan and Ollie find a wallet belonging to a cop, and in* Pack Up Your Troubles *(1932) they are guardians to a human valuable, a girl entrusted to them by her missing father.*

medium. Laurel made several films with Semon at Vitagraph, years before he was paired with Hardy. Semon's extensive use of surrealism rubbed off on Laurel. In *Huns and Hyphens* Semon plays a humble waiter pretending to be a wealthy paramour. Upon leaving the fancy house of his deluded sweetheart, Semon pauses on the pavement, makes sure his girlfriend's door is closed safely behind him – then gets into a child's toy car parked at the side of the road. A full-sized vehicle drives past him and Semon hitches a ride by chucking a tow-rope at it – and being whizzed out of frame. Later in the same picture Semon – having knocked out an annoying diner – pins a large menu to the prostrate man's chest like a sail, puts a powerful fan on the floor by the fellow's feet, and blows the man like a sailing boat out through the door, into a stream in the gutter, and down the drain.

In Laurel & Hardy films, the surrealism was on occasions as bizarre, but never gratuitous. The cycling goat in the closing frames of *Another Fine Mess*, the manipulation of shadows in *Blockheads*, the rubber neck-twisting in *Way Out West*, Stan's cartoonish distended belly in *Below Zero* after being plunged in a barrel of icy water by a malevolent restaurateur – these bizarre images were characteristic of Laurel. Although his performance was a sublime achievement of restraint, and the Stan character a wonderful example of almost non-acting, there always existed under the surface a touch of the manic, an impish desire to play with reality.

So although it had its roots in the antics of vaudeville and music hall, this was a new comedy being created on the lot at Culver City. And Laurel knew it. By the time the boys were famous and were fleeing adulatory mobs in London in 1930, he gave an interview to the *East Anglian Times*, which neatly summarised his philosophy of the comic:

> The slapstick of today is more refined than the slapstick of twenty years ago. Its wit is sharper and its capers are more extravagant. Slapstick more closely approximates to the daydreams of childhood than any other form of screen entertainment. The antics of the funny men in the custard-pie comedies are an exaggeration of those which keep children in the heights of laughter. You may not see the similarity at first, but on thinking it over the resemblance is very definitely there. The comedian who knocks down the policeman is the small child rebelling against authority. The custard pie is the symbol of revolt – revolt against an ignorant world of grown-ups which cannot appreciate that the dirty puddle at the end of the garden path is really the most romantic of lakes, on which there are boats to be sailed and bridges to be built.

For Chaplin, comedy was a social force – for Laurel it was psychological. Laurel recognised that all comedy at bottom is the inability of the comic character to operate successfully in the adult world. This includes the social rebel – for in knocking off the policeman's helmet he is not being political, but is swiping at a parent. In Chaplin's films one always feels that the Tramp could win: in fact, he often does. With Laurel & Hardy, their entire aesthetic is fail, fail – and fail again. More recently the comic Larry David expressed an identical philosophy of comedy when he said 'My comedy is all about pretending to be an adult, and pretending to be able to operate in the adult world.'

Film after film displaying the finest examples of visual comedy yet produced poured out of the Hal Roach lot: *Towed in the Hole* of 1932 where the hapless duo attempt to get ahead in the world by restoring a fishing boat; and *Busy Bodies* of 1933 where the boys play workers at a sawmill – more sophisticated and slower than their earlier completely silent carpentry comedy of 1929 *The Finishing Touch*, and further evidence of their continued commitment to pantomime.

When they moved into feature films, once again pantomime predominated: indeed, the most memorable scenes from their canon throughout the 1930s are visual: their dance in front of the saloon in *Way Out West* to 'At the Ball, That's All' played by the Avalon Boys; the running gag of Ollie falling in the pond in the same picture; the extended silent routine in *Swiss Miss* when Stan attempts to trick a St Bernard dog into giving him his barrel of brandy by lying on the floor and fabricating a snowstorm with goose feathers; the routine in *Blockheads* when Stan is left behind in the trenches of the First World War and we see him twenty years after the war has ended still performing his same daily routine, marching up and down, setting out his stove, and throwing his tin of beans onto a refuse heap of tins now the size of a small mountain.

It is fair to say that, by the end of the 1930s, the fast-talking comedy had won; the Cary Grant style of chat, farce and romance held sway over the waning world of the visual comedian; and Abbott and Costello's cross-talk patter was on the ascendant. Hal Roach's stable of silent comedy stars had moved on to become gag-writers or supporting artistes at the big studios; and by 1940 the Lot of Fun was not producing any comedy at all, focussing on B-pictures and dramas and what were called mini-features.

Laurel & Hardy moved to Twentieth Century Fox, where they made a series of – by their own admission – sub-standard pictures, largely because creative control was out of Laurel's hands and Fox were forcing them to emulate the dialogue-heavy comedies of the era. They were no longer the comedy kings of the screen, though they enjoyed a rich renaissance on stage as they spent the late 40s and early 50s touring England and Europe in vaudeville.

The fashion for talkies may have won, but this was not quite the triumph it is generally believed. When James Agee's article appeared in 1949 in *Life* magazine in praise of Comedy's Golden Age, it was silent comedy he was praising. His was the most eloquent voicing of the growing awareness that the appearance of the microphone had, very probably, thrown the baby out with the bathwater.

CHAPTER 4

Swansong of a Pantomimist: Chaplin

Chaplin responded to the advent of the talkies by raising his game. Far from being cowed by the new aesthetic, Chaplin's response was to lift the art of silent comedy to a higher level. *City Lights* and *Modern Times* are considered two of the finest cinematic masterpieces of the twentieth century: both were created in the sound era, and both are pure pantomime.

As ever with Chaplin, a certain anxiety fuelled his drive for excellence: his concerns about the arrival of sound were palpable to all around him. He became very nervous. He had watched Laurel & Hardy make the seamless transition to dialogue and recognised that whereas speech had enhanced their comedy (he wrote a fan letter to director Leo McCarey extolling the team's films and predicting a great future for them) if the Tramp spoke it would decrease his power as an Everyman. The Tramp's character was a complex creation fuelled by fight and flight, infused with the cunning of the streets. His survival hinged not on language but on dance, evasion, escape, physical trickery. Years later Chaplin would write in his autobiography, 'The silent picture, first of all, is a universal means of expression. Talking pictures necessarily have a limited field, they are held down to the particular tongues of particular races.' He approved of the talking picture as 'a valuable addition to the dramatic art regardless of its limitations, but I regard it only as an addition, not as a substitute,' because, he said, 'Pantomime lies at the base of any form of drama. To continue with a feeling that the art of pantomime was gradually becoming obsolete was a discouraging thought … But – if I talked I would become like any other comedian.'

These mixed feelings coloured his approach to his work: Chaplin wrote a dialogue script for *Modern Times* – then abandoned it. He and his brother Sydney had been shown Monsieur Lauste's fledgling synchronised sound technology as early as 1918, and in 1926 Sydney himself was the star of Vitaphone's second (recorded) sound movie, *The Better Ole.* No-one understood the serious implications of the innovation better than the Chaplin brothers. By July 8 1928 Chaplin was in the early stages of preparing *City Lights*. From its inception the film had been intended to be pure pantomime, although a synchronised soundtrack must have been planned for gags such as the 'swallowed whistle' routine. In April 1929, during pre-production, Alf Reeves wrote to Sydney Chaplin saying '... sound effects, if required, can be added afterwards', and on May 16 1930 he wrote again confirming that 'Charlie ... intends to synchronise it for sound and music ... no dialogue.'

Unfazed by the arrival of audio, Chaplin makes City Lights *(1931), cinema's first visual comic masterpiece in the age of sound.*

Nevertheless it was an anxious Chaplin that attended its premiere on January 30 1931 at the new Los Angeles Theatre on Broadway. His anxiety had been fuelled by an earlier preview eliciting a mild response from an audience who, while not indifferent, were not enthusiastic.

He needn't have worried. The premiere was attended by Albert Einstein, the Vidors, the de Milles, Hedda Hopper, Gloria Swanson – in front of whom the greatest silent comedian in the world placed himself in the critical arena to be judged. With silent comedy already an anachronism, mime itself was on trial that night.

It was a triumph. From the somewhat defensive opening caption – 'A Comedy Romance in Pantomime' – and the statue-unveiling sequence of the first few frames, to the closing scenes later to be described by

James Agee as the '... greatest piece of acting and the highest moment in movies', the film scaled new heights of picture-making. It was to become many directors' (including Fellini and Tarkovsky) favourite movie of all time and was registered by Congress as being of historical and cultural significance. After its opening, the reviews were largely euphoric. *The Record* stated: 'Nobody in the world but Charlie Chaplin could have done it. He is the only person that has that peculiar something ... to defy the popular penchant for pictures that talk'. The box office matched the superlatives of the reviews: the movie took more than five million dollars, half of which went to Chaplin following his renegotiation with United Artists.

City Lights has an unjust reputation for excessive sentimentality, a judgement I believe that diminishes the sublime physical routines the movie contains. From the outset Chaplin's clowning is fresh, socially satirical and funny: as a crowd gathers before the unveiling of a statue dedicated to Peace and Prosperity, Chaplin delivers the first blistering satire on the advent of the sound picture when the dignitaries, in tinny and squeaking voices, emit gibberish pronouncements on the significance of the occasion – establishing the genre of his film as a movie with a soundtrack, but no actual words. When the huge drape is raised it reveals, of course, the little Tramp lying asleep on the lap of one of the statues, to the snobbish horror of the throng. To the furious silent commands from the police and dignitaries to get down, Chaplin gets his trousers caught on an upturned sword, and his struggles to free himself are punctuated by a hilarious interruption of the national anthem, which instantly freezes the hostility of the cops who have to stop, stand to attention and salute, as well as Chaplin, whose attempts to pay respects to the anthem whilst hanging from a broadsword, show that he had lost none of his acrobatic skills.

With *City Lights*, however, a new subtlety had crept in to Chaplin's performance – indeed, by the close of the picture his Tramp figure has descended to a state of reality that is actually hard to watch; no longer is he the cheerful crafty rascal who always has the last laugh, but a downbeat, haggard figure displaying all the mentally unbalanced hallmarks of a real vagrant, his clothes more ragged and torn than usual and his rants at two kids who fire their peashooters at him possessing the hard, dry, sterile anger of a weakened hobo. Although the film is pierced with this new dimension of realism, the story is balanced with some fine madcap physical clowning reminiscent of Chaplin at his Mutual best. The boxing sequence in particular demonstrates that Chaplin had lost none of his nimbleness of footwork: the classic sidestepping routines were reprises of previous antics, as were the punchings of the referee, but original physical gags abound such as the Tramp becoming tied to the string that pulls the bell, resulting in him ringing it every time he falls. It was a boxing routine emulated by his old pal Laurel the following year in 1932 in the short *Any Old Port.*

In the drunkenness sequences with the millionaire (Harry Myers), Chaplin revisits not only his Mutual masterpiece of 1916, *One A.M.* – his first solo film (apart from Albert Austin's cameo as his driver) in which he plays an inebriated aristocrat attempting to get to bed but whose household objects conspire against him – but also his old routine that made his name, the sozzled Viscount in Fred Karno's *Mumming Birds.* In *City Lights,* however, Chaplin advances the routine by adding another character, the wonderfully pickled tycoon. Their dual clowning has a magnificent rapport; the restaurant sequence in particular being a tour de force of extended mime. Chaplin lights his companion's cigar in mistake for his own; he eats a long party streamer thinking it is a strand of spaghetti; and mistakes a couple's Apache Dance for the real thing – leaping up and removing his dinner jacket in preparation for defending the woman he believes is being attacked.

The escalating anarchy of this restaurant sequence bears some similarity to the restaurant sequence in Jacques Tati's much later *Playtime,* in its gradual build, its crowding dance-floor, its sense of slowly, slowly, becoming increasingly out of control.

Indeed, it becomes bacchanalian: as Chaplin and the lord become more and more drunk, the rhythms of the dance-music begin to infuse them; their feet begin to drum on the floor and – unable to contain himself any longer – Chaplin rises and grabs the nearest woman, twirling her around hysterically. Once the woman is grabbed back by her husband, Chaplin grasps a waiter and dances with him – nothing can restrain him.

Use of sound permeates the movie, from the tinny squeaking of the dignitaries speeches at the top of the film to the whistling and *pop!* of varying lengths of spaghetti strands as they disappear into Chaplin's mouth. With *City Lights* Chaplin was inventing a new type of film: a visual comedy with sound. With his next picture, *Modern Times,* he advanced yet further.

*

Despite the great reception accorded *City Lights* and its instant recognition as a masterpiece – or perhaps because of this – there was a hiatus between its release and starting work on *Modern Times.* If Chaplin had hesitated on

In Chaplin's Modern Times *(1936) the Tramp not only becomes mechanical but is – like Oliver Hardy in* Busy Bodies *– literally swallowed by a machine. The comedian's moral point that the industrial age is turning humans into mechanical objects is not the cause of the laughter – for such an observation comes in hindsight. The laugh emanates from the sudden unexpected treatment of the body as a mere 'thing.'*

Not only was Chaplin the greatest protagonist of silent comedy but he also invented the modern 'visual comedy with sound'. In City Lights *(1931) and* Modern Times *(1936, above) he applied soundtrack comedy to the visual – the intelligible speech of a politician, a rumbling stomach, a gibberish song. Above, the Little Worker is tyrannised by a Big Brother Factory Boss – an image that must have burned deep into the young Jacques Tati's mind, for the Frenchman paid homage to it in his 1967 film* Playtime.

In Modern Times *(1936) Chaplin spoke for the first time on film. Only he didn't speak at all – he sang. But in line with his dictum that 'actions speak louder than words,' his song was utter gibberish – Edward Lear-like passages of nonsense befitting the century's greatest mime.*

the threshold of sound, he dallied even more as dialogue comedy became more entrenched. The fact that a dialogue script exists of *Modern Times* is evidence of this crisis. Could he continue making pantomime? Early in 1931 he had been unequivocal: 'I give the talkies six months more. At the most a year. Then they're done.' A mere three months later, in May 1931, his view had softened into 'Dialogue may or may not have a place in comedy ... What I merely said was that dialogue does not have a place in the sort of comedies I make ... for myself, I know that I cannot use dialogue.'

There is talking in *Modern Times*, but predominantly non-diegetic, emanating from a source not within the live action of the scene itself. For example, in the demonstration of the fast-food invention, when Chaplin as the hapless factory worker is strapped into a chair and force-fed by a mechanical device, the spoken instructions come from a gramophone record. The factory bosses' orders come, Big Brother-like, from a huge screen on a wall – and the only speech from a living human being within the scene itself comes from Chaplin: but it is gibberish, a jabberwocky language invented deliberately to prove, once again, the paucity of language as a vehicle for humour.

When challenged to explain why he had resisted dialogue and would continue to do so, Chaplin observed that '... for years I have specialised in one type of comedy – strictly pantomime. I have measured it, gauged it, and studied it. I have been able to establish exact principles to govern its reactions on audiences. It has a certain pace and tempo. Dialogue, to my way of thinking always slows action, because action must wait upon words.'

The story of film-making in the ensuing decades was to prove the prescience and accuracy of this observation: while through the 30s, 40s and most of the 50s fast-talking speech dominated screenplays, from the 60s onwards it did not. The word once more withdrew and acquiesced to action: indeed, any tutor of screenplay writing today will tell you that the meat of the craft of screenwriting is action, action, action – show, do not tell.

Yet despite Chaplin's absolute belief in the dominance of action over words, it is a measure of his insecurity and susceptibility to peer pressure that he spent several weeks shooting dialogue scenes for *Modern Times*. Thankfully they were discarded and the movie remained purely visual. Although he rejected dialogue, he did not reject sound – and he set to work creating an innovative comic soundtrack, though he did retain title cards. Audio-tracks for the new sound pictures were normally handed over by directors to musical arrangers, but characteristically Chaplin oversaw every step himself. He even created the effects himself. Production manager Alf Reeves came into the studio one day and found Chaplin crouched down blowing bubbles into a bucket of water. It was to become the sound for the stomach-rumbling scene, in which the warden's wife sits next to Chaplin drinking tea, both attempting to cover up the fact they are emitting bodily noises. A memorandum from Chaplin states his firm intention for the use of noise: 'Natural sounds part of the composition, ie. Auto horns, sirens and cowbells worked into the music.'

Music, of course, was also key. Chaplin worked deep into the night with his orchestra under the directorship of Alfred Newman and the composer David Raksin to weave a musical score that wasn't mere accompaniment to a scene but fundamentally attached to the action: again, this was innovative.

While *Modern Times* justly possesses the reputation of being an important satire on the age of the Great Depression and the effect of industrialisation on the soul of modern man, in purely comedic terms it has a picaresque, episodic structure, which led critic Otis Ferguson to describe it as 'really a collection of two-reelers that might have been titled *The Factory*, *The Jailbird*, *The Watchman*, and *The Singing Waiter*.' Each episode, however, contains sublime physical routines – the manic tightening of the bolts on the production line as the conveyor-belt speeds up; the falling into the whirling machinery; the jail escape; and the flag routine. The latter was a neat sideswipe at Hollywood critics who were branding him a leftie – Chaplin has a lorry judder over a pothole and dislodge a red warning flag; the Tramp picks it up and follows its owner simply in order to give it back, and in so doing inadvertently becomes the head of a group of unionised marchers. This is Chaplin the misunderstood social critic: I am no leftie, he is saying – I am an observer of the suffering of the human soul, whichever class you are.

The Tramp and the Gamin (Paulette Goddard) are outsiders par excellence, their only home a shack on the edge of a mud-bank and a miserable stretch of river. They are on the fringes of the city – but they could be on the fringes of the world. Even the river proves an illusion: on his first morning in his new abode the Tramp wakes bright and optimistic and, clad in bathing suit, prepares to plunge deep into its luxurious waters a mere ten yards from his porch. It turns out to be only a few inches deep. His pratfall brings him sharply back to life: he woke up as a successful homeowner – two minutes later he knows that he is really only a tramp sitting in a muddy river next to a hut.

There is more than a hint in the film that Chaplin knew this would be the Tramp's final appearance: the entire movie is an unfolding of scenes depicting society rejecting this odd little vagrant who had spellbound the world for twenty years – culminating in the final iris shot of the pair disappearing into the undefined distance.

Why does society reject the Tramp? Or, conversely, why does the Tramp reject society and why is he unable to settle down?

My theory is that the Tramp is a character who plays around too much. Who plays around? Kids. Chaplin's screen character is a stunted ten-year-old – the age, roughly, when his father died and his mother was incarcerated in an asylum. Living on the streets with his brother Sydney, on his wits, he not only developed sharp survival instincts, but retained that sense of anarchic play that only someone outside society can cultivate. Chaplin – I believe – never became socialised. The rebellious, childish anger he had when he was 10 years old never left him, and it found its way onto the screen.

Above and beyond its themes, of course, the routines in *Modern Times* are to be enjoyed for their own sake as masterly gags that represent the distillation of a lifetime in silent comedy. All the comic scenarios stand up well today – the chase of the secretary following his breakdown on the production-line when the Tramp transforms himself into a kind of Shakespearian Bottom-as-Donkey using two lowered wrenches for drooping ears, his ribald comic libido released from mechanical drudgery; the foreman (Chester Conklin) stuck in the machinery while Chaplin kindly feeds him his lunch; the jailbreak sequence – and the final scenes in the restaurant when for the first and last time the Tramp opens his mouth and speaks.

Fittingly, it is gibberish that he emits: words that exist beyond language and are therefore merely sounds. Obtaining a job in the restaurant where his gamin companion has secured work, he launches into a (brief) career as a Singing Waiter. He loses the lyrics –hastily written onto his shirt-cuff – a few seconds after his entrance, a flourish of his arm making the cuff fly off. The jabberwocky verses that emerge summarise his comic schtick: the full meaning and story of the song is conveyed in mime. In short, he is saying, I am making a sound picture, yet look – I don't actually need words at all.

With *Modern Times* Chaplin's wholly visual career came to an end. The man who had pioneered the transfer of comic pantomime from the stages of small theatres in provincial England to the global audience of international cinema had made his last visual comedy.

*

Or had he? Almost immediately he began work on his next picture, which from the start he was determined would be about Hitler. For the first time in his life he was commencing pre-production with a dialogue script. Yet the power and enduring appeal of visual comedy is evidenced by the fact that the best-remembered sequences are silent: the acrobatic balancing act with the inflated globe; the shaving scene performed in perfect rhythm to Brahm's *Hungarian Dance No 5*, and the coin-in-the-cake routine – a cousin to the many hidden object/poison gags in numerous pictures since.

The shaving sequence is a glorious demonstration of the supremacy of Chaplin as mime, and – despite his subsequent nostalgic work in *Limelight* – is perhaps his swansong. Set up vocally with the radio announcer instructing listeners to instil rhythm in their work by listening to music, the routine is a pleasant counterpoint to the speeded-up conveyor belt routine of *Modern Times.* Each flick of the razor, each application of the shaving foam, is utterly precise. Chaplin filmed the routine in time to a gramophone record, but then re-recorded an orchestral accompaniment – which remarkably was achieved in the first take.

It wasn't the first time he had performed a comic barber routine: in his 1919 short *Sunnyside* for First National he filmed an extended eight-minute long scenario with his old stalwart from his Fred Karno days, Albert Austin, but the entire routine was cut from the picture. The gags are different – the comedy of the earlier routine is derived from the Tramp's utter incompetence as a barber – applying shaving foam to

Austin's face as though it were whitewash, getting the handle mixed up with the blade thus making Austin think his throat has been cut, and so on – but there is a piece of mime identical in both movies: the rhythmic stropping of the razor on the leather strap. In *The Great Dictator* Chaplin replicates the neat, upward swing of the hand as he works, a small comic detail that he must have remembered and reproduced twenty years later.

For all his fears at not being able to break into sound pictures, *The Great Dictator* turned out to be Chaplin's biggest financial success, making more than $11 million worldwide. His prescience had captured the mood of the Allied West: when he had begun work on the film, the UK signalled its intention to prohibit its release, owing to the then Government policy of appeasement or rapprochement with Nazi Germany. By the time of its release of course, in 1941, Britain had been at war with Hitler for nearly two years. It was exactly the film the world wanted to see.

Yet despite the huge success of *The Great Dictator* no one would deny that by 1941 Chaplin's greatest work was behind him. His last three films, *Monsieur Verdoux*, *Limelight* and *The Countess of Hong Kong* were admirable in their way – the jewel at the centre of *Limelight* being a silent duet with Chaplin and Keaton – but there can be no doubt that technology had rendered Chaplin's art and modus operandi of film-making anachronistic. His talkies were not as good as his silent pictures. He was anxious about his legacy: in his last two decades he believed that his silent films would not be appreciated beyond his lifetime, so in the 1950s he relentlessly re-edited and re-packaged them, adding spoken commentaries, in the belief that this would make them more appealing to a modern, and a less forgiving, audience.

CHAPTER 5

Out and Down: Buster Keaton

The received story of Buster Keaton's middle and final act is altogether curiouser and somewhat sadder than Chaplin's: the script we read for his life and career in the 30s and beyond is one of steady decline, rejection by the movie industry, and descent into a string of humiliating jobs as gag-writer for lesser comics.

This is actually a crude distortion of what really happened. True, there was a period in the early 1930s when his only income was royalty payments from Japan where his movies from the 1920s were still being shown (Japan made no sound pictures until the mid-30s); and a combination of alcoholism and lawsuits by an ex-wife appeared to batter him into acceptance of a minor role in the brave new world of sound.

The reality was far more complex than the headlines: what is often forgotten, or simply not told, is that many of the movies he made after he made the switch to M-G-M in 1928 were big financial successes, as were the films he made with Jimmy Durante. His shorts with Educational Pictures – the company that after the coming of sound became a kind of refuge for silent comics of the 20s – were mildly successful, as were his shorts for Columbia.

So while his later career was not as outwardly triumphant as his glory days, Keaton's output in the sound era both on film and on stage represents a somewhat neglected body of work that carried the beacon of visual comedy right through the decades when everyone thought it was dead and buried. Furthermore he exerted a profound influence upon later comedians such as Jacques Tati, who saw him onstage in Paris just after the war – and grasped the torch that Keaton handed out to him.

Keaton's return to the stage in the 40s is a story that has not been fully told – a rediscovery of his vaudevillian roots that arguably had more influence on the next generation of visual comedians than his films, which did not enjoy a renaissance until the mid-to-late-50s when TV pumped out re-runs of his own work plus that of Mack Sennett, Laurel & Hardy et al.

Despite two years of sound technology, Buster Keaton continued to remain silent in his 1929 film, Spite Marriage, *his final wholly dialogue-free movie. Here he props up Dorothy Sebastian, with whom he developed the 'helping the drunken woman into bed routine' which he performed onstage at the Cirque Medrano, Paris.*

Keaton's last truly independent silent feature, *Steamboat Bill Junior*, was made in 1927: thereafter, his old friend and mentor Joe Schenck announced that he was now to be subsumed beneath the ever-growing M-G-M umbrella. Schenck would go on to form Twentieth Century Fox in 1933. This was the story mirrored across the industry – the smaller independent studios that had given birth to and nurtured the great comedy of the 10s and 20s were fading in power before the growth of big business. The cottage-industry days were over – days when you could go to a park in the morning with a film camera and a few friends, and by evening you had a comedy movie that would make you thousands of dollars. Famous Players-Laski Corporation had become Paramount; Carl Laemmle's Universal City Studios had become Universal; and in 1924

Keaton and Sebastian developed into a formidable double-act. Here, in another scene from Spite Marriage, *they manage to convey a comic restraint in their amorousness, in an increasingly moralistic Hollywood.*

Metro, Goldwyn and Mayer had fused into their famous triumvirate. Dozens of other smaller studios were swallowed up by the big fish. Some persisted, like Educational Pictures, Republic, Monogram and Grand National – and it was these smaller lots that continued to produce many of the low-budget but sometimes innovative comedy work of the era.

*

Keaton's first movie in the sound era was *Spite Marriage*, released by M-G-M in 1929. Unlike Chaplin, Keaton was keen to embrace the new technology: he wanted sound, but the studio insisted it be dialogue-free. There are some sublime visual routines in *Spite Marriage*. The opening set-up includes a great reveal with Elmer (Buster Keaton) ostensibly a gentleman in high society endeavouring to court the sought-after Trilby Drew (Dorothy Sebastian). His clothes and polite manners dupe us into believing that, in a departure from his previous Everyman character, Keaton has joined the ranks of the aristocracy. Hints are made as to this being a ruse, however, when we see him struggle to ride a horse; and the penny is fully dropped minutes later when his true identity is laid bare – that of a dry-cleaner who has borrowed one of his customer's fancy frock-coats and transformed himself for the day. 'Your suits had a good airing,' he assures the customer as he returns it, stone-faced. This gag is reminiscent of Larry Semon's routine in *Huns and Hyphens* released in 1919, when we see him leave his house in full finery, puffing on a big posh cigar, but on arriving at the restaurant we assume he owns, he gradually sheds all his outer layers of wealth and dons a humble waiter's clothes.

There is a nice running gag of Elmer lifting his top hat and extending his hand for a shake – just out of synchronicity with the man he is greeting – which goes on for several attempts until Elmer abandons the robotic ritual and simply ends up grabbing the man's mitt. And the top-hat gag even has a topper, when Elmer turns and – almost bumping into a lamp-post – automatically launches into the top-hat-lift-handshake before recovering himself.

As with Chaplin's *City Lights* and *Modern Times*, *Spite Marriage* contained full musical score and synchronised soundtrack – again, a new mode of visual comedy movie was being invented here. There are sound effects in abundance – odd trombone noises for sneezes, theatre audience applause, laughter, swanee-whistle accompaniments to slip-ups, a melée of crowd noise as passengers scramble to flee a sinking yacht – even a gobbledook speeded-up cartoonish argument between two sailors.

The stylistic tone of the first two-thirds of the film, however, is of a talkie – a domestic rom-com. Gone are the ambitious stunts, the chases. There are one or two pratfalls, however, and a sublime extended physical routine where the newly married Elmer helps his drunken semi-conscious bride into bed. This sequence was to achieve longevity and not a little notoriety – producer Lawrence Weingarten wanted the scene cut from the picture for being 'blue'. The scene remained and became a fixed feature of Keaton's stage act when he returned to vaudeville.

A new realism permeates the 'rom-com' part of the film, at odds with Keaton's previous work which always hovered on the edge of the bizarre: when Elmer is enlightened as to the truth behind his marriage to Trilby Drew, his reaction is quite brutal – he floors the guy with a single punch.

And whereas in his previous films he would have fled with cartoon speed, now he simply walks off, striding down the sidewalk casting nervous glances behind him. This is Keaton settling down into the realistic world of the talking picture, but the lack of dialogue makes him look uncomfortable. At times he seems rooted to the spot and appears in some scenes to be on auto-pilot. There is an air of him having been pitched into a new world in which he does not belong: the straight actors are favoured, and although he is clearly still the star of the piece, there is a hint of the beginnings of the era of the comedian-as-support. The entire film is shot through also with a marriage-weary cynicism, perhaps reflecting his own domestic troubles: one title-card declares, tellingly, 'There are only two cures for love: Marriage, and Suicide'.

However, immediately after this sequence, as if rebelling against it, suddenly we are pitched into the old familiar Keaton world. Elmer jumps into a taxi but finds it's actually a getaway car containing a bank robber, is pursued by the police, ends up in the harbour, and gets taken on as deckhand by a private yacht owner. Once we've returned to this picaresque world of the Keaton comedy-adventure, we never leave it until the final credits. We are treated to a display of his acrobatics when he is ordered to varnish the mast – cue for rope-entanglement business fifty feet in the air and much dangling with said rope entwined round ankles – followed by a great visual gag down below when the boozing engine-room steward reveals that he keeps a secret store of alcohol in the fire extinguisher. Of course Elmer has recourse to use the extinguisher – and promptly creates an inferno. That Keaton had lost none of his athleticism is proved minutes later when he performs an amazing display of acrobatics while hanging from the yacht's boom.

*

Despite the huge success of the near-silent *Spite Marriage*, Keaton was still anxious to prove himself in talkies. In 1929 he and Norma Shearer did a sound-test that has gone down in Hollywood legend. A crowd gathered outside the recording booth on the M-G-M lot. Minutes later a technician ran out, yelled 'Keaton talks!' – and the air became full of hats. His first dialogue movie was *Hollywood Revue of 1929*, M-G-M's showcase for its new stable of all-talking, all-singing stars. But there was still no dialogue for Keaton – in a dancing Salome routine he reprised the descending-the-stair gag from his 1921 short *The Haunted House* and his amazing lifting-both-feet-onto-the-edge-of-the-chair gag, a speciality he reproduced throughout his long career. His first starring talkie proper was *Free and Easy*, released in 1930.

It is undeniable that the sound movies he made for M-G-M from 1930-34 were the nadir of his career; although they contained glimpses of the fine slapstick of the former decade, they represent a prime example of the way the new sound technology exerted a dreadful impact on cinematic comedy. Watching them now it is as if suddenly all energy has been drained from Keaton's onscreen world: the pace is leaden, the dialogue unfunny. He does insert physical play into the storylines, such as the undressing scene in *Doughboys*, when as Elmer – his new, slower and more dim-witted persona – he finds himself inadvertently signed up to the army and is instructed to remove his civilian attire, resulting in an acrobatic routine where he ends up swinging from a light-fitting, but the majority of the action flounders with the necessity of a static camera, two-shot and close-up.

He was no longer in control of his films: M-G-M supplied gag-writers and scenario writers, and although he was still working with his familiar director Edward Sedgwick, this was not sufficient to recapture or recreate the brilliance of his former output. Years later in interviews, Keaton blamed this lack of control for the relative mediocrity of these M-G-M pictures, but in reality they were hampered simply by dint of being sound films. In the movie *What! No Beer?* released in 1933, Jimmy Potts (Jimmy Durante) is lathering his face with shaving foam and gets some in Elmer's eyes. 'Watch out, you're getting it in my eyes!' says Elmer. The superfluity of this line perfectly demonstrates the inferiority of dialogue over visual comedy – not only is it superfluous, it is also not funny!

Like Chaplin, Keaton was not a dialogue comedian. Furthermore, the writers at M-G-M gave him a dumb persona, leaning towards that of Stan Laurel, whereas his previous screen character had been vital and energised – not a rascal like Chaplin, but a stoical fighter. In the M-G-M pictures he is an idiot who drifts through the action in a complete state of victimhood. This was not Keaton.

All in all he made six features for M-G-M – *Free and Easy*, *Doughboys*, *Parlour, Bedroom and Bath*, *Speak Easily*, *The Passionate Plumber* and *What! No Beer?* before a combination of disillusion and his heavy drinking led to the studio firing him in 1933. Ironically this was nothing to do with the failures of these movies at the box office – paradoxically Keaton's sound pictures made more money than his silent features, and his teaming with Jimmy Durante was a critical and commercial success. Whatever the causes of his drinking – self-awareness of his decline and knowledge that he was producing sub-standard fare, or domestic strife – the result was a once-great silent comic reduced, in 1934, to signing up with one of Hollywood's Poverty Row studios, Educational Pictures.

Poverty Row studios were those companies who continued to produce low-budget movies, often two-reelers but also hour-long supports, in the era when features ruled the roost: Republic Pictures, Grand National, Monogram Pictures, PRC, and Educational Pictures, among many, who battled on through the 30s and 40s until the big studios set up their own B-movie units, TV appeared with its half-hour comedy genre, and in cinemas the two-feature programme vanished.

*

Keaton made sixteen shorts for Educational Pictures. For many years these movies were unavailable, and for this reason, combined with Keaton's later pronouncements of disdain for the work he did in the 30s and beyond, people believed that every movie he made in that decade represented a trough in the great comic's career. However, since his death and the release of these shorts, as well as the ten two-reelers he made with Columbia between 1939-41, a re-evaluation of his work in the sound era can be made. As James Neibaur states in his 2010 book *The Fall of Buster Keaton*, Keaton's two-reelers, the Columbia tenure in particular '… may very well represent the best of the comedian's work in sound movies.' I don't quite concur, believing the Educational shorts superior, but the general point is valid.

After shooting the first two shorts for Educational, Keaton made his first foray into Europe, flying to Paris to make a French comedy feature, *Le roi des Champs Elysées*, shot in twelve days. While vaudeville was declining in the USA, visual acts were still thriving on the Continent because of the language differences; they persisted through the war and beyond. Keaton was an act they wanted: and whereas *Le roi* is not quite a magnificent return to form, it contains some fine visual comedy. Shot in French with no US release, there is no documentary proof that Jacques Tati saw the film, but there is compelling evidence enough in that a scene in *Le roi* depicts Jim le Balafré (Keaton) taking pity on a caged bird and placing it outside the window of an apartment so it can be bathed in a ray of sunshine. Tati reprises this touching scene twenty-five years later in *Mon Oncle* when he adjusts the window of his apartment so it reflects a beam of sunlight on a similarly caged canary. In later years Keaton was to say that, of all his sound features, *Le roi* was the one in which he was allowed free rein to play to his strengths; in short, he was allowed to … 'keep quiet with lots of sound all around me.' For most of the picture he remains in dumb-show while his fellow actors talk in French around him, and there are some splendid pantomime antics such as when he is attempting to get onstage and gets tangled in a ladder.

Hampered by the arrival of dialogue in films, Buster Keaton was forced to lower his sights and work for one of the 'poverty row' studios, Educational Pictures (and subsequently as a humble gag-man for M-G-M). Here in The Gold Ghost *(1934) the director stops the characters talking for few minutes and allows Keaton to display flashes of his old brilliance.*

He followed up *Le roi* with another European movie, this time a British production shot in Spain, *The Invader*, which wasn't a major success but which contained sufficient quality business for him to reproduce it in his later film for Columbia, *Pest from the West.*

Returning to Educational Pictures after his European ventures, Keaton ploughed himself into a relentless routine of making two-reelers, and produced some flashes of genius. Once again the best of these are the ones that contain most visual content: *One Run Elmer* (1935) features a delightful set-up with an immediate visual impact: Elmer runs a tiny gas-station in the middle of the desert. No bigger than a shed, the cash-desk is cobwebbed and the rocking-chair in which Elmer sits waiting patiently for a customer while puffing on a corn-cob pipe has been rocking for so long in that position that it has formed a small pit, reminiscent of Stan Laurel's boot-worn military trench in *Blockheads* of 1933.

Much is made of the silence and desolation of the location – you can hear the whisper of tumbleweed – and each sound effect (door slam, disobedient till ring) is stark and clear, surrounded as it is by the silence of the desert. Suddenly, out of nowhere, a lorry-load of timber pulls up. A rival store and gas-station is being built directly opposite Elmer's solitary little establishment. A perfect engine for twenty minutes of comedy has been constructed – and a classic tit-for-tat escalatory conflict unfolds, with virtually no dialogue at all. A lovely routine comprising the two gas-station owners slashing their prices to lure customers culminates in the lone customer choosing Elmer's rival because he doesn't want any cheap old gas. The movie veers off towards the end with a comic baseball game routine that doesn't quite live up to the gas-station tit-for-tat in the first reel, but nevertheless there is a hint of the old surreal Keaton world here. And in *The Gold Ghost*, another Educational Pictures short, there were flashes of visual comic brilliance. Wally, Keaton's character, rejected as a suitor by a well-to-do family, declares that he wants to be alone, and drives miles into the middle of nowhere. He is in ghost-town country. The scenes of his lone wandering in the dusty streets and buildings of the abandoned town are beautifully shot, and a welcome echo of some of the most powerful scenes in his former films: Keaton at his best when alone in a hostile or alien landscape, like the classic hurricane sequence in *Steamboat Bill Junior*. Keaton's visual business is not dramatic or stunt-filled in *The Gold Ghost* – he wanders through the empty world like a spirit. He finds the old Sheriff's office, and pinning the badge to his lapel, declares himself Sheriff – of a deserted town. There is a magical, almost Chaplinesque sequence in the town saloon, when he cranks up an antiquated pianola and plays a melody of the Old West. Before him appears a phantom girl from the 1890s, and other long-dead figures from the town's past. He dances with the ghost-girl, has a shoot-out with a gang of phantom cowboys, and waves goodbye to the girl as she fades into nothingness once more.

Other visual delights in *The Gold Ghost* are a card game on a table so filthy it sends up clouds with every card slammed down on its surface, until the saloon is full of dust; and a bowling game when Wally hurls barrels at a gang of crooks and scores his hits on a chalk-board as they topple like skittles.

But Keaton is at best in this film without other actors crowding out his comedy with needless talk and plot. As soon as they turn up, his comic power is diminished. These shorts are far better than the M-G-M sound features but Educational Pictures still didn't seem to recognise the fact that if you stick Keaton alone in a landscape, or with objects large or small – preferably railway engines or buildings – then he becomes a genius. Stick him in a scene with other talking actors and he becomes a weakened reactor. In *Allez Oop* of 1934 the best comedy is, once again, visual: Keaton plays a watch-mender hell-bent (as ever) on courting Paula, a girl of his dreams – to win her from the arms of a lascivious trapeze artist in the local circus he attempts to become an acrobat himself. There is a lengthy and splendid sequence of him training in his backyard being observed only by a laconic schoolboy lapping at a lollipop. His training does not make him a fitting competitor for the attentions of Paula however – played by *Spite Marriage*'s Dorothy Sebastian – but pays off in the tag of the movie when he rescues Paula from her burning apartment by recreating his rope-swinging-rescue routine from 1920s *The Balloonatic*. Sebastian and Keaton perform wonderfully together in this movie, and develop a rapport of visual business – missing each other going in and out of doors, bumping into each other – that is subtle and in no way laborious. Sebastian had a lightness of touch and a comic sensibility that perfectly complemented Keaton's, and one wonders why they didn't make more films together as a double-act.

In *Palooka from Paducah* and the final movie he made for Educational, *Love Nest on Wheels*, Keaton was reunited with his father, mother and sister – Joe, Myra and Louise Keaton, the old vaudevillians back together: again, there are flashes of great visual gags, memorably a horse pulling a cable that hauls the elevator of a run-down hillbilly hotel from floor to floor.

Keaton's contract with Educational expired in 1937 when the studio went bust, and he spent two years as a gag man for M-G-M on $200 per week. In 1939 he signed on to shoot ten two-reelers for Columbia – movies which did well at the box office but which displeased Keaton in that he felt he was recycling old material from his silent days. *Pest from the West* and *She's Oil Mine* proffer glimmerings of earlier genius, but when Columbia asked him to renew his contract, Keaton refused. He was about to turn his life around and to return to his roots – theatre.

The seeds of the final act of the great Keaton's career had actually been planted earlier, when he had made a return to the vaudeville stage in 1933 at the Hippodrome Theatre, Baltimore. It had been the first time he had stepped onstage with his mime act since the days of the *Three Keatons* in 1917, and, at first wary, he had been boosted by the great reception hed received – not to mention the pay-check, which was a handsome $8,000 for one week's engagement.

When he decided not to renew his contract with Columbia, Keaton returned first to gag-writing at M-G-M while his wife Eleanor worked as a dancer for the same studio; then, after hostilities had ceased in Europe, he packed his bags and set off to Europe to return to a life on the cabaret stage, and the circus.

His life had come full circle.

*

Cirque Medrano, in Montmartre, had been famous for its music-hall and circus acts since the late nineteenth century in its earlier incarnation as Cirque Fernando, and had been immortalised on canvas by Degas and Toulouse-Lautrec. In addition to being highly lucrative for Keaton – he was paid $1,500 per week – after an initial uncertainty he fell in love all over again with the stage, and returned on numerous occasions to both the Medrano and other venues on the international cabaret circuit.

For his return to the stage he revived the drunken act he'd performed originally with Dorothy Sebastian in *Spite Marriage*. This time he performed the routine with his wife Eleanor. It was a sensation. With other routines, such as the duelling scene from *The Passionate Plumber*, Keaton was an international hit, and the Medrano attracted fans from across the continent. A fellow American clown employed at the Medrano testified to his immense popularity, saying of Keaton: 'He was in fantastic physical shape. Every performance the Medrano clowns would hang out in the entrances watching him work. His comedy was completely different from the French clowns. Everyone was in awe of the man.'

Novelist Paul Gallico attended one of the shows, and wrote afterwards of Keaton's delivery-boy routine: 'a sad-faced little fellow wearing flat porkpie hat, string tie, too big clothes and flap shoes. He was carrying a mouldy-looking dress suit on a hanger, obviously looking for a cleaner. Before he had finished, the suit was a wreck on the arena floor and the audience was in hysterics. The French called Keaton *Malec*, and in their eyes he was a member of that favoured pantheon of clowns Grock and Orlando.' Other intellectuals and critics agreed – Edmund Wilson wrote: 'In February 1954 I saw Buster Keaton perform at the Cirque Medrano in Paris, and was confirmed in my opinion of twenty-eight years before that Hollywood had not made the best of him. He is a pantomime clown of the first order ... His loss of reputation in the United States and his appearance in an engagement abroad is only another example of the perversion and waste of talent for which Hollywood has been responsible.'

Wilson was right: the blip of the newly born sound era had straitjacketed Keaton, and by the 40s and 50s people were beginning to apprehend the damage that had been inflicted on a particular form of comedy which had conquered the world only a couple of decades earlier. It took Keaton's return to the stage to ignite the third and final phase of his career – a phase that would prove triumphant. Although he never made any more starring features, his star was nevertheless in the ascendant: post-Agate, one by one his silent films were rediscovered, preserved, and shown. He made numerous TV appearances in the 50s, including his own series *The Buster Keaton Show*, and his international profile was maintained through guest roles in big movies such as *It's a Mad Mad Mad Mad World,* and *A Funny thing Happened to Me on the Way to the Forum.* At the age of 55 he was still reproducing the perennial gag of propping one foot up on a table, swinging the other up by its side, then crashing to the floor. How he kept performing that particular gag into middle-age and beyond is not a mystery. When asked by Garry Moore, the host of *I've Got a Secret,* how he manage to achieve his physical routines at an age when most comedians would have slowed down, Buster simply replied: 'I'll show you' – and opened up his shirt to reveal a plethora of bruises. 'You have to care enough about the gag not to care,' he added.

Perhaps Buster Keaton's greatest legacy is that, unlike dozens of silent comedy stars, every single one of his movies has been preserved. And when in 1959 he received an Honorary Oscar for his pioneering contribution to the art of film comedy, any clouds of low self-esteem that must surely have gathered around him throughout his wilderness years, when his masterpieces of the 20s were not being shown in cinemas, were blown away.

CHAPTER 6

Long Live Vaudeville – Harpo Marx

At 8am on the morning of May 20 1924 an excited Groucho Marx called up his younger brother Harpo. They'd just opened in their first Broadway show, *I'll Say She Is*, at the number one vaudeville theatre in the land, the fabled New York Palace – and the reviews were in. An irritable, slumbering Harpo propped up the phone on his pillow and listened as Groucho read in full a piece by the theatre critic of *The Sun*, one Alexander Woollcott. By the time his brother had finished, Harpo was sitting bolt upright in bed. He knew why the call had come so early. He and his siblings had become major stars overnight.

Only it wasn't overnight, of course. It never is. Success had come after fourteen years of hard slog around the vaudeville circuit of America – a vicious grind of flea-ridden hotels, pawnshops, semi-starvation, setback, poverty, despair and hope. The eulogy by Woollcott – one of the major critics of the day who hadn't even wanted to go along to the show in the first place – set the seal on their careers, and was the springboard to their future glory. While Laurel & Hardy had been stars of the silent screen who had become even bigger with the advent of sound, the Marx Brothers can be called the first true comedy stars of the new era.

'Harpo Marx and Some Brothers,' ran Woollcott's review, ' … Hilarious Antics Spread Good Cheer at the Casino':

> As one of the many who laughed immoderately throughout the greater part of the first New York performance given by a new musical show, entitled, if memory serves, *I'll Say She Is*, it behoves your correspondent to report at once that that harlequinade has some of the most comical moments vouchsafed to the first-nighters in a month of Mondays. It is a bright-coloured and vehement setting for the goings on of those talented cutups, the Four Marx Brothers. In particular, it is a splendacious and reasonably tuneful excuse for going to see that silent brother, that sly, unexpected, magnificent comic among the Marxes, who is recorded on some birth certificate as

> Adolph, but who is known to the adoring two-a-day as Harpo Marx ... Surely there should be dancing in the streets when a great clown comes to town, and this man is a great clown. He is officially billed as a member of the Marx family, but truly he belongs to that greater family which includes Joe Jackson and Bert Melrose and the Fratellini Brothers who fall over one another in so obliging a fashion at the Cirque Medrano in Paris. Harpo Marx, so styled, oddly enough, because he plays the harp, says never a word from first to last, but when by merely leaning against one's brother one can seem richly and irresistibly amusing, why should one speak?

Why indeed? Since the age of eight as a semi-vagrant on the streets of the East Side of New York City, Harpo had been getting laughs by pulling faces; in particular, his famous Gookie in imitation of the intense expression adopted by a local cigar maker of that name as he toiled away rolling cigars. When the Marxes hit the vaudeville road in 1905 they were a singing act; by the time they hit the big time in the early 20s, the intermittent comic schtick that had gradually been fed into the act by improvisation had swollen into entire routines, and the music became incidental. Unlike European music-hall where visual acts were the norm because of national language differences, the stars of American vaudeville were mainly singers, musicians, and patter comics: Bert Lahr, Marie Dressler, Jimmy Durante. But over their years in the business, the Marxes learned that the more visual an act, the more you got paid. Spearheaded by their dynamic mother Minnie, their sets grew more and more ambitious: at one stage they had an entire ship onstage for their grand exit, which would sail into the wings to thundering applause.

Groucho developed a fine line in erudite wisecracks; Chico built a faux-Italian persona nurtured from his early youth on the East Side when a young Jew often found it expeditious to pretend to be from another ethnic background. In the early days Harpo would talk, sing and play the harp. But after one performance, in which he'd been struggling to keep up with his fast-talking elder brothers, he exited into the wings and decided that – unable to compete – he would never again talk onstage.

And he never did. It was in Champaign, Illinois when Harpo made the momentous plunge into pantomime. Their show 'School Days' had been such a success that the theatre wanted them to expand it into two acts, so their uncle Al Shean, himself a star on the vaudeville circuit, had written them a follow-up: in Act Two, years have passed, the pupils have grown up and have a reunion, along with their head teacher, Groucho.

When he received the script for the new show, Harpo was surprised to discover that he hadn't been given a single line. Al said that dumb-show would add fantastic contrast to the wisecracking Groucho and the fast-talking shyster Chico. Harpo protested, and insisted on ad-libbing lines. But after the show opened, a critic wrote: 'The Marx Brother who plays Patsy Brannigan is made up and costumed to a fare-thee-well and he takes off on an Irish immigrant most amusingly in pantomime. Unfortunately the effect is spoiled when he speaks'. Years later Harpo wrote: 'After I read this I knew Uncle Al had been right. I simply couldn't out-talk Groucho or Chico, and it was ridiculous of me to try. I went silent. I never uttered another word, onstage or in front of the camera, as a Marx Brother.'

*

There had always been visual routines in the Marx Brothers' act but now Harpo had fallen completely quiet the silent comedy blossomed, and his momentous decision to stop talking was to lead directly to Alexander Woollcott's review of 1924 when he ranked Harpo with other great stage clowns of the age, Joe Jackson, Bert Melrose and the Fratellini Brothers.

A serendipitous rainstorm in San Francisco led to his obtaining a costume that would achieve comedy-movie immortality – diving into a pawnshop, he grabbed a huge trench coat for three dollars. Getting it home, he realised it was way too big – big enough, in fact, to house the dozens of props he would stuff into it over the years. 'I couldn't have come up with a better comedy coat if I'd had one custom made,' he wrote years later in his memoirs, *Harpo Speaks*. 'It was perfect, with my battered plug hat, ratty wig, and underslung pants with the clothesline belt. I lined the trench coat with huge panels and pockets, enough room to stash half a trunk's worth of props in.'

This coat would be the source of many of Harpo's most famous gags, including the falling knives routine which he devised in New York in 'On the Mezzanine'. In a hotel foyer a detective is on the trail of the hotel's stolen silver. After grilling Harpo and concluding he is totally innocent, the detective shakes him apologetically by the hand – and a knife falls from the clown's sleeve. In a building routine of impeccable timing this single knife is followed by more and more items of cutlery – half a dozen knives, forks, spoons. The detective gives another shake, and yet more purloined articles clatter to the stage – culminating in a big silver coffee pot. In one form or another Harpo performed this routine not only onstage but also in the movies and all over the world; it was a particular hit in Soviet Russia when he toured there in 1934 – the international language of

Harpo's clowning was not lost on American diplomacy, when in 1934 he was invited to become the first US entertainer to tour the newly recognised communist empire. During the tour the concealed-knives-routine had a bizarre mirroring in reality when Harpo was recruited as a spy, smuggling secret papers – strapped to his leg – out of the country and back to the US.

It was in Elko, Nevada, about the same time as he went silent, that Harpo invented the sliding-under-the-carpet gag. Chased by a cop and desperate for somewhere to hide, he lifts up the edge of an onstage rug and – as the audience sees it – slides under it feet first, vanishing completely as if he has suddenly turned into a sheet of cardboard, without the slightest bulge showing in the carpet. This gag never failed to kill, the huge laugh being topped with an even bigger one when he would poke his finger up through a hole in the carpet. The trick was neat and simple, the carpet being laid on a false level above the stage with a concealed entrance for Harpo to slot himself into.

In his years on the road traipsing round the vaudeville circuit, Harpo became a movie fan, in particular a devotee of Chaplin. Although the Harpo persona is drawn with bolder strokes than that of the Tramp, one can see an affinity between the two: both are rascals, under-miners of authority. Both are types, but while Chaplin's character still exists in the everyday social world, the Harpo character is a surreal exile who enters polite society like a bizarre whirlwind. He and Chico are outsiders in all their movies, with Groucho as the foothold in the arenas of authority they set out to lambast, ridicule and destroy. Groucho plays societal figures like college principals, lawyers, famous explorers, then systematically undermines the pomp and the mores with wisecracks: Chico is the slippery, conniving, scheming outsider content only in the company of cardsharps, hookers, gangsters – and Harpo is the wild undisciplined jester, the Lord of Misrule so beyond society he cannot even speak its language. But these three personae are not inventions – they are caricatures of the performers themselves. Groucho was an avaricious reader from an early age; Chico was a gambler and hustler who spiritually never left the twilit bars and hangouts of his East Side days, and Harpo was a loner who spent his formative years wandering New York alone, learning how to get laughs and stave off bullying by pulling faces at shopkeepers and cops. These characteristics nourished their routines firstly on stage and then in the movies – sneaking cutlery, hiding blankets in otherwise empty suitcases, fleeing gambling dens ... all three were anarchists and outsiders.

As the physical routines expanded, Harpo's destructive persona ripened: in 'The Cocoanuts' of 1925 he enters a hotel foyer and starts ripping up dozens of telegrams; he jumps over the hotel desk and reduces the letters in the pigeon-holes to shreds. His wild enthusiasm is so infectious that even Groucho joins in. When every scrap of paper in the place has been torn up, Harpo looks forlorn. Groucho: 'Sorry the afternoon mail hasn't come in yet.'

This anarchic comedy was totally fresh and new and made the Marxes the biggest theatrical comedy act of the 20s. Their transition from stage to screen at the end of the decade was a natural step and they signed a deal with Paramount. Harpo had already attempted to make a break into films – in the early 20s his brothers had persuaded him to do a screen test at M-G-M. 'While I was playing the Orpheum in Los Angeles, the boys convinced me I should try for a job in the movies,' he wrote years later, 'I was a natural for silent pictures, they said. I didn't talk anyway, and I was pretty good at stunts and pratfalls.' But he flunked it – and never heard from the studio. It must have been shortly afterwards that the entire team made their first movie: *Humour Risk* is a legendary lost picture that had a limited release in New York. Harpo makes a cameo appearance in another movie, *Too Many Kisses*, released in 1925 and lost for decades but rediscovered in the early 1990s. A period film, Harpo turns in a fine and charismatic performance as a rustic servant, showing distinct signs of his later onscreen persona.

*

Despite these early efforts it would be nearly another ten years before the boys made their next movie, *The Cocoanuts*. It was a smash hit, and the team followed it up with five more movies for Paramount before signing with Irving Thalberg at M-G-M and making a further five, all of which are regarded today as masterpieces. By employing the finest humorous writers – including George S Kaufman, S J Perelman and Morrie Ryskind – they ensured that Groucho's wit became the mainstay of each picture, but equally memorable are the physical routines: the crowded stateroom in *A Night at the Opera*, the mirror routine and popcorn scene with Edgar Kennedy in *Duck Soup*, the war sequence in the same movie, the medical examination in *Day at the Races*, the gorilla on the trapeze in *At the Circus*, and the wood-chopping routine aboard the train in *Go West*.

Quick visual gags are also legion, Harpo's method of ordering food and drink being endlessly inventive – honking his horn for a hard-boiled egg in *Night at the Opera*, doing a Highland jig for Chico to order a glass of scotch in *Horse Feathers* (which extends into him secreting the bottle so he can pour a never-filling glass – a trick explained seconds later when

Despite the onset of sound, the dumb-show of Harpo Marx carried the torch of pantomime between 1927 and its revival by Tati in 1946. Mischievous, anarchic, anti-authoritarian, Harpo is the heir to Scaramouche of the Commedia dell'arte – a scamp known for his grimacing and for creating 'skirmishes.'

we see a further bottle beneath his glass, which he is slowly filling with purloined whiskey). Moments later in the same scene he passes two poker-players. 'Cut the cards!' drawls one – and in a flash Harpo produces an axe which he brings down with a crash! to slice the pack in two.

They loved substitution or switch gags – the classic was Harpo proffering his leg instead of his hand whenever anyone tried to give him a handshake; but objects behaving like other objects were also a favourite. In *Horse Feathers*, exiled from the gaming tables, he wanders forlornly past a coin-operated public phone-box which he promptly begins using as a fruit machine, dialling to play the game – and of course winning the jackpot. Harpo's outsider persona is further deepened in this film when he literally finds himself outside eating with the horse. Yet he is not morose at being shoved out with the animals – he relishes it, tucking in happily to the food in the nosebag, adding salt and pepper to the hay, then eating part of a banana and zipping up the skin to save the rest for later. In *Horse Feathers* the boys reprised part of the show that had first made their names all those years ago on the vaudeville circuit, 'Fun at High Skule' with Groucho as the teacher accusing Harpo of burning the candle at both ends – an object which he promptly produces from beneath the folds of his gigantic coat. The banana leitmotif continues in the big football

Shot through as they were with Groucho's verbal wisecracks, the Marx Brothers' movies were also notable for Harpo's anarchic dumb-show. Here in one of his numerous extended visual sequences he reduces a ship to chaos in the classic stateroom scene in Night at the Opera.

sequence at the end, with Harpo dropping dozens of skins to thwart the rival tream, and when it doesn't work, riding a horse and chariot Ben Hur style across the pitch, touching eight balls down in one go. In their next movie, *Monkey Business* in 1931, Harpo transcends reality so much that he becomes a puppet, joining a Punch and Judy show to evade capture from the cruise ship captain and his crew.

In *Duck Soup* (1933) and *Night at the Opera* (1935), once again it is the visual routines that burn into the memory: the mirror sequence in *Duck Soup* between Groucho and Harpo, although a well-worn vaudeville and music-hall staple, becomes more than just a clever trick through the nuances of their characters – Groucho's scheming as he leaves the mirror frame; Harpo's faux-corpsing as his mimicry begins to show cracks; Chico's oblivious wandering into the action. This, plus the precision timing, make it the finest example of the routine on film.

The other classic physical routine in *Duck Soup* is the lemonade-selling scene with the triumvirate of Harpo, Chico and Edgar Kennedy. The director of *Duck Soup* was Leo McCarey who had shot many of Laurel & Hardy's best shorts for Hal Roach, so it is probably him we can thank for casting Kennedy – a Roach stalwart and Laurel & Hardy foil – as the stallholder who becomes victim of the boys' destructive anarchism. In an interview given in 1967, McCarey reminisced: 'As my experience of silent films had very much influenced me, it was Harpo that I preferred.' Which is probably why there is definitely a touch of Stan and Ollie in some of the business – McCarey even introduces a mixed-up-hats routine into the lemonade-stand scene, only this time they have three hats to get confused with. Kennedy gives one of the greatest performances in cinema history of a bewildered foil as Harpo and Chico reduce him to a state of staggering frustration and despair. The boys unleash the full armoury of their physical schtick – the leg-handshake-switch, the comedy kicks in the seat of the pants, the car-horn full of lemonade, the nicked hat. It is a *tour de force* of pantomime from three comics at the top of their game.

Yet there were more hits and classic routines to come: when Thalberg signed them up to M-G-M in 1934 they given bigger budgets, which resulted in higher production values and more ambitious slapstick routines: *Night at the Opera* contains one of their most famous sketches, The Stateroom, in which Harpo delivers a sublime performance. Asleep throughout, he flops and collapses like a rag-doll over anyone and anything, appearing so inanimate that at times you surely believe he has no bones; he curls round one of the many girls in the crowded room, prompting Groucho to crack – 'He's doing better with the dames than I do when I'm awake!' The scene culminates with three waiters entering, bearing large trays of food at shoulder height – across which the still-somnabulant Harpo proceeds to crawl, like a dozing tortoise. In the medical examination scene in *Day at the Races* Harpo once again steals the scene as Dr Hackenbush's assistant, drying his hands on the coat-tails of a fellow doctor, launching into a paper-selling mime after Chico has shouted X-Ray! X-Ray! Xtra... – and turning on the overhead sprinklers. The scene culminates in all three brothers – at their anarchic best – riding out of the surgery on a horse.

With *A Night at the Opera* and *A Day at the Races*, Thalberg had steered the team in a slightly different direction: their madcap antics are pot-shots aimed at undermining villains rather than tearing apart the fabric of rational behaviour itself. Thalberg insisted on stronger plotting and more rigorous scripting, which lent itself to lengthy dialogue routines, but visual comedy still remained a key component.

At the Circus (1939), by its very title alone, indicates the plethora of visual comedy – culminating in the trapeze sequence at the film's close, with all three brothers plus Suzanna Dukesbury (Margaret Dumont) forming a human chain between two trapezes while Gibraltar the Gorilla walks across them as a tightrope. And a visual highlight of *Go West* of the

In I Love Lucy *of May 9 1955 the 67-year-old Harpo joins Lucille Ball for an affectionate recreation of the famous mirror routine from* Duck Soup *of 1932. Only it wasn't a Marx Brothers routine: such is the continuum of the visual comic tradition that even when* Duck Soup *came out the reviewer in Variety called it 'the old Schwartz Bros. mirror routine,' referring to a vaudeville act. The gag had also appeared in French comedian Max Linder's* Seven Years Bad Luck *(1921) and Charlie Chaplin's* The Floorwalker *(1916). Bugs Bunny did it with Elmer Fudd in* Hare Tonic, *the Three Stooges did it in one of their shorts, and Abbott and Costello borrowed it for* The Naughty Nineties *(1945). Two guys in gorilla costumes even do the routine in Blake Edward's* The Pink Panther. *Proof that visual comedians are a family connected across the decades, and even the centuries.*

following year was the train chase sequence during which Harpo chops up practically the entire train for firewood to keep it moving.

Their M-G-M career came to a respectable close with *The Big Store* in 1941, with its chase sequence during which the boys tip over dozens of carpet rolls, causing the pursuing villain to roll along them like a fallen lumberjack sliding along a rack of logs. Then there is Groucho fending off flying bullets with a shovel; Harpo falling into a pair of roller-skates (the ensuing chase turning the store into a skating rink, reminiscent of Chaplin's routine in *Modern Times*); and Harpo swinging between overhead light-fittings then riding on Groucho's shoulders on a unicycle.

Before the release of *The Big Store* the team had announced their retirement from motion pictures, but Chico's severe gambling debts pulled them back into the business in 1946, when they released *A Night in Casablanca.* While Groucho reinvented himself as a TV panel show host and Chico gambled and played piano round the nightclubs of the world, Harpo's last twenty years were a drifting in and out of retirement. He kept himself busy with numerous stage appearances, sometimes with Chico, sometimes solo; and in 1955 he was lured out of happy family life with a film that perhaps belied its name, *Love Happy*, a vehicle conceived first as a solo for Harpo but which owing to the financiers' threat to pull the plug if the other brothers were not on board, ended up as the final Marx Brothers picture. It is not the hapless result history has labelled it: Harpo still produces some fine mime, especially in the seduction scene with the beautiful Madame Egelichi (Ilana Massey) where he turns to cartoon jelly as she turns on the charm – like a lascivious Wolf in a Tex Avery animation he becomes putty in her hands, leaning forward towards her at an unfeasible angle like Chaplin in *Pay Day* when his feet are stuck in the tar.

TV appearances followed – the *Spike Jones Show*; an appearance on *I Love Lucy* in 1955 when Harpo and Lucille Ball reunite after her performance in *Room Service* of seventeen years before to perform a fabulous version of the classic *Duck Soup* mirror routine; the *Kraft Music Hall* in 1959 when he dusted off his clarinet blowing bubbles act; and a dramatic role in *Silent Panic* in 1960 where he gave played a clockwork marionette in Santa's grotto who witnesses a murder.

At Harpo's final appearance on Allan Sherman's TV show in early 1964 he surprised everyone by speaking for the first and last time in public; and it was to announce his retirement. While a tearful Allan Sherman looked on, the great silent clown bowed out from show-business, hung up the wig and raincoat he'd bought forty years earlier from the pawnshop in San Francisco, and returned to his family in Palm Springs. Six months later he was dead.

CHAPTER 7

Diehards: Visual Comedy on Stage & Screen 1930-45

While Laurel & Hardy took the coming of sound in their stride and the Marx Brothers developed a unique blend of firecracker wit and inspired pantomime, other comics did not fare as well.

When the studios had all been wired for sound, the final all-silent pictures (apart from Chaplin's) were Chester Conklin's *Tell it to Sweeney*, Monty Banks' *Weekend Wives*, Syd Chaplin's *A Little Bit of Fluff*, and Harold Lloyd's *Speedy*. Thereafter, many silent comics descended a few rungs of the ladder and went to work for lesser studios like Educational Pictures (Keaton) and Columbia (Lloyd Hamilton) or gave up performing altogether and became writers for the new sound stars (Langdon). As the 30s progressed and the Depression deepened, visual comedy on screen was pushed to the sidelines.

During the period 1930-45 there was such a cross-over between the artistes and comics who appeared on stage and on screen that it is virtually impossible to disentangle the two, such was the symbiosis of their development: indeed, a whole genre of film appeared that was a hybrid of the two, the *cine-variety* movie, such as *Elstree Calling* and the weekly *Pathe-Gazette.* In Britain, cinema audiences began embracing new screen stars like suave Jack Buchanan, cheeky northerner George Formby, eccentric bumbler Will Hay, and the earthy optimistic delights of Gracie Fields. All these stars came from the variety stage, and in the first decade of sound it was the patter acts and character acts that took prominence: fast-talking cockney Max Miller made *Educated Evans*, there was Will Fyffe in *King of Hearts*, Lupino Lane in *Hot News*, and Aldwych farceurs Ralph Lynn and Robertson Hare reproduced their stage hits like *Pot Luck* for the big screen. British cinemas were obliged by law to book a quota of British-made films, so in many ways the 30s became a renaissance of opportunity both for these stage comics and for the studios. The results, in terms of quality, were mixed; gems emerged of course like *Oh Mr Porter* and *Thark*, but as John Montgomery concludes, 'Most of the pictures were prolonged music-hall acts, musical comedies, and stage farces –

photographed from a limited number of angles.'

It wasn't all talk: there was the Crazy Gang, that hotch-potch of zany double-acts that became, almost, the British Marx Brothers. From early stage success at the Palladium in 1931 with *Crazy Week*, this collection of duos – Nervo and Knox, Flanagan and Allen, and Naughton and Gold – mixed visual routines with cross-talk patter, graduating to films in 1937 with *Okay for Sound*, followed by *Alf's Button Afloat* and *Gasbags* (1941). Separately, they had specialised in pantomime routines such as Nervo and Knox's slow-motion wrestling (the men were a former circus act). Their films had dialogue, to be sure, but were packed with sight gags and silent vaudeville, such as their high-speed charade routine in *Okay for Sound*. Often the films would also include guest visual acts, such as spectacular displays of *apache* dancing – a form of speciality act originating in the variety theatres and cabarets of Paris and consisting of a man and a woman throwing each other around the stage.

Comedy acrobats Nervo and Knox, whose 'slow-motion wrestling' routine in the 1930s led to their teaming with two other double-acts to become The Crazy Gang – the Monty Python of the 40s/50s.

Despite the threat to live variety from the 'all-talking, all-singing, all-dancing' sounds films, it was ironically a film company that saved live comedy performance in Britain. While the Stoll theatres had converted to sound technology so they could show films, the Gaumont British Film Corporation – to prevent a similar conversion on the part of the Moss Empire Circuit – bought the theatres, lock stock and barrel, and kept them as live venues, staging variety shows but films too. Led by George Black and including the London Palladium, this new Moss circuit became the biggest theatrical chain in the country, and took modern variety into the post-war era.

*

Two visual British acts who had built major reputations as silent clowns but who suffered unjustly in the new decade of sound – by which I mean they were underused – were Lupino Lane and Walter Forde.

Lane, just one member of a vast and illustrious performing dynasty, returned from Hollywood and a stint with Educational Pictures to sign up at Teddington, where he was misused. Rather like Keaton, he suffered from having his visual schtick subordinated to plot and dialogue, with *Picturegoer* summing up his 1936 offering *The Deputy Drummer* rather sadly and tellingly by saying 'Lupino Lane's dances are its only asset.' It was on stage that he was to achieve his greatest success, directing and touring in highly popular musical comedies 'Twenty to One', and the long-running spectacular 'Me and My Girl', which made Lane a very rich man.

While not scoring particularly well in Hollywood with his silent series of *Walter* comedies, by the end of the 20s Walter Forde had struck it big in his home country with *Wait and See* and *Would You Believe It!* The advent of sound found him drawn to directing, first at Gainsborough with Michael Balcon then at Gaumont British, where his skills were applied equally to comedies and thrillers, ranging from *The Ghost Train* in 1931 to the Sid Field vehicle *Cardboard Cavalier* of 1946. Forde directed the leading comedians of his day, from Jack Hulbert and Arthur Askey to Alistair Sim and Tommy Handley – stamping his movies with the visual flair he'd acquired in the golden years of silent film.

Harry Tate had been plying his trade in the music-halls since 1905, with his largely pantomimic sketches 'Motoring', 'Golfing', 'Fishing', 'Billiards', 'The Office', and 'Selling a Car'. Their popularity continued into to the 30s, and he enjoyed a successful run as guest comedian in several films and in his own series of shorts filmed at Pathe-Studios in 1934. A blustering, bumbling buffoon with a crazy false propeller-like moustache, his routines – despite his larger than life persona – brought an element of realism to stage-comedy, drawing as they did on everyday situations and confrontations.

In addition to the sketch comics were the visual speciality acts – acrobats, dancers, magicians, escapologists, dog-acts. Eccentric dancing was a perennial favourite, the most famous exemplars of course being Wilson, Keppel & Betty, whose Egyptian sand-dance burlesque is one of the few purely visual variety acts that still lingers today in the British public consciousness: at the height of their fame they played the Royal Variety Show at the Palladium supporting Frank Sinatra and their performance at Nuremberg Germany was famously condemned by Goebbels as 'decadent.' As with many variety acts of their time they

Not quite slapping with a stick but slapstick nevertheless, Moe Horwitz was the Pulcinella of visual comedy, the number of blows inflicted on his Three Stooges cohorts – Curley and Larry – over a forty-year career surely running into the thousands. Since Fatty Arbuckle first began throwing bricks at people in his movies, the centuries-old tradition of comic violence merged seamlessly into the medium of film.

found occasional spots in movies, many of which are sadly lost such as *In Town Tonight* and *On the Air* (both 1934) – but their act is wonderfully preserved in the films *Starlight Serenade* (1943) and *Variety Makers* (1948).

Another famous dancing act of its day was Burke and Head, consisting of Johnny Cooper and Bill Burke, who – after stints with the Eight Lancashire Lads (a long-standing team of clog-dancers whose members included Charlie Chaplin and Rubberneck Nat Jackley) – formed their own double-act routine. Cooper remembers the original Lancashire Lads act thus: 'The curtain would rise exposing a cinema screen hung from the flies so that the bottom of the screen was eighteen inches above the stage. Immediately behind the screen we did a clog dance wearing gold clogs and black tights. Behind us was a black drop which made our legs invisible so that it would appear as though only the clogs were dancing. While this was going on, slides of the original Eight Lancashire Lads were shown on the screen.' Their new act was an inspired insertion of mad dance-routines into almost cinematic situations, such as a house-fire. There are no records of any film appearances for Burke and Cooper, but they enjoyed a flourishing stage career right up to the decline of variety at the end of the 1950s.

Nat Jackley, another graduate of the Lancashire Lads school, built a unique reputation as a tall, gangly, tap-dancer whose non-verbal act with his sister Joy involved manic terpsichore atop a steel table to the accompaniment of furious xylophone-playing. Like many other variety performers, he enjoyed a movie career as a side-line, appearing as support for Norman Evans in *Demobbed* (1944) and *Under New Management* (1946), and even experiencing a late-career renaissance in the 60s by being cast alongside the Beatles in *Magical Mystery Tour* and *Mrs Brown You've Got a Lovely Daughter*, starring Herman's Hermits. Not as famous as Jackley, but just as successful a visual speciality act, were Horace Mashford and his wife Edna, whose Scottish Dance, Military Dance, and Dutch Dance took them from seaside pierrot shows in the 1920s to the European Cabaret scene of the 1930s and beyond.

The crucial weapon of these visual acts was that they were international, and with a flourishing European cabaret scene it was no longer necessary to continue plying your trade in your own country. And it wasn't just Europe – variety acts whose comedy did not rely on language also had the vast cabaret circuit of South America.

In the USA, 1920s vaudeville act The Three Stooges blossomed into a movie success when they signed with Columbia to make a series of two-reelers. Generally considered to be the team's finest work, these Columbia shorts (and between 1934 and 1958 they made 190!) were a rich pageant of wild, and at times violent, slapstick and were characterised by a surreal detachment from reality. Altogether broader and ruder than Laurel & Hardy, and lacking the finesse of the Marx Brothers (and without the warmth of either), the Three Stooges pulled in vast paying audiences in their day. Curley, Moe and Larry even won an Academy Award in 1934 for Best Short Comedy *Men in Black*.

The Ritz Brothers were another, largely physical, vaudeville team-act who achieved some success in pictures, but not on the scale of the Three Stooges. Relying on grotesque bodily distortions, face-pulling and disguise, Al, Jimmy and Harry (of the independently swivelling eyes) began in their own starring vehicle *Hotel Anchovy* in 1934, thereafter appearing mostly as a guest-act in movies like *Sing Baby Sing* and *On the Avenue*. Fox and Universal signed them in the late 40s for their own starring vehicles, but they never attained the status of Laurel & Hardy or Abbott & Costello.

The weakness of these comics in relation to the greats was their subordination of character to stylised comedy: the truly great do both. The Marx Brothers had set off a trend for the zany and madcap, but few could pull it off. Olsen and Johnson were another pair who perhaps epitomised the genre, and with more success than the Ritz Brothers; their *Hellzapoppin* of 1942 is a firecracker movie version of their wild Broadway hit, including taxi cabs journeying to hell; a feast of non-sequiturs; the film itself turning upside down, and reversed; Indians galloping through the set on their way to another studio; and a nerdy-looking fellow wandering through the film carrying a shrub that gradually grows into a tree. Such surrealism and caper was without doubt the roots of the post-war zaniness that created the Goons, Monty Python and Mel Brooks. But zaniness without a modicum of gravity does not endure, and in my view the stylised nature of *Hellzapoppin* suffers from the same absence of truth as *The Goons.*

After silent success at the Hal Roach Studios, Charley Chase – seen here with co-star Katherine Grant – took sound in his stride and moved to Columbia Studios to make a series of largely visual shorts, as well as directing Andy Clyde and The Three Stooges.

Abbott and Costello were such verbal comics that they have no real place in this book; but other American comedians of the era, while not achieving the fame of that double-act, include great silent comedian Lloyd Hamilton, a much-neglected star of the 1920s of whom it is said he was the one comedian Chaplin felt was better than him. After making numerous highly successful shorts in the 20s, Hamilton continued turn out two-reelers for the lesser studios like Educational Pictures and Columbia. Mack Sennett, that former giant of the early days, even oversaw Hamilton's final pictures, which were visual comedies in everything but name: as a stout, overgrown boy in pork-pie hat, Hamilton maintained the loser character he had invented in the 20s for the *Bud & Ham* pictures, and his last movies, though talkies, were filled with splendid mime – such as the routine in *Camera Shy* (1930) when the hungry Brennan (Hamilton) peers through a restaurant window at a dining couple then keeps coming back to gaze covetously at the rich food within. Hamilton died in 1935, but his contribution to visual comedy in the first decade of talkies is considerable, and he is ripe for rediscovery.

Another masterly protagonist of comic dumb-show, Charley Chase, was one of that raft of performers that not only survived the transition to sound but whose career was buoyed by it. After writing and appearing in many two-reel shorts for Hal Roach in the 20s – including *Mighty*

Like a Moose directed by Leo McCarey (whose penchant for character and farce over broad slapstick lent a finesse to the Chase pictures) he made the seamless slide into two-reel talkies in the 30s, until Roach moved exclusively into features. In 1936 Chase signed to Columbia, directing Andy Clyde and The Three Stooges, and starring in his own series of shorts that were more purely physical than his films made with Roach.

Italy had its own supreme pantomimist, Toto. Born Antonio Clemente in 1898, his 97 films spanned a career between 1937 and 1968 and were Commedia dell'arte farces in all but name. An illegitimate son of a marquis, Toto was bought up in a poor district of Naples and cut his teeth as a member of the *giutti*, or scriptless comedians. Performing in small theatres, these troupes were direct heirs of the Commedia dell'arte companies, and the young Toto was soon armed with all the tropes of the tradition such as wild physical exaggeration, mobility of the face and heightened expression, and portrayal of extremes of emotion such as lust or hunger. He moved to Rome and played the larger theatres with *avanspettacolo* – a bill of burlesque, dance and comedy that was a genre whose lineage stretches right back to the sixteenth century. Like Grock, however, Toto eschewed the movies until relatively late in life, making his first film at the age of thirty-nine. *Fermo Con le Mani!* (*Hands Off Me!*) was a rumbustious farce that laid down many of the tropes of his future work, and included memorable routines such as fishing from a fishmonger's slab, and giving a bald man a haircut. While his films were crisply played dialogue movies, from his debut it was clear that they were silent comedies in all but name, for they are replete with sight gags, reveals, and grotesque clowning.

*

In addition to film and variety of course, there was the world of the circus – that ancient temple of amusement seemingly immune to all technological advances and changes. And the clowns remained the perennial favourite of the ring. Grock, born Charles Adrien Wettach in Switzerland in 1880, became the world's most famous white-faced red-nosed fool of the twentieth century, making the move from the ring to the music-hall and variety stage with ease and becoming the highest-paid stage entertainer in the world. Though making few films – *Clear the Ring* in 1950 and the biographical *Grock* in 1959, his dominance of the world variety scene throughout the 1930s was unchallenged, and his renown spread from Europe to Britain to the USA. Grock was probably the greatest visual comedian not to become a film star; there is no doubt his comedy would have been perfectly suited to the camera, for although he performed in several thousand-seat venues across the world, his style of comedy was quite minimalist: 'The genius of clowning,' he wrote in his memoirs, 'is transforming the little, everyday annoyances, not only overcoming, but actually transforming them into something strange and terrific ... it is the power to extract mirth for millions out of nothing and less than nothing.'

When Harpo Marx first attracted the praise of critic Alexander Woollcott in the brothers' first Broadway hit 'I'll Say She Is!' in 1925, he wrote: 'He is officially billed as a member of the Marx family, but truly he belongs to that greater family which includes Joe Jackson and Bert Melrose and the Fratellini brothers, who fall over one another in so obliging a fashion at the Cirque Medrano in Paris.' And it is to Paris that we turn for the next chapter in our story, for it is there that the tradition of visual comedy not only thrived in the decade or so after sound, but actually became a crucible of innovation. The reason France – and principally Paris – flourished as the home of visual comedy was that in addition to the venues for the popular presentation of pantomime, artists and teachers founded schools devoted to physical performance.

His film career more than a decade away, a confident young Jacques Tati straddles the European cabaret stage of the 1930s, dreaming of glories to come.

CHAPTER 8

At Odds with the World – Jacques Tati

In the summer of 1936 a young novelist called Colette took her seat in the ABC Theatre in Paris to watch a tall gangly man perform a mime act. It was an act he'd been performing for years, in the tatty music-halls and clubs of Paris, ever since he'd stood up to entertain his fellow rugby players at social events between matches at the Racing Club de France in the Bois de Boulogne. As the 29-year-old performed his series of *impressions sportives* – minimalist silent depictions of a goalkeeper, a tennis player, an angler, and a horseman – the novelist sat entranced.

Her review of his performance was nothing less than a paean:

> From now on no celebration, no artistic or acrobatic spectacle can do without this amazing performer, who has invented something quite his own ... His act is partly ballet and partly sport, partly satire and partly charade. He has devised a way of being both the player, the ball and the tennis racquet, of being simultaneously the football and the goalkeeper, the boxer and the opponent, the bicycle and the cyclist. Without any props, he conjures up his accessories and his partners. He has the suggestive powers of all great artists. How gratifying it was to see the audience's warm reaction! Tati's success says a lot about the sophistication of the allegedly 'uncouth' public, about its taste for novelty and its appreciation of style. Jacques Tati, the horse and rider conjured, will show all of Paris the living image of that legendary creature, the centaur.

While it is an exaggeration to say that Colette's review established Tati overnight as a star, it was without doubt the critical impetus he needed and an important validation of his career choice to date.

Jacques Tatischeff was born in 1907 into a prosperous middle-class family of Dutch, Russian and Italian ancestry. Raised in a wealthy suburb of Paris, he followed a spell in the military by joining his uncle's picture-framing business in the centre of the city where he trod water for several years, becoming gradually dissatisfied with the path laid out for him by his family. As he drifted through his twenties he discovered that his heart belonged not to the stolid upper-middle-class into which he had been born – but to the theatre.

His early forays into the world of performing took him first to social events, parties, charity occasions, and then to the music-hall proper. Gradually Tati left behind his comfortable bourgeois life and embraced the uncertain, classless society of variety – and once embraced, he would never leave it: even after he became an international star his favourite people were circus and variety folk, his cinematic swansong, *Parade*, being a homage to that colourful, ramshackle world.

It was clear from the outset that his ambitions were not restricted to the stage. With a few friends and with scratch finance he made three experimental short films in the early- to mid-30s – *Oscar, Champion de Tennis* (1932), *On demande une brute* (1934), and *Gai Dimanche* (1934), the last two with his friend Enrico Sprocani, well-known in Paris as the clown Rhum at the Cirque Medrano. The only one of these films still in existence is *Gai Dimanche.*

After Colette's review of his stage act, he went on to make another short, *Soigne ton Gauche*, then launched himself into full-length films with his first feature, *Jour de Fête.* But between *Soigne ton Gauche* and *Jour de Fête* was an intervening period of almost ten years – as for millions of others across Europe, the small matter of the Second World War came along to derail Tati's momentum.

Tati's act did not suddenly appear out of nowhere, but from a long tradition of French mime dating back to Deburau in the mid-nineteenth century, through Jacques Coupeau and Etienne Decroux, Georges Wague, Max Linder, Jean-Louis Barrault, and more. In the 1920s Etienne Decroux's theatre school was becoming the vortex of a remarkable group of performers, Decroux's invention of corporeal mime spearheading a more realistic acting style than the flamboyant gestural pantomime of a previous age. While Tati he must have been aware of this tradition, he was not a member of any group belonging to it, rather sidestepping into vaudeville from a stolid bourgeois milieu without any acting background or training.

Therein lay, perhaps, his originality. The existing tradition served to ease his way into theatrical success, for managers were booking mimes. But his style was sparkling, minimalist, realistic – and new. Which is why he became a star.

His lack of association with the more serious mimes of the day is evinced by the fact that as he began to be sought-after in clubs and theatres across Europe, he started to sue other mimes for stealing his act. Imitation is, of course, the sincerest form of flattery, but when Jean-Louis Barrault began performing a routine involving an imaginary horse, Tati transformed indignation into legal action. Naively, he did not realise that you cannot copyright an idea: if the acts had contained dialogue then there might have been grounds for a case, but movement cannot be owned – and the litigation petered out.

*

In between theatrical engagements across Europe, Tati made short films and with each he made advances in both the sophistication of the story and film technique. In 1936, the same year of his fêting by Colette, he made his most accomplished movie to date – *Soigne ton Gauche* ('Take Care of your Left'). In this film he is not yet his famous creation, Monsieur Hulot, but rather a well-meaning dimwit, eager to please, full of energy but suffused with a dozy, rustic otherworldliness. The character has the air of Stan Laurel: indeed, Tati apes Laurel's slightly slow, side-to-side gait as he is summoned back to work by the matriarch of the farm on which he works.

From the opening shot of *Soigne ton Gauche* you might be forgiven for thinking you are watching his first feature-length film, *Jour de Fête*, where Tati plays a postman doing his rounds in a rustic French village. In the earlier film we see a postman cycling manically along a country lane to the accompaniment of bright, cheery music – the same theme, in fact, as in the later picture, part of the score by Jean Yatove. But the postman is not Tati, it is Max Martel, a comic actor Tati would use again as The Drunk Man in his masterpiece of the 50s, *Mon Oncle*.

Tati instead plays a farmhand, whom we see pretending to be a sportsman receiving a trophy from a group of children who are playing at being news reporters, complete with fake camera and microphone. At once Tati is established as a grown-up child – he is playing along happily with the youngsters until he is caught out by his mother, who summons him back to his haymaking with a series of barking shouts.

A boxer is training in the farmyard, and Tati uses the scene to shoot what would be the first of many his trademark double-textured gags – the contrast between what is happening in the background, and what is happening in the foreground. While Tati the farmhand gives us a display of his boxing mime, the real boxing is continuing on the right-hand side of the screen in the background.

It is a tantalising first glimpse of Tati's sporting stage-act. Over the years he would reproduce parts of his live show onscreen: the horse routine in *Monsieur Hulot's Holiday*, the fishing routine in *Parade*. We are treated to further displays of his comic pugilism when the boxer's sparring partner is knocked out cold and the manager – clocking Tati's deluded shadow-boxing in the barn – nabs him to take the unconscious man's place. At first delighted, and then uneasy, Tati enters the ring, basing all his moves on an instructional booklet which he places carefully on a stool in his corner. There follows a wonderful display of his athleticism and balletic ability as he prances about the ring. It is not an original comic setting by any means – Chaplin had covered boxing as early as 1915 in *The Champion* for Essanay and again in *City Lights* (1931) and Stan Laurel had stamped his own on a boxing routine in *Any Old Port* in 1932. In the same year as *Soigne ton Gauche* was made, Harold Lloyd was playing a milkman mistaken for a boxer in *The Milky Way*.

Tati's use of the instruction booklet, however, is original and very funny: he pauses between punches to turn a page with his boxing glove and mug up on the next exercise. And the topper to this gag is when the postman inadvertently turns the booklet over to the back page where there is an advert for a Fencing School – and Tati promptly adopts a fencing pose in front of his opponent.

The final shot of the film is pure Tati: a child at the side of the road with a toy film camera filming a postman cycling off into the distance. Throughout his movies Tati was obsessed with including an observer in his scenes, so instead of simply watching comic action we are also watching someone else watching it. As a trope this device would recur in all his films, right up the gag in *Playtime* (1967) when two workmen carrying a plate-glass window are being observed by a group of onlookers on the pavement. By including an observer in the scene, Tati is making the comedy more real. He is saying that, even in the world of the picture, the comic action is worth watching.

Tati had high hopes of *Soigne ton Gauche* establishing him in the cinema – but despite modest international sales it sank without trace. The war then effectively put a stop to his career for four years.

*

Following his military service and France's surrender Tati got married, made a meagre living plying his music-hall trade, and was ironically rescued by the very group of people to whom he had never belonged and with whom he had had legal contretemps – Marcel Carné and Jean-Louis Barrault. When in 1943 Carné mooted Tati to replace Barrault as Baptiste in his epic homage to the Théâtre de Funambules, *Les Enfants du Paradis*, he set a chain in motion that would lead directly to Tati's launch onto the big screen. As it happened Barrault was able to free himself from his commitments to the Comédie Française, so Tati did not get his chance in that movie – but in the casting process he met the producer Fred Orain, who would prove vital to his career from then on. Orain cast Tati as the ghost in his film *Sylvie et le Fantôme*, and fruitful creative collaboration was born.

The two men hit it off from the start – Orain was a fanatical enthusiast for silent comedy from Mack Sennett onwards, so when Tati suggested a series of silent shorts, Orain embraced it. In the event, they made only one film – but it nevertheless became the springboard for Tati's cinematic career.

In *L'Ecole de Facteurs*, made in 1945/6, Tati plays a rural mailman instructed by his boss to deliver the post faster. The movie follows Tati's efforts to fulfil this remit, and a series of hectic gags follow – many of which would resurface in his first feature a year later. In his manic attempt to deliver his mail in record time he places a letter under a horse's tail, sets a pair of parcelled boots down in front of a butcher who promptly slices the toes off with a cleaver, is hauled into the air by a bell-rope, gets his bicycle stuck on a level crossing barrier, and attaches himself to the back of a lorry where he does his mail sorting while hurtling along at fifty miles per hour.

There is a delightful routine when, stopping at a café for a well-earned drink, Tati joins a group of youthful dancers jigging along to gramophone jazz. Tati's dancing is very reminiscent of Laurel & Hardy's, and he gets so carried away that he's only snapped out of it by the sudden noise of the the air-mail plane overhead. Racing to the landing strip, he manages to hook his entire mailbag onto the tail of the bi-plane ... and the film is done.

Though not a satire, but rather a fun exhibition of Tati's pantomimic and comic physical ability, *L'Ecole des Facteurs* nevertheless contains the central theme of Tati's subsequent comedy ... his antipathy to the modern fetishising of progress. He is establishing himself at the outset as an outsider at odds with the world – his postman would rather stop off at the local café for a refreshing glass of *vin de table* than deliver his mail at breakneck speed – and why not? In his full-length follow-up film, *Jour de Fête*, the enemy becomes more explicit – Tati once again plays the same rustic postman but now it is not simply an over-ambitious boss who instructs him to go faster, but an American Educational film demonstrating the speed and efficiency of the US Postal Service – planes skim through the air, cars zoom along highways, even mailmen drop through the air by parachute. Capitalism itself has become the foe. It is a simple thing, and it is not *Modern Times*, but Tati is hinting that this modern obsession with speed will at first erode rural life, and then destroy it. By 1967 when

Playtime was released, this demon progress has not only affected the postal service but has built glass and steel tower-blocks across the whole of Old Paris, and Tati is adrift in a vast soulless hell of grey, unable even to navigate through a maze of parked cars. From *L'Ecole des Facteurs* to *Trafic* there is a through-line; the films are both elegy and criticism. And at the centre of the critique is the personality of Tati himself, extended and redrawn into his persona first of the lazy, simple postman who takes his time to get to know each and every one of the people he delivers to, then of Hulot – a man so at odds with the modern world growing up around him that he cannot connect with anyone, and whose attempts to relate to the normal world are doomed to failure.

L'Ecole des Facteurs won the Max Linder Prize for best comedy short in 1947, and this publicity, coupled with the relentless faith and drive of his mentor and champion Fred Orain, secured the finance for Tati's first feature.

*

The release of *Jour de Fête* in 1948 was a landmark in the history of film comedy. It was as if the art of screen humour was straightening out a kink in its lineage, righting a wrong that had been inflicted nearly twenty years previously. Soundless film was reasserting itself as a valid genre. Of course this reassertion could only work if the film in question was not old-fashioned – it had to be bold, cutting-edge, fresh – there would simply have been no point rehashing the tropes of the silent comedy of yesteryear. *Jour de Fête* succeeded on all these counts, and not only established Jacques Tati as a major cinematic comedy star, but also put visual comedy back on the contemporary map.

Strictly speaking, however, it is not a purely visual film. More accurately, it should be described as dialogue-free. It is peppered with speech, but at no time do the vocals serve – as they do in other pictures – to advance the plot. They are garnish, tantamount to background noise, functioning in a similar way to the music and sound effects. The old woman character who serves as the film's narrator certainly supplies us with brief poetic streams of monologue as she hobbles round the village bent over her crooked stick, but her comments are judgements upon the tale rather than part of the action itself: like us she is merely a spectator. And Tati's character, though on occasions voluble, is without exception filmed in long-shot or mid-shot, which deliberately serves to reduce his vocals to a mumbling and as a consequence increases the superiority of his actions over his words.

So subordinate is speech to action, that many viewers erroneously remember the film as being purely visual.

The plot is fairy-tale-like in its simplicity: a fair comes to a small village in the middle of nowhere and causes a brief ripple of change in the otherwise slow and predictable routine of a sleepy community. The local postman is drawn into the fun and excitement, becomes the dupe of the more worldly wise fairground folk, and seeks to impress them by aping the amazing hi-tech efficiency of the American Postal Service. He fails, the fair leaves, and the village returns to its dozy agrarian stasis.

That is it. Tati plays – as he did in *L'Ecole des Facteurs* – a village postman, François. He appears to have no family or home – at least we never see it in the film – and although he is an important part of the small rustic community, his outsider-ishness is established from the very start. He is duped by everybody, including children who place fake letters in the mailboxes; his fellow villagers who trick him into drinking cognac when he thinks he's knocking back wine, and by the fairground workers who give him an ink black eye with a conch shell.

Jour de Fête is a huge leap forward from *L'Ecole des Facteurs* both in terms of roundedness of character and cinematic technique. The earlier shorts look heavily influenced by the silent directors of the past such as Keaton, Chaplin and Laurel; in *Jour de Fête* Tati, who directed as well as starred in the picture, stamps his own authorial style on the movie. While not as advanced in terms of surreality or ingenuity of gags as his later works *Monsieur Hulot's Holiday, Mon Oncle* and *Playtime,* it prefigures those films by displaying several unique characteristics that came to justify the soubriquet Tati-esque.

Tati-esque, for example, is his favouring of the long-shot: more often than not, the spectator's eye is well back from the action, observing the comedy as if from afar in a locked-off shot that is not only unobtrusive but also allows several things to go on at the same time. Certain French commentators have pointed to the director's apprenticeship as a picture framer as being a source of his style: Tati treats the camera-frame as a canvas, with action occurring in both foreground and background.

This technique occurs at the very outset of the film: following the opening scene of the fairground trucks trundling along the dusty highway towards Sainte-Sévère we first see François cycling along a narrow twisting lane, his mailbag on his back. But it is not us observing him: it is a farm-worker halfway up a hill in the foreground. Bothered by a bee, the peasant flaps it away. There is a beat, and we now see François bothered by (we presume) the same bee. It is a simple gag told uniquely: the camera remains firmly planted behind the farm-worker – a different director might have insisted on cutting to a close-up of the postman being harried by the insect, but Tati does not. From this very first scene Tati was laying down the law of his comedy: the comedy of shape and form, not subtext. His characters lead interior lives, to be sure, but that is not his business: their comedy lies in how they look, and they are best seen from the middle-distance.

The second great stylistic decision that makes the film Tati-esque is the simplicity of its story. It takes place over two days and although it contains all the vital ingredients of any story (a big event, change, challenge, and character development), these elements are so subtle as to make the movie appear almost plotless. All Tati's films have the leisurely pace and near-drift of the documentary – as though the film-maker is not making all this up but is simply cataloguing what he is discovering as his camera rolls. It is this that marks him off most distinctly from his earlier counterparts in the genre of silent comedy: for them, story was paramount. The extreme opposite of Tati's almost-languid approach is the manic hysteria of someone like Mack Sennett, whereas Tati's style in terms of his characters' performance owes most to the art of Laurel & Hardy, who under the guidance of Leo McCarey, James Parrott and Laurel himself, slowed the comic tempo right down. Cinematically, however, perhaps the greatest influence is that of Keaton, in his use of the long-shot and the manipulation of the action within the frame as if he making a painting and standing outside it.

It is perhaps invidious, however, to tease out the influences of other film-makers on Tati's first feature, for its chief power lies in its originality. Remarkably, there are only three close-ups in the entire film – a squinting peasant, a post-box, and a shot of François examining a black circle around his eye. There are several medium shots – such as François hitching his bicycle to the back of a truck and performing his franking duties while he shoots along at 40mph – but apart from these rare moments the entire movie is filmed in long-shot. We are observers watching the comedy from a distance, invited to spectate but not become too involved in the emotions of the characters.

Some intellectual commentators have observed that this style is the cinematic fulfilment of Brecht's theory of alienation, and there is no doubt that Tati's decision to make his comedy in this way is an intellectual one. But for all that – and perhaps unintentionally – *Jour de Fête* and *Monsieur Hulot's Holiday* are imbued with a warmth and empathy for his characters. This is not cold abstract art. Even though we are engaging with their exterior shape and motion rather their thoughts, we are nevertheless engaged in a sympathetic relation with them. All the characters in *Jour de Fête* are rounded and identifiable, from the stout peasant working the hillside flapping away a bee, to the fairground traveller who tricks François into aping the American way of delivering the mail. In his third and fourth films, *Mon Oncle* and *Playtime*, a certain harshness and coldness of attitude creeps in to his portrayal of protagonists, but in the late 40s and 50s Tati still retained a more playful, somewhat more humane, world-view. *Jour de Fête* has been described as a perfect mixture of slapstick and satire, yet it is not the bucolic townsfolk of Saint-Sévère who Tati is satirising but rather the threats to the village from the outside world – in particular the modern obsession with speed and efficiency. Tati's film is a eulogy to the rhythms of rural France.

Tati's slapstick throughout the film is sublime: liberated from the stage-bound performance of the sporting routine, he displays a dazzling athletic comedy ability, from his trademark long-legged gangly running to his straight-backed, somewhat pompous bicycle riding. His bicycle, indeed, features so prominently in the routines of the movie that it becomes almost an extra member of the cast. There is a marvellous routine where it becomes accidentally hitched to a truck and the hapless mailman sets off in pursuit: the bike, with a life of its own, doesn't merely roll down sloping lanes, but turns corners, necessitating a manic scramble up a hill on the part of François to head it off at the next bend. The bike passes several citizens on its journey, all of whom pause to observe its ownerless escape – a man sticks his head out through a car sunroof, a peasant woman turns from her goats, a traffic gendarme even directs the empty bicycle across the village square. Finally it comes to rest outside the café, and Tati runs up, breathless. He explicitly imparts life to the machine by admonishing it for running off, then tethering it to the café by a long chain, as if it is planning to make another escape.

Some of the most memorable routines in *Jour de Fête* involve the bike: on the day of the fair he is whizzing down a street towards the central square where a huge flagpole is being erected – having planted in an earlier scene that this massive pole is prone to fall every which way, François gasps as he clocks the wobbling object, then promptly steers to his right, shooting – bike and all – into the tavern. Immediately he is upstairs, emerging blinking at the window; clearly an unfeasible gag achieved through a simple cut in the film, but it doesn't come across as surreal or magical – we assume he has simply been carried upstairs by the momentum of his bike.

We never see where François lives, for he never reaches it: as night falls across the village, he wobbles slowly to a grinding halt next to a fence. Attempting to remount his steed, he swings his leg not only over the bike but the fence as well, and after several manic bursts of cycling that get him nowhere, the inebriated postman – plied with cognac by the fair-workers – gives up, staggering across the dark field and crawling gratefully into an empty railway carriage to spend the night. This was the first of many of Tati's night-time scenes throughout his films – from the firework scene in *Monsieur Hulot's Holiday*, to the scene in *Mon Oncle* where he sneaks back to his sister's house to snip away at her garden vine, to the nocturnal city scene in *Playtime* where he is stuck outside a friend's modern apartment block.

Much of the originality of the film lies in Tati's use of sound. Whilst the slapstick is traceable to the influence of silent comedians and directors of former decades, his use of audio is wholly his own. We've seen how Laurel & Hardy pioneered sound-gags in their pictures of the early 30s, later enhanced by Chaplin particularly in *Modern Times*, but Tati's use of a post-recorded soundtrack is utterly fresh and establishes a trademark style for all his films.

Non-diegetic sound – that is to say, audio that does not derive from a person or object within the frame being seen – is fundamental to his pictures, and is introduced at the very outset of *Jour de Fête*. This was a revolution in itself, given that the synchronicity of noise and image had been considered to be the be-all-and-end-all of movies since 1929. Tati played around with the grammar of sound, giving us the noise of the French countryside – chickens, sheep, cows – without the sources necessarily being seen. He added sound afterwards, like paint from an artist's palette.

From the outset, he plays with the grammar of how audio should be employed in cinema. In the first bee-gag, for example, the sound of the insect is at the same level whether it is buzzing around the peasant's head (standing near the camera in mid-shot) or a hundred yards away buzzing around the head of François. Tati is flouting aural perspective, and this is not the only instance in the film – it pervades *Jour de Fête* just as it pervades his subsequent pictures. The slightly muffled tinkle of the bicycle bell, for example, is at the same level irrespective of whether François is cycling in the distance or right past the camera: it is a signature splash of noise as close up as an image, and therefore of equal significance.

One sound gag might owe something to René Clair's *A Nous La Liberté* from 1931. In that film a hobo awakens in a field and the camera pans to a flower vibrating in a breeze accompanied by the tremulous warbling of a woman's singing. We are meant to believe that the flower is singing; when the woman reaches a passage of vibrato, the petals of the flower tremble. The source of the song is revealed to be a gramophone, but the surreal implication has been made. In one of the fairground scenes in *Jour de Fête* Tati has a fair-worker make eyes at a local girl and the pair exchange flirtatious looks for several moments. On sound is the dialogue from a cowboy film being broadcast in an adjacent tent, dialogue which we are at first intended to believe is emanating from the playful couple. Once the source of the soundtrack is revealed, the joke continues, the man's movements becoming increasingly cowboy-like, to the extent of him tipping his hat with his spanner as though it is a gun.

These kinds of gags abound in *Jour de Fête* and – whether influenced by Clair or not – Tati made the devices his own and in so doing virtually invented a whole new genre of film comedy. Dialogue is often half-heard, mumbling noise, words reduced to background, establishing a style that set the template for many a visual comedy in later decades from Jerry Lewis to Ronnie Barker. Human utterances are distilled into grunts, exclamations, verbal gestures on a par with the bleating, mooing and clucking of the farmyard animals. Indeed, the parity of human and animal is made explicit in a routine when François discovers the black ink circle on his eye that the fairground workers have inflicted on him: his head movements become fowl-like as he inspects himself in the mirror, and the sound of chicken-clucking colours the point.

François' attempts to turn the village of Sainte-Sévère-sur-Indre into a little America is, of course, doomed, and the last act of the film is a playing-out of his manic failure. Naturally his increased speed proves his undoing: like a Keystone Kop whose rapidity never catches the crook, his efficiency as a postman actually decreases by going faster – until he plunges his bike into the local river, and the magnificent pell-mell fifteen-minute sequence comes to an end.

Drenched, he joins the female narrator of the tale and they totter back to the village on her cart. As they pass the crops that are being harvested by the toiling peasants, she utters the moral of the film: 'The Americans won't make all that grow any faster. And as for good news, it doesn't go bad for waiting a little while.'

After various stumbling attempts to find a distributor, during which Tati returned to the music-hall stage, *Jour de Fête* finally obtained a release in London in March 1949, and a limited release in Paris in May of that year. It was an immediate hit with the public, if not with the critics. A grand showing was arranged in Sainte-Sévère-sur-Indre with a huge screen, coach-parties, bands, almost like a scene from the film itself – and, ever since, the remote bucolic community has become the town of *Jour de Fête*, with even a statue of François adorning the main square.

Initially many critics were suspicious of the languid, almost free-form plot-lessness, not realising that the skeletal narrative was an artistic choice. The movie was generally criticised for being a puffed-up short, although in the same review by Jeander in *Libération* of May 1949, it was admitted that Tati had created a 'new international language of comedy,' like Chaplin or Keaton. The sniffiness of the French critics was gradually contradicted, however, by the film's growing success abroad. Twenty years of sound had begun to root films in the country of their origin, being filled, naturally, with culturally specific references embedded in language – and now suddenly a film appeared that managed to be both nationally referential (it is clearly a French film about France) but at the same time expressed by means of a universal language: mime.

The burgeoning success of *Jour de Fête* led to Tati being inundated with requests from international distributors for a series of François pictures: *François in Love*, *François goes West*, and even a proposal to team him up with Italian comedian Toto. It is a testimony to Tati's vision and his own quite ruthless artistic integrity that he resisted all these demands. The world would wait a further four years before the release of his second feature – but it was a wait well worth enduring, for it would prove to be one of the greatest comedy films of the century.

*

Unlike Chaplin's invention of the tramp character on the back-lot of the Mack Sennett studios in 1914 for the movie *Mabel's Strange Predicament*, Tati's discovery of Monsieur Hulot seems to have been a more gradual creative process. In the hiatus prior to the release of *Jour de Fête* Tati had returned to the stage, but as the movie gained popularity he was granted the financial freedom to slow down and ponder his next move. Once again he collaborated with writer Henri Marquet and, together with the painter Jacques Lagrange, set about planning his next film. The fact that at this time he was raising a young family and consequently going off on seaside holidays probably informed the theme and setting of his next picture: a vacation in a small hotel on the coast.

His creative collaboration with Marquet and Lagrange proved fruitful: Lagrange's designs and drawings of beach-huts, hotels and characters brought Tati's visions to life, and his discussions with Marquet produced some of the most wonderful visual gags ever seen on screen. Once again the shape and structure of the picture was to be less plot-driven and more picaresque, possessing the episodic nature of a Dickens novel or – as some commentators have pointed out – a kaleidoscope of scenes akin to the

Praxinoscope, a proto-cinematic invention popular in turn-of-century France. The Praxinoscope was a sophisticated slide-show projector that threw comic images and vignettes onto a screen through a moving celluloid strip. The inventor, Emile Reynaud, had created one particular story, *Autour d'une Cabine,* a fifteen-minute narrative concerning the comic exploits of various characters at the seaside. In 1946 the Praxinoscope was a prominent feature of the fiftieth anniversary celebrations in Paris of the invention of French cinema, leading Tati's biographer David Bellos to conclude that the film-maker was at a showing of this primitive seaside comedy.

Whatever the influences upon the theme and setting of *Monsieur Hulot's Holiday,* central to its huge success was the character of Hulot himself. Like the other great visual comedy characters, Hulot is a complete outsider. His body itself does not belong in society – and he knows it by adopting the most deferential, almost self-hating posture imaginable. He is in an almost permanent stoop, as if ashamed of his height. His gait is halting, apologetic, his footsteps short and unobtrusive. His head bobs and bows in a near-Oriental manner of deference. He defers to everyone. He hides, he sneaks around – one suspects he would rather not be in the presence of humanity all. He is in the company of others only because he has to; we experience the sense that he just passing through, without any desire to make any actual connections with other people at all. And yet he is deeply lonely. At the end of his holiday he sits on a sand-dune watching the other guests saying goodbye to each other, and makes a doomed attempt to bid them farewell. They studiously ignore him. He is an oddball who has spoiled their vacation with his strange ways.

Like Tati himself, Hulot is at odds with the modern world. He can never hold down a job, he is never married, preferring to glide through life skimming social reality. He gets trapped in a block of parked cars; he is baffled by the technology of the modern kitchen; a machine in a factory producing hosepipe gets the better of him; the architecture of an office block defeats him in his quest for a businessman who is meant to interview him. On a human level he rarely interacts with others – which is, of course, the hallmark of the great silent comedian: Laurel cannot conduct the simplest of conversations with anyone, be it a nurse, a policeman, a toff, or a factory boss. Without Ollie he is a doomed wraith. Chaplin sleeps in the streets. Keaton is mostly alone and dreaming in his films, living inside his head so much that we often see filmed sequences of his dreaming.

So too Hulot – with one exception. In *Monsieur Hulot's Holiday, Playtime* and *Trafic* he makes hesitant gestures towards striking up some kind of relationship with a young woman. Yet she too is an outsider: in *Monsieur Hulot's Holiday* she is the only other fellow holiday-maker who has come away on her own; throughout the film she smiles at and laughs at the same things we are invited to smile and laugh at – the foibles and idiocies of the other, mainly bourgeois vacationers. In this way she is allied with Hulot, whose eccentricity throws into relief the staidness and pretentiousness of the others. In *Playtime* too, he has a similar ally in the young woman in the coach party visiting Paris; she is totally unlike the rest of the group, who are uniformly mid-West, stout, hen-like and shrill – examples of that breed of American tourist that had started to appear in the cities of Europe in the 50s and 60s. And in *Trafic* of 1971 he makes a significant romantic gesture to the young woman who he accompanied on the long journey to Holland from France in their delivery of a camper van he has designed: in the final shot we see Hulot linking arms with her as they both disappear down the stairs into a metro station in a flurry of opening umbrellas.These tentative forays into the world of social normality never blossom; they are left as tentative explorations. In many of Chaplin's films, from *The Immigrant* to *Modern Times*, Chaplin wins the girl – Hulot never does.

Watching *M Hulot's Holiday* is like leafing through an album of holiday photographs: the only structure of the film is the structure of a holiday itself – episodic and with that air of timelessness that vacations by the sea possess, when the days seem to melt into each other. That's not to say the movie is simply a series of sketches or gags: true, the characters do not follow the same kind of journey of transformation as in orthodox feature films, but as we accompany them we can see that they possess goals, and are subject to challenges, setbacks, and opportunities – but these ingredients are far more nuanced than in traditional movies.

With his second feature, Tati made more explicit his intention to present onscreen a new type of mime: intentionality and self-consciousness. When his characters mime, their performance manages to be both realistic yet deliberate. They are aware they are miming, so exaggerate their gestures to highlight a particular mode of behaviour. This is not the mime of the Funambules or the circus – it is behavourial, modern mime rooted in reality but enhanced to send up that reality. Take the early shot of the woman running down the beach. A simple shot, a simple act: and yet her slowness is exaggerated, her steps just that little too heavy – she is a statement of what it is *like* to run down a beach. Actors in his films would speak year later of Tati demonstrating how he would like them to walk: and as they watched him, they realised he was taking elements of their own walking style and exaggerating them – not for satirical effect, but simply to *show* the camera how that character behaves.

Similarly the keep-fit fanatic in *M Hulot's Holiday* is every seaside keep-fit fanatic we have ever seen – his arm rolls are just that little bit too pronounced, his knee-lifts a tad absurdly high. By directing such exaggeration Tati is saying – look, this is how we behave, all our actions are actually a performance …

The opening gag is one of the great sound-jokes of cinema. In a locked-off shot of a French provincial railway station we see a crowd of holidaymakers sent hither and thither from one platform to another by an unintelligible tannoy announcement. This is a gag that immediately unites a modern world audience, for despite technological advances it seems that railway tannoys have never and will never, be perfectly heard. Though it is unprovable, I would venture to suggest that in the creation of this gag Tati was influenced by the opening gag of Laurel & Hardy's *Berth Marks* (1929). The gag in the earlier picture is identical, yet more

As master of the visual gag, Tati's favourite device was 'information withheld from the protagonist.' Here Hulot is the last to know – indeed, he never actually finds out – that far from drying himself with his beach-towel he is in fact simply drying the pole around which it is inadvertently draped.

A classic example of the 'misunderstanding' visual gag where a scenario is construed as something other than what it is: Hulot sees what is ostensibly a peeping-tom outside a woman's beach-hut so decides to deliver a kick to the apparent offender.

At the last second we – at precisely the same moment as Tati – clock that the man is simply bending to take an innocent photograph of his family. Once again full information has been withheld – but this time it has been denied both Hulot and the audience.

surreal – for the railway announcer is standing right next to them when he utters forth his stream of unintelligible gibberish.

From the outset, we see Hulot is an outsider: first, he is not travelling the seaside by train with the others but in a bizarre, homemade-looking vehicle that is not only driven off the road by other cars but also halted in its progress by a dog who potters lazily into the middle of the road and settles down comfortably to sleep.

His arrival is a distillation of all our experiences when we enter a hotel – that overwhelming sense of entering a place with rules. It is one of the odd conventions of a hotel vacation that one leaves one's own home in which one (usually) behaves just as one likes, and goes off to spend a period of time in what is effectively someone else's house, with its own strict codes of social behaviour. We are treated to the formal and staid atmosphere of the lobby of the Hôtel de la Plage with the guests seated in silence playing cards, reading newspapers, knitting and listening to a dull programme on the wireless. Hulot opens the door and lets in a huge gust of wind that shatters the air of boredom and restraint: playing cards are scattered, papers tossed everywhere – even a man's moustache is blown upwards by the incoming sea-gale..

That is the essence of Hulot: at times desperate to fit in, his presence in the normal social world is that of the anarchist – just as he destroys the posh new trendy restaurant in *Playtime* and reduces it to a shambolic, anarchic café of the Paris of old, he renders the staid Hôtel de La Plage into chaos from his very first appearance.

The film is rich with sound gags: as in *Jour de Fête*, Tati employs no perspective with his soundtrack – the cries from the beach are as close-up as they would be if the holidaymakers were standing right next to the listener. Even someone whistling on a bike in the middle-distance is whistling right in our ears.

Despite the film having a flavour of the avant-garde, Tati is not averse to using classic sight gags. As the guests drift in to the Hotel restaurant, the waiter adjusts the width of the meat portions he is slicing according to the size of the diner – edging the carving knife to a very wide slice as the rotund businessman enters. Another waiter is cleaning out the fishtank when – so engrossed is he in Hulot's antics – that he drops the net. Rolling up his sleeve in preparation to recover the net, he is once again distracted by the maverick guest, so plunges his clothed arm into the tank. There is even the age-old gag of a waiter being asked the time while he is holding a glass of beer, tipping his arm to look at his watch and thus spilling the drink. In an exquisitely timed stunt Hulot is strolling along the promenade and is propelled into the harbour by the cable connecting two vehicles, which suddenly tautens as one vehicle pulls forward. Later in the film he helps a woman carry a trunk which he is holding in front of his eyes: his vision obscured, he imagines a top step that isnt there and so is carried forward by both his stumble and the weight of the luggage all the way through the house and out the other side into her back garden.

The gags are non-stop, both subtle and broad: on the beach Hulot is drying himself and throws the towel behind him. As he is standing up against a pole, the towel naturally flies behind it – so he ends up drying the pole rather than himself: there is a wonderful misunderstanding gag when Hulot spots what he thinks is the rotund businessman spying on the young lady in her beach-hut. He finds out the man is simply stooping to take a photograph of his family – but only after Hulot has given him a hefty kick up the backside.

The mistake is handed on to the businessman like a comic baton, for he then clocks a man rubbing his foot (actually removing sand) and assumes that he is the deliverer of the kick. This handing on of misunderstanding is a device used by Laurel & Hardy, a perfect example being the ripping clothes routine in *Berth Marks*, where a chain of people tear each other's clothes in the mistaken belief that they are enacting revenge.

In one of his ubiquitous gags involving vehicles, an inflated inner-tube (to which Hulot has just applied glue) rolls off down the lane and – seemingly with a mind of its own – enters a cemetery during a funeral. As it rolls, the sticky tyre picks up leaves, so that by the time it reaches the funeral gathering it bears a striking resemblance to a wreath: at once an undertaker stoops and picks it up and adds it to the commemorative display.

The supporting cast all have wonderful visual routines, including the British couple – she always walking ahead like a dog-owner dragging along a reluctant dog, he dawdling behind, tossing away the shells and pebbles passed to him by his crooning wife and gazing with a hint of envy at the bachelor Hulot. This implicit admiration for the 'freedom' of the Hulot character is a theme Tati was to draw on further: indeed, the children in the film miss Hulot when he goes absent one night, one of them rushing into the music room when the loud jazz starts up, thinking the eccentric guest has returned, only to be disappointed when he finds out it is only the waiter who has accidentally turned the electricity on. At the beginning of the film a group of children gather round Hulot's bizarre vehicle as it splutters up to the Hôtel de la Plage, and it is this same group of children that Hulot joins on the sandbank on the last morning of the holiday, as they all sit morosely, waiting for the parents to finish packing.

Hulot also gets on far better with the band of scouts camping on the hill above the town than with the staid middle-class guests. He joins them for an evening's spree that turns into a night of drinking and singing, to the annoyance of the hotel residents, whose umbrage is expressed by the lights in their windows going on one by one – another leitmotif of Tati's work that would be returned to in *Mon Oncle* and *Playtime.*

This is a clear statement that Hulot represents an idea of freedom: while he makes sporadic attempts to join in the normal social world, he actually embodies a certain bohemian liberty that some bourgeois adults in his stories recognise and yearn for, and which most of the children acknowledge as matching their wilder sense of existence.

Waiters feature prominently in *M Hulot's Holiday*, and their comic potential was not lost on Tati, who would bring them back to dominate the entire last half hour of *Playtime.* In *M Hulot's Holiday*, waiters serve as custodians of the constricting rules of the hotel, Hulot treating them like adults he must please or avoid. After he becomes soaking wet as a result of a boating accident, he makes wet footprints across the lobby, then hides from the eagle-eyed waiter in a coat-stand. Magically he escapes from the coats, leaving a puzzled waiter ruffling through the empty hanging garments before clocking a series of wet prints on the stairway. Had Chaplin shot the escape he would doubtless have featured a long-shot of himself nipping athletically up the stairs – here, Tati simply uses a set of prints, and the off-screen thump of his footsteps. There is a beat, then a single canoe paddle rattles down the stairs all the way to the lobby.

On its release in March 1953 *Monsieur Hulot's Holiday* was an instant success both with critics and the public, and made Tati an international household name. Its influence was incalculable, even on comedians and writers not specialising in visual comedy. Perhaps the most eminent British comedy writers of the last fifty years, Ray Galton & Alan Simpson, creators of *Hancock's Half Hour* and *Steptoe and Son*, told me (at the British Film Institute in 2012 after a reading of one of their 'lost screenplays' for Hancock, *The Day Off*) that part of Hancock's difficulty in choosing a subject for his transition to movies was down to Tati. 'Everyone was in awe of Tati,' Ray Galton said, 'and we couldn't help but be influenced by him. One screenplay suggestion of Galton & Simpson's was 'Hancock on a Cruise' – which, despite the comedian wanting to be 'international,' he dismissed as 'Monsieur Hancock's Holiday.' The script they ended up writing for him – and which Hancock also rejected, *The Day Off* – is particularly Tati-esque in its episodic structure, its wilful abandonment of heavy plot, and it beautiful sense of drift, or *derive*: Hancock simply wanders round his hometown on his day off, encountering various characters. But again Hancock (foolishly, in my view) rejected it. 'He wanted to be international like Tati,' Alan Simpson told me, 'but at the same time he wanted to be original. 'And of course he then went on to make *The Punch and Judy Man*, which is set by the sea but which couldn't be more British.'

Comedy actress Liz Fraser – stalwart of several Carry On films as well as appearing with several of the greatest comedy actors of the post-war era from Hancock and Peter Sellers to Sid James – also testifies to the immense influence of Tati on British comedy. I had the great fortune to have Liz appearing in my radio comedy series *Truly, Madly, Bletchley* and we talked at length of her work: 'Everyone asks me about my work with Sid James,' she told me, 'but the two people I worked with who were more serious about comedy were Hancock and Sellers. And both of them loved Tati. They'd both go on about him. Particularly Sellers – because I suppose he could see himself being influenced by him more than Hancock (could), who had one character and was sticking with it. But Peter could be anybody.'

After the success of *Hulot,* Tati was now in a position to embark upon a third film almost immediately. A legal wrangle with his producer Fred Orain – over the amount of money Cady Films (the parent company) were receiving from the sale of *M Hulot's Holiday* – together with family problems with Tati's ageing parents, was to lead to a five-year wait for his follow-up, *Mon Oncle,* but it was a wait well worth enduring.

*

The evolution of each of his films was slow and painstaking, building gradually frame by frame like a series of paintings progressively forming an exhibition. This approach was allowed partly because he stood firmly outside the French film establishment, obtaining funding from private business rather than arts organisations. Even though he was lauded by critics and other directors alike – attracting plaudits from scholars like André Bazin, Francois Truffaut, and august journals like *Cahiers du Cinéma* – he remained an aloof figure, his own man and his own boss. The kind of accolades and praise he did enjoy were those received from other artistes – when Harpo Marx expressed his admiration, Tati responded with delight.

One might say that *Mon Oncle* picks up where *M Hulot's Holiday* leaves off, in that we are now seeing him at home. And just as we suspected, he inhabits an eccentric, crumbling part of the Parisian suburbs under threat from the stark, clean lines of the new modernist capital growing up around it. The plot of his new film is simple: he plays the brother of a well-to do woman married to a prosperous bourgeois businessman, whose young son prefers his more shambolic company to that of his oppressively middle-class parents. His mother stifles him with obsessive hygiene, his father with cold distance and formality. It is the uncle who introduces into the young boy's life a world of boundless play, untidiness, and a taste of Huckleberry Finn-like existence – and Tati is demonstrably saying that such a life is under threat from the encroachment of the modern world. It is a subtle film, as languid and drifting as *M Hulot's Holiday*, and yet it contains a barely concealed satire on post-war Europe. It's as if Tati – as he moved into middle-age – looked around and saw the fruits of the Marshall Plan and the building boom and the desire to get rid of the past, and wanted to release a paean to the beauty and value of the old pre-war Paris in which he had grown up.

For all its satire, *Mon Oncle* is still a remarkable comedy, full of gags – but the comedy is less slapstick than in his previous films. We first meet Hulot in the market square of the Old Quarter in which he resides, the huge fish poking out of his shopping basket frightening a terrier crouched beneath a stall. In a famous scene he ascends a stairway into his ramshackle home in the attic flat: after a series of twists and turns in which he goes up, down, and even round the back of the building, he finally arrives at his topmost apartment. Some writers have observed that this manner of living – perfectly suited to the eccentric Hulot – is a nod towards a school of French architecture dubbed the Irrational Style, a movement running counter to the functionalism of modernism and incorporating staircases that lead nowhere, rooms too small for occupation, windows on the floor and so on.

The engine of most of the comedy in *Mon Oncle* is an old-fashioned character in collision with the modern world. Hulot is only relaxed and happy when drifting in his old tatty neighbourhood of flower-sellers, cafés, roadsweepers and landladies. Once out of this environment he is gawky, hesitant and destructive; and in his confrontation with the trappings of the modern world, they are made to look ridiculous.

In contrast to Hulot's rambling, characterful dwelling, his sister's house – beautifully designed by Jacques Lagrange – is a clean white geometric box devoid of soul; the front garden a similarly patterned display of mathematical precision that Hulot's presence can only disrupt and subvert. He mistakes a lily on the pond for a stepping-stone; he mistakes a glass receptacle in the ultra-hi-tech kitchen for an indestructible plastic one, dropping it confidently on the floor expecting it to bounce and being shocked when it shatters into fragments. Staying over one night, he tips a modernist sofa over onto its side and makes a bed out of it. He destroys the perfect symmetry of the climbing-plants on the outside wall, so creeps back at night and attempts to rectify it by snipping the tops of the creeper. His loud snippings break the silence of the night and wake his sister and her husband, their heads popping up into the round windows like the two pupils in a pair of giant eyes.

Further confrontations with the modern world involve a sequence in which the eternally jobless Hulot seems to have found gainful employment in a plastics factory, a post admittedly procured for him by his brother-in-law. A series of routines designed to secure his sacking in the quickest possible way ensue. Two of them are based on Tati's use of misunderstanding as a basis for the gag: in the first, he is walking along a corridor when he pauses to pet a dog. In a series of carefully modulated moves he ends up on the ground, patting the dog's head. The dog trots off, leaving Tati ostensibly lounging lazily on the floor – a sight which is immediately presented to his boss, who rounds the corner at that precise moment.

The second misunderstanding gag is an extension of the wet footprint routine from *M Hulot's Holiday*. In *Mon Oncle* Hulot gets white paint on the soles of his feet, and in his attempts to clean it off, places suspicious white footprints on the secretary's desk, situated below a window onto the ladies' rest room. Of course, on her appearance in the office, she immediately deduces that Hulot has climbed on her desk to indulge in a spot of voyeurism.

What finally gets him sacked, however, is not a misunderstanding joke at all but a mechanical and slapstick routine that would not have been out of place – and indeed may even have been inspired by – Chaplin's *Modern Times*. Put in charge of a hosepipe-making machine, Hulot falls asleep at his post, and the resultant faulty batch of hose begins to bear a resemblance to some kind of mutant serpent. Belching out yards and yards of bulging coloured plastic, the machine finally wakes Hulot up, and he is faced with getting rid of a mountain of rogue product.

In his films Tati loved pursuing the consequence of gags. All gags, if they happened in reality, would have a consequence – yet few comedians pursue this notion. In *Mon Oncle* Tati pursues consequences twice. First, when he breaks a garden creeper in the house of his sister and goes back at night to try and rectify it, leading to more problems; and secondly, when he enlists the help of his local rag and bone men to get rid of the faulty hosepipe. They pull up outside the modern factory in their horse and cart – another example of the old world meeting the new head-on –

and willingly help Hulot bundle the offending plastic on the back of their vehicle. But even they, who can see money in the most useless of items, can discern no profit in this chemically produced garbage, and Tati gets another gag out of the routine when they throw the bundle of hosepipe off a bridge into a canal, and a passer-by dives in, thinking it's someone hurling themselves to a watery death.

Though subtle of plot, *Mon Oncle* nevertheless has more of a story than its predecessor, and the leading characters have arcs. In *M Hulot's Holiday* everyone is more or less the same at the end as at the beginning – it is as if we have been riffling playfully through a set of postcards. In *Mon Oncle* the young boy's father, growing jealous of Hulot's benign influence on his son, realises he must change in order to bond with him – so sends Hulot away to some unexplained foreign posting. The final scene is at an airport, and we see the gawky Hulot disappear into the crowds. Is that the last we will see of him? It would certainly be a long wait – it was not until 1967, nine years later, that audiences would once again be entranced by this odd-man-out of film comedy, in *Playtime.*

Mon Oncle was released in May 1958 and was an instant success. It had already won the Special Prize at Cannes, and in the ensuing year the movie became an international hit and won the Oscar for Best Foreign Film. In the USA to collect his trophy in April 1959, Tati was asked by the Academy if there was any special treat he would like: he requested meetings with his silent comedy heroes – Buster Keaton, Stan Laurel, Harold Lloyd, and Mack Sennett. Sennett summed up Tati's art – and indeed the art of visual comedy in general – when he responded to Tati's stumbling efforts at speaking English by replying 'I understand you much better when you don't say anything.'

*

Playtime may have been ten years in the making but the film wasn't Tati's sole focus. Much of it was spent on raising the finance – but interspersed with his pre-production activities were stage appearances, experimental in themselves in that they contained a fusion of film and live performance. He also shot some new scenes for *Jour de Fête,* leased a cinema – L'Arlequin – and showed not only his own but other directors' comedy shorts. Other tentative ventures in the 60s included adding soundtracks to the films of Mack Sennett and Buster Keaton, and developing his screenplay *The Illusioniste,* a film that would not get made for fifty years when Sylvain Chomet adapted Tati's script into an animated film in 2010.

Playtime finally went into production in 1963, but its progress was intermittent and the finished film was not released until 1967. It was one of the most expensive films of its day – and it broke Tati. His artistic ambition for his fourth picture was such that it became at best fantastically quixotic, and at worst self-destructive. His poetic dream simply ran away with him. His biographer David Bellos' observation that 'Playtime distils the accidental beauty of modern life,' is a perfect summation of the film. It makes it sound like anything but a comedy – and yet it is. In the history of cinema I believe it to be unique. Experimental, art-house, yet full of sight-gags, it was the culmination of Tati's career.

Tati's vision was nothing less than a complete satire of modern Europe. He wanted to portray the contemporary architectural urban world that was destroying the old continental cities – but when he began searching for locations he couldn't actually find anywhere suitably and extensively, brutalist. Paris was being developed, certainly – Tati himself was part of the protest movement against office development in the heart of the city – but it hadn't yet been spoiled sufficiently to provide the perfect setting for send-up.

His solution was simple. He would build a city. On a vacant lot on the outskirts of Paris the construction of Tativille became legendary. Streets, buildings, hotels, restaurants, apartment blocks, even an airport – from the designs of Tati and his old collaborator Jacques Lagrange sprang a futuristic vision that turned *Playtime* from being a satire of contemporary humanity into a comic vision of the future. Set-building in the days of Cecil B de Mille and Chaplin was impressive, but they couldn't hold a candle to Tativille. Chaplin built a factory for *Modern Times* – Tati built the town in which the factory stood.

It was into this bleak, sterile vision of the future that Tati deposited M Hulot. We see him first attempting to navigate his way through a labyrinth of cars outside the airport – twisting and turning, finding his way blocked, back-tracking. The continuum between *Mon Oncle* and *Playtime* is explicit and deliberate: at the end of the earlier film the irritant Hulot is packed off to the airport to some obscure destination; and here he is, in the new film, re-appearing at an airport. A decade has passed, and Hulot is even more at odds with the world. He has a job interview, but such is the power of the modern environment to alienate that he only gets to meet his potential employer much later in the film when they happen to bump into each other in the street. From his embarkation on a bus from the airport to the following morning – the timespan of the entire film – he is plunged into a surreal, almost hallucinatory comic dream. I will not call it a nightmare, because of the films elegiac relationship with its subjects – Tati does not *hate*

The continuum of 'visual comedy with sound' between Chaplin's pioneering masterpiece Modern Times *and the work of Tati is evinced by Tati's use, thirty years later, of a central image from Chaplin's film. Adrift in the industrial wasteland of contemporary Paris and stuck in a sterile modernist waiting-room, Hulot the outsider is watched over by the corporate oligarch – who, three decades later, is still in power.*

the modern urban world, he is alternately gently appraising it and acerbically critiquing it. The whole work is satire, to be sure – evinced by the American tourist vainly attempting to gain a glimpse of the real old Paris and only managing to obtain a fragmentary hint when a reflection of the Eiffel Tower suddenly appears in an opening glass door. Yet in other episodes in the film features of the urban landscape are eulogised, made poetic, such as the tall graceless streetlamps lining the motorway on the edge of the city suddenly given great beauty when likened to flowers in the hand of one of the coach-party.

Hulot's journey across the city is one of drift, *derive*, and is a perfect cinematic example of the French situationist school of psycho-geography that made art out of aimless wandering. He is like a bagatelle ball bounced from one place to the other: roaming a vast Kafkaesque office complex in search of his potential boss, then pitched into a city he no longer feels at home in.

In a city of steel and glass, it is hardly surprising that reflection gags abound: Hulot and the interviewer see each other through a series of gigantic glass doors and windows, only to realise that – like in fairground hall of mirrors – they are actually not where they appear to be. The boss is behind Hulot, not in front of him – he collides with a glass door, and limps away, stricken ...

Critics sometimes bemoan the lack of plot in *Playtime*, but not only is its sense of drift deliberate, there is a method and a story in its meandering. Tati hit upon a sub-plot for the film that proved the perfect

A major recurring device in visual comedy is the 'object switch,' – one thing behaving like another thing. Tati employed it on numerous occasions, memorably in Monsieur Hulot's Holiday *when the inner-tube of his car tyre becomes a funeral wreath after leaves become stuck to it. Here, in* Playtime *(1967), a traffic roundabout becomes a fairground carousel.*

Tati's elevation of visual comedy to hitherto unreached heights culminated in Playtime. *He may have begun as a pantomimist on the cabaret stages of 1930s Europe performing imitations of sporting characters – but his growth into one of the greatest artists of the century is evinced by this 'window-cleaning' sight-gag in which a tilted window swings the occupants of the reflected coach upwards.*

His years of working in an art gallery imbued Tati with a love of perspective and depth of field. Here in Playtime *he uses it to good effect when he makes an electrician inadvertently light up a 'halo' above a priest's head: later in the same film a waiter ostensibly waters the flowers on a diner's hat – only of course he is merely pouring champagne into an unseen glass. Some of these gags in* Playtime *are very subtly placed in the frame; like a painter, Tati crammed his canvas with so much material that it is only on repeated viewings that they become discernible.*

vehicle for depicting a tour around the brave new Paris he had created. A party of Americans are on a weekend's visit to France. During their stay the tourists eagerly seek the Paris of old, but they seek in vain. They are driven into squeals and paroxysms of delight by a tatty little flower-stall; are taken on an excursion to a business fair where pointless products such as vacuum cleaners with electric lamps for under-sofa cleaning are demonstrated; and are herded into a futuristic restaurant, which the shambolic Hulot sets about gradually – and inadvertently – to destroy. By the end of the film, in a sense, the foreign visitors *do* encounter the old Paris: through the character of Hulot. He has deconstructed the geometric formality and pretentiousness around them and restored to the restaurant the anarchic ambience and *joi de vivre* of France's yesteryear. It becomes a film of hope.

Despite its underlying seriousness, gags abound. Though the credit sequence is a lyrical pan across blue sky to the accompaniment of Francis Lamarque's soundtrack, the opening shot proper is a surreal sight gag – two nuns in big white hats, the points of which flap like the wings of swans. Cutting inside the airport, we have a protracted locked-off shot of a waiting area. Characters come and go, and no one is favoured: the camera remains in long-shot. A seated husband and wife observe the action as various people enter the frame, cross it, and exit. For Tati the film-frame is a stage. This is theatre: a military man enters at the top left of the frame, marches up and down, consults his watch, pauses, does an about-turn, and exits. A nurse follows. A stout cleaner with wide broom and bucket edges into visibility, scans the antiseptically clean floor – and withdraws.

This is a new genre of visual comedy: the comedy of everyday life, of what Tati called 'democratic mime.' None of the characters are being intentionally funny, and yet the way they are directed and behave is intended to *show* how funny they – and by implication we – all are. When I first saw *Playtime* the film didn't exercise its fullest effect until I emerged from the cinema into reality. I began to see Tati-esque characters and behaviour all around me – the self-conscious manner of a businessman consulting his watch; the studied, deliberate manner in which a woman walked down the street. Tati is saying we are all actors, and all our behaviour is performance. His aim for Hulot in *Playtime* immediately becomes clear – he has no intention of placing the character centre-stage as in the previous two films, but to set him among dozens of Hulots. To hammer home the point, indeed, he actually introduces three Hulot look-alikes into the story. There is a classic mistaken-identity routine in the Business Fair, when one of the Hulot-clones with identical tan mackintosh, umbrella, pipe, hat and gait, annoys the supervisor of a display stand by his oafish behaviour. When, minutes later, the real Hulot wanders by the manager takes him to be the offender, his gentle mocking escalating into furious outrage. There is something hilarious about a person behaving insanely in front of someone who has absolutely no idea why they are acting as they are – and this is one of the few traditional gags in the picture, akin to the misunderstanding gags in Laurel & Hardy's *Berth Marks.*

Playtime also contains new genres of sight-gags. A traffic roundabout behaves like a fairground roundabout, operated by the coins inserted into a parking meter; a coach lifts up into the air simply because its reflection is lifted up in a tilting window; the flowers on the hats of the tourists are standing proud and fresh when they set off in the morning for a day's sightseeing – when they return in the evening, weary and footsore, the blooms have drooped and wilted.

The opening of a new restaurant, The Royal, takes up the final half hour of the film, and could almost be a complete movie in itself. The sequence is, of course, a metaphor for the entire film: grappling with newness. Hulot has no intention of spending time at the restaurant but is cajoled into entering by an old army pal working as the doorman. Hulot smashes the huge glass door fronting the eatery, and in another glass-transparency gag the doorman quick-thinkingly holds up the door-handle in its former place, swinging his arm to open the now non-existent door for arriving customers.

Comic entropy ensues: chefs cannot fit large dishes such a whole salmon through the narrow hatchways; customers get their heels caught in loose floor-tiles, a waiter keeps snagging his uniform on the protuberances of the modernist furniture. Gags related to the innate hostility of inanimate objects are interspersed with surreal sight-gags: a waiter pouring wine in the distance looks – from the perspective of the camera – to be watering flowers on the hat of a woman seated in the foreground; a model aircraft at the bar melts in the heat, but when a fan is switched on it unmelts to the point of seeming to take off, with accompanying 'jet-engine' sound effect provided by the electric fan. As the atrophy reaches the point of chaos the power begins to fail: the electricity system short-circuits and sparks shower onto the dance-floor. Hulot attempts to fix things – and pulls the ceiling down.

At first we are led to think he has contributed to the destruction, but the dangling fragments and detritus of the destroyed restaurant becomes in itself a smaller, more romantic section, towards which the diners are drawn. A few tables are pulled into the area and covered with tablecloths, the young woman Hulot has befriended sits at the piano and plays a gentle romantic tune. The modern establishment lies wrecked around them, and while the architect and staff run round like headless chickens the anarchist Hulot recreates what once might have stood in its place – an old French café that would not have seemed out of place in the village of *Jour de Fête.*

By the time Tati released his comic epic, he was ruined. All his own personal wealth had been poured into the making of the film, and it broke him. After a limited showing in Paris the movie did not secure the vital US distribution deal it needed in order to recoup its money – and so Tati was doomed. He suffered the fate of the pioneer. He could so easily have produced a family-friendly, cosy clone of *M Hulot's Holiday,* and kept on doing that. Instead he chose to make an odd, alienating, sometimes cold, sometimes slow, experimental epic. From a critical point of view, the film was a 'sleeper', attracting a growing following over time: in 1969 *Cahiers du Cinéma* devoted an entire edition to the film.

*

Tati didn't vanish after *Playtime.* He was still a major figure abroad, especially in Holland and Scandinavia, and his last two features, *Trafic* (1971) and *Parade* (1974) were both low-budget international productions. They lack the high production values of his former works but nevertheless contain episodes of great comedy.

In terms of the way it was shot, *Trafic* was a patchy affair, several times grinding to a halt until more money was found. More than one director was used. Yet there are sublime moments. One of the greatest sequences is the choreographed car-crash: at a crossroads a skidding lorry and the manic gesticulations of a traffic policeman cause a multi-vehicle pile-up that in real life would be horrific, but which in Tati's hands becomes a magical, beautiful thing. A Citroën DS skids forwards, tipped up at an angle of 45 degrees; another car spins like a roundabout; a Volkswagen loses its wheel and chases it like a mechanical animal, the bonnet opening and closing like the beast's metal jaws; a priest involved in the crash kneels before his broken vehicle and administers what looks like the last rites; drivers emerge slowly and painfully from their cars and embark on slow, exaggerated physical exercises on the now silent highway. It's a breath-taking sequence.

A notable misunderstanding gag is when a woman thinks her dog has been squashed beneath the wheels of her open-topped sports car. In reality it is merely her fur stole, the result of a prank by a couple of youths. Hulot's increasingly desperate efforts to prove to the grief-stricken woman that it is not her pet, culminating in him wiping his feet on it like a doormat – look, it's inanimate! – causes her to be engulfed by even bigger paroxysms. It is a perfect example of a pure visual gag, for if this was a normal speaking world he would simply tell the woman rather than launch into mime. Another notable sequence involves two car mechanics who have just watched a moon-landing on television. After marvelling at the slow-moving astronauts fixing their buggy on the moon, the mechanics then launch into their own slow-motion repair of a car – handing over spanners painfully slowly, moving round the vehicle at a snail's pace. Uniquely in Tati's *oeuvre* there is also a fly-on-the-wall candid camera sequence – perhaps the most famous sequence in the film – of a row of stationary drivers stuck in traffic and picking their noses. It is perhaps the ultimate expression of the democratic comedy theory Tati had come to espouse: in his pursuit of the comedy of everyday life Tati finally dispensed even with actors, and ended up pointing his camera at real people without them knowing.

Tati's swansong, *Parade*, released in 1974, was an affectionate *homage* to his old circus and music-hall days, and was populated by acrobats and other performers he'd known for years. Tati was the centrepiece of the film as ringmaster, and fittingly his last appearance on screen was a performance of his *impressions sportives* act – the angler and the horseman – that Colette had seen forty years earlier and that had projected him into stardom. Seconds after filming his last sequence, Tati collapsed and was rushed to hospital. He would live for a further eight years, but would never appear on screen again, save for the occasional interview at film fairs and conferences. If, at the time of his death in 1982, his sense of his own worth had weakened – he never really got over the battering he had received for *Playtime* – he received a boost when in 1977 a Paris film distributor paid off all his debts and re-released his four masterpieces: *Jour de Fête*, *Monsieur Hulot's Holiday*, *Mon Oncle*, and *Playtime*. He lived just long enough to see a new generation of cinema-goers rediscover his magic.

From street urchin to superstar: in his heyday more popular than James Bond, here Norman Wisdom greets fans on the set of The Early Bird *(1965).*

CHAPTER 9

The Kid: Norman Wisdom

In 1924 a boy of nine scrambles up a wall in Paddington, London. Evading the clutches of a burly copper he lunges for the top and gets his hand caught on a nail. Screaming in pain, he hangs there like a puppet for what seems an age until suddenly he feels a pair of rough strong hands around his waist. Lifted off gently by the benign policeman, the boy – nursing his wound – darts off into the fog to re-join his urchin gang.

Flash forward to 1956. The same kid is hanging off a window ledge. Only this time he is filming a slapstick window-cleaning routine for the film *Up in the World.* It is the kid's seventh picture and he has already won a BAFTA and become one of the biggest box-office draws in the country.

That slapstick is in large part derived from the violence of working-class life is borne out by the extraordinary parity between the lives of Chaplin and Norman Wisdom. In childhoods almost identical, both were brutalised by neglect, both shaped by the streets of poor districts of London, and (perhaps irrelevantly but certainly interestingly) both had elder brothers with whom they forged a bond based on mutual survival. Chases, fights, hunger, envy of the rich, pratfalls, petty thievery – all the tropes that found their way into Chaplin's movies also became the staple of Wisdom's comic farces of the 1950s. If ever two artists spun gold from straw it was Chaplin and Wisdom.

Wisdom's autobiography, *My Turn,* published in 1996, tells a sorry tale of this early hardship. Abandoned by his mother by the age of five and by his father by the age of ten, he and his brother had to fend for themselves. They stole from shops, went to school barefoot, and spent whole days in the British Museum because it was free. Farmed out to foster homes then thrown out for disobedience, a still-young Wisdom found himself homeless on the streets of London and – in a poetic echo of Chaplin's opening sequence of *City Lights* where the Little Tramp is discovered sleeping on a monument before City Hall – he dossed behind the statue of Marshall Foch near Victoria Station. Ahead of him lay a bleak and uncertain future. With a friend he walked all the way from London to Cardiff and was signed up as cabin boy on a merchant ship by a sympathetic Chief Mate. After a trip to the Argentine, during which he experienced as much brutalism as his childhood (his fellow sailors entered him for a boxing match in Buenos Aires where he was battered senseless: he won the match but never saw a penny of his winnings as the crew disappeared with all the money), he found himself back in London, penniless and alone. He returned to a life of drifting and begging until finally, he signed on to the army who, in his own words, saved his life.

Mention the name Norman Wisdom today and more often than not people will describe a flat-capped diminutive clown who mugged and fell over and pleaded for sympathy with his audience in a series of light knockabout farces of the 50s and 60s. It would be true to say that while many millions of fans still admire and love him, his work has not fared well with the critical establishment in our more cynical and knowing age. This, I would argue, is a misjudgement of his achievement. While on the surface light-hearted and easily summed up, Wisdom's schtick was more profound: I believe he did nothing less than restore the primal agony and subversive struggle of the universal clown to the big screen. Wisdom may act with broader strokes than Tati, but he is still nevertheless a similar 'Outsider in the modern world,' an archetype of someone socially and psychologically excluded from the norm. The source of Wisdom's psychological alienation is a browbeaten, emotional stuntedness – he is a child who has never grown up. In the wrong hands this trait can lapse into the kind of mawkishness Harry Langdon fell prey to, but although sentimentality does creep into Wisdom's films it never displaces the comedy and, I would argue, derives not from artifice but from an artistic truth.

Wisdom's Gump persona – the little man in the ill-fitting suit and the flat cap – exhibits all the behaviour of a child. His moods fluctuate wildly from excessive excitability to despair in a matter of seconds; he gets excited at the sight of sweets or buns; he displays a complete lack of inhibition amongst his social superiors. His single-minded focus on extreme desires, such as lust in the presence of a woman and hunger in the presence of food, is pure Commedia dell'arte, an echo of Chaplin's libidinous pursuit of the woman in *Modern Times* following his mental breakdown on the conveyor belt.

In *One Good Turn* (1955) there is an extended scene set in a railway carriage where, on his way to Brighton for the day, Norman attempts to engage his stuffy fellow passengers in banter: 'Come on, let's have a sing-song!' His co-travellers remain silent and stiff-lipped behind their newspapers and their sixpenny novels. Not to be silenced, Norman stubbornly continues: 'I expect we'll go paddling', he pipes up, in what becomes a futile one-sided monologue. It is a scathing indictment of British society in the 50s, and wonderfully played by Wisdom and his supporting characters. He offers them a sandwich from his rumpled paper bag. They sniff and refuse.

This lack of inhibition in the presence of social 'superiors' is a more radical trait than Wisdom has hitherto been credited with. His movies were far more subversive than they seem now to our more socially mobile age. Post-war Britain was still virtually feudal in its stratification of the classes, yet in Wisdom's films there is absolutely no deference to anyone above him: in fact, not since Chaplin has the establishment been so mocked and undermined. George Formby was the cheeky lad from Lancashire, but at no point in his films were the upper classes brought down a peg. Will Hay had cocked a mild snook at pillars of the establishment such as the police or the local 'toffs', but in Wisdom's films no tier of elite British institutions escapes unscathed – the military, the police, the aristocracy, the plutocracy, all have their noses tweaked and the rug pulled from under their feet by Wisdom's anarchic whirlwind. In *Up in the World* (1956) he gate-crashes an aristocratic party at the stately home at which he is working as a window-cleaner in the belief that it is the staff lunch canteen. He breezes into the rarefied, stuffy environment, cutting through its pretension, heaping his plate high with cakes and sandwiches, urging the others to 'go on, get stuck in!'. He is the force of uninhibited classless joy, greeted with frowns of disdain by most, but welcomed by Maurice, one of the guests – in a marvellous camp cameo by Michael Ward – who gleefully abandons his upper-crust persona and joins in with Norman's joyful antics. With a whoop of ecstasy he spots a drum-kit and a piano and in place of the genteel music seeping into the room, launches into a frenzy of free-jazz, he and Maurice jamming happily, oblivious to the stares of shock and disdain from the upper-class gathering.

This is the premise of most of his films – to cock a snook at these upper echelons of British society, whether it's destroying a business magnate's garden, wrecking diplomatic missions, wreaking havoc at a posh orchestral concert or drenching a police commissioner with a hose. He yearns for the pretty girl, woos her, is rejected, and bounces back. He is on the side of the little man, the outsider – an entire film, *One Good Turn*, is devoted to buying a present for a young boy in an orphanage; and in *The Early Bird* (1965) he battles a corporation to protect a small milk delivery business, his outsiderishness so complete that he sleeps alongside the horse.

This social mission in Wisdom's films is not accidental: he co-wrote most of his movies, feeding elements of his life into the stories just as Chaplin did. In this sense Wisdom is not simply a comedian but a comic artist, and his entire *oeuvre* is overdue for a reappraisal.

The physical skills he acquired on the streets of Marylebone and Paddington as a boy were shaped by the army into clowning. His occupations prior to joining up: – hotel bellboy, cabin boy on a merchant ship – also fed his slapstick and supplied material for later routines, for there is comedy in a small man carrying a huge breakfast tray or swabbing a deck. He would later say he owed everything to the army, and he'd be right. A nascent comedian is nothing without an audience, and his fellow recruits became just that. Signing up as Drummer Boy in the 10th Hussars, he sailed for India. Five years later he sailed back a comic. Around the same time as Jacques Tati was showing off his sporting mimes to his friends in the Racing Club de France, a young Norman Wisdom was performing a shadow-boxing routine for his mates in the barracks at Lucknow. While his bandmates were his audience, his commanding officers were the talent-spotters who nurtured him. Recognising his penchant for clowning, they cast him as the front man in shows, urged him to perform his horse stunts in equine displays. The first applause Norman heard was the clapping of officers and memsahibs. After five years in the Hussars he moved to the Royal Signal Corp, and when war broke out in 1939 worked first for the embryonic GCHQ in Cheltenham, then in a secret underground bunker off the Edgware Road, relaying messages from the allied leaders to the Prime Minister himself.

Wisdom's war work has up to now never been cited as crucial nourishment of his later comedy movie schtick, but his mingling with the top brass of the British War effort during those years – and you can't get more top brass than Churchill – must have influenced the onscreen relationship of his character with his straight men. His job was to speak to world leaders like Eisenhower, Roosevelt and Stalin, and relay the messages to Churchill. He was once told off for calling him Winnie. Proof, surely, that his cheeky film persona was no invention but an expression of an ingrained and authentic subversiveness. His role as sidekick to the Prime Minister and his aides prefigures the comic dynamic between him and Edward Chapman, the actor who played the stolid, pompous Captain Mainwaring-like Mr Grimsdale, Wisdom's most famous foil.

Traditionally the 60s is seen as the decade of satire – and certainly it was the boom years for political comedy – but there is a strong argument to be made that the previous decade was equally strident in questioning the old certainties of class and hierarchy in British institutions. The films of Norman Wisdom were part of that wave. While the Boulting Brothers were making their series of social satires of the army, academic life, big business and the church between 1956 and 1963 in *Private's Progress, Lucky Jim, I'm Alright Jack* and *Heavens Above,* Wisdom was lampooning the establishment in his own, less subtle, way. Wisdom's social satire was done through puncturing of pomposity with slapstick: he blasts a businessman with a hose, wrecks his garden with a runaway motorised lawnmower, ruins a military drill on a parade ground by shouting out contrary commands before ducking down into the hole he's digging at the edge of the base. As Andrew Roberts points out in his article on Wisdom for the BFI (Nov 19 2013) '… he would sing, dance and slapstick his way through spivs, teddy boys, assistant managers and other post-war folk devils.' This is comedy of revenge: the cinema-goers who consistently made Norman Wisdom one of the top box-office draws during his golden decade – from the mid-50s to the mid-60s – relished such retribution.

In his films Wisdom has the jester's license to spread folly amongst the ruling classes and he does it with a gusto and sense of joy and abandon not seen on screen since Chaplin. That is why, for example, his 1963 picture, *A Stitch in Time,* knocked *From Russia with Love* off the top of the box-office charts.

*

His professional journey had begun in 1946 when, recently demobbed, he was spurred on by some encouraging words from Rex Harrison who had visited him backstage at a troop show in Gloucestershire, urging him to try his hand at making a living at entertainment. With Harrison's fillip ringing in his ears, Wisdom pestered Lew Lake, manager of Collins Music Hall on Islington Green, north London, for an open-spot. 'I was more warm-up than stand-up,' remembered Wisdom years later, 'but that cold December night I didn't care'. Collins was famous as a launching pad for young hopefuls – agents would gather on the Monday night at the long bar which ran the length of the theatre behind the stalls, to drink and watch the acts at the same time.

He goes on to describe his act, and from his description it becomes clear exactly why his rise in the world of variety was so remarkably rapid – in a mere two years he was performing at the Palladium. The reason is blindingly simple: his act was predominantly visual. 'I billed myself as The Successful Failure,' he said. 'My act began with just one prop on stage: a piano. I was a clown let loose into a virtually empty arena, and somehow I had to fill it with mime, imagination and fantasy.'

Unjustly remembered solely for his supreme slapstick, Norman Wisdom – like Tati – employed many clever switch gags in his films, including this cleverly constructed candy-floss-stick-as-conductor's-baton routine in One Good Turn *(1955). This is no throwaway sequence: Wisdom sets the conceit up so believably that he includes an acceptable reason for his wearing a tuxedo – he is a West End sandwich-board man …*

… and also adds the device of having his mouth clogged up with candy-floss to prevent explanation. Which makes his arrival onstage in front of a crowd expecting an orchestral performance utterly acceptable. Even the conducting itself is not gratuitous – in shaking his hand Wisdom is simply attempting to remove the sticky 'baton,' so all the 'conducting' is completely inadvertent.

His early routine was not yet the downtrodden Gump in ill-fitting suit and threadbare cap – he was a well-meaning eager entertainer in bow-tie and tails. He'd start to sing, but in the wrong key, and never got more than one word out. His act was Tati with a dash of English showbiz. His tap routine involved placing a mat in the centre of the stage and dancing round it, but never quite reaching it. On that first night the manager Lew Lake went backstage and promptly booked him for a week.

Such was the freshness of his act that he was signed up by an agent immediately and plunged into the variety circuit – a world of train journeys and digs at eccentric boarding houses. Quickly promoted from the opening spot to the second half, traditionally the more superior part of the bill, Wisdom extended and developed his act. In Basingstoke in the winter of 1946 he stayed up all night writing himself a twenty-minute routine:

> It opens with the curtain slowly rising to reveal me in my misfit evening suit, leaning on a grand piano, reading a newspaper and munching a sandwich, oblivious to everyone. When I realise in horror that I'm being watched, I hurriedly try to conceal the half-eaten sandwich by stuffing it into the piano. Of course my hand gets stuck under the lid – and when I walk away I'm jerked back and end up on the floor. I fool around on the keys and suddenly launch into *I'll Walk Beside You* – only to find the orchestra are playing in the wrong key, at least an octave too high... I ended the act by picking up my tenor sax and finishing with some jazz and a spot of tap-dancing for a bonus.

Single-handedly, Wisdom had reinvented dumb-show for the English stage. Just as Tati had conquered the European stage with pantomime, so too was Wisdom allowing the British public to rediscover the joy of wordless comedy.

For two years Wisdom slogged round the variety circuit, getting further up the bill. Far from adding speech to his act, he reduced it, extending the mime sections until his act was practically entirely dumb-show. This was partly owing to an appearance at the notorious Glasgow Empire, traditionally dubbed the graveyard of English comedians. So feared was this venue by southern comics that Des O'Connor legendarily pretended to faint just before going onstage. At the first house, Wisdom went out and tasted his first defeat – he played to complete silence. Between shows he pondered the problem: though words hardly featured in his act, the few sentences that did were delivered, naturally, in his broad cockney street-urchin brogue. 'Desperate situations call for desperate measures, as they say,' he wrote years later, and they don't get more desperate than a comic dying the death at the Glasgow Empire. 'With a stand-up comic, in the words of Frank Carson, it's the way you tell 'em. With me, it's the way you do 'em. Mime saved me that night … Ironically I shall always be grateful to the Glasgow Empire, because I found a new dimension to my performing ability which would later play an important part in my films.'

A string of successful revues, summer seasons, pantomimes and variety bills followed, with Wisdom topping the bill after a mere two years in the professional business. As the 40s came to a close he began making his first TV appearances: on July 8 1950 he debuted in *Music Hall* produced by Richard Afton, and the following month he was given his own show, *Wit and Wisdom.* Although the reach of TV shows was obviously far smaller than it is today, his face was gradually becoming a presence in people's homes. A review in *The Observer* declared 'Television has discovered a clown so prodigally endowed with talent that he might become another Grock.' Another three years of bill-topping stage performances culminated in Rank offering the thirty-eight year old Wisdom a seven-year film contract.

*

His movie debut could not have been more successful: with a great team around him consisting of John Paddy Carstairs, Maurice Cowan, Ted Willis and Jerry Desmonde – a team later enlarged by the presence of one of the greatest light-comedy screenwriters of the postwar era, Jack Davies – his first film, *Trouble in Store,* broke all box-office records in London, winning Wisdom the BAFTA for best newcomer.

Although Wisdom's debut movie came out in the same year as Tati's *M Hulot's Holiday,* the two films could not be more stylistically different. Wisdom and his team were not setting out to invent a new aesthetic, but rather to reinvent the brash slapstick of the 1920s. A year after the film was released, Wisdom defended this revival of broad slapstick in a revealing introduction to John Montgomery's book *British Comedy Films:* He writes – 'In this book the late W.C. Fields is quoted as having once said that film comedy is often too refined. Well, isn't that true? I think audiences still enjoy knockabout, still want to laugh at visual gags and broad slapstick humour. People tell me that they enjoyed my first film *Trouble in Store* because it was good honest knockabout, with a touch of sentiment.'

Indeed, cinema audiences had not seen such a combination of knockabout-plus-sentiment since Chaplin – and comparisons were quickly made. 'People call me Chaplin's successor,' he said in Montgomery's book. 'I do not mind being called anything, but not Chaplin's successor. To me Chaplin is unique, and always will be. And in any case, I want to be myself.' Himself, to be sure, but all his movies contained the Chaplin-esque leitmotif of the underdog's struggle, and during a brief visit to Hollywood in 1950 before his British film career had started, Chaplin was the one person he eagerly sought to meet. Chaplin was filming *Limelight*, and unusually – for towards the end of his career Chaplin would rarely welcome visitors on set – he embraced Wisdom with open arms. The two sat and chatted for an hour, showed each other their comedy walks, discussed slapstick, exchanged theatrical gossip. 'You will follow in my footsteps,' the great man told Wisdom – and he was right.

Wisdom's debt to the comedy stars of the silent era is obvious from the very first scene of, *Trouble in Store*: we see Norman ostensibly seated in a limousine alongside wealthy businessman Major Willoughby (Jerry Desmonde); the car pulls away and reveals Norman sitting on a bicycle. A funny gag, but not wholly original – Harold Lloyd employs the same reveal in the opening to his 1932 picture *Movie Crazy*.

Ably supported by straight men Jerry Desmonde and Edward Chapman, through all his films for Rank and others, Wisdom constructed some brilliantly original routines. In his second feature, *One Good Turn*, the orchestra-conducting routine is a masterpiece of invention and execution. The set-up of the routine is perfect: Norman is working as a sandwich-board man in the West End of London. Tempted by the wares of a nearby candyfloss seller, he buys some and sits on the steps of a theatre stage-door to consume it. This sets up two crucial components of the ensuing routine: he is holding a stick in his hand that is subsequently mistaken for a conductor's baton, and the candy-floss is so dense that it renders him unable to speak and therefore explain that he is not actually a conductor. Whisked into the theatre by two over-eager managers, he is thrust onstage (appropriately garbed in white tie and tails, which is his sandwich-board outfit) – and the scene is set for a prolonged visual musical routine involving Norman, a full orchestra, and a full theatre.

It's a masterpiece of mime. At first oblivious of his expected role, he tries to remove the sticky candy-floss 'baton' from his hand. He shakes it. The orchestra responds to his shaking with a few blurted-out musical notes. He repeats the action. Ditto the orchestra. Still failing to see the connection between his actions and the action of the musicians, his shaking hand gradually becomes wild and manic – as does the playing of the orchestra.

Then he twigs – and it is from that moment that Wisdom's character infuses the scene, for instead of fleeing as many comics might do, Norman embraces the comic potential of his new-found situation. The playful imp, trickster and faun inside completely consumes him, banishing all vestiges of socially aware behaviour (if any existed) and, relishing the sudden power in his possession, he dissolves the formal structure of the orchestra into a cacophony of chaos. It is a joyous scene, topped by the arrival of the real conductor who attempts to wrest some semblance of normality back to the occasion, launching the orchestra into the William Tell Overture, which becomes the accompanying music for the ensuing chase of the now-fleeing Norman.

It is not the only routine in the movie worth pinpointing: Andrew Roberts, writing for the BFI, highlights a stand-out routine centred on a telephone box in which Norman's efforts to retrieve a number scribbled on the wall while arguing with an arrogant queue-jumper, ends with the booth wrecked and the dial jammed into the queue-jumper's mouth.

Spurred by the huge success of *Trouble in Store,* Wisdom went on to make five further films in the next three years, not only taking the comedy world by storm but also restoring the finances of the Rank Organisation. As the 50s progressed, the films retained the same theme of the underdog battling to survive in a British hierarchy while nurturing an Everyman's dream of romance, but the routines became more sophisticated. In *Trouble in Store* the chase on roller-skates of the bus is pretty crudely filmed, with much cutting and back-projection. By 1956 and his fifth picture, *Up in the World,* both the routines and the filming had become more ambitious. Wisdom had always performed his own stunts, but with each picture they became more and more elaborate, with a touch of the Harold Lloyd thrill about them.

His relationship with his straight men, in particular Jerry Desmonde, also deepened. In *Up in the World* his first encounter with Major Willoughby (Desmonde) is a finely constructed, lengthy sequence rendered utterly original by the fact that they are fifty yards apart, and never actually meet. Norman is the socially uninhibited window-cleaner arriving to start a new job at the gigantic mansion belonging to Lady Banderville: Willoughby is the crusty Secretary running the place. Norman shouts up to Willoughby's office in his raucous cockney brogue – 'Major! Hey, *Major!!!*' – and after being told to keep his voice down is given instructions on where to get the hose, bucket and chamois leather. In a wonderfully building, physical sequence, Norman keeps returning to bother Willoughby, until the fractious Major is so apoplectic you can practically see the veins sticking out on his neck. Norman protests that the hose isn't long enough, and of course runs with it until he reaches the end and he is jerked back. The sequence integrates a running gag where he is ordered to 'keep off the grass!' – Norman anticipating the fourth such command by skipping jauntily and cheekily back onto the path literally one second after Willoughby has started bellowing. It's a masterly piece of timing.

Up in the World yields two more great routines a mere five minutes later – the tea-dance routine described above where Norman mistakes an aristocratic gathering for the staff canteen – and a routine immediately afterwards where, now installed in the correct quarters among the other underlings, he helps one of the maids by holding her knitting. Character actor Cyril Chamberlain, as Harper, is his foil: Norman answers the phone whilst holding the loop of wool and passes the receiver to Harper through the loop. With Laurel & Hardy finesse, the entanglement then escalates – not too slowly, not too quick – with Norman's pauses perfectly timed as he urges Harper to 'calm down!' As they both become completely wrapped in the knitting, Norman picks up the phone and says 'he'll be with you in a minute' before resuming his efforts to get the knitting off his legs. Such routines look simple but have to be impeccably timed and rehearsed in order not to come across as laboured, or indeed too rapid: escalating complication has to proceed at precisely the right pace for the comedy to work.

As the 50s came to a close and the 60s began, Wisdom's films continued to top the box office – *The Square Peg* was the seventh most popular film of 1959 and *A Stitch in Time*, as we have seen, toppled *From Russia with Love* off its number one position in 1963.

Yet movie stardom did not mean Wisdom neglected his stage career. Indeed, the pattern of his year was such a relentless combination of revue, summer season and pantomime interspersed with daily shoots at Pinewood and elsewhere, that on occasions his health suffered. If there was any doubt about his supremacy as the nation's greatest living physical comic it was dispelled by his now-legendary appearance in *Sunday Night at the London Palladium*.

*

Since 1955, *Sunday Night at the London Palladium* had steadily proved itself one of the most successful variety show in TV history, establishing Bruce Forsyth as king of the compères. The edition of April 1961 has gone down in showbiz history. A Variety Artistes Federation strike led to the bill becoming suddenly and completely empty, but because Norman Wisdom had already signed his contract to appear, he couldn't pull out – and as a vocational trouper whose motto was 'the show must go on', he had no intention of withdrawing. Producer Val Parnell was all set to cancel the broadcast, but Wisdom called up Forsyth on the phone and suggested they perform the entire show on their own. Despite harbouring a few reservations, Forsyth agreed.

Legend tells it that the pair improvised much of the performance, but Wisdom's lifelong commitment to painstaking rehearsal meant that he insisted that he and Forsyth spend the next week going over the material for eleven hours a day. It showed: the broadcast was a spectacular success. Everyone remembers the perfect double-act slapstick wallpapering routine, but the stand-out sequence for me was a solo spot where Wisdom plays a tramp waking up in a barn and imagining he is at an upper-class party. It is classic mime of the French school. Here he is not the Gump but a perennial Commedia dell'arte vagabond, bringing to life through sheer mime an entire ballroom full of invisible guests. He grabs a scarecrow and, pretending it is a fair maiden, launches into a series of whirling dances. Though mining the same trope of the dreaming tramp as Chaplin did in *The Kid* and *Sunnyside*, this is mime far older than Chaplin, delving right back to the mid-nineteenth century and Grimaldi. Had it not been for the strike, this routine would probably have not been allowed an airing on TV, with Wisdom sticking to safer, brasher material, so we have to thank industrial action on the part of the entertainers union for the preservation onscreen of one of Wisdom's most skilful and memorable routines.

The wallpapering sketch is a masterly study in co-ordinated double-act slapstick worthy of Laurel & Hardy: two men in overalls, two planks, a trestle table and a roll of wallpaper – resulting in a ten-minute routine that once again preserves on the screen a form of entertainment now lost: the extended stage pantomime. The exquisite timing of the two performers as first one, then the other, then both, become trapped between the two planks of a trestle table, is a delight. Wisdom, naturally the underling of the double-act, is ordered to measure the wall with his hands, a measurement which of course shrinks as he walks back to the paper, his arms getting closer together. The slapping of the paste onto the wallpaper is also a routine worthy of Laurel & Hardy, the rhythmic motion of the paste-brushes as they are slapped from side to side segueing into a cha-cha-cha – echoing Stan and Ollie's cleaning-up routine in *The Music Box*.

*

On the Beat, made in 1962, contains in my view some Wisdom's finest routines. Too short to be accepted into the police force like his father, Norman resorts to wearing stilts for his application: the ensuing extended sequence with the police doctor (Eric Barker) exploits the mileage of the stilts to the full, from his approach along the pavement towards the station where (now at least eight feet tall) he ascends the steps like a uniformed clown; to the physical examination by the doctor, who of course taps Wisdom's knee with a little hammer to test his reactions – and the entire leg flies off.

Wisdom's performance in the same film as crooked Italian hairdresser Giulio Napolitani allowed him – under the skilful directorship of Robert Asher – to give free rein to his physical comedic genius. His performance as the flamboyant, camp Mediterranean *coiffurist* demonstrates just how versatile an actor he could be, for Napolitani is the exact antithesis of the Gump. Where the Gump shuffles and sniffs, barges about, bumps into people, falls over and is prey to extremes of emotion, by contrast Napolitani is all finesse and control, studied gesture and gaudy, flashy displays. One of Wisdom's finest moments onscreen comes during the scene when we first encounter Napolitani, while an undercover policewoman (Eleanor Summerfield) secretly films him with a camera strategically placed in her handbag, Napolitani – infused by the heady swing of the bossa-nova – launches into a spirited dance/haircutting routine that ranks with Chaplin. Without missing or fluffing a beat he prances between his clients, beautifying them with a snip of the scissor here, a flick of the comb there. The bossa nova becomes the cha-cha-cha and the quickstep, and he frolics like a faun, like Chaplin liberated from the conveyor belt in *Modern Times* – and in an instant the glory of silent comedy of the 20s is recreated.

The success of *A Stitch in Time* was followed by *The Early Bird* (1965), Wisdom's first colour film. Once again he is paired with Mr Grimsdale (Edward Chapman) as two small-town milkmen battling the machinations of a big conglomerate. The entire opening sequence is a ten-minutes of sublime dumb-show, as the household wakes. In an odd *ménage-a-trois* – Grimsdale and Norman share the house with the housekeeper (Paddie O'Neill) who is secretly carrying on an amorous relationship with the officious Grimsdale – the trio stumble out of bed, stagger along hallways half asleep, carry cups of tea precariously up and down stairs, forget to light the gas-stove for the kettle, crawl back into the wrong beds, and tumble downstairs again.

There are some fabulous sight gags and routines in *The Early Bird*. Breaking away hastily from a stolen kiss with his housekeeper, Grimsdale double-takes as he realises his spectacles have stuck on his sweetheart's face. In an attempt to ingratiate himself with the boss of Amalgamated Dairies – played by the ever-bristling and outraged Jerry Desmonde – Norman mows the lawn of his manor house garden, reducing it to chaotic ruin, the motorised mower dragging Norman through greenhouses and garden ponds. Once again he performed all his own stunts. *A Stitch in Time* features a particularly dangerous routine where, fully encased in plaster and bandages, he scrambles into a wheelchair which then smashes through a brick wall and propels him on top of a moving ambulance, which then screams at seventy miles an hour through the streets. Naturally the studio wanted a stuntman to stand in for him – but Wisdom insisted on performing it himself. Ever since he had spent the day practising tumbles from his horse way back in his army days in Lucknow, he had learned the value of preparation. A physical comedian is not only an athlete but also a technician: when the stunt depends on equipment, it pays to check, re-check, and re-check again. Wisdom had special handles constructed on top of the ambulance and a rubber mat put in place – and the stunt went without a hitch.

He prided himself on his stunt-work, right up until his later films. There is a wonderful sequence in his last film for Rank, *Press for Time* (1966). As a reporter for a small-town newspaper, he visits the wife of the Mayor. The simple act of wheeling his bicycle into the living-room (he's had it stolen before, so is taking all precautions) is developed into an extended piece of solo business that results in him dangling by his shirt-cuff from the light-fitting in the middle of the ceiling. By the time his hostess appears, Norman is hanging like a rag doll, swinging slowly to and fro. It is a masterly pantomime of escalation.

The Early Bird was the last of Wisdom's films that had the involvement of writer Jack Davies, and although *Press for Time* has some marvellous sequences and was directed by Wisdom stalwart Robert Asher, it possesses a slightly different character to the other films; there's a hint of brashness about it, as if everyone is trying to move along with the times into the slightly heady atmosphere of the late 60s. But once again it proved the continued satirical mission of Wisdom's comedy above and beyond mere slapstick. While the Beyond the Fringe comics and the Establishment were garnering praise and plaudits as the principal proponents of 60s satire, Wisdom's films were firing salvoes at similar targets – this time local government and press corruption. The movie culminates in that familiar trope of late-60s British comedy movies, the Beauty Contest, and the moralising speech at the end, while a tad forced (Wisdom's character suddenly opines volubly about the need for all political parties to stop fighting each other and pull together) it nevertheless is consistent with the inner story of his movie character – the underdog criticising society from the outside.

A similar cry of outrage occurs at the end of *A Stitch in Time*. In the climactic scene at a big televised charity benefit for abandoned children, Norman rounds angrily on the assembled throng of bejewelled aristocrats: 'These kids shouldn't need your help in the first place!' he shouts – a cry of rage at the parents who abandoned Wisdom all those years before. The wealthy audience are shamed into silence, and after a dramatic pause throw banknotes into the middle of the floor. It is a powerful scene and one which both sums up his film career and belies the fact that he was a shallow knockabout clown. His films had a depth – a simple depth – but a *raison d'etre* nevertheless above and beyond the sight gag.

*

By 1966 his film career had reached its zenith, and *Press for Time* was his last Rank picture. That year, he moved to New York to star on Broadway in the James Van Heusen-Sammy Cahn musical comedy *Walking Happy*, his highly acclaimed performance nominated for a Tony Award. Attracting the attention of Hollywood producers, his ambitions to become an international star were realised when director William Friedkin cast him in the joyous tribute to American Burlesque, *The Night They Raided Minsky's*.

It was an inspired casting. Starring alongside Jason Robards, Bert Lahr and Britt Ekland, Wisdom was virtually playing himself. As Chick Williams, sprightly stage performer, the film gave him the opportunity to draw on his vast repertoire of theatrical mime, and his routines stole the show. *The Night They Raided Minsky's* was his first American film, and he received good notices. *Variety* wrote: 'So easily does Wisdom dominate his many scenes, other cast members suffer by comparison', and *Time* compared him to America's comedic Old Guard: 'Wisdom recalls Keaton in his split-second spills and deadpan pantomime'.

The movie is a joyous hymn both to a lost genre of entertainment and the city that spawned it. From the opening dumb-show footage of 1920s New York, to the pratfalls and onstage slapstick of the Minsky Theatre's double-act – Wisdom and Jason Robards as Chick Williams and Raymond Paine – it is a fitting big-screen climax to one of the longest movie comedy careers in British history.

Although he had more than thirty years left as a stage performer, playing to packed houses across the UK and beyond, *The Night They Raided Minsky's* was in a profound sense Wisdom's big-screen swansong. He had come full circle. His own brand of knockabout had in itself become an object of nostalgia. Between 1954, when he made his debut film *Trouble in Store*, and the late 60s, times – and audiences' tastes – had changed. Wisdom's Little Man Battles with the Establishment routine had become old-fashioned, replaced by the bitter surreal critiques of British society from dark comedy films like *If* and *The Ruling Class*, and serious films had appropriated social critique such as the brash, cynical upward punching of Richard Harris in *This Sporting Life* and Albert Finney in *Saturday Night and Sunday Morning*. Wisdom's anarchic Worker reducing establishment events to chaos was no longer enough for a new, radicalised, younger movie audience – so he took his flat-cap and his ill-fitting suit, and returned to the stage.

Not before making an attempt to fit in with new culture of the Swinging Sixties, however. In his 1969 film *What's Good for the Goose*, Wisdom plays Timothy Bartlett, a disillusioned middle-aged businessman who falls for enticingly liberated Nikki (Sally Geeson) on a business trip to Southport. It was a brave yet perhaps slightly misguided attempt to reinvent himself, and whilst an anomaly in his output, it stands as a quirky and historically significant product of the times. There was a brief period in the late 60s and early 70s when comedy actors felt constrained to acknowledge the world of sexual liberation and other aspects of the Swinging Era – memorably Alf Garnett experiences an LSD trip in the second *Till Death Do Us Part* film – and this was Wisdom's stab at addressing the new culture.

For the last thirty years of his life Wisdom toured virtually non-stop, making occasional forays into TV acting such as *Last of the Summer Wine* and the critically-acclaimed Stephen Frears drama *Going Gently* in 1981 in which he played a dying cancer patient. But for the most part the latter third of his life was spent re-treading his beloved boards with the old physical routines he had dreamt up way back in 1946

His movie career was – and still is – unprecedented for a British comedian. Twelve years of topping the box office was an achievement that perhaps might never be replicated. No one since Chaplin had so profoundly and prolifically stamped their comic persona on an era: and it is more than significant that it is two visual comedians who still hold that accolade.

CHAPTER 10

The Nebbish: Jerry Lewis

Of all the comics celebrated in this book, the one who most seems to have been plucked straight from the world of silent film and set down unalloyed in the sound era is Jerry Lewis, a performer who, despite making numerous dialogue films, nevertheless retained a style of performance labelled (in his politically incorrect day) as *spastic* – but which can best be described now as unabashed gyratory burlesque clowning. In his work Lewis makes no concessions whatsoever to the subtlety of performance seemingly demanded by the new medium, mugging and grimacing his way through dozens of pictures with unashamed celebratory excess. When he sees his girlfriend in the arms of another man, he buckles, screams silently, and collapses, clutching his chest (*The Ladies Man*, 1961): a Lewis performance is emotion physicalised. It was a schtick born out of the mime acts of 1920s burlesque (his early bill matter

Beginning as a Catskills Tummler – an audience-pleasing showman of the upstate Jewish Borscht Belt in the 1930s – Jerry Lewis became America's most accomplished comic mime. At 17 he was performing a 'pantomimicry' act in vaudeville, and twenty years later – following his necessary split from Dean Martin – his 'idiot' style metamorphosed into maturer, more considered routines, such as the famous 'Pretending to be the Boss' sequence above in The Errand Boy *(1961).*

boasts 'Jerry Lewis! Pantomimicry!'). Lewis' success came at such a young age (he was only 15 when he made his professional debut, and by 19 was a household name) that he straddles almost an entire century of American showbiz, from the silent days to the present.

Born in 1926 to variety parents working the US East Coast Hotel circuit, his career began when – aged five – he sat in the stalls of the Loewe Pitkin theatre in Brooklyn about to watch his first film. His parents were off on tour (again) in the Catskills and his grandparents had packed him off to the movie-house with a dollar bill and a packed lunch.

The film was Chaplin's *The Circus* – and it was to change his life. Little Lewis had gazed spellbound at his parents from the wings of various vaudeville houses many times in his few short years (by the age of ten he could imitate practically every single act on the 'Borscht Belt' circuit, much to the amusement of his mother and father's colleagues) but it was Chaplin's 1928 silent that exerted a career-defining influence on the young boy. Apart from being a masterpiece containing some of Chaplin's most inventive and broad routines, it was in itself a masterly essay on the nature of comedy: the story involves a budding comedian (Chaplin) *trying to become* a clown, and as such contains rehearsal scenes, the mechanics of building physical business, and the problem of not being funny when you try too hard. It is, in short, a movie *about* comedy, and it stuck in Lewis' mind.

He fell into performing more inevitably than perhaps anyone ever did, starting work as a Tummler (a Catskill version of a British Butlins Redcoat) – a member of the hotel staff that functioned as both busboy and entertainer. The Tummler moved among his audience and engineered a comedy of interplay, so the act was necessarily more visual than spoken: there was no microphone. The young Lewis would get caught on tablecloths, drop trays, cover himself in food. He was building an act and a repertoire of facial tics and comic gestures that would stay with him for the rest of his career. Working vast dining rooms, those facial expressions had to be big.

And they stayed big. Promoted from the dining hall to the stage, he debuted at the Arthur Hotel New Jersey in the winter of 1938 when Red Buttons failed to turn up. Lewis chose to premiere his miming-to-gramophone-records act, a routine that he had been practising with a girlfriend. He was not an instant hit – there were numerous such mime or lip-synching acts on the circuit, known as dummy acts, the railway train impersonator Reginald Gardiner being the most notable – but for the young Lewis it was a toehold in the business he was to dominate for the next thirty years.

Perhaps the closest record of his early stage-act we have are two great routines in his later solo films (he did reproduce some routines in the long-running TV series *The Colgate Comedy Hour* but the feature films show the acts at their pristine best: the first from *Cinderfella* (1959), the second from *The Errand Boy* (1961)). In both sequences he accompanies music with mime, but in the earlier film he fastens a sublime dumb-show onto Count Basie on the radio in which he portrays the entire orchestra – from drummer to bass-player to flautist – whereas in the latter he substitutes music for words. The sequence in *The Errand Boy* is a tour de force of mime. Alone in the boardroom, he lights up a cigar and fantasises being the boss. And the music becomes his voice, each note and phrase portrayed in swift changes of modulating mood. It is a truly great piece of acting, and although based on old vaudevillian routines that other entertainers had begun, it is a comedy Lewis had made firmly his own over years of honing on stage and TV. These filmed routines came thirty years after his early stage performances, but they are an echo of what audiences must first have been entranced by when a gawky young 15 year old took to the stage in the holiday hotels of the 30s.

The word 'vaudevillian' has been used to describe Lewis, but in truth his origins were burlesque. The difference is more than subtle: while vaudeville had its brash and slapstick moments, it was the more sophisticated of theatrical traditions – vaudevillian fare was smooth-talking comedy routines, double-acts, song-and-dance: burlesque was cut from an altogether brasher cloth. In danger of being raided for obscenity in the creepingly puritanical 30s, burlesque shows became increasingly fast and frenetic: knockabout slapstick was favoured over languid cross-talk, big pratfalls over the built routine. Lewis was nurtured in this crazy cauldron of high-kicking dancing girls and tumbles, of comics chased across the stage, of breaking the fourth wall and falling into the orchestra pit. Many comedian indeed worked both circuits, and had two acts – one for the vaudeville circuit and a faster, more strident and clownish version for the burlesque. Lewis was fashioned firmly in the latter – and it is this fact, interestingly, that both made him a star, and twenty years later caused his star to wane. For by the time he was paired with Dean Martin in 1946 and became, literally overnight, a household name, burlesque theatre had been dead for years. Lewis was bringing physical anarchy back onto the stage, and his friction with Martin as the smooth-talking, urbane vaudevillian song-and-dance man was a breath of fresh air: their emergence in the immediate post-war period was literally as new and exciting as Monty Python in the late 60s. It's hard to understand now, but when Martin and Lewis took to the stage at the 500 Club in Atlantic City or the Copacabana in New York, crowds of thousands would mob the place. This was cutting-edge comedy, as explosive as Lenny Bruce or Andy Kaufman. Lewis' brand of high-concept physicality had largely been banished from the big-screen in the eighteen years since the advent of sound: Hollywood embraced him like a long-lost son. He reigned supreme as a stage and film comedian for twenty years, from 1946 to 1966 – by which time, of course, audiences had forgotten all about burlesque: now he simply came across as an over-the-top, grotesque, twitching cardboard puppet. He had lost his audience. And when the audience regained their taste for flamboyant clowning it was Jim Carrey and Steve Martin who they looked to.

*

When Lewis met Dean Martin in 1946, they quickly teamed up and pursued a meteoric rise, Hollywood snapping them up in 1949 for their first of seventeen films together, *My Friend Irma.*

Although the films made him a huge star, Lewis was never well-served by the Martin-Lewis movies. Mostly standard B-picture fare with plots borrowed from stage-hits, the excessive romantic interest edging any imaginative visual routines to brief corners of the story, and mostly they woefully short-changed the young comic. There are flashes of quality clowning – a song and dance sequence in *At War with the Army* is a straight lift from the team's stage show, with an impressive jumping-over-the-cane routine, a memorable boxing act (that perennial favourite of the visual comic) in *Sailor Beware* (1951), in which Lewis runs around the ring getting faster and faster until he runs out of breath and gets slugged by his opponent. In the same routine there is also some delightful backwards dancing, punching of his opponent's knees, and sprightly ballet-work with the ropes worthy of Laurel in *Any Old Port* (1932).

Lewis' schmuck character – his childish falsetto particularly grating after 20 minutes – was unpalatable, but when they allowed him to stop talking and simply be visually funny there were glimpses of an extraordinary physical ability. The jitterbug sequence in *Living it Up* (1954) for example is jaw-droppingly brilliant, with a display of comic dancing not seen onscreen since Chaplin. And in *Three Ring Circus,* released in the same year, it was clear that as Lewis' creative control over his pictures increased, so too did the imaginative quality of the comedy. In *Three Ring Circus* his persona is stripped down to the bare essentials: there is no artifice of character or contrivance of comic scenes – in this film he literally is a clown, called, in a further undisguised nod to the fact that he is playing himself, Jericho.

In *Three Ring Circus* Lewis is hinting at what he could do as a visual comic if he was un-tethered from the romantic crooning leading man he'd been shackled to for eight years: he tumbles, climbs and frolics like the great silent stars of yesteryear, while Dean Martin literally looks on from the sidelines, occasionally holding a blanket to catch his old partner. As Jericho the Wonder Clown it is Lewis' film – Martin doesn't even get to sing until at least an hour into the picture. Like Harold Lloyd, Lewis climbs a hundred-foot ladder holding a unicycle round his neck and faking strangulation, joins in the other Keystone Kops in a classic house-on-fire routine, and executes a fine lengthy sequence alone in the circus tent dreaming of glory. It is Lewis unchained.

Reviewers were ecstatic: Jack Moffitt in the *Hollywood Reporter* invoked the shade of Chaplin, saying 'Jerry has learned to blend pathos with his slapstick, until he has begun to show the potentialities that can make a great actor and a great star.' It's perhaps no coincidence that Lewis chose a circus as the scenario for the film in which he chose to emerge from the shadow of his comedy partner and exercise his wings: was he remembering the very first movie he saw, aged five, in the Loewe Pitkin Theater, Brooklyn? Was he making a bold statement that he could be the second Chaplin?

It's evident that, from early on, Lewis perceived and understood the tradition in which his talent lay: that of silent film. He had invented a fast-talking childish *nebbish* persona for himself for the Martin-Lewis act and it had been a wild success, but deep down he sensed that this was a red herring: with each film he was injecting more and more of the physical comedy with which his career had begun. Martin noticed this and at times resented it: writer on *Scared Stiff*, Ed Simmons recalls (in Shawn Levy's book *King of Comedy: the Life and Art of Jerry Lewis*:

> When we were on set for *Scared Stiff*, there was one scene where Jerry has been a stowaway on a boat and has been in steamer trunk for a few days … the trunk is opened and he gets out. I'm standing watching them shoot and again, I'm standing with Dean. Jerry gets out and looks like he's bucking for an Academy Award. He was showing pain, he was showing ache, he was showing crippled … And I turned to Dean and I said 'what is he doing?' and he says 'Chaplin shit.' And he rubs his cigarette out with his shoe and walks away.

It wasn't the first time his hero-worship of Chaplin had crept into the films: there is a distinctly Chaplin-esque routine in *Jumping Jacks* (1952) where he and Dean cavort with hat and cane; and in the publicity materials for *That's My Boy* Lewis outlined exactly where he intended his ambitions to take him – he referred to Junior Jackson (his role in the picture) as a pathetic figure very reminiscent of Charlie Chaplin and others of his era. 'At heart,' he said, 'I really belong to the old school which believed that screen comedy is a combination of situation, sadness and gracious humility ...' But to circumvent any accusations of hubris he went on to add a hasty caveat, saying that he had 'no intention of imitating Chaplin or any of the other great humourists of his day, hoping only to catch the same warm, sympathetic quality which Chaplin and a few others had.'

This was a comedian in search of a deeper visual persona than that which he had been delivering, or been allowed to deliver, thus far. After *Three Ring Circus* the Martin-Lewis partnership was to struggle on for a further two years, but the film sends out a powerful signal that, creatively, Lewis was already independent. By 1956 he was free. And over the following decade he was to make half-a-dozen fabulous and innovative movies that stand as a great contribution to the continuation of the slapstick tradition. Significantly, he hired Frank Tashlin, who had served his time as a writer and director for both Looney Tunes and Hal Roach, and Bill Richmond, jazz drummer turned comedy writer, and set about carving out a niche for himself as a post-Chaplin visual comic.

*

The timing of Lewis' renaissance and self-discovery was in line with James Agee's article in *Life* magazine, Jacques Tati exploding onto the world screen, and Norman Wisdom's movies topping the box office in Britain. Lewis knew he was part of that revival. Dean Martin was not.

When, in 1958, Lewis hosted the Oscar ceremony at which Jacques Tati won Best Foreign Language film for *Mon Oncle*, Tati's acceptance speech must have fanned the flames of a desire within Lewis to become his American equivalent. Tati's speech was a plea for Hollywood not to forget its rich comic heritage of slapstick: 'From Mack Sennett to Chaplin and everyone else, you invented it,' he said. 'I am doing pantomime; but I am the nephew, you are the Uncle. I respect Hollywood.

But to become a major visual comic you need a character, and Lewis' falsetto nebbish was not enough. So he went in search of another. His first few solo films, *The Delicate Delinquent*, *Sad Sack*, *Rock-a-bye-Baby* and *The Geisha Boy* were tentative traditional pieces that recycled his squeaking-

Jerry Lewis brings his vaudeville clowning to the small screen in his NBC show of 1958.

clown persona yet nevertheless explored more contemporary mores than his double-act films – including teenage rebellion and the world of beatniks.There are some memorable visual routines in all these early solo pictures, and clever ideas such as the scene in *Visit to a Small Planet* where Lewis magically plays a set of bongos from acoss the other side of the club by means of gesticulations alone – but it wasn't until Lewis began to direct himself in his own pictures – starting with *The Bellboy* in 1960 – that he began to stretch himself and come into his own as a solo visual comic.

Lewis was adamant that his next picture was to be in line with the silent film tradition; so adamant that he employed Stan Laurel as a consultant on *The Bellboy*. Lewis had been introduced to Laurel – now in his seventies – by Dick Van Dyke, and one Sunday morning he drove out to Santa Monica to pay him a visit. Biographical elements in common – son of showmen, one half of a double-act – they hit it off. Laurel would have been heartened by the flattering attention he was being paid by the new wave of comedians; his films were a huge hit on TV in the 50s, and his star had arisen anew, culminating in the honorary Oscar for Lifetime

Achievement awarded him in 1961. The impact of Laurel on Lewis' film is hard to pinpoint – he refused a salary – but Lewis went through the script with him, and Laurel's shadow certainly lies across it. Co-writer Bill Richmond even performs, in tribute, a Laurel imitation as a hotel guest. Lewis's character of the bellboy himself is even called Stanley.

The influence of Tati is also evident. Gone are the corny storylines of the Hal Wallis years; even the trailer announces it as '… a visual diary, a few weeks in the life of a humble errand boy' – a pre-emptive strike at those who might bemoan the paucity of plot. Lewis could have stuck with what he knew he was good at – a hackneyed rom-com with a couple of serious supporting stars and a melodramatic plot. But instead he presented his public with a drifting, narrative-free, dialogue-less exercise in comic invention.

The film is a picaresque chronicle of a week in the life of a nebbish, a clear emulation of *M Hulot's Holiday* and *Mon Oncle*. It's even set in a hotel. As with Tati's films the comedy is episodic rather than cumulative, and whilst perhaps lacking the humanity of the Hulot films, *The Bellboy* contains several truly great routines and many imaginative gags.

An example is the chair-setting routine; it opens with a locked-off shot of an hotel ballroom theatre of such vastness that Stanley becomes a mere dot amid the whiteness. Charged with setting out all the chairs for a performance, Stanley crosses the floor as someone might cross a desert. We don't go with him: the camera stays rooted to the long-shot. As he reaches the farthest corner of the room he assumes the appearance of a shadow-puppet, faithfully picking up a single chair, then travelling back to the middle of the acreage of floor and setting it down. Of course it is in the wrong place, so he spends several minutes adjusting it. We cut back to the lobby, expecting, of course, the hapless bellboy to take hours to complete his task. But Lewis didn't employ Laurel as an advisor on the picture for nothing: the magical ability of Laurel's persona rubs off on Stanley, so when his two colleagues peer through the ballroom door seconds later he has by some mystical means set out hundreds of chairs.

It's a lovely twist, and not one which the Lewis of previous years would have gone for. In his earlier pictures we would have seen him struggling with dozens of chairs, falling over, panting hammily, wheezing, collapsing. In *The Bellboy* Lewis finally joins the pantheon of the great silent comics by not simply relying on his mugging and pratfalls but mining comedy from the environment. The hugeness of the room itself in the chair-setting routine is part of the comedy: in using the filmic shot itself as the fuel of the gag, Lewis ceases to be a clown and becomes a fully-fledged screen comedian.

There is still clowning, of course, in *The Bellboy* but of a more sophisticated and inventive kind. Yes, he falls through an elevator door, struggles with luggage, and he certainly doesn't abandon his facial tics – but the picture also includes classic routines such as the orchestra-conducting scene, a masterly mime where the humble hotel serf conjures up music and adulation from imaginary musicians and an equally invisible applauding audience. Put in charge of the bank of telephones at the front desk, Stanley darts manically from receiver to receiver, always missing the call, becoming tangled in the wires, in a finely-played escalation where the only sound is the raucous ringing of the offending instruments.

A masterly gag involves a camera flashbulb that lights up the entire night: once again Stanley becomes magical when he permanently turns night to day, banishing even the moon with a single shot. Perhaps influenced by the work of Ernie Kovacs and Tati, this is nevertheless evidence of a comedian seeking to extend himself and enrich his films with a comic intelligence beyond mere slapstick.

He followed up the success of *The Bellboy* with *The Ladies Man*, with what at the time was the most expensive set built for a Hollywood movie (a foretaste of Tati's later albatross of a set in *Playtime*) – a vast mansion apartment block complete with huge open courtyard for ambitious crane shots.

The Ladies Man is a remarkable production in many ways, once again directed by Lewis, and although a dialogue film contains numerous novel visual scenes. He plays Herbert, an incompetent who – crossed in love – works as concierge of a vast mansion complex in which dozens of young women reside. Lewis makes the setting a crucial ingredient of the comedy: in a scene in which the occupants of the house rise from slumber, Lewis masterminds a crane-shot of breathtaking skill. All the actors' movements are perfectly choreographed to the rhythms of a jaunty, waking soundtrack – they yawn, stretch, climb out of bed, and parade up and down stairwells in uninterrupted unison in time with the music. A girl smooths her stocking to the ankle, a dowdier woman adjusts her pyjama-bottoms in an identical movement. Lewis' swooping, rising, falling camera captures every comic nuance– it is a superb display, and in this single shot alone Lewis announces his talent as a director.

What is more, he was on a roll: his next film, *The Errand Boy*, was released in the same year. Once again co-written with Bill Richmond, in some ways it's a stitch-back to the style of *Bellboy* although containing dialogue. The film is episodic or – as Richmond described it – a plotless thing about the studio losing money. Wherever Lewis' bumbling Morty S Tashman goes at Paramutual Pictures, hapless disaster follows: movies

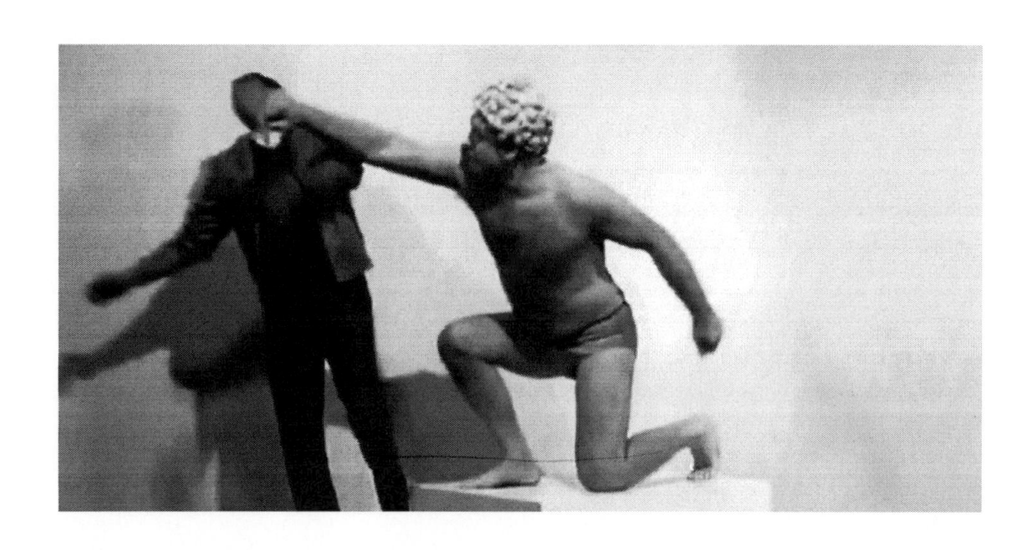

get dubbed with his voice instead of that songstress, a tractor is driven through a soundstage, background actors are almost drowned with a bottle of bubbly. And it features some great mime routines, including the aforementioned sequence where the hapless Morty strolls around the boardroom and, puffing on a huge cigar, launches into an extended mime, mouthing to a non-diegetic jazzband soundtrack (again his favoured Count Basie, this time playing *Blues in Hoss Flat*), just as he had done years before when, aged 15, he touted his miming to a wind-up gramophone routine round the Borscht Belt. Bill Richmond recalls that this was Lewis' party-piece at dinner tables on tour – the plates would be pushed back, the cutlery cleared, the music turned on, and Lewis would be off. It's one of his most famous routines, and has been transmitted to a new generation by being reprised by Peter in *Family Guy*.

Another notable sequence is the elevator scene. Taking the claustrophobia of being stuck in a lift with a crowd of people to new comic heights, Morty finds himself squashed up close to a grim-faced businessman. It is a perfectly timed sequence of escalating gags that never flags: the businessman's toothpick gets transferred from his mouth to Morty – who then swivels round to escape a possible sneeze, only to confront a man puffing on a huge cigar. Wriggling away from this annoyance he then finds himself confronted by a dizzy blonde chewing on bubble gum. The gag is signposted but not undermined: Lewis watches in horror as the bubble expands to hot-air balloon dimensions then we cut to the corridor outside the lift for the off-screen non-diegetic 'POP!' A comic beat, then the doors open to reveal a staggering Lewis with an unfeasibly huge quantity of gum spattered across his face. There's a topper to the gag as another hapless victim steps out, also covered in gum.

His next collaboration with Bill Richmond, *The Nutty Professor*, was arguably Lewis' greatest solo movie success, released in 1963 and selected in 2004 by the Library of Congress as being culturally, historically and aesthetically significant. Despite being a dialogue film it nevertheless contains a plethora of visual routines, and sees Lewis returning to his wild pantomime: emotion writ large. If he had been edging towards a

Opposite page: Post Tati and Etaix, Lewis' films began to include cleverer gags that transcended mere pantomime, and as he became more appreciated in France his work fell under the influence of European clowning and surrealism. In his experimental feature Cracking Up *(1981), he slips and slides on a shiny floor (as in Tati's* Playtime*), a painting comes to life (as in Etaix's* Yoyo*), a sculpture delivers a blow to the comic (as done by Ernie Kovacs), and a cowboy on TV fires bullets out of the screen. This playing with reality had been absent from Lewis' oeuvre until then. Embraced by French intellectuals and critics, his reputation in Europe never diminished – and though his reputation in the US and the UK has waned, his stylistic influence can be discerned in Steve Martin and Jim Carrey.*

more restrained style of performance in *The Bellboy*, perhaps under the influence of Stan Laurel, he abandons it here, his Professor Julius F Kelp a gangly buck-toothed falsetto maniac as starkly surreal as one of the Three Stooges. But the film also provided him with an opportunity to portray a cooler, more suave alter-ego, a counterpoint to the clown – as the character Buddy Love, he is a smooth ladies' man, following his invention of a secret serum. There are some funny routines in the gym as the loser Kelp attempts to shape up, a typically grotesque and embarrassing dance sequence, and an inventive scene where Kelp attempts to run a class with a hangover. Although a tried and tested staple of comedy now (memorably in Ronnie Barker's *Futtock's End* of 1970), the magnified noises inflicting themselves on the headache-ridden Kelp are well-escalated, building from the painful scratch of chalk on the blackboard to a student's thunderous mastication of chewing gum.

There is, however, a paucity of pure pantomime in *The Nutty Professor*, a deficiency reversed in his next picture, *Who's Minding the Store?* in which Lewis produces one of his most memorable dumb-shows, a reprise of one of his skits in the *Colgate Comedy Hour.* Once again performing to music, he recreates the typing of a letter without a machine, but this time the music is purely percussive and the synchronisation of his hands' movements with the rhythmic soundtrack is a display of genius. Rowan Atkinson's piano-playing routine is a clear descendant, and one almost wishes that Lewis had pursued more of these routines in his pictures rather than chasing the plot. It's too damning to describe it as a deficiency because it is clearly a conscious artistic choice, but Lewis' wilful sticking with his childish clown act meant that his star throughout the 60s was to wane. Similar to the pattern of Norman Wisdom's career, along the way it seemed the audience grew up: they gradually no longer embraced the staggering, face-pulling clown, and despite continuing to make movies right into the early 70s, his standing declined.

*

His reputation in Europe, though – especially in France – remained undiminished. For me, Lewis's greatest moments are those in which it is clear he has come under the influence of Tati and Laurel – *The Bellboy*; his physical routines in *Ladies Man*; *The Errand Boy*, and *The Disorderly Orderly.* But his problem was that he never created heart in his persona: we may laugh at his gauche gyrations and admire his mime and his inventive gags – but unlike with Chaplin, Laurel, Keaton and even Wisdom, we do not love him. He was a comic actor in search of heart, and who displayed his genius only sporadically. A late curio of his career actually hints at what could have been his true path: a distinctly Tati-esque picaresque of a movie called *Cracking Up* – a series of comic episodes linked by the theme of a middle-aged man undergoing something of a nervous breakdown. It was only released in continental Europe and was not a critical success, but it contains some of his most inventive work. A suicide attempt in his apartment, a running gag of an absurdly slippery floor in his psychiatrist office, cowboys on TV shooting out of the screen and breaking the glass, a sweet with so many wrappings he can't get at it despite scrabbling away at the innumerable layers, a painting of a bull that charges out of the canvas at the sight of a red handkerchief: *Cracking Up* is a movie chock-full of surreal gags and marvellous pantomime. Shot in a very European style, with modernist furniture and clean, clinical sets, gone is Lewis' squeaky voice, facial tics and flailing limbs. Despite being an odd film, it is one of his finest works – yet is almost completely unknown.

Perhaps Lewis' greatest legacy is his influence on the subsequent generation of comedians, in particular Steve Martin and Jim Carrey, who just as Lewis' star was waning, picked up the baton of the crazy clown persona.

CHAPTER 11

Diehards II: Visual Comedy on Stage & Screen 1945-1960

It would be an exaggeration to state that when James Agee's article praising silent comedy was published in *Life* magazine in 1949 it sparked off an instant revival – but it undoubtedly lit a slow-burning fuse.

Best remembered today for his classic study of tenant farmers in the mid-West of the 1930s, *Let Us Now Praise Famous Men,* Agee was a novelist, screenwriter, journalist, film critic and alcoholic, whose untimely death aged only 45 cut short a life of versatile if discursive creativity. He worked on the screenplays for *The African Queen* (1951) and Charles Laughton's *Night of the Hunter* (1955), wrote an unproduced screenplay for Chaplin, and his novel about the death of his father, *Death in the Family,* (1957) won him a posthumous Pulitzer Prize.

Agee's film criticism was the most influential of its age; he perceived a decline in the nature of comedy between 1927 and 1945 and decided to bear witness to it. Arguably his was the first major assessment of silent comedy as a cultural phenomenon rather than as mere light entertainment, and his essay plunged deep into the aesthetic with the forensic skill of a literary critic. Above all, he demonstrated an understanding of the language of visual comedy and its immense heritage, expressing an awareness that the film clowns hadn't sprung from a historical vacuum:

> When a silent comedian got hit on the head ... he gave us a figure of speech, or rather of vision, for loss of consciousness. He gave us a poem, a kind of poem, moreover, that everyone understands ... He might make a cadenza of it, look vague, smile like an angel, roll up his eyes, lace his fingers, thrust his palms downward as far as they would go ... until, with tallow knees, he sank down the vortex of his dizziness to the floor, and there signified nirvana by kicking his heels twice, like a swimming frog.

But this was an assessment of silent comedy in its infancy, and 'the man who could handle them properly combined several of the more difficult accomplishments of the acrobat, the dancer, the clown or the mime.' There were some artists who elevated these performance tropes to the level of high art: 'The more gifted men ... simplified and invented, finding out new and much deeper uses for the idiom. They leaned to use emotion through it and comic psychology, more eloquently than language has ever managed to, and they discovered beauties of comic motion which are hopelessly beyond reach of words.' Agee not only eulogises those supreme artists of the genre – Keaton, Chaplin, Lloyd, Langdon and Laurel & Hardy – but also the early, cruder pioneers. Of Mack Sennett he says: 'He took his comics out of music halls, burlesque, vaudeville, circuses and limbo, and through them he tapped in to that great pipeline of horsing and miming which runs back unbroken to the fairs of the Middle Ages at least to Ancient Greece.' He also praises silent film as the training ground for those who became the greatest directors of the sound era: 'Frank Capra, Leo McCarey and George Stevens also got their start in silent comedy; much that remains flexible, spontaneous and visually alive can be traced, through them and others, to this silent

Back to their roots ... in an almost unbearably poignant collaboration towards the end of both their lives, two of the supreme artists of silent comedy unite for the first and last time, in Limelight *(1952), to recreate the music-hall pantomime that gave rise to all visual comedy on film. Despite Chaplin's reputation for egotism, his son, who was with his father during post-production, confirms that Chaplin edited the sequence to include more of Keaton than himself.*

apprenticeship.' Though lavishing admiration upon all the greats of the pre-sound era he saves his most abundant fervour for Chaplin, for being the 'first to give silent language a soul.'

Throughout, Agee is no mere nostalgist – a crucial section of the piece includes a blow-by-blow technical demonstration of how visual comedy and the techniques of the silent practitioners were superior to the verbal comedy of the time. Citing Bob Hope's *Paleface* he compares it to Keaton's *The Navigator*, explaining that the routines in the latter are more cinematic and are allowed to breathe, each comic idea being exploited to its utmost rather than being neatly curtailed because of reasons of plot. In a visual comedy, physical event is plot, so everything onscreen has potential for laughs, whereas in a verbal comedy there is restraint and let-up.

At the time of the article's appearance, sound comedy had had a run of nearly twenty years, and there was a sense that audiences were becoming receptive to change. The return of silent comedy to the screen wasn't instant but there is no doubt Agee's piece contributed to a gradual growing realisation of two things: that the silent clowns of yesteryear were still incredibly funny, and that visual comedy had far from exhausted itself creatively by 1927. Jacques Tati was busy proving the latter: a man called Robert Youngson proved the former.

*

Born in 1917, enterprising Brooklyn producer-director Robert Youngson – more than anyone else – re-introduced vast TV audiences in the post-war era to the work of the great silent comedians. Feeding a passion for all things pre-war, and perhaps mining a seam of nostalgia in the public for an age less anxious and uncertain, Youngson began compiling miscellanies of 'thrills and spills' shorts for Warner Brothers, such as *Roaring Wheels* (1948) and *Spills & Chills* (1949): these first collections were essentially benignly comical celebrations of 'life in the old days,' focussing on sport, lifestyle and technology (the clips from the early days of flight in particular proving very popular, and providing inspiration for the 1965 movie *Those Magnificent Men in their Flying Machines).*

These amusing 'social histories' soon graduated into clip-shows of favourite movie moments from the silent days, such as the Western collection *Horsehide Heroes* (1951) and *Magic Movie Moments* (1953). But it was his feature-length plundering of the works of the great silent clowns that yielded Youngson's greatest contribution to the 'Silent Renaissance' of the 50s and 60s. *The Golden Age of Comedy,* released by Twentieth Century Fox in 1957, is accredited with rehabilitating the reputations of Laurel & Hardy, containing as it does choice clips from some of their finest silent work such as *Two Tars* and *You're Darn Tootin.* Both Laurel and Hardy lived to witness this renewed appreciation of their art, Hardy passing away in the year of the film's release but Laurel living to enjoy an Indian summer of stardom culminating in his receipt of an Honorary Oscar in 1960.

The Golden Age of Comedy not only reawakened the public to the genius of Laurel & Hardy but also to the work of minor comics such as Andy Clyde, Ben Turpin, Thelma Todd, Roscoe Arbuckle, Charley Chase, Snub Pollard, Billy Bevan, and Mabel Normand. Youngson followed this up in 1960 with *When Comedy was King* – by which time visual humour was not only back on the map as a curiosity, but as a creative comic force in its own right.

It wasn't merely in the USA that there was a revival of interest in the old silent greats: in the UK, producer James Anderson released *Made for Laughs* in 1952, a compilation similar in structure to that of Youngson's, consisting of an assemblage of choice work from Chaplin, the Keystone Kops, Edgar Kennedy and others. Post-Agee, silent film was gradually moving out of the obscurity of film-society showings and repertory art-house cinemas and back into the mainstream. By 1952 a cursory glance at the Readers' Letters page of *Picturegoer* tells a story of ordinary people making the discovery that purely visual comedy, far from being consigned to oblivion, was not only still funny, but should have a future. Miss Joyce Clegg of Rochdale, Lancashire, wrote: 'At a cinema repertory club recently I saw the 1923 silent picture *Safety Last* starring Harold Lloyd. I have never seen anything so funny! The audience was in hysterics throughout. Film producers today could learn much about cinematic technique from some of the silent comedies, which depended on action and the creation of amusing situations for ther appeal, rather than upon slick dialogue and lavish settings.' In the same month another reader, Gerald Emanuel of London, pays tribute to the genius of Keaton: 'Recently I saw Buster Keaton's silent picture *The General.* It is certainly the funniest film I have seen in a long time. I hope someone will realise that Keaton, no less than Chaplin, can stand the test of time.' It wasn't just the public; film producer and historian John Montgomery would write: 'Yesterday's vintage silent comedies are often more amusing than modern humorous films.'

*

In 1950, perhaps bolstered by Agee's article, Chaplin re-released *City Lights* to great acclaim: indeed, *Life* magazine hailed it as 'the best picture of (the year).' His *Limelight* of 1952 is perhaps clouded by controversy in his personal life when, during his promotion of the movie in Britain, he received news that he would be refused re-entry to the United States: but for visual comedy historians the film is rather more memorable for its uniting of Keaton and Chaplin in the famous music-hall performance scene. With Chaplin as a down-at-heel clown and Keaton as his short-sighted pianist, the two former giants of the golden age of screen pantomime draw on two lifetimes of experience and skills to recreate a burlesque routine that would not have looked out of place on an Edwardian music-hall stage. It was their (big-screen) swansong, with Keaton thrilled to be in the picture, and rumours of Chaplin 'cutting' his old rival's business in the editing room being firmly quashed by Chaplin's son Sydney, who said if anything his father had trimmed his own material in favour of Keaton's.

In exile for his (perceived) politics, Chaplin – inspired by the success of *City Lights* and *Limelight* – spent his time re-editing and scoring his old pictures for re-release. In 1959 he produced *The Chaplin Revue*, a compilation of three First National Films, *A Dog's Life*, *Shoulder Arms*, and *The Pilgrim*. With newly written commentary replacing the old caption cards, the tone of Chaplin's introduction is somewhat apologetic, pointing up the 'old-fashionedness' of the dialogue-free films, a defensiveness that a decade later he would not perhaps have adopted.

*

The trend of comedy films after the war was to cast actors rather than comedians: whereas before 1945 movies drew on the world of variety, now they drew from repertory theatre. In Britain the big comedy stars of yesteryear were fading – the likes of Will Hay, George Formby, Max Miller and Norman Evans being dropped from feature films in favour of actors who happened to excel in comedy, like Alec Guinness and Alistair Sym. Michael Balcon at Ealing was making his series of delightfully English and liberal comedies from *Hue and Cry* (1947) to *Barnacle Bill* (1957); the Boulting Brothers were making satires like *Private's Progress* (1956), *Lucky Jim* (1957) and *I'm Alright Jack* (1959). Knockabout slapstick had been subordinated to a more literate, gentler narrative imbued with overt 'message.' As we have seen, the work of Norman Wisdom was flowering in the same decade, and for all its broad dumb-show was delivering no less a profound 'message' to audiences than the Boulting's satire – namely, that a working-class clown could spread anarchy in the upper echelons of the British Establishment. In the USA there was much free-and-easy slapstick in the Road Movies of Hope and Crosby, but by 1945 there were only four more to be made in the series, and though containing much visual shenanigans, song and dance were dominant tropes.

In Europe, the career of Toto, the Italian cinematic clown, was going from strength to strength, his films made between 1946 and 1968 being *commedia dell'arte* farces in all but name and propelling him to national stardom. But whereas Tati's films achieved great success abroad, Toto's work – which stuck to dialogue-based scenarios – remained largely unappreciated outside his native country.

France not only had Tati but Jean-Louis Barrault, whose *Les Enfants du Paradis* of 1946 was an epic hymn to the silent stage traditions of the Théâtre des Funambules. The film serves as an historic record of the grand tradition of French mime, but also re-introduces it to a new post-war generation. Barrault portrayed the great nineteenth-century mime artist Deburau in the film, alongside Etienne Decroux; highlights include the reproduction of the classic pantomime *Baptiste.* To have pantomimists as protagonists in film was Mime Artist as National Hero, and it is fair to say that mime underwent a renaissance in post-war France.

Another member of Charles Dullin's acclaimed mime school was Marcel Marceau. Like Jerry Lewis, Marceau (1923-2007) had been spellbound by watching a Chaplin film as a boy, and during the war in Occupied Paris had learnt many mime techniques by teaching fellow Jewish children how to communicate quietly when in the proximity of prowling Germans. In 1949 he enrolled in Etienne Decroux's school, and his accomplishment in corporeal mime made him perhaps the most famous silent stage performer of the post-war era. Achieving instant fame as Arlequin in Dullin's production of *Baptiste* inspired him to set up his own school in 1959, and his Théâtre de Poche ('Theatre of the Pocket') in Montparnasse became the most famous silent theatre in Paris.

Spellbound by a Chaplin film as a boy, Marcel Marceau took mime from the theatre schools of Paris in the 1950s to the international stage.

While in France silent stage performance enjoyed what might be described as 'high-culture' status (though it also flourished in more popular and broader venues such as cabaret clubs like Le Lido and theatres like the Cirque Medrano), elsewhere – in Britain and America particularly – it remained chiefly the province of cabaret and variety. The rise of television in the 1950s was eroding variety audiences, but international cabaret still provided a home for speciality acts of all types, including acrobats and other visual comics. We have seen how Keaton returned to the stage after the war – so too did Laurel & Hardy, performing in two stage tours in 1952 and 1953, including shows at Le Lido on the Champs Elysées, which had opened in 1946.

Over in England, Max Wall had been dancing eccentrically for variety audiences since the 1920s, billed as *The Boy with the Educated Feet.* A stalwart of the theatrical circuit, Wall's act found a home in international cabaret with the decline of the variety business in the 1950s. He toured the Continent for years, and the working men's clubs of Northern England, uncompromising in his commitment to a largely visual show. His 'clown' persona was Professor Wallofski, who – clad in skin-tight lycra and long clownish boots – would spend an age attempting to play Liszt's Second Hungarian Rhapsody, then launch into a display of such mad terpsichore as would bring the house down wherever he played. Despite success in musicals and notable cameos in films such as *Chitty Chitty Bang Bang* in 1968, household-name status eluded Wall until the late 70s and beyond, when he was 'rediscovered' by a new generation, and appreciation for his 'lost art' grew to such an extent that he was offered large theatres and a less restricted slot of two hours, during which time he could relax and build a relationship with the audience.

Acrobats, too, found a home in cabaret as post-war variety declined, and in moving out into the theatres into the clubs gradually put more and more comedy into their routines. Ted Durante toured as an acrobat in Continental cabaret right up to 1985, first with his brother Ted then with his wife Hilda. 'We did comedy acrobatic work – no patter as we were supposed to be French,' he told comedy historian Roger Wilmut. 'It's always been assumed that the continental acrobats were the best. The bill matter stayed with us for years – *direct from the Bal Tabre, Paris.*' Durante was one of hundreds of tumblers who were continuing an ancient tradition stretching back centuries:

> A pratfall is when you fall on your bum; a one-oh-eight is when you go half forwards and land flat on your back; a butterfly is a cartwheel in mid-air without your hands touching the floor – a side somersault; a layout is when you go over backwards and instead of curling up you keep straight – hollow back – and land on your feet; a roundel is like a forward somersault with

a cartwheel – as you go forward you twist your back so you land on your feet facing the way you came; flip-flaps are going forward onto your hands, then back onto your feet – hands, feet, hands, feet. I've seen all-in wrestlers doing some of these falls – they're visual knockabout comedians, these fellows.

*

A chief factor in the revived interest in silent comedy during the period 1945-60 was, of course the ascent of television as the dominant mass-medium of the day. In Britain alone, more than two million sets were being watched in 1953, compared to one million the previous year. The Coronation, of course was the spur, and statistics are misleading as it is estimated that with 'public' TV audiences factored in (viewings in churches, village halls etc.) approximately twenty million viewers watched Elizabeth II crowned. In the same year the BBC switched its transmission from Alexandra Palace in North London to the far more powerful Crystal Palace in South London; two years later the country's first commercial TV station was established – and the revolution proceeded apace. In the USA figures were even more startling – by 1960 fifty-two million people owned a set.

In 1951 the US TV distributor Regal Films had bought up the rights to the entire output of Hal Roach Studios, and TV re-runs of the old silent greats became a staple of viewing throughout the decade. Despite some occasional heavy-handed editing of the original films (Laurel would sometimes be pained by the inevitable cuts for a commercial break that would, naturally in his view, interrupt the flow and spoil a gag) these re-runs, like Robert Youngson's big-screen compilations for theatrical release, re-planted silent comedy in the minds of a generation. There is much debate today about whether TV companies showed these old silents at 'the wrong speed.' This topic – that of silent film either being shown too fast or too slow, is a controversial one amongst film historians, for throughout the silent era itself there was no standard speed at which comedies were filmed or shown – it depended utterly on the choice of the director, and indeed cinema projectionists would also either slow them down or speed them up according to the time of day, or indeed the taste of their audience.

The power of TV is proved by the simple fact that the one silent clown who stubbornly refused to sell his films to the networks was Harold Lloyd, whose reputation as a consequence declined in comparison with that of Chaplin, Keaton and Laurel & Hardy. 'I want $300,000 per picture for two showings,' explained Lloyd, '... that's a high price, but if I don't get it, I'm not going to show it.' Perhaps regretting his recalcitrance upon seeing the burgeoning acclaim being accorded his fellow clowns of the silent days (Laurel received an Honorary Oscar in 1961) Lloyd switched tactics and assembled his own compilation in 1962, *Harold Lloyd's World of Comedy.*

The television sitcom in the 1950s was universally verbal, most of the shows transferring from or building on existing radio successes: growing out of the variety format they were not yet, of course, half-hour 'playlets' as they quickly evolved into, but 'presentations,' with constant breaking of the fourth wall and characters stepping out of action to adopt the role of compère. In the US they had *Burns & Allen*, *I Love Lucy*, and *The Honeymooners*, while in the UK there was *Take it From Here.* It took Galton

In addition to the long-running 'ditzy sitcom wife' persona of her sitcoms, Lucille Ball was also an accomplished slapstick comic, performing several memorable routines with Danny Kaye including the 'Getting Drunk on Salad' sketch for NBC in 1962, and here in Lucy's series of 1964.

& Simpson in *Hancock's Half Hour* to dispense with musical breaks and main-character-as-host to establish the dramatic format we know today.

So the variety show effectively divided into two, spawning the sitcom but also remaining as a standard bill of fare for viewers from the late 1940s to the present. And it is the TV variety show that became the home of many a visual act in the 50s. There was NBC's *Colgate Comedy Hour, Texaco Star Theatre* with Milton Berle, *Your Show of Shows* with Sid Caesar, *The Jack Benny Show, The Kraft Music Hall* and many others; while in Britain there was *The Good Old Days* and *Sunday Night at the London Palladium. Café Continental* (1947-53 on the BBC) was a direct reinvention of a cabaret for TV audiences and even included a *maitre-d'* who led the spectators to their 'table.' These shows offered occasional slots for visual acts – drawn from the circus, vaudeville and cabaret – but the general trend in TV in the 1950s as far as comedy was concerned was the nurturing, and indeed the very invention, of the sitcom. It would not be until the 60s and 70s that the TV variety show matured into what we now know as 'the sketch show'.

Another clown who perhaps achieved his greatest success on TV in this era was Richard Hearne, better known as his stage and screen character, Mr Pastry. Born in Norwich in 1909, the son of an actress and a circus acrobat, as a young man he appeared in everything from circus to variety to pantomime, and developed his immortal character while appearing in a play at the Saville Theatre in 1945, *Big Boy,* written by Fred Emney among others. Over the next twenty-five years Hearne starred in dozens of TV shows, either in his own series or as a guest segment in sketch formats such as the BBC show *Kaleidoscope.* It was on an episode of *Kaleidoscope* that Hearne performed one of his most famous routines, known as The Lancers, in which he cavorted and frolicked around a ballroom entirely on

Richard Hearne, aka Mr Pastry, was perhaps the most accomplished physical performer on British television in the 1950s and 60s, his deceptively slapdash persona disguising pantomime skills every bit as precise as those of Marcel Marceau – and with the common touch, he brought circus clowning to small-screen audiences of millions.

his own, being swirled around and into the air by a host of 'invisible' dancing partners. Hearne appealed equally to children and adults, and would appear on TV early in the schedules for young audiences, then later in the evening in something slightly more sophisticated. The key to his success was character; while Max Wall's persona of Professor Wallofski was slightly sinister, Mr Pastry was altogether a more likeable chap, an eccentric and affable uncle who – though bumbling and clumsy – was so well-meaning that one couldn't help but warm to him. Everyone's funny relative, his scatterbrained antics belied an accomplished physical performer, and all his routines were meticulously rehearsed, whether it was attempting to board a train with loads of luggage or feeding animals in the zoo. Though he did make feature films – *Mr Pastry Does the Laundry* (1950) and the short *Mr Pastry at the Circus* (1960) – it was television that made him a star. When ITV was launched in 1955 they made Hearne a flagship performer, giving him his own series of six 45-minute episodes, *Richard Hearne as Mr Pastry*, and in 1958 he made a show that truly deserves the name 'special', for he co-starred alongside none other than Buster Keaton. *The Adventures of Mr Pastry* (ATV), had Hearne attempting to learn Method Acting from Keaton's Professor. Intended as the first episode of a series, sadly Keaton fell ill and the enterprise never materialised. Hearne's career went from strength to strength in the ensuing decade, the story of which will be picked up in a later chapter – suffice it to say that his work perhaps above all others turned a whole post-war generation of young people onto the joy and potential of visual humour. In addition, international success was his, and he became popular all over the world, in France being known as *Papa Gateau* and in Germany as *Herr Zucker Tart* (Mr Sugar Tart).

CHAPTER 12

Television's First Genius: Ernie Kovacs

Mention the name Ernie Kovacs in a crowded room and the chances are only a few comedy aficionados will raise their heads in recognition, yet at one time this pudgy, dour, cigar-chewing Hungarian was not only American TV comedy's biggest star – but its first.

Although Kovacs' reputation in the decades following his death has waned and he lurks merely in the history books or on occasional clip-shows, in the 1950s Kovacs –a moustachioed box of anarchy and firecracker sight-gags – formed part of that extraordinary renaissance of visual comedy jump-started by Tati. Unlike Tati or Jerry Lewis or Norman Wisdom, however, Kovacs brought his genius for purely visual humour to the new, exciting medium of television. Also unlike those three film comics, Kovacs' background lay not in variety but – oddly for one who was to become remembered for his outlandish visual imagination – in radio.

American wireless in the 1930s and 40s had been a fertile breeding ground for comedians, only relinquishing its hold on the US public when TV took off in the ensuing decade. The Smothers Brothers, Bob Hope, Amos 'n' Andy, Burns & Allen – like their British counterparts Tommy Handley, Al Read, Spike Milligan, Peter Sellers and Tony Hancock – were icons of radio who became as big as movie stars. If you had your own show on radio it guaranteed you a sell-out tour of variety theatres, to packed houses. And with the transfer of many of these shows to TV, they became and defined the term 'household names', for this new type of star literally performed in your household.

Commercial television fed off its invisible counterpart not only for its stars but also its formats: as broadcast historian Les Brown points out, 'Radio not only developed the stars and program formats that were to be adopted by commercial television, but also the entire modus operandi, including the economic system and the affiliate relationships.' And it was America's oldest radio station, NBC, that first ventured into TV broadcasting – the station that embraced the talents of Ernie Kovacs and made him one of the world's first TV stars.

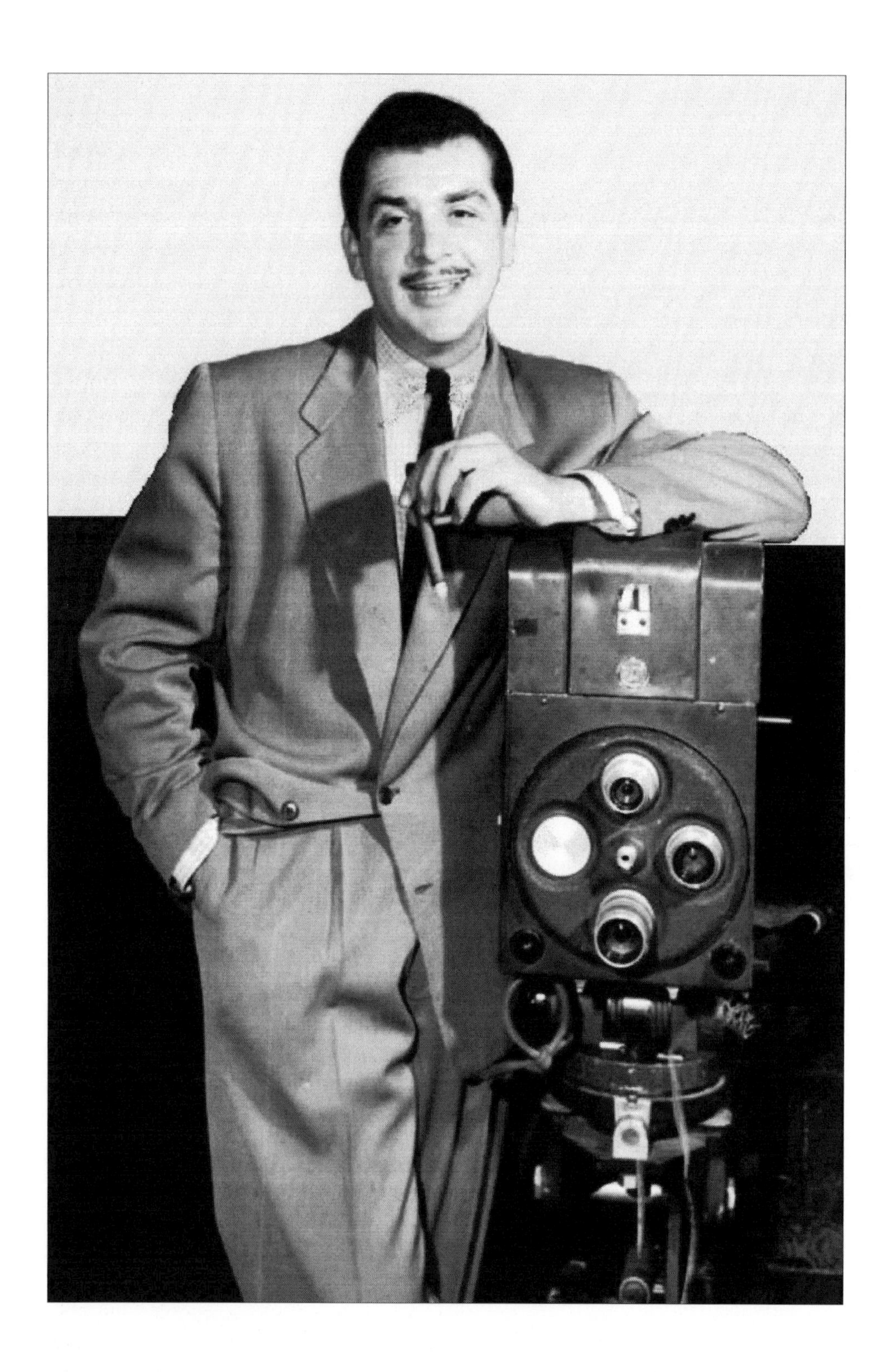

'We didn't tear up the rule book – there was no rule-book.' Ernie Kovacs entered the brave new world of 1950s TV and re-invented the visual comedy sketch.

TV stardom was a wholly different animal to the Hollywood movie star. The latter was a remote godlike figure whose art was, in a profound sense, aloof: to experience their art you had to make a journey to a special building. It was akin to visiting an art gallery. The TV star, on the other hand, performed his or her antics in the corner of your living room, while you carried on your family life: so they became part of your family, imprinting themselves week after week onto your consciousness as you sat having dinner.

Such was Ernie Kovacs.

Timing was all. An awkward, stocky, socially difficult child from a broken home in New Jersey, he rose from presenting innovative shows on local radio in the late 40s to the giddy heights of NBC.

His innovative style of comedy immediately caught on, grabbing the attention of producers and listeners alike. Very quickly his freshness, anarchy and originality gained him a reputation as the *enfant terrible* of comedy broadcasting. Just as Lewis and Martin were subverting the tropes of the variety double-act with their spirit of breezy indiscipline in the clubs and movie theatres, so Kovacs completely shattered the form and structure of radio: his madcap, fast-moving, improvisational free-wheeling comedy was a total revolution, containing sound gags, spoof news reports, mock-interviews – tropes that would go on to influence dozens of comedy stars of later years, from Benny Hill to Monty Python, Kenny Everett to Reeves & Mortimer and Harry Hill, and even the 'Zoo'-type chat shows (a mix of chat, sketch and solo act) of Jonathan Ross and Chris Evans.

*

When he made the transition from sound to sight in 1949 with shows like *Three to Get Ready*, for WPTZ, *Deadline for Dinner*, (a comedy cookery show), *Kovacs on the Corner* and *Today*, there is no doubt that the early silent comedians were a major influence. But it was Jacques Tati in particular who cast a stylistic shadow. Tati's first films were spreading from Europe to the US, and word of this eccentric re-discoverer of visual comedy reached the ear of Kovacs. So when he began developing material to effect the transition from pure audio shows to TV, he looked to Tati for inspiration.

Kovacs' regular TV persona in many of his sketches was Eugene – a rather bland, rain-coated nebbish-like character with large spectacles who drifts through a surreal landscape interacting with objects and scenes but rarely with other human beings. Eugene has been compared to Keaton and Chaplin – and indeed his famous tilted table routine has an ancestor in Chaplin's swaying ship in *The Immigrant* – but he undoubtedly owes a lot to Hulot, and indeed the whole tenor and style of Kovacs' TV work bears all the hallmarks of Tati's pace and avant-garde approach. One of Kovacs' writers Mike Marmer bears this out: 'Jacques Tati was one of Ernie's idols. He always mentioned (him). Tati used lots of sound effects with visuals, and had that slow pace to his comedy.' (quoted in Diana Rico's book, *Kovacsland*).

His early forays into TV were live 90-minute shows for WPTZ, an extraordinary baptism of fire in those heady days of pioneering TV. Here, the rule-books for the new medium were being written: these were the golden days of an art form when no one bothered to sit around thinking up reasons why you couldn't do something – they simply let you get on with it. In this fresh, can-do environment, Kovacs flourished.

Some of his early sight-gags and routines in these first TV shows were also reminiscent of Jerry Lewis: Kovacs would twitch his face in synch (or out of synch) to records; deliver a report to camera with a live jaguar on his back; and pure pantomime routines were regular features, often shot on location with a 'vox-pop' type camera locked off in long-shot. Early examples of these visual quickies included Kovacs haggling with a salesman in the street, reaching a deal with a handshake, the salesman then throwing him over his shoulder and marching off: entering a barbershop, emerging seconds later completely bald and chasing the barber down the road: Kovac's watch chiming like Big Ben, with him putting his hat over it to muffle the noise … these were quick, sharp, stylistic gags perfect for TV – and utterly new. They were new because they exploited methods not seen before even in movies – even in 1950. For example, Kovacs was the first performer to break the fourth wall and show viewers the cameras, technicians and crew. It was as if no sooner had television been invented, then along had come a comic anarchist hell-bent on subverting it. He was the first Jester of TV whose mission was to be Lord of Misrule. As Diana Rico says in her biography of Kovacs, 'Theater and its descendants – movies, radio, TV, require an understood contract between creator and audience. The audience is asked to suspend its disbelief in exchange for the creator's promise to convince the audience that what it is seeing or hearing – which is an artifice by definition – is in fact real. Ernie's refusal to fulfil that tacit promise was a form of theatrical anarchy, and it set him far apart from the mainstream of American television's creators then and since.'

Kovacs' early TV shows caught on like wildfire, and he was quickly promoted from the (bizarre, for today's scheduling) daytime early morning slot to prime-time 7:00pm to 7:30pm with NBC's *Ernie in Kovacsland* for Channel 3.

The perceived excitement of those early pioneering days of television is not illusory, based on nostalgia – it genuinely was a golden age. Every aspect of making shows for TV was being built from the ground up, so each day was filled with a sense of experimentation. Even something as ostensibly minor as lighting-design was ground-breaking: Karl Weger Jr was Kovacs' lighting man in the early series. 'Most of the people at Channel 3 were young and anything was possible,' he reminisces. 'Nothing had been done previously, so when somebody said 'why can't we do it thus and so?' we would try to do it – and many times we'd succeed.' (Rico, ibid). Weger was the first to bring sophisticated lighting techniques to TV, and personifies the innovative team surrounding Kovacs enabling him to achieve his extraordinary – for his day – 'special effects' comedy.

Therein lies Kovacs' uniqueness – his special effects. Comedy of light, shadow, perspective, shape: he would shoot entire sketches containing no human beings, merely objects. This was comedy as art, and what is more it was happening on mainstream TV being watched by millions. With technicians as eager as he to exploit the new set of electronic toys a TV studio contained, Kovacs ran amok and set the benchmark for avant-garde TV comedy. When it was over, mainstream TV would never again allow itself such off-the-wall experimentation. Akin to Dennis Potter's reinvention of TV drama in the 70s, Kovacs' era was almost over before it was begun. He had to race to get it all done – and when he died prematurely in a car accident in 1962 there was an air of 'Wh-what just happened?'

He was the first comedian to employ the reverse-scan function, enabling us to see him looking at a sign outside the studio reading Fly-Man Wanted – then entering the studio upside-down like a fly. He played cards with himself, fenced with himself, and gave himself the body of a dog. As his poet character Percy Dovetonsils, he could recite a poem then sink as if by magic into his chair and disappear – a pioneering TV use of the 'wipe-down' trick. And remember, all this was live transmission. Set-designer Rene Hickman has no doubt that 'This was impromptu theater, really. It was like a bunch of kids putting on a show in a garage. With a show like that we could experiment, and if it failed it failed. I mean, who cared?' (quoted in Rico, ibid). Other colleagues recall that Kovacs never minded if a gag didn't work. If it went well he'd come off and say 'What a boffo!' (a trad comic expression for a big laugh); if it didn't go over, he never bothered. 'Everything was just a big joke,' remembers audio engineer Bill Hoffmann, 'He was just like the big kid who never grew up.' (quoted in Rico, ibid). If the big kid couldn't find a toy in the studio that made something happen that he wanted to happen, then he invented it. He and Weger came up with a home-made 'image inverter' constructed from a couple of mirrors in a tin can. Sets were built where the furniture was upside down, then the image flipped to make it seem like a normal room. Ernie would stroll in on the ceiling and start hoovering.

Weger was also a pioneer of 'matting' in TV – merging the image from camera with another; a trope so common on TV today we see it virtually in every studio non-fiction genre from sports-desks to newsreading: then it was being seen for the first time. Ernie and his team also invented 'abstract' comedy, by way of placing a kid's kaleidoscope inside a tin can and fixing it to the camera. With accompanying comedy sound effects, these astonishing pieces were surely the first examples of 'video art.'

*

On December 12 1955 his years of hard work on local radio and TV were rewarded by NBC giving him his own series – the *Ernie Kovacs Show* – and it was this series, along with his taking over of Steve Allen's *Tonight* show (which Kovacs, predictably, twisted into a surreal assemblage of sketches all his own) – that elevated him into a household comedian. With a small team of writers including fellow-Hungarian Deke Heyward and associate producer Shirley Mellner, Kovacs encouraged and fostered what Producer Perry Cross recalled in later years as '... a spirit and a love of experimentation. He tuned into that. He stimulated us to be different and to have fun while we were doing it, and it came across that way.' (quoted in Rico, ibid). From the outset, surreal, firecracker sight-gags peppered the show: Kovacs would fasten a moustache to the lens of the camera, then shave it; drops of sweat would fly across the screen; goldfish would sit in the audience watching the show. And while a storm raged outside, and a lifelong stamp collector prepared to mount his collection of a thousand stamps in an album, Ernie would enter and – subverting expectations – the entire contents of the room would be blown about yet the stamps would remain in neat, unmoving piles.

The show spawned the 'visual quickie' – a comic genre that would become the staple of most sketch shows ever since. The perfect example of one of these 30-second mini-masterpieces is *The Blindfolded Chess-Player*, recalled by writer Deke Heyward:

> You did everything upside down when you worked for Ernie. Ten chess tables set up. Ten guys behind each one. And the World's greatest Chess Player is about to play them all blindfolded. Ernie makes his appearance blindfolded, and you

> *know* he has got to bump into the tables. Any (other comedian) would have done that. We don't do that. Blindfolded, with great surety, he walks to the first table, second table, third table, tenth table, makes a move at each one of the tables, and then looks at the audience through the blindfold and walks off – at which point all the tables collapse without anybody touching them. That's the difference!' (quoted in Rico, ibid).

He was not averse to the odd *homage* to the visual comics of yesteryear: one distinctly Laurel-esque gag consists of him seated on the branch of a tree holding a saw: after a few methodical sawing strokes there is a mighty creak and he plunges haplessly to the ground below. He even proffers a Hardy-esque look to camera – a technique that was to become one of his staple links between items: '... the camera (would move in) for a close-up on Ernie's face,' remembers Heyward, 'looking for all the world as if he had a question-mark in each eyeball – which he could do! It's like, 'what the hell's going on here? Why is this happening to me?''

The brash, anarchic, fast-talking 'presenter' persona Kovacs invented as the host of his shows is very similar to the behind-the-desk madness of Reeves & Mortimer years later, and is oddly a complete contrast to the quieter, calmer, more innocent character he created for his visual routines. Again Deke Heyward has an explanation for Kovac's specific reasoning:

> He took a forlorn, lost soul, and made him into a hero in certain aspects of his comedy. He was almost patterned along the lines of the Talmudic innocent ... The Talmudic innocent would be walking down the street as a safe was hoisted above him; the rope would break but (Ernie) would be unscathed because it would crash just behind him or in front of him. Buster Keaton, also a non-Jew, instinctively went to the Talmudic innocent. When a building crashed in its entirety around Keaton, not a fleck of brick came near him: he went through everything unscathed. And this was a substantial part of what Ernie was doing.

Unlike Keaton, however, whose big-screen routines were principally shot on locations like mountainsides, railway tracks or rivers, Kovacs' comedy playground was small and contained: the first visual comedy, in fact, to be shot inside a studio.

Even his 'outside' routines were shot indoors; one might say that the discipline of the TV studio in many ways dictated the format of the comedy. Kovacs would be seated in a chair in a living-room: we fasten in on a close-up. On sound, there comes the galloping of an approaching horse. He looks up, but the camera stays on his face. His eye-line travels across frame as he follows the path of the (unseen) stallion; the sound of galloping stops; we hear the (out of vision) door opening; a few more hoof-steps, the door closes, and the galloping resumes.

It was, perhaps, the cheapest comedy sketch ever shot. Another example of these sharp, quick 'TV cartoons' (of the kind that influenced many comics afterwards and even permeated whole movie genres such as the *Naked Gun* franchise) is: 'Man with stubble in front of mirrored medicine cabinet ... opens door ... Tiny barber inside sharpening razor.'

Milligan-style comedy was prefigured in Kovacs' work: perhaps one of his most famous routines was the musical 'Nairobi Trio' sketch. It is pure Milligan's 'Q.' The format is simplicity itself – there is no set-up, no interior development, and no punch-line, yet its comic impact is immense. It possesses a strange, drifting dreamlike quality that actually borders on nightmarishness. Three men in gorilla costumes sit on stage and play three minutes of bizarre, rhythmic music. That is it. It is more Absurdist Theatre than TV comedy, and on its own is proof enough that Kovacs was laying down the template for dozens of comedy shows that came thereafter.

*

It was on *The Tonight Show* on October 15 1956 that his silent alter ego, Eugene, made his first appearance, in what became a regular running scenario known as 'The Library Bit'. The schtick of 'trying to keep quiet in the library,' a familiar comic trope today but innovative in the mid-50s, was fresh and surprising.

In a way *The Tonight Show* was a dress-rehearsal for the famous *Silent Show* of a few months later, a special that would reprise much of the material showcased in *The Tonight Show* and confirm Kovacs as the biggest TV comedy star of the decade. It fizzed with dozens of ideas; Producer Roger Gimbel recalls a favourite – 'He had one sketch where he was a baseball player, and he hit the ball and it went out of the park and around the world. You saw Eskimos looking at it, you saw all these things.' But the audience in the huge Hudson theatre on West 44th street didn't always get the gags. 'The ideas were so terrific ... (but) it was a very mild reaction, which made us nervous,' continues Gimbel (quoted in Rico, ibid). Here was the first comedian on TV making jokes that would *only* actually work on TV. More than any comic before him, Kovacs truly understood the medium he was working in – his visual gags were not the variety-born tumbling and mugging of a Norman Wisdom or a Buster Keaton; they were smaller, subtler, more contained – they had the ambience of the European avant-garde rather than the Vaudeville stage.

His solution to the quietness of the live audience? They put up screens in front of the proscenium, forcing the crowd to watch what the TV audience would eventually see – *on the monitors*. Today this is commonplace at live studio recordings, but in 1956 it was unheard of: you book a ticket to go and watch an NBC show, and you end sitting in an 800-seat theatre watching TV?

But this was comedy specifically designed for the small screen – and it worked. Audiences across America were treated to a spectacle of visual humour a step beyond the pratfall: this was a playing with reality in the Bunuel or Tati mould.

Diana Rico writes of the kinship between Tati and Kovacs: 'In spirit and in the form their comedy takes Eugene and M. Hulot might be cousins – the one bumpkinly American, the other solemnly Gallic.' Kovacs without doubt borrowed the sense of drift from Tati: in his extended visual routines his alter-ego Eugene wanders cipher-like through the world with the minimum of engagement. As Yvonne Gerald has written of Tati in *Films in Review*, December 1958, 'Hulot is a situational, not a personality, comedian. Hulot does not go out and make funny things happen. He is a magnet which attracts contretemps to himself. Tati says Hulot is, as it were, invisible, and it is for the audience to find him and to decide whether or not he is their friend, or someone they would pass unnoticed in the street.'

As Kovacs reached the height of his powers in the *Tonight Show* he was unquestionably emulating Tati's vision. Gone was the manic cheerful host of local Philadelphia Radio chucking out jokes and wisecracks: in his extended visual routines Kovacs became Eugene, the slow, almost Chauncey Gardner-like victim of the bizarre, clad in raincoat and pork-pie hat; an Alice-figure floating through a looking-glass, topsy-turvy universe where planes of reality collide and where anything can happen.

To bring such brave, edgy visual comedy to mainstream American TV is a quite extraordinary achievement. As Producer Roger Gimbel puts it: 'He was trying things that didn't seem like big jokes, and they were funny in a totally new, different way. Sort of avant-garde, experimental television.' (quoted in Rico, ibid).

How the legendary *Silent Show* came about is a landmark in TV comedy history in itself. Jerry Lewis and Dean Martin had announced their split only a few months before and NBC commissioned a TV special from each, salivating at the vast audience figures such shows would attract. They contracted Lewis to do a ninety-minute spectacular – *Saturday Colour Carnival* – but Lewis demurred. He would only do an hour. Left with a spare thirty minutes, NBC execs panicked – who could they get to fill the floundering half hour?

They approached Kovacs. Sensing the network had been backed into a corner, he used the situation to persuade them to let him undertake one of the riskiest ventures in the history of broadcasting: half an hour of all-silent comedy augmented only by music and sound effects, on prime-time network TV. Kovacs knew the risk but embraced it.

It was a dream project that Kovacs and his fellow-writer Deke Heyward had actually nurtured for a while. Now they'd been given the green light, ambition fuelled the enterprise from the very beginning. Kovacs wanted all the TV commercials in the breaks to be silent (a demand he almost achieved, but not quite): he also wanted Harpo Marx to guest star (a request that sadly never came about). Despite these logistical setbacks (and in truth, Harpo in the mix might have unbalanced the aesthetic somewhat: a burst of applause on his entrance and exit could well have demoted the show to the trad TV-variety fare Kovacs was attempting to subvert) the *Ernie Kovacs Show* as recorded the night of January 19 1957, produced and written by Kovacs and directed by Barry Shear, has gone down in broadcasting history as one of the classics of television comedy.

Although called *The Silent Show,* it was, of course, anything but silent. Sounds abounded and Kovacs utilised music and FX to an extent never before seen on the big or small screen.

The culmination of years of experimentation in a new mass medium, Ernie Kovacs' NBC special The Silent Show *of 1957 announces itself to the world as a dialogue-free half-hour.*

The grammar and vocabulary of the show was established from the outset – an orchestral drummer lifts a drumstick to beat a mighty tattoo on his huge bass drum but the drum suddenly becomes instead a huge bowl of mud or soup and his stick produces an unexpected soft 'plop' (a gag reprised twenty years later by Morecambe and Wise). From that moment the TV audience was lured into a strange, twilit world of non-verbal sound and dreamscape that on occasions morphed into a Lewis Carroll-like nightmare. Throughout, Kovacs as Eugene makes a squelching noise with his feet. Trapped in a corridor that shrinks, Alice-in-Wonderland-like, he escapes by 'drawing' a door on a wall with sticky tape – that then becomes a real door. He enters a living-room that is actually not a living-room but an empty landscape of the mind. A TV repair man crouches at a cabinet containing nothing but an empty space, ostensibly fixing a set but in reality working at nothing.

Ernie Kovacs' seminal The Silent Show *incorporated special effects never before seen on TV. Kovac's technical director Karl Weger recalls 'nothing had been done previously, so we would try to do it – and many times we'd succeed.' So Kovacs draws, in the air, an entire room of furniture which then comes to life – thirty years before Kenny Everett did the same thing – and here a whole library comes to life in sound, Tolstoy's epic releasing first thunderous gunfire, then a dove.*

He sets about creating furniture for the room, once again drawing pictures on walls that demonically become real. An illustration of a lamp magically lights up, a scrawled picture hangs down, lopsided.

Now the TV repairman has now finished his work, and switches on the set. Lo and behold, it appears. Kovacs wanders over to an invisible sash window, opens it, and a gust of wind blows hat off. A maid uses an invisible hoover to suck up items of rubbish from the floor: an invisible dog pulls his chain free from the wall and the lead runs off.

This is a human Looney Tune – a performer and his production team experimenting with the toy-box of the TV studio in a way that can only be compared to what the Beatles and Pink Floyd were to do ten years later in the music studio with *Sergeant Pepper* and *Piper at the Gates of Dawn* with their wind-up clockwork toys FXs, galloping horses, reversed-tape loops and Moog synthesisers.

The Silent Show aired in a prime-time comedy slot, yet there were moments in the show that extended beyond comedy and became poetically surreal. In one scene Eugene walks through a gallery of sculptures, each of which make sounds as he passes, culminating in a female statue reaching out to touch him. When he returns the stone woman's kiss, the woman crumbles. This is like something out of Ovid, or mid-European folk tales.

The show spiralled onwards into ever-more surreal episodes: Eugene hangs his hat on the antlers of a moose's head stuck on the wall, passes through the door and discovers that the entire animal is stuck through the wall. In a gag that years later Jerry Lewis would use in *Cracking Up*, Kovacs stares at a painting of a boat at sea. The boat sinks with accompanying gurgles. In Lewis' picture it is a bull that gallops out of the canvas, but the influence is indisputable.

The whole show was a firework display of visual treats, Kovacs at the height of his powers, the culmination of fifteen years of creativity but shorn of the anarchic indiscipline of his formative work. This is a contained, artistic Kovacs, displaying precision-engineered jokes with technical expertise. In the days before instant push-button digital effects, a sound-man sat behind the set in front of a bank of monitors and numerous record turntables, playing the effects in live as Kovacs performed. A Mona Lisa doesn't just smile, she audibly giggles: as Eugene browses in a library the books make noises: a history of the Luftwaffe fills the room with the sounds of an aerial dogfight and machine-gun strafing; similarly a volume of 'War and Peace' produces a cacophony of conflict, until the final page when Kovacs becomes a stage magician and releases a (real) white dove of peace from the pages. And the gunfire comedy continues when Eugene sits and begins cracking his knuckles, each scrunch creating gunfire of increasing decibels until his thumb goes off like a rocket.

He brings out an egg-timer that ticks like a clock, and which chimes the hour. He produces a miniature record player which he plugs in to a socket on his stomach and which then plays a song in elf-like falsetto. He takes a packed lunch over to a long refectory table, and launches into his famous tilted-set routine.

The tilted-set routine, which Kovacs reprised many times in his shows and which became a favourite, was not mere camera trickery but involved genuine athletic strength: to maintain the illusion of sitting up straight and performing complex routines with props required both artistic discipline and physical stamina. When the body is angled at forty-five degrees the strain on the muscles is doubled, and the simple act of reaching an arm out 'horizontally' to a water-jug whilst maintaining the illusion of uprightness is no easy task. Kovacs had performed the tilted routine before on the *Tonight Show* but nevertheless it took a toll each time he executed it. An olive rolls magically down the 'flat' table; a stream of poured water flouts gravity and hangs suspended in the air as it rebelliously avoids his glass. It was a surreal artist at work, of the calibre and imagination of Keaton, something that the critics recognised immediately the show was off air. Jerry Lewis' show was universally panned – and it was Kovacs who was heralded as the solo comic genius. This must have been particularly galling for Lewis, whose first solo TV outing this was and whose 60-minute special which aired immediately before Kovac's innovative half-hour was meant to be his big bold statement – 'Look at me, here I am and I don't need Dean Martin!'

Kovacs bringing the ingenuity of the silent film-makers of the 1920s to the small screen in his tilted-table routine. The comic device of matching the angle of the camera with the angle of a surface had certainly been done before and would be done many times afterwards, but in these lengthy visual sequences Kovacs was proving that an extended dialogue-free sequence could be part of mainstream entertainment.

The critics uniformly crowed that Lewis did indeed need Dean Martin. Jack O'Brian's stark assessment in the *New York-Journal American* spoke for all the papers: 'Lewis: No. Kovacs: Yes.' The public wholeheartedly agreed with him.

Post-show, as Kovacs was relaxing backstage and his dressing-room filled up with friends and cigar-smoke, the NBC switchboard was being bombarded with more calls than they'd ever had in their history.

'Where Lewis relied on frenzy, Kovacs' humour was fresh and wildly inventive. Look on Lewis, and learn something,' proclaimed the *New York Daily News*, and Harriet Van Horne in the *New York World-Telegram and Sun* went further: 'In technique, sophistication and charm, the Ernie Kovacs 'Dumb Show' was light years ahead of the Jerry Lewis spectacular.

Coming as it did right after this tedious and costly hour, it was a gem of the purest ray serene.' And John Crosby in the *New York Herald Tribune* said 'it was all pretty weird and wonderful and avant-garde.'

The accolades didn't fade after the airing: *The Silent Show* became the only TV programme to represent America at the Brussels World Fair, and Kovacs himself was nominated for an Emmy. He used the success of the show to step aside from the small-screen and present it as a calling-card to the moguls of Los Angeles.

With mixed success.

*

It is fair to say that his foray into feature films yielded Kovacs lesser rewards: although he received plaudits as a character actor, signing a deal with Columbia, he was destined always to be second-fiddle on the big screen. After all, he was competing with the likes of Jack Lemmon, Walter Matthau and numerous other accomplished movie comedy actors. It was the Golden Age of the Character Actor, and in Hollywood Kovacs became, bluntly, a smaller fish. Perhaps like Tony Hancock, and indeed many other TV comedians, Kovacs' eye was always on something 'bigger and better.' Both he and Hancock failed to see that their unique and peculiar genius lay in TV. Although a star-maker, TV in its early days was very much looked down as a medium: for ambitious comedians and actors it was perceived as a stepping-stone, not an end in itself. Certainly stage actors looked down on it – ('slumming it on telly, darling!') – and comedians of the ilk of Kovacs, Hancock, Sellers, and even Morecambe & Wise, held cinematic stardom in their hearts as a personal Holy Grail.

So, Kovacs went to Hollywood – and, laudable though his ambitions were, he failed to become a major star. Some comics shine on the small screen, others light up the cinema. Despite appearing as notable characters in *Bell, Book & Candle* (1958), and *Our Man in Havana* (1959), his true genius lay on television – so he returned to it.

But the clock was ticking, both on the comic's life and on his innovative style of TV. As Diana Rico puts it, 'Kovacs' work, ironically, was totally indigenous to the medium, but as it became more offbeat and original, it fit less and less into television's increasingly conservative game-plan.' We have to be doubly thankful, therefore, that when he returned from Hollywood to TV he was allowed by ABC to make eight half-hour specials that would consolidate his reputation as one of TV most innovative comedians, and which contained some of his finest work. Sponsored by Dutch Masters (and when has there ever been a more apt sponsor, given Kovacs' Churchillian passion for cigars?) *The Ernie Kovacs Show* aired between May 18 1961 and January 23 1962. The final of the (monthly) shows became an obituary, for ten days before the last show went out – Kovacs was dead.

His swansong thankfully contained some of his finest work. Between forays into films Kovacs had made the one-off special *Kovacs on Music*, in 1959, hosted the quiz series *Take a Good Look*, and anchored a homage to the greats of silent comedy, *Silents Please* – but it was the first of these, his exploration of all things music, that fed into his last great series.

Music infuses these last shows like the vital ingredient in a recipe: from the opening sequence when Kovacs welcomes the audience like a top-hatted Barnum-esque circus hawker, hardly a word is spoken throughout the half-hour. Surreal and bizarre concoctions are heaped on the viewer relentlessly: a man in chains is lowered into a harbour to the strains of *Mack the Knife* (the sound intermittently displayed on an oscilloscope); two chefs beat each other with frying pans; a picture of a dam bursts open and floods the studio; a three- legged man ties up three pairs of shoelaces; a singer hits a top note and crack the lens of the camera; Kovacs hammers a nail though the wall into someone's head; a high-jumper rebounds on the bar and is thrown out of the stadium.

Each episode contained a lengthy visual centrepiece, usually not involving human beings at all, but objects. One such famous episode is what became known as the Kitchen Symphony in which – in time to the ever-present melange of music – inanimate objects come to life and perform for us: three taps (hot, cold and lukewarm) pour out their water in rhythm; a banana unpeels itself like a stripper; sardines stand up in their tin and dance; slices of toast leap into the air in joy; pots, pans and dishes become percussive; and a roast chicken dances on a table-top. It makes Monty Python look positively humdrum.

Another long sequence included an extended pantomime showing the comic difference between the ways men and women get dressed in the morning, the females elegantly applying lipstick and drawing on stockings, the men scratching themselves and slapping on shaving foam with the finesse of drowsy apes.

This same sequence develops into a choreography of Busby Berkeley complexity, with a remarkably under-floor shot of a ballerina displaying expert point-work that morphs into a reveal that she is standing on a man's feet who's guiding her round the dance-floor. The routine ends with an overhead shot of two rooms whose walls then fold flat.

The only words Kovacs utters throughout are the intermittent ads for Dutch Masters, and the occasional verbal quickie. In one show he follows a sequence where a scientist is extolling the value and quality of corks for their ability to seal links inside bottles. Kovacs is revealed sitting behind a huge desk, the President of Konosky Corks, where he utters the six words – 'I am proud of my corks.' This behind-the-desk non sequitur comedy would become the dominant style of two British surreal comedians of the 1990s, Reeves & Mortimer.

The closing title sequence of the series was a comic *tour de force* in itself: names appear from underwater, drift on the surface for a moment, only to plunge down into the liquid depths.

The ABC series contained another landmark piece of television in Kovacs' 'Street Scene', an extraordinary, almost cinematic dumb-show enacted to the accompaniment of Bartok's Concerto for Orchestra. This was an entirely new genre of TV entertainment – not a sketch, not a sitcom, not a quickie, but a comedy-noir, the natural home of which might be a European arts cinema rather than prime-time US TV.

Kovacs died in a car crash on the morning of January 13 1962. He lost control of his Chevrolet Corvair station wagon while turning fast and crashed into a power pole at the corner of Beverly Glen and Santa Monica Boulevards. When the police arrived Kovacs was sprawled on the tarmac, arm reaching out lifelessly for the cigar that lay inches from his hand.

If he had lived, how long would he have been given free rein on the networks to showcase his unique gifts? The television industry was changing; it was no longer longer a free-and-easy environment where innovators could exercise their idiosyncratic and experimental genius. Kovacs' luck was to have entered the industry at a time when the rule-book was still being written and, although clearly run by the money-men at the outset, it had not crystallised into the rigid and prescriptive hierarchy it became in ensuing years. Some dismiss Kovacs today as being 'weird and too brainy' for TV comedy, a judgement that perhaps explains his relative obscurity. But it is, of course, precisely his 'weirdness and braininess' that made him great. Kovacs suffered the fate of many originals in that we look back on his output today and recognise so many familiar tropes and techniques that influenced subsequent comedians, that our appreciation of them is often muted.

His influence on TV comedy has been immeasurable, from Python to Milligan to Rowan & Martin to *Saturday Night Live*, to Steve Martin, to Reeves & Mortimer – in all the work of all these artistes one can trace the hand of Kovacs.

In respect to one particular comic it is particularly gaugeable. While Kovacs was creating avant-garde waves on US TV, a rising star of British variety was sitting in his digs in Southsea watching *The Silent Show* on a flickering black and white Rediffusion set, feverishly and unashamedly scribbling down ideas in a notebook for his own first forays onto the small-screen. His name was Benny Hill – and he was to become Britain's first TV comedy star.

CHAPTER 13

Kid in a Sweet-Shop – Benny Hill

In September 1967 a dough-faced comic with an infectious cheeky twinkle sat in the sunshine in the German village of Rothenburg-ob-de-Tauber chatting with a taller, lankier comedian. They were discussing their three heroes: Chaplin, Buster Keaton and Stan Laurel.

'We both thought we were born in the wrong era,' the taller comedian recalled in 1997 in the British TV series *Heroes of Comedy*.

Benny Hill met Dick Van Dyke during the shooting of *Chitty Chitty Bang Bang* and the two men bonded over their mutual love for the silent greats. In fact they hit it off so well that Van Dyke saw to it that Hill became a co-writer on Roald Dahl's screenplay, adding material during the shoot. In fact, Hill ended up contributing most of the visual routines in that picture, memorably the dancing 'doll' sequence. He had had plenty of practice – for the previous fifteen years Hill had not only forged a career as one of Britain's biggest TV comedy stars, but had also written most of his scripts, along with cohort Dave Freeman.

Benny Hill has two life stories. The first is of a comedian of such inventiveness, ambition and originality that he became Britain's first big TV comedy star and then the world's biggest TV comedy star. The second story is that of a sad, lonely, traditional, variety comedian who stuck to the same format for three decades, outstayed his welcome, and whose anachronistic portrayals of women led to a banishment from the small screen and a lonely death in a Teddington apartment. Unfortunately, and unjustly, it is the second story that has held sway in the public imagination.

A more balanced view would be to re-assess Hill's contribution to comedy (and in the context of this book, physical comedy), to connect him firmly to the tradition of European cabaret mime blended with Donald McGill-postcard-style seaside humour, and to view his later toppling by Ben Elton et al and his subsequent sacking by Thames Television in 1989 as more an expression of changing social mores than a judgement of the talents of the man himself.

Born in Southampton the son of a prophylactic salesman, Hill's 'nudge-nudge' comic leitmotiv was perhaps nurtured in this childhood atmosphere of English reserve and euphemism. There followed a youth spent entranced by the big seaside variety shows of the 1930s, and a child-like veneration of the Star Comic in such shows.

Introverted comedy writer Benny Hill singlehandedly invented the British television comedy sketch show and brought continental mime to mainstream TV.

Hill took to the stage. But it was rude awakening. He discovered that live theatre was not for him. In later years he freely admitted that in front of theatre audiences he was constantly, cripplingly nervous. Like Kovacs, it took the entirely new medium of TV to embrace Hill, to allow him to relax, breathe, and shine. Indeed, such was Hill's aversion to live performing that it was actually as a scriptwriter that he landed his first series at the BBC in 1955. He'd made a few solo-spot appearances on various live TV specials from 1949 onwards but by 1955, his nerves had got the better of him. He had slunk back to his parents' house in Southampton, where he saw a brighter future as a comedy writer. So wrote a speculative comedy script – intending it as a vehicle for another performer – and sent it to BBC Producer Ronnie Waldman. The prescient Waldman immediately invited him in to Television Centre. Waldman praised the script to the skies and promptly offered him a series. 'Who's going to star in it?' asked the naïve Hill. 'You are,' replied Waldman.

*

There followed fourteen years of major TV stardom at the BBC. Why did he fail in the theatre but become an immediate star on TV? A combination of two major factors. Firstly, he was a 'telegenic' comic: the facial expressions that had proved ineffective in variety halls beyond the first two rows of the audience, worked magically in front of the TV camera, allowing Hill to virtually singlehandedly invent the TV comedy reaction shot. In the King's Theatre, Southsea, his wicked glint was invisible – down the lens it became charismatic. Secondly, he injected into his shows two elements that – in the early to mid-1950s – were utterly radical: visual comedy, and spoofs of other TV shows. For a medium that had only just begun to flower – ITV itself had only begun broadcasting in 1955 – a comedian lampooning series like *Film Night, This is Your Life, Armand and Michaela Denis, The Perry Como Show* etc etc. was cutting edge.

But spoofs date – and it was Hill's use of mime in his TV shows that was to ensure his longevity.

To perform in your own prime-time comedy show on the BBC is one thing: to write it all is another. Yet this is what Hill did. The Oxbridge university wits are usually awarded the accolade of ushering in the age of the writer-performer (a ubiquitous phenomenon today when most comics write their own material) – but Benny Hill got there before Peter Cook and before the Pythons. In an age when most comedians would hire 'comedians labourers' to churn out their material, Hill ploughed the furrow of the auteur, like Eric Sykes, Spike Milligan, and his comic heroes Chaplin, Laurel and Keaton.

A major source of Hill's comic archaeology was his deep love of European travel. Between TV shows he would go to Paris, Berlin, Rome, Madrid for months on end, seeking out the cabarets, music-halls and circuses in order to steep himself in its mimes, acrobats, comedians, magicians.

It was the Golden Age of European Cabaret. In Paris one could visit the Lido, the Moulin Rouge, Olympia, Casino, Crazy Horse, the Folies Bergères and the ABC Music Hall in Montmartre. Mark Lewisohn writes: 'Already a passionate devotee of the great silent-film comedians Chaplin, Keaton, Lloyd, Langdon and Laurel & Hardy – Benny Hill added continental mime to his repertoire: the genius of Marcel Marceau and his many imitators, and the visual humour of the French dialogue-free movie creator Jacques Tati. From this point on, a good deal of Hill's comedy would be silent. He little knew it, and he certainly did not seek it, but this, above all else, would provide the key to his eventual global domination.'

His principal originality, for me, was that he took English music-hall and gave it a European, or world-wide, twist.

This absorption of the language and grammar of international visual comedy was no secret: in 1957 a *TV Times* article declared, with an appropriate tone of surprise at the novelty of the phenomenon, 'Benny Hill Goes to Paris – to write a script!'

'Yes, it's easy to write in Paris,' Hill enthuses in the same article, 'and this lark gives me the same thrill every time I'm booked for TV. I must write a script – so Paree here I come again. I write much better abroad ... One of the best programmes I've ever done was dreamed up in Paris. There's so much to write about. It makes scripting easy.'

Some critics, and indeed friends and colleagues, have imputed a degree of plagiarism to these forays into the world European cabaret. Certainly Hill nourished his TV shows with visual routines inspired by continental comics – but he would always describe them as inspirations rather than thefts. No comic routine is gestated in a vacuum – from Chaplin's appropriation of some of Max Linder's mannerisms to Les Dawson's absorption of Norman Evans' 'over the garden wall' frumpy old northern lady routine, hundreds of examples can be cited that prove the dictum 'there is nothing new under the sun.'

There is a point, however, when influence does becomes theft: in the second *Benny Hill Show*, broadcast in February 1955, Hill and Beryl Reid performed a sublime pantomime routine entitled 'The Bathing Huts'. In adjacent beach cubicles, unseeing of each other, Reid and Hill set about changing their clothes: as they change, they sing sweet love songs, laugh merrily, and clearly and visibly create wild fantasies of how handsome and beautiful their unseen equivalent is.

Until, of course, they emerge from their respective huts and catch sight of their *real* selves. Punctured by reality, their imaginations fall flat to earth like deflated balloons.

The dumb-show was singled out by reviewers: 'Delightfully witty, straight from the intimate review,' declared *The Stage*. The delightful wit, however, was not Hill's at all, but revealed to have been French comedian Robert Dhéry's all along. Nine months after Hill's routine was televised, Dhery brought his visual revue *La Plume de Ma Tante* to London and presented an identical Bathing Hut routine to laughing and applauding theatre-goers, some of whom surely must have recognised it.

But to Hill this theft was little more than unpunishable and completely permitted influence: in his mind he was doing Dhéry – and numerous other European cabaret performers such as Dutchman Wim Sonneveld – a favour by showcasing their routines on British TV and paving the way for a tour of their own. On numerous occasions in interviews he used the word 'steal', 'stolen', 'nicked' when discussing his comic influences from abroad.

Hill hadn't abandoned his stage work, and off the back of his TV success he (somewhat reluctantly) appeared in revue tours for impresario Bernard Delfont – like *Fine Fettle* in 1959. Although he disliked doing them, they gave him a chance to develop some fine mime routines, such as the 'Kid at a Country Fair' sequence. His co-writer Dave Freeman is in no doubt that Hill's aim, in both his stage and TV work, was to recreate the spirit and the content of a French cabaret. 'He didn't hate 'Fine Fettle' as much as he hated 'Paris By Night'' Freeman recalls, 'but it certainly hadn't gone as well as he hoped. He had wanted to do a real, modern, surreal 'La Plume de la Tante,' and we had failed to achieve it.' (quoted by Mark Lewisohn in his book *Funny Peculiar: the True Story of Benny Hill*).

The critics of Hill's early work were mixed, but Milton Shulman was in no doubt of his genius and prospects: 'His cherubic face, with eyes fluttering like some berserk windscreen wiper, represents on the surface the orthodox little man buffeted and baffled by fate. But he brings to this traditional comic characterisation a secret, lip-smacking irreverence which gives his humour a boisterous, bawdy quality.'

The pitfall of hindsight is to warp what was once innovatory and see it as something old-fashioned. Comedy is no exception, which makes it extremely difficult to portray Benny Hill as anything other than an old-time variety comic. But if we exercise a certain archaeology of the mind and dig back through the years, we can *just about* appreciate how revolutionary and avant-garde he actually was. Like Ernie Kovacs in America, Hill was doing things on television that had never been seen before. In addition to infusing his shows with continental humour, another major innovation was his use of film. Inspired by the revolutionary work of Kovacs, he hired M-G-M film director John Street to direct his series, and from that point on ascended to being the most sophisticated sketch comedy on air. 'TV needs to be rejuvenated' said Hill at the time, and his show became the first British sketch comedy to use filmed inserts. In 1961 the opening show of his series included items (shot in 'Benirama Hillascope') filmed in Paris, Columbia, Tokyo, Mexico, Hong Kong, and inside an aeroplane. He was stamping TV comedy with an internationalism never before seen on the small screen: in the age before the package holiday the vast majority of the British public had never set foot abroad. The series was inspired by Hill's own world tour of 1960 when he plunged himself into cabarets and circuses across the globe, adding South America and the Far East to his itinerary.

That Hill was principally a visual comedian was borne out in 1961 when George Martin turned him down as a potential recording artist. Peter Sellers had achieved massive success with his comedy LPs made for the fledgling Beatles label Parlophone and other comedians were clamouring to jump on his bandwagon, but when Hill auditioned at Abbey Road, Martin was in no doubt that his strengths were as a pantomimist. 'Benny's talents seemed visual in origin' remembers Martin, 'so we never proceeded.' (quoted in Lewisohn, ibid).

The nine TV specials made by Hill between November 1964 and January 1966 are regarded now as among his finest. An imaginative visual routine from a show recorded in April 1965 achieved a longevity unforeseen at the time: two women making breakfast to the rhythms of a bossa-nova cha-ca-cha – slicing toast, cracking boiled eggs, filling a kettle. Nine years later Ernest Maxin recreated the piece for Morecambe & Wise, in a routine that has gone down in comedy history. This was either subconscious influence or mere co-incidence – in comedy there are very few new things under the sun – but coincidence or not, it is testimony to Hill's ability to come up with great enduring ideas. Another great physical routine was his 'Overweight Acrobat' which featured as a slot in his spoof of *Opportunity Knocks*. Accompanied by two agile young women, the portly Hill strains and gyrates and contorts in a progressively exhausting and pain-inducing display of hilarious gymnastics. Miming to a pleasant ballad, his voice ascending to a squeal as he attempts to lift one of the girls. In another piece he lampoons the very avant-garde French films that were such an influence on him, playing Mervyn Twit in a short film called *The Knock*. Hill – in his familiar persona of the lusty young man – pursues various females with unremitting lack of success, but achieves fulfilment with a marvellously black-wigged Patricia Hayes, with whom he performs an extended dumb-show depicting their courtship and married life. Odd gags abound, often very near-the-knuckle: a close-up of Hayes' face in what we are meant to believe are erotic contortions of pleasure is revealed to be the result of Hill tickling her feet. He keeps one shoe on in bed; in one sequence they both watch television, laughing and crying alternately but never together; it is a bizarre avant-garde sequence which at the time of recording received big laughs from the studio audience, but the precise target of which now seems lost in the mists of history.

Despite his reticence for live performing, his TV success led to offers of theatrical shows – *Music, Mirth & Mime!* – visual routines in particular proving popular hits, such as his fashion parade pantomime in which Hill plays a mannequin à la Marcel Marceau, and the 'Square-Dancing' routine, in which despite all the terpsichorean complications of the dance and his machinations, Hill always, to his chagrin, ends up with least attractive partner.

These TV shows reveal a Benny Hill not often commented on today: a Hill who saw himself in the avant-garde European visual tradition but who found himself feted, courted, lured, and finally trapped in British TV light entertainment. It's difficult now to perceive just how different his light entertainment fare was to that of his contemporaries such as Dickie Henderson, Max Bygraves or even Ken Dodd. Hill was Europeanising British music-hall, and not by accident but by design. One masterly extended mime sequence reveals Hill in a cinema watching a film, his silent actions providing a perfect comic counterpoint to the onscreen dialogue: the hero proposes to his girl and offers her a ring – Hill offers a sweet to the female seated next to him. As the girl describes her lover's face – strong chin, wonderful smile – Hill's facial expressions match her eulogy, predictably attracting the disapproval of his neighbours. The onscreen girl exhorts her fiancé to give up drink – so Hill tosses his carton of Kia-ora over his shoulder, causing a woman in the back row to scream. Gradually emboldened by the growing romance of the film, Hill sidles in for a kiss. Here the mime becomes more elaborate, an armed intruder onscreen being echoed by a cinema-goer behind Hill entering with an umbrella, which Hill takes for a gun and so sticks his hand up. His imagination now running riot, he flails out with his limbs right and left, attracting the attention of the cinema manager, and just as his celluloid alter ego is led out to be 'bumped off,' so too the real Hill is guided to the door marked 'Exit' by the manager.

It is an expert extended sequence of the kind not seen since Tati – indeed, the conceit of action providing mundane counterpoint to onscreen hyperbole is one seen in *Jour de Fête* when the fairground worker adopts the body-language of the cowboy as he watches an (unseen) Western through the flaps of a tent. Years later Rowan Atkinson would devote a quarter of a Mr Bean episode to a similar scenario, with perhaps less inventive results.

For Hill's shows abounded in inventiveness: the reversing of stock news footage five years before Python and fifteen before *Not the Nine O'Clock News*; a dancing duo in leder-hosen that builds into a fight; and an extraordinary extended sequence from one of his shows in 1965 involving a television that literally comes to life. With eyes forming on its screen and talons growing out of its legs, the gogglebox rampages through the house, pursuing its occupants and killing them with a deadly spray. It's surely not fantastical to infer that this depiction of TV as a ghastly succubus reflected Hill's growing attitude towards the medium. By the mid-60s he was getting restless – he took to describing TV as little more than 'photographed radio,' and set out his ambition to work in films firmly and unequivocally.

'I realised that I'd been making a very comfortable living on television for fifteen years,' he said after he'd been voted BBC Personality of the Year in 1965, 'and if I wanted to meet other challenges it would have to be elsewhere.'

*

Hill wasn't alone among British TV comedians to attempt the leap from parochial to international stardom – after all, Norman Wisdom and Peter Sellers had done it. Morecambe & Wise too were making forays into cinema, with mixed results. Their big-screen appearances in *The Intelligence Men, That Riviera Touch* and *The Magnificent Two* were creditable, though lacked the charm and frisson that their TV live audience shows possessed.

Hill sensed it was his time. In an untypically revealing interview for *TV Times* in 1968, he said 'I don't get excited any more. I'm doing the same thing as I was seventeen or eighteen years ago. Nothing's changed except the money. What I'd really like to do is direct feature films.'

But this confession was made after his two years of struggle to 'crack' motion pictures – revealing that, on balance, his attempt was a disappointment. It was an attempt that began with *Chitty Chitty Bang Bang* and his fruitful partnership with Dick Van Dyke. As a result of his fine performance in that international blockbuster (many routines of which he wrote) he signed a deal with Paramount, and acquired the soubriquet 'The Peter Sellers (Hollywood) can afford.'

They may have been able to afford him, but they didn't know how to use him. His cameos in *The Italian Job* and *Those Magnificent Men in their Flying Machines* increased his profile but did not launch him into the higher echelons of the film business.

It was a rude awakening. Whereas in the world of TV Hill had commanded his domain, in the world of international film-making

Bonded through a mutual adoration of the silent greats, Dick Van Dyke asked Benny Hill to write much of the comic material for Chitty Chitty Bang Bang *(1968,) including the famous 'live-puppet' routine. Underrated now, Hill's visual work on TV was pioneering – he was the first comedian to include filmed sketches and injected the tropes of Continental mime into the British sketch show.*

he found himself a small fish, and didn't much like it. He argued with Paramount when they insisted he dub his character in *The Italian Job* – (he'd performed in Yorkshire dialect but the US bigwigs wanted British RP) – and he argued with Blake Edwards. Sellers' director had invited Hill to a meeting and during the conversation asked him – somewhat patronisingly – if he could do a French accent. Hill replied tersely, 'Would that be a Parisian, Southern, or *Français du Midi*?' (quoted in Lewisohn, ibid).

Edwards regarded him for a long moment through the silver curlicues of his cigar smoke then replied equally tersely, 'M. Hill, God doesn't like a smart-ass.'

It was the end of Hill's film career. Or would have been, had he not been possessed of sterner stuff. Spurned by Hollywood, he returned to England and signed up with a small company, Fanfare Films, owned by veteran producer George H Brown. His aim? To make a silent film. His hero was still Jacques Tati, and on his numerous trips to Paris he'd often stay at the Hôtel des Tuileries Montana on the rue Saint Roch where he'd attempt, as he told Kenneth Passingham in a 1968 interview with *TV Times* 'to crash into French films ... The French go in for a lot of funny films of the sort that are badly neglected by the British,' he added, making it clear where his ambitions lay.

He actually met Tati, though oddly not in Paris but in London. Friend Peter Charlesworth remembers: 'Tati was shooting in the east end of London and Benny went down there to meet him. They spent a good few hours together, talking about the business of making comedy films. Benny came back and told me he'd had a marvellous afternoon – it was a big moment in his life.' (quoted in Lewisohn, ibid).

The Waiters, Hill's debut solo-authored and directed film, was a curate's egg. From the outset he set out to emulate not only Tati but the silent comics and directors of yesteryear. Co-star Pamela Cundell recalls him saying to her 'We're going to make a film without any words, a silent film, like in the old days. It'll be a laugh and we'll have a good time.' The film co-starred the sublime character actor David Battley, who alongside Hill played one of the eponymous waiters whose incompetence and shenanigans wreak havoc in a middle-class household. Even he was critical of the result: 'To my mind,' recalls Battley, 'none of the people were acting properly. Even in a ridiculous comedy you wouldn't have people who were being treated like that just sitting there quietly. That was the director's fault. I was (also) a bit disappointed in the way it was shot,' he continues, 'Some of the gags needed more impact. It could have been a lot more slick.' (quoted in Lewisohn, ibid).

Hill's character in the thirty-minute silent was altogether harder and meaner than his jovial TV persona – one suspects he may have been trying to emulate W C Fields. The movie is memorable for its introduction of what was to become one of Hill's most ubiquitous pieces of comic business, the *slap*. Where in later years it was just the old bald Jackie Wright who would be the recipient of Hill's harsh patting, in *The Waiters* no one was safe from the palm of his hand – Battley, the guests, the other staff, you name it.

It is clear that Hill had pinned all his hopes of becoming an international visual comedian on the odd little movie, but his ambitions were not realised. With a delayed and limited release (as the support for *Catch 22 !*) *The Waiters* foundered and has become a curiosity of Hill's canon. Biographer Mark Lewisohn's summation is perhaps the most accurate: '... an unfunny and ultimately disturbing piece, dreary and lacking both atmosphere and comedy invention. It was not in Tati's league.'

*

But even when he was being wooed back by TV, Hill clung stubbornly to his dream: 'I don't want to do another TV series,' he said in 1968 whilst his agent Richard Stone was in negotiations with the BBC, 'I really want to develop in films as a writer and performer. But an occasional one-shot TV, that's fine.'

The occasional one-shot became fifteen years of television stardom – not on the BBC, but on ITV. After three more specials, he decamped to Thames Television in 1969 – cunningly securing a commission for his next silent film project as part of the deal.

Disgusted by his flight to the opposition, the BBC responded by removing Hill's portrait from the hallowed walls of Television Centre and erasing the last three shows he made for them.

Hill wasn't bothered – he'd been given *carte blanche* to make his follow-up silent movie. For him this was the *raison-d'être* of his move to Thames, not the series at all. Indeed, when promoting the switch to independent TV he barely mentioned the series, choosing to speak only about his next big venture onto the silent screen. He told *Reveille*, 'I have already taken a step in the direction I want to go. I am playing in and directing my next film, which is being made by Thames Television. My directing job is the attainment of a very strong ambition. In fact, if I made it as a director I would be quite happy to bow out as a performer.'

Eddie in August is an altogether more accomplished work than *The Waiters*. The spirit of Tati abounds. Episodic – a month in the life of a sad,

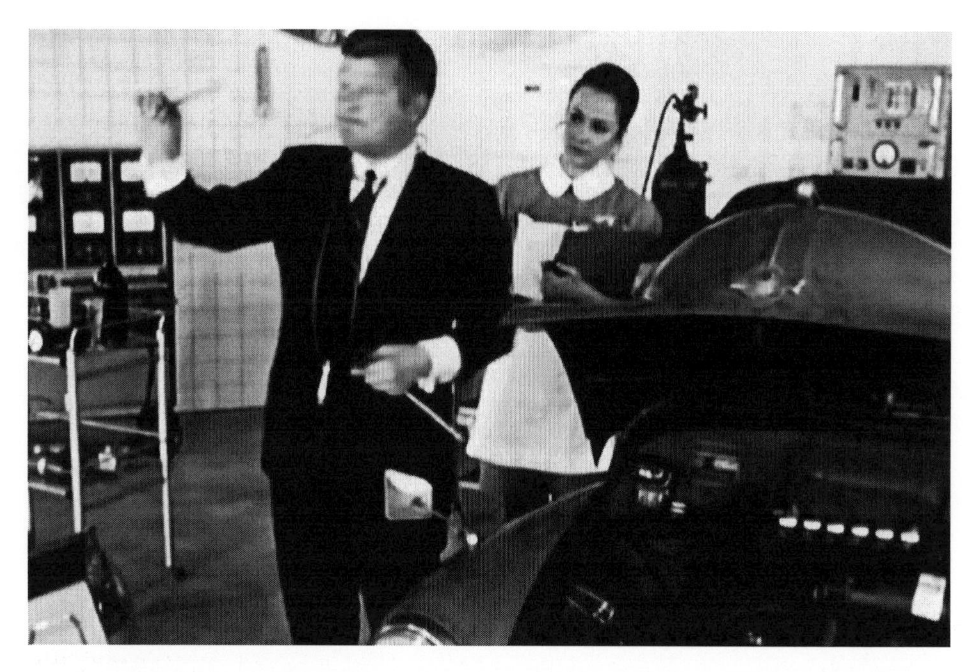

Another example of the 'object switch' gag, here in Benny Hill's second attempt at a solo all-visual film, Eddie in August *(1970), he takes his car in for repairs and the garage becomes a hospital, his vehicle an ailing patient.*

lonely, love-seeking bachelor – the film contains familiar Hill-tropes that would certainly not pass muster in today's climate (the routine of four men attempting to look up a woman's skirt for example), but the gags are inventive and the pace consistent. From the opening, mistake gags and reveal gags are dominant: a road-sweeping van passes Eddie's basement flat, squirting water through the open window. A flustered and soaked Eddie wakes to see a dog on the pavement looking in. Eddie is about to administer a slap to the rear end of a woman cleaning her doorstep and almost immediately transforms it into a salute to the revealed husband who steps out menacingly from inside the apartment.

Again, like Tati the plot is minimal: Hill plays his ubiquitous young man in search of love. If in structure it resembles *M Hulot's Holiday* – there is even a tennis playing sequence – Hill's character is no Hulot drifting through each tableau undesirous of meaningful contact with society. Although he is an outsider, Eddie is constantly attempting to enter the normal world of relationships and success: approaching girls, acquiring a dog as an ice-breaker, buying a new shirt. Like Chaplin he is a loser but nevertheless aspirational – there is even a Chaplin-esque fantasy sequence where Hill imagines he is an ace tennis player impressing the girl of his fancy by defeating her boyfriend opponent; we then dissolve to the reality in which he is actually being trounced by a suave louche rival, who – to add insult to injury – even smokes a pipe on court whilst thrashing him. Further evidence of the Chaplin influence is in the picnic scene where Hill's stomach emits embarrassing noises after gulping a cup of tea – a nod perhaps to the Tramp's gag in *Modern Times* in which Chaplin is seated alongside a female prison official whose tea-sipping produces similar sounds.

In a finely played scene with a dodgy car salesman (Tommy Godfrey, stalwart of many a 60s comedy), Hill buys a clapped-out car. As the transaction progresses more and more bits come off the vehicle – a bit of wire here, a windscreen wiper there – topped with a Laurel & Hardy style gag when the car drives off leaving a trail of mechanical innards on the tarmac. The fantasy element is pursued when Hill imagines he is a top surgeon operating on the car, with his paramour as his glamorous assistant nurse, an extended sequence in which the ailing car coughs and splutters like a suffering patient and even gives a sample of oil in a flask.

Eddie in August contains some good visual gags but at bottom it is Hill's character, or rather lack of it, that lets the piece down. As Chaplin said, 'nothing transcends character,' and you can string as many clever gags together as you like but if there is no comic heart at its centre – a finely-drawn hero with subtle light and shade – then you are lost. Hill is anodyne, charmless, and although we are invited to sympathise with his plight and his quest, our empathy is never quite ignited. The fact that (a leitmotiv throughout Hill's work) he is tied to an unattractive woman whilst lusting after the obvious beauty – is a trait that evokes a smirk in some but repulsion in most.

Eddie in August was Hill's final attempt to establish himself as a comedy film *auteur*. The world, it seemed, preferred him as a hybrid of TV variety entertainer, monologist, comic-singer, and occasional creator of inspired pieces of mime that maintained his connection with European dumb-show and vintage silent screen comedy. Despite the lukewarm reception to his work in *The Waiters* and *Eddie in August* these silent films were templates for the kind of comedy that would fill his Thames show – cerebral visual sketches, inventive mimes and, in what would go down in television history as his speciality, manic chases. The famous 'yakety-sax' pursuit of Hill by scantily clad girls, policemen and other authority figures has become his signature, and is of course a homage to the under-cranked camera technique which began in the Mack Sennett era, evinced by Hill's scripts which specified 'Go to 6fps with police ladies chasing Benny,' – where 'fps' is 'frames per second.'

His series with Thames ran for twenty years between 1969 and 1989 and became one of the richest repositories of inventive pantomime anywhere in the world, doubtless the prime reason for its gigantic international success.

He hit the ground running – the very first sketch in the first show broadcast on November 19 1969 being the silent Chaplinesque 'Wishing Well'. Strolling past a magic well with his frumpy wife, he tosses a coin in and she transforms into a young beauty. Hill then subverts himself by having the young beauty toss a coin in to produce a muscle-bound hunk. Just when you don't know where the tag is going to come, the muscle-man then tosses a coin in to make the young beauty disappear, and takes the arm of Benny who, with suitably raised eyebrows, flings a final coin into the well to restore his frumpy wife – and they exit arm in arm.

*

On December 28 2006 Channel 4 broadcast the documentary *Is Benny Hill Still Funny?* The programme featured an audience that comprised a cross-section of young adults who had little or no knowledge of Hill. Participants were asked to watch a 30-minute compilation that included examples of Hill's humour from both his BBC and ITV shows. The responses and results demonstrated that none of the sample of viewers took offence at any of the sketches shown. And the most popular? Hill's silent 'Wishing Well' sketch.

The visual sketches in his TV series had a joyous uninhibitedness, a confidence and pace that the films lacked. Hill was at his best perhaps when he shrugged off the attempt to emulate the genius of Tati and was true to himself and his origins: the broad, brash, laugh-a-minute world of 1950s variety. Some of the funniest physical routines were his historical lampoons such as the fifteen-minute 'Robin Hood' sketch in which Hill plays a camp (yet determinedly heterosexual and lusty) robber, aided by an incompetent band of men. These long visual items were invariably shot on location, usually under-cranked, and utilised the eccentric and visually hilarious support actors Henry McGee, Bob Todd and Jackie Wright, a motley repertory company based on Hill's admiration for Laurel & Hardy's use of James Finlayson, Charlie Hall and Billy Gilbert.

A question-mark hovers over much of Hill's legacy. But there is an argument to be made that his leering attitude to women was not so much his own invention but a product of the times. All British comedy at that time seemed to have 'leering at women' as its dominant trope: it was a brief, crazy era in light entertainment when comedy took a look at permissiveness and male lust and fashioned a take on it. How else can comedy have a reaction to a social and cultural movement such as 'sexual liberation' but by lampooning repressed men? The Hill leer was not simply of its time but was also perennial. Hill was a sexually-aware Harry Langdon, a leering Pan or Bacchus, childish and uninhibited in his love and pursuit of women but perennially doomed never to succeed. His comic persona was a refraction of his own life, a grotesque magnification of a patently visible arrested development. One could say that, like him or not, Hill's comedy persona was actually a searingly honest depiction of his inner life, a baring of his soul just as truthful as many a modern 'confessional' comedian.

CHAPTER 14

Diehards III: Visual Comedy on Stage & Screen 1960 to 1970

The two major British protagonists of the silent comedy genre in the 60s were Eric Sykes and Peter Sellers, whose contributions were so significant they deserve chapters in themselves. But there were numerous other comics who experimented with dialogue-free films whose work paved away for the popularity of the later more well-known features like *The Plank* and *The Party*. It is to Sellers, however, that we turn first, for it was an early work of his that ushered in – or at the very least heralded – the new wave.

The gestation of *The Running, Jumping and Standing Still Film* of 1959/60 is, in typical Milligan/Sellers fashion, disputable, the two giant Goon egos both laying claim to being the sole begetter of the first completely silent British film for thirty years. In January 1959 *The Goon Show* had reached the end of its extraordinary tenure as the zaniest show on radio, and Spike stated that in spring of that year he said to Sellers (who had bought a 16mm cine camera) 'Look, films are being made for millions – I think we can make one (not very long) for – how much does a cameraman cost? He said 'Seventy-five pounds.' So we paid that, and the sound engineer was fifty. We had about twenty ragged characters in a van and we just drove up the Great North Road until we saw a suitable field … We just went to a hill, and I wrote the script out, what I wanted roughly, and had just to improvise how to do it.' ('Spiked,' *Daily Express*, February 13 1960). While acknowledging that Richard Lester had 'given excellent advice, and helped with the editing,' he told biographer Pauline Scudamore that he directed it. This is contradicated by designer and director Joe McGrath, however, who told Humphrey Carpenter that Spike had only been there for one day's filming, and that Lester had directed from the outset.

Peter Sellers had his own take on the matter. In *Films and Filming* (March 1960) he said: 'I only made (the film) as a demonstration to show what can be done without dialogue. I want to inject this thing into British comedy.' Ten years later he was saying pretty much the same thing: 'It all started when Spike Milligan and I once said we wanted to

Milligan and Sellers kick-start the Silent Renaissance of the 1960s by messing around in a field off the A1 and inadvertently making the first underground art-house movie of the decade. Plotless and surreal, this was Bunuel meets the Marx Brothers, narrative-free abstract comedy made not by university intellectuals but by ex-forces variety comedians. Already a major player in international movies, by choosing to make a silent film in 1959 Sellers was already dropping hints of his ambitions to become a British Tati, evinced by his future work in the 'Pink Panther' films and The Party.

experiment in visual humour ... We shot ideas, that was all, and linked them together.' After the film was shot Spike went off to Australia and Lester and Sellers apparently edited the movie 'in (his) bedroom at Whetstone,' not only adding the credit 'Devised by Peter Sellers' but also headlining the film with the soubriquet 'A Sellers/British Lion Production.'

The Running, Jumping and Standing Still Film bears hallmarks of both the gravity-free zaniness of *Hellzapoppin* and the surreal short films of Louis Bunuel. More accurately, it is of course, Goon-Vision, a pictorial expression of the abstract radio comedy Milligan and Sellers had been creating since 1951. They'd tried bringing their wild streams-of-consciousness to television before, with mixed success – *Down Among the Z Men* (1952), *The Idiot Weekly (price 2d)*, and *A Show Called Fred* (both 1956). These early shows attempted to capture the free-form surrealism of *The Goon Show*, and though studio-bound and largely verbal, contained occasional imaginative visual vignettes. Dick Lester directed *A Show Called Fred* so it was natural to ask him to helm their first film proper.

Untethered to plot or central character (Sellers plays a squire complete with plus fours, binoculars and blunderbuss who wanders as a detached observer through the action) the film is a series of unconnected sight-gags and non-sequiturs. With a cast including Mario Fabrizi, Leo McKern, Noman Rossington, Graham Stark and David Lodge as well as Milligan and Sellers, it was only after the film was entered into various international festivals and, to the surprise of its makers, won prizes (and an Oscar nomination) that Sellers began talking of it as if it had been pre-planned as an avant-garde abstract comic masterpiece.

In reality, of course, it had been a spontaneous, jazzy outburst of ideas dreamt up either on the day or not long before: as Lester said, 'it was really just a chance for Peter to play around with his camera.'

As Sellers never strictly wrote a thing in his life it is fair to say that the script – such as it was – had to be Milligan's; and the gags, assuredly, are pure Spike: a man holds a stylus onto a gramophone record and runs round the machine with increasing speed to make the vinyl play; a big hand in close-up beckons a distant Graham Stark who gradually comes closer to the camera only to be punched out by a massive boxing-glove; Leo McKern attempts to play the violin but his music-stand is miles away so he has to read the music through a telescope; a parlour maid scrubs a patch of grass; a woman sits for a portrait with her face covered in painting-by-number sections.

The entire film inhabits the crazy Edwardian attic of Milligan's mind, and like *The Goon Show* is stuffed full of turn-of-the-century tropes – old gramophones, deerstalkers, brass bedsteads, circus weight-lifters. 'The broad framework,' said Sellers, 'was one person looking at another person looking at another person, and it carried on like that. Each person brought you into the next scene.' Shot on 16mm and blown up, the resulting blurriness added to its dreamlike quality, and lent the film an ethereal look. Though Milligan disapproved of the jazz soundtrack added by Lester, one can't help but conclude the director was right, for the free-form music perfectly complements the images.

Its big impact derives from its freshness: here were the new kids on the block, the Pythons of the Beat Generation, the Sex Pistols of film comedy. Home movie or not – or precisely *because* it had the quality of a home movie – it couldn't but make a splash. With its startling jump-cuts, bizarre imagery, and nod towards the film styles of the silent age, it fed a certain youthful rebellious streak that is the joyous fuel of many a cultural movement – and all these factors made it the odd, quirky, very British-yet-European icon of the Silent Renaissance. Tellingly, it became a favourite of the Beatles, who promptly hired Lester to direct their first feature, *A Hard Day's Night* (1964).

*

While Sellers and Milligan were creating surreal dialogue-free comedy on a field off the Great North Road, ATV were filming a surprisingly innovative sitcom starring singer Anthony Newley. *The Strange World of Gurney Slade*, written by future Morecambe & Wise writers Dick Hills and Sid Green, is a startling prediction of late-60s surrealism, a kind of comedy version of Patrick McGoohan's *The Prisoner*. Though containing dialogue, the six-part series, broadcast in October-November 1960, contains long stretches of pure vision, and has Newley reject the confines of an orthodox domestic sitcom by refusing to speak to his 'family' and walking out of the house/studio set, past the TV camera and a flabbergasted floor manager, and out onto the streets of London. There then follows a Tati-esque drift or *dérive*, during which Newley falls in love with a shop window mannequin, dances with a vacuum cleaner, and engages in social interaction with a dustbin. This is Lewis Carroll meets Jacques Tati, and is remarkable for its early escape from and destruction of already-accepted television tropes. This is Sid Hills and Dick Green bursting out of the restrictive confines of early TV production, several years before Dennis Potter: all three writers are saying 'hang on, can't TV be like *this*?'

For ITV the answer was – no, it can't. Proving too much for a prime-time early evening audience, from episode three onwards *The Strange World of Gurney Slade* was shunted to a late-night slot, and the series quietly expired. But as with many innovative creative works, since its demise it has acquired a cult following, and is appreciated now as a vital part of the visual renaissance.

*

A more orthodox example from that exciting period of pantomimic experimentation was Bob Kellett's *A Home of Your Own* (1964). What started life as a corporate film intended to advertise Terson's building firm – a typical company 'review of the year' – the silent half-hour achieved success way beyond its remit, managing to gain a theatrical release through British Lion. Producer Bob Kellett recalled years later (in an interview with Mark Wright on the DVD release of the film) that he wanted to 'show the truth of what happens on a building site – which is usually chaotic.' It was a classic silent comedy setting – back in 1920 Buster Keaton had made house-building comedy *One Week*, ditto Laurel & Hardy in 1928 with *The Finishing Touch*. In hindsight it seems that Kellett attracted a stellar cast of the comedy stalwarts of the day, but at the time of course these were comic actors on the cusp between early cameos and later household-name status: Ronnie Barker (whose role in the film we discuss in a late chapter devoted solely to him), Bernard Cribbins, Richard Briers, Peter Butterworth, Bill Fraser, Fred Emney. Cribbins and Fraser were perhaps the biggest names at the time – but the whole enterprise proves that there was a host of performers eager to take part in a purely visual movie.

Written and directed by Jay Lewis, director of seminal 1962 British film *Live Now Pay Later* starring Ian Hendry, *A Home of Your Own* became, perhaps inadvertently, a satire of British working life of the time, and tapped in to the 'workplace' comedy genre that the Boultings had established with such success in *I'm Alright Jack*. A building-site is particularly rich territory for visual gags: before laying water-pipes Peter Butterworth goes divining with a rod; a short-sighted Bernard Cribbins has a running gag as a stone-mason, whose repeated attempts to carve the name of the house in a block of slate result in escalating mishaps. The architect, played by Ronnie Stevens, dives over patches of cement and has his car hoisted fifty feet in the air by crane: the film is packed with the kinds of gags not seen since the 1920s, with accompanying filming techniques from the era, such as reverse-action, all with a jaunty musical soundtrack by Ron Goodwin.

It certainly resonated with the audience, for when this humble 'corporate' film was shown as support at the premiere for *A Shot in the Dark* starring Peter Sellers and George Sanders, the latter leaned forward to Sellers during the film and whispered 'this is much funnier than ours ...'

The success of *A Home of Your Own*, in addition to perhaps influencing Sellers and the director Blake Edwards (who would have been at the premiere) to make their own wholly visual movie, also impacted on distributors, establishing a tradition throughout the 60s and 70s of showing a short comedy as support to the main feature in British cinemas: a tradition that only died out in the 80s.

Producer Bob Kellett followed up *A Home of Your Own* the following year with 'British holidaymakers abroad' silent comedy *San Ferry Ann*, similarly featuring a colourful host of comedy character actors – Barbara Windsor, David Lodge, Graham Stark, Joan Sims, Rodney Bewes, Wilfrid Brambell and Ron Moody. With a screenplay written by Kellett and the film directed by young talent Jeremy Summers who had previously directed *The Punch and Judy Man* for Hancock, *San Ferry Ann* followed the peradventures of a motley group of comic types – pretty girl hiker and her gigantically rucksacked partner (Barbara Windsor and Ronnie

Stevens), voyeuristic old man (Brambell) young newlywed (Bewes) – and pursued their sunny mishaps with no narrative save the natural shape and structure of a vacation.

More ambitious than *A Home of Your Own,* (it ran to 55 minutes), it hits the ground running by establishing each character with set-up gags: the besotted Bewes and his new wife romantically engrossed in each other to such an extent that their Morgan drives itself up the ramp into the ferry while they are locked together in a fond embrace; Stevens constantly propelled onto his back by his huge back-pack so he resembles a turtle; David Lodge the pipe-smoking patriarch in charge of long-suffering wife Joan Sims and their VW camper van. With a fabulous score by Burnell Whibley (conducted Ron Goodwin), an opening credit sequence sees a French border control officer laughing in turn at each of the characters' passport photos. It is difficult to comprehend now but this was the mining of new comedy territory, the 60s being the first time many ordinary people began travelling abroad, and what became staple material of comedy feature films and sitcoms for years to come – Brits overseas – in *San Ferry Ann* was being tackled for the first time. So the engine of the gags are Duty Free Drink, Sunbathing, Unintelligible Tannoy Announcements (a gag that reaches back to both Laurel & Hardy's *Berth Marks* of 1929 indeed the opening sequence of *M Hulot's Holiday.* The gags come thick and fast: Ronnie Stevens almost toppling over the side of the ferry; David Lodge bizarrely thinking his wife has had a baby (she is simply holding it); Wilfrid Brambell in a never-ending quest for a patch of unbroken sunshine to sunbathe in; seasickness. Punctuating the drifting plot are visual highlights such as Ronnie Stevens and Barbara Windsor tying to put up a tent in a wind-storm; Brambell inadvertently pitching his tent on the traffic island of a busy roundabout; Warren Mitchell as a French waiter offering Fred Emney a live frog in a restaurant; Ron Moody and Wilfrid Brambell getting sozzled in a bar then crawling through mud to rescue a tent from the harbour; Rodney Bewes and his new wife emerging blinking into the sunlight after spending the entire holiday indoors.

These are all comic tropes that would have been recognisable but fresh to a mid-60s British audience. The film climaxes with a traffic pile-up mismanaged by bumbling gendarme Graham Stark, caused – naturally – by a French onion seller spilling his wares across the highway. A crane-shot ascends to reveal the same collective chaos as characterised the close of many a Laurel & Hardy picture: everyone crying from the onions, or slipping on the onions – until the offending vendor takes his bike, tosses it into the river, and dives in after it.

There are some nice touches in *San Ferry Ann* but, perhaps understandably, Jeremy Summers, the director, seems to build to the gags far too quickly. Understandably, because he had indeed been criticised for applying too much pace to the climactic sequence of *The Punch and Judy Man*, in which a group fight at a civic event picks up speed a tad too briskly. In comparison, Tati sets out each of his jokes in a very measured and leisurely way, a studied pace that magnifies the punchlines: *San Ferry Ann* tends to dash gags off in a slightly perfunctory manner. This niggling criticism apart, Kellett can nevertheless be afforded the title of an early founder of the new genre of the *sound effect comedy*. Without *A Home of Your Own* and *San Ferry Ann*, arguably that there would have been no silent Eric Sykes films or silent Ronnie Barker films.

*

On TV, *Goon Show* co-founder Michael Bentine was busy divesting the crazy visual contents of his mind in a BBC series that combined mind-boggling Terry-Gilliam-esque animation nine years before Python with wild Goon-esque conceits in *It's a Square World*, that ran from 1960-64 and won a BAFTA and a Press Award at Montreux. Memorable highlights included BBC TV Centre being blasted into space, miniature plays supposedly acted by invisible fleas with accompanying sound effects, and the source of the River Thames discovered to be a leaking tap.

*

Over in France, a clown every bit as talented as Jacques Tati (but who was neglected until 2012 primarily because of prolonged distribution problems) was making a series of short visual films and features that earned him the sobriquet the 'French Buster Keaton.' Pierre Etaix was one-time assistant to Jacques Tati, and an aspiring artist and clown. He worked on *Mon Oncle*, but temperament and personality clashes led to him leaving Tati after the movie's success, together with a fellow-employee, Jean Claude Carrière, who had been taken on to write the novelisation of *M Hulot's Holiday*. Etaix and Carrière set up on their own to write and star in a series of visual shorts.

The tradition of the visual short in France had persisted since the war, and right up to the end of his life Tati praised the genre as essential training ground for a writer and director. With Jean Claude Carrière directing, Etaix proceeded to create some of the most marvellous and accomplished visual comedies of the 1960s. His first, *Rupture* (1960) has – understandably – a similar ambience to Tati's work: though shot in a less

Out of the shadow of the great Tati, French comedian Pierre Etaix went on to make a series of highly original films in the 60s, bringing to the big screen the minimalist corporeal mime developed in France in the 1920s.

Having emerged from the shadow of Tati – Etaix worked as his assistant and co-writer on Mon Oncle *– Etaix bloomed into an original clown in his own right, producing a string of whimsical and dreamlike silent masterpieces throughout the 1960s. Here in perhaps his greatest work,* Yoyo *(1965), dream becomes reality when a thirsty butler takes a drink from an oil-painting – a gag Jerry Lewis emulated later in* Cracking Up *(1981).*

painterly way it is nevertheless very contained, with subtle movement, clean precise actions, and enhanced soundtrack applied post-filming. Etaix's persona in his films is delicate and charming; he is a dapper smartly dressed little man with a warmth and ordinariness that is both studied yet endearing – a well-meaning everyman, an outsider like Hulot but less eccentric and more affable. He is a loser, but his defeats are humble and everyday – a hook falls off a coat-hanger, a fountain pen spills ink over the paper when he is trying to write an important letter. Small surreal moments pepper his films; in *Rupture* he blows a kiss to a picture of his lover, and it promptly falls over. The film takes place almost wholly in one room with him seated at a desk, and is a music-hall act in everything but name. This is comedy of the minutiae of life: the escalating squeak of an opening desk, the loss of a nib down the tube of a pen, the loss of the pen in the lining of his jacket, the difficulty of putting a stamp on an envelope. Etaix has the delicate expressive hands of the expert mime – he toys with the handle of a drawer, brings out a revolver, and just as we think he is about to commit suicide, he lights a cigarette with it. But there is a twist – having lost the love of life, he picks his way across the wreckage of his little office, sits on a large rocking chair – and his promptly propelled out of the open second-floor window.

The plot of his Oscar-winning second short, *Heureux Anniversaire* in 1962, is simplicity itself – a man attempts to get home to celebrate his anniversary. Watching the film now, one cannot help thinking it must have grown out of discussions with Tati for there are themes and routines that will find an echo in Tati's work; chiefly the comedy of traffic. The humorous possibilities of the new automotive age were to supply Tati with the entire plot of 1971's *Trafic* – it is clear Etaix got there first. A man having a shave in a barber's shop shifts his car so Etaix can move his, then cannot get back in to the parking place so is forced to drive round and round, still wearing shaving foam and white barber's gown. Though traffic jams had been mined for comedy purposes since Laurel & Hardy's *Two Tars*, Etaix comes up with some inventive gags – the driver in pilot's leather helmet and goggles 'zooming' forward a mere two inches, piles of cigarette stubs in the road indicating the smoker has been stuck in the jam for hours; one driver reading a book, another fast asleep; a businessman catching up with his office work while in the driving seat; someone even washing his car. Nipping out to buy a bottle of champagne for his patiently waiting wife, Etaix returns to find his car wedged in by two other vehicles. Resorting to climbing into the (empty) adjacent car, he is then accused of attempting to steal it.

As Etaix's epic cross-Paris journey becomes fraught with setback after setback, we intercut with his wife waiting at home and watch her gradually become tempted by the sumptuous anniversary dinner she has prepared. Soon plates are empty, bottles are drained, and ashtrays are full. While Etaix buys a very tall sunflower for his wife that he has to stick out of his sun-roof, the man from the barber's has a lovely pay-off, for when he finally abandons his car and makes his way back to the hairdresser's – still in his white robe and face covered in foam – he finds the shop closed and the barber gone. Finally making it home – brandishing an exceedingly shortened sunflower for it has been severed by the closure of the sun-roof, Etaix finds his wife slumped asleep on the detritus of the dinner, and we fade to iris as he nibbles on a piece of bread. *Heureux Anniversaire* is a delightful visual gem rightly awarded Oscar for Best Short Film of 1962, and the win kick-started a productive career in that decade for Etaix, as he went on to make five feature films and two further shorts.

Etaix's first feature, *The Suitor* (1963) is highly Keaton-esque in that it establishes his persona as unworldly and dreamlike with a strong fantasy-life: to emphasise the character's outsiderishness he even begins the film with outer space imagery, as if to misdirect the audience into thinking the protagonist is an alien (as Curtis and Atkinson would do in the opening credits of *Mr Bean*). In *The Suitor* Etaix plays a married man whose yearning for the fantastical, unattainable image of female beauty overtakes his reality: in a precisely-choreographed breakfast sequence he gazes, rapt, at a woman singing on the TV, while his real wife attempts to give him breakfast. His fixed gaze never wavering from the television, he spreads jam on a saucer, drinks from the milk jug, bites on a china plate etc, all without averting his focus on the dream-like beauty of the woman on the screen.

Although a comedy, *The Suitor* is shot through with a melancholy, and plays out a serious theme: that dreams are often more powerful than reality, and divert us from appreciating what we have. There are many stand-out scenes, one such being the hide and seek sequence, a beautifully fluid series of consequences with Etaix first choosing a tree behind which two lovers are already hidden, then hiding directly in the eye-line of a painter who promptly depicts him on his canvas. Etaix runs past the painting and seeing himself in the picture, helpfully rubs it out while the artist is not looking, then he borrows another of the artist's pictures to hide behind, leaving it on the grass behind a man – who lies back and imprints the freshly-painted work on his leather jacket.

Gags with consequences pepper the film: in a restaurant Etaix attempts to engage the attention of a beautiful woman; asking her for a light he mistakenly takes her lipstick by mistake and rests it on an ashtray next to the stub of a cigar, the owner of which then picks up the lipstick in mistake for the cigar and takes a puff that naturally smears his mouth – at which point his wife approaches and slaps his face. The pace of this sequence could so easily be laboured, resulting in us predicting each step before it happens, but Etaix and Carrière's direction is so rhythmic and exact that we cannot see the next moment coming, resulting in comic surprise and delight. In another sequence Etaix puts earplugs in to blot out intrusive piano-playing from downstairs: we the audience are plunged into his silence, and when the father of his sweetheart enters the room and delivers a prolonged and heartfelt 'man-to-man' speech, complete with gestures and impassioned entreaties – of course, we are oblivious to every word and the entire monologue is delivered in dumb-show.

Yoyo (1966) was Etaix's second feature film and is rightly acclaimed as his masterpiece. A more surreal and stylised picture than *The Suitor*, *Yoyo* is an almost fairy-tale fable and a hymn to the love of Etaix's life, the circus. In an extraordinary first act Yoyo (Etaix), a vastly wealthy man, is seen to live alone in a huge chateau, attended upon by an army of servants all of whom move regimentally around the palace in highly meticulous unison. The first twenty minutes of the movie are entirely silent save for the enhanced use of non-diegetic and diegetic sound applied post-filming. Doors creak, footsteps squeak, hands brushed together make a noise like sandpaper. There are passages of dreamlike surrealism: a weary butler pauses beside an ornate still life of bottles, glasses and fruit – and idly reaches a hand inside the painting to bring out the carafe and pour himself a drink. The arrival of a circus interrupts this opulent *ennui*, and amongst the troupe is a girl Yoyo was once in love with (played by his real-life wife Anne Fratellini), who has given birth to their son, a marvellous young clown played deftly by Philippe Dionnet. In a sublime scene Young Yoyo roams about the chateau, hides from the servants, and is rescued at a window by a circus elephant.

Yoyo Senior is inspired to run off and join them on the road, and there follows the most lyrical and Jean-Renoir-like episodes in the film, not without humour but full of a romanticism not seen since Chaplin. Reunited with his lady-love and son, the three set off along the dusty golden lanes of France – a three-person touring circus – and pursue a life of rustic bliss. The travelling montage, interspersed with the performances of the little troupe in village squares, is expertly directed and contains a fluid Keaton-style routine, beginning with Etaix in the driving seat passing a lighter to his wife at the back of the caravan by placing it on a fence-post at the side of the road, then her getting it back to him by placing it onto the rim of a passing cyclist's hat, who then slowly overtakes the car, enabling Young Yoyo to reach out and reclaim it. The spirit of Keaton is even more in evidence seconds later when Etaix crawls up and over the top of the caravan to kiss his wife, then on his way back is scooped up by the overhanging branch of a tree, left suspended in mid-air, then drops on to a passing hay-cart which then draws up alongside the car enabling him to hop back on his vehicle. These comical stunts are all performed in long-shot, with Etaix exhibiting an athletic grace Keaton would have admired.

There is a passage of time in which Young Yoyo grows up – and is then also played, obviously, by Etaix. The War comes and goes in montage (allowing a marvellous gag where a soldier is seen dodging around ostensibly to avoid gunfire, but actually playing in goal in a football match – diving not for cover but for the ball).

Here the picture becomes episodic and resembles Fellini's work: the young clown grows up and abandons the circus (his parents have vanished, presumably victims of the war but this is unsaid) and returns to his father's chateau, which he restores to its former glory by prostituting his clowning talents on TV and in the merchandising of comedy props and accessories. But like father, like son – a lover begins to pull him back to the life of the circus, and the final act of the film is a party in the newly restored chateau – a very Great Gatsby affair where Young Yoyo, now a tycoon, invites the great and the good into his palace. The film ends in a delightful circularity, with the same elephant that rescued him from the chateau years before when he was a boy, now rescuing him again, appearing at a window and carrying him off from the false life of wealth and commercial prestige back to the simple, pure life of the small circus.

Despite the serious underlying message of the final act – and indeed the entire film – it is nevertheless packed with inventive sight gags: at the party a reporter mistakes a champagne flute for a microphone; a lady mistakes her own beads for grapes and pops them into her mouth – whilst it is a moral and psychological fable, Etaix never loses sight that he is making a sparkling comedy.

Yoyo received some negative criticism in the press for its obscurity, which perhaps led to Etaix's next film returning to more orthodox physical comedy. *Tant qu'on a la santé* (*As Long as You've Got Your Health*) (1966) is a portmanteau of four comic shorts; Etaix struggles to find a seat in a cinema, struggles to get to sleep, struggles to survive in a dystopian vision of a polluted Paris where everyone has to visit the doctor, and in the final episode, struggles to survive in the wilds of the countryside.

His final feature was *Le Grand Amour* (1969) and once again his

Yet another 'object-switch,' – here in Pierre Etaix's Le Grand Amour *of 1969 a bed takes to the road and becomes a vehicle, passing other divans that have variously crashed at the side of the road or are stuck in a 'traffic jam' of pyjama-clad drivers.*

character is a mild-mannered victim of ennui dreaming of better things; although it is a dialogue film, speech is minimalist and there is more comic mileage extracted from diegetic and non-diegetic sound than there is through verbal interchange. In a scene where three people including Etaix sit round a table cracking nuts, it is the nut-cracking and not the conversation that is forefront. The sound of the cracking itself is presented first as a reveal: with the camera focussed on a sleeping dog, the animal suddenly jerks its limbs as it's startled by a strange *crack!* – the origin of the disturbance is then presented as Etaix cuts to a mid-shot of the three seated round the table.

A highlight of *Le Grand Amour* is the magnificent bed sequence, which at the beginning is reminiscent of the storm winds edging Keaton's hospital bed out into the street. In Etaix's case it is pure dream that drives the divan out onto a fantastical long avenue lined with trees, along which Etaix glides along, seeing other beds similarly behaving like motor-cars; one is broken down at the side of the road, its stout driver lying underneath it attempting to 'fix' it'; another bed has ploughed into a roadside tree; and further up the lane, a whole queue of beds are stuck in a traffic jam.

Le Grand Amour was to be Etaix's last (fictional) feature. In 1971 he directed an experimental documentary, *Land of Milk and Honey*, a rather inward-looking study of his own film-making redolent of a certain introspection and self-doubt that was redolent of the times; after which, true to the story of *Yoyo*, he went back to the circus with his wife Anne Fratellini, thereafter only occasionally popping up to direct the odd television special.

The artistic accomplishment of Etaix is only now being fully appraised, as all his films were locked away until 2012 owing to legal disputes over their distribution. Thankfully he lived to see the resolution of the case, following which all his films were completely restored and given a worldwide release. In the ensuing two years his reputation has rightly been renovated, and aged 84 he was given a standing ovation at the Slapstick Festival at Bristol in 2012, where he was presented with a special award.

With all his films now back in his ownership and fully restored, elderly French clown Pierre Etaix smiles as he is honoured at the Slapstick Festival, Bristol 2012.

While Tati and Etaix were reinventing visual comedy in France, British TV audiences were being reawakened to the delights of silent humour from the old days. In 1966, comedian Bob Monkhouse – an avid collector of 8mm and 16mm silent movies – produced, presented and syndicated worldwide the series *Mad Movies* on ATV. A clip-show of all the silent greats from Ford Sterling to Harry Langdon, the show ran to 17 episodes and was a huge hit; so much so that the format was copied by the BBC who came up with their own visual comedy extravaganza, this time hosted by Michael Bentine at the National Film Theatre, *The Golden Silents.*

*

Comedian Roy Hudd always had one foot in the music-hall past, straddling as he did the age when variety moved from stage to television (he appeared on the same bill as Max Miller at the Finsbury Park Empire in 1959). It is perhaps inevitable then that his soul was also partly infused with the spirit of silent comedy, and many of his TV shows in the 60s included a feast of physical humour. For TV producers he was a tricky performer to provide a vehicle for, as his style didn't sit comfortably with the new wave of satirical and cerebral performers like Peter Cook and the other University wits of the satire boom. Nevertheless he was cast in the BBC's follow-up to *That was the Week That Was,* which had been hosted by David Frost. *Not so much a Programme More a Way of Life* took over the mantle of topical satire and aired thrice weekly between 1964 and 1965. Hudd's talent as a 'satirist,' however, proved something of a red herring, a fact perceptively spotted by Norman Wisdom's producer John Paddy Carstairs, who enlisted writers George Evans and Derek Collyer to devise and write an almost all-visual sitcom for Hudd, simply titled *Hudd.* Exploiting the performer's flair for concocting comic business often with props alone, *Hudd* ran for seven episodes in 1965. His career was given a further boost the following year when writer John Law (writer for Tommy Cooper and Marty Feldman, as well as having scripted one of the most famous sketches in the British canon, the 'class' sketch for *That was the Week That Was* featuring Ronnie Corbett, Ronnie Barker and John Cleese) and producer Dick Clement created a half-hour silent (or 'sound effect') comedy for Hudd entitled *The Maladjusted Busker.*

The Maladjusted Busker (1966) became Roy Hudd's curious contribution to the silent renaissance of the decade; more continental and subtle in its style and content than the broader British offerings from Bob Kellett, this 30-minute television special resembles the work of Pierre Etaix rather than Benny Hill or Eric Sykes. Its plot is a perfect expression of the French *derive*, or 'drift,' with Hudd as a London busker who becomes separated from his fellow-musicians when they crowd on to a bus in Trafalgar Square, and spends the rest of his day trying to re-join them. Along the way there are some inspired scenarios – conducting the gramophone players in a record shop in Denmark Street (tin pan alley); cavorting like a Pan in Kensington Gardens. Although stylistically shot like a documentary (the crew seemingly simply roamed the West End in pursuit of Hudd, in the process recording and preserving many fabulous street scenes of the mid-sixties) the post-filming overlaying of the music and sound effects once again lends an air of unreality to the piece. To the accompaniment of free-wheeling jazz xylophone and flute, Hudd skips and frolics across the rooftops of the West End, spotting his musical mates in the cavernous streets below, descending rapidly through a building in the process of construction, pausing for a breather and taking a swig of a welcome mug of tea – only to realise it's a mug of turps, as revealed when a labourer pops up out of a trench wielding a paintbrush.

Hudd is like a puppet hurled every which way by a swirling fate – or (more aptly) a hapless snooker ball buffeted and propelled in different directions: he is lifted into the air by a building-site elevator, whisked off by a taxi-cab after pausing to rest on the runner, thrown off at the feet of a young woman. Mid-film, he seems to abandon all desire to find his mates, and simply wanders, entering a state of limbo where he stops *pursuing* and starts living. He buys a carton of milk from a slot-machine; passes a television shop and waves at an onscreen newsreader (Richard Baker) who promptly waves back; and enters a park.

From the moment he enters the park the film assumes an air of poetic unreality, and in a beautifully directed sequence by John Duncan we are shown Hudd abandoning all routine and reverting to an almost prelapsarian state. He has left the city behind, and the park becomes a veritable Garden of Eden: indeed, the first sign he sees is 'Children Only.' He ploughs through a forest of swinging youngsters, meets the young woman again, and bringing out his flute becomes the Pied Piper, dancing nimbly off through the ethereal ground-mist, in such a state of Sufic bliss that he fails to notice he is dancing into the lake.

A highlight of *The Maladusted Busker* is when Hudd enters a record shop on the corner of Denmark Street and Charing Cross Road and 'conducts' the occupants of a row of listening-booths, all of whom are of listening to different records ranging from Beethoven to jazz to country, but whose music – under the direction of Hudd's baton – all blend into one.

He drifts in and out of various shops and establishments – a laundrette, an amusement arcade – before meeting up with the young woman again and finally being reunited with his fellow musicians. *The Maladjusted Busker* becomes, at bottom, a hymn to the West End of the 60s as well as being a worthy contribution to the genre of 'sound-effect comedy.'

*

Another comic performer to make an assault on the genre was Lance Percival. After making a splash as a cabaret artiste in the late 50s, he was offered a regular spot by David Frost on *That was the Week That Was*, and in 1964 was rewarded with his own show, a six-part visual series entitled *Lance at Large* written by David Nobbs and Peter Tinniswood.

Nobbs – author of such future classics as *The Fall and Rise of Reginald Perrin* – told me at a BBC Christmas party in December 2014, 'That visual series was the most difficult series I ever wrote. It was a blank canvas, creating comedy out of nothing.' Nobbs was heavily influenced by the Absurdist dramatist N F Simpson, writer of the innovative comic stage-plays *The Resounding Tinkle* and *One Way Pendulum*. The latter was filmed in 1964 starring Eric Sykes and Jonathan Miller, and although it had dialogue, it contained a plethora of visual imagery, the memorable centrepiece being Miller's attempt to conduct an orchestra of 'Speak Your Weight' machines. Simpson's influence on 60s TV was profound, and contributed to the extraordinary culture of experimentation in the medium during that decade.

*

Robert Youngson's compilations of silent classics in the 50s and early 60s created ripples that reached the mainstream movie industry: in 1965 comedy screenwriter Jack Davies and director Ken Annakin created an all-star homage to the madcap days of early flight with *Those Magnificent Men in Their Flying Machines*. Having worked together on *Very Important Person* (1961), *The Fast Lady* (1962) and *Crooks Anonymous* (1962), Annakin and Davies created a sparkling feast of visual thrills, the film capturing the knockabout zest of the 1910s and becoming one of the most successful movies of the decade, earning $31 million dollars from a budget of $6 million. The film was topped and tailed by two appearances of the American physical comedian Red Skelton – first popping up as the protagonist of a series of faux re-creations of man's early attempts at flight from caveman days to the Edwardian era, then reappearing in the epilogue of the movie as a disgruntled passenger waiting in a fog-bound Heathrow Airport – and resorting to flapping his arms up and down as he scampers off to the closing credits. Skelton was an apposite choice for the role: the son of a former clown for the Hagenbeck-Wallace Circus, Skelton cut his teeth like Keaton in a medicine show, followed by stints on a showboat and in vaudeville. Though accompanied by patter, the laughs from his 'dunking doughnut' routine were purely visual, deriving from his portrayal of a range of characters and the different ways they dip their doughnuts into coffee. In 1943, Skelton began a fruitful association with Buster Keaton, who was working a gag-man and story-liner for M-G-M: Skelton's film *I Dood It* was effectively a remake of Keaton's *Spite Marriage*, and Keaton's 1926 film *The General* was also later rewritten to become Skelton's *A Southern Yankee* (1948). Keaton perhaps saw himself in the young Skelton, and he asked Louis B Mayer to create a small company within M-G-M for himself and Skelton, where the two could work on film projects (sadly Mayer turned him down).

A hit on radio in the 50s and given his own NBC series in 1951, Skelton experimented with some bizarre visual skits that – while broader than Kovacs' work – became TV highlights in that boom decade, including the 'Willie Lump Lump' routine in which his wife walked up the wall of their living room. In 1960 Skelton bought Chaplin's old studios where he recorded many episodes of his TV series, now extended and retitled *The Red Skelton Hour*, that ran until 1970. It was for this series that Skelton received most acclaim, in particular for his regular 'silent segment' that often included his character Freddie the Freeloader, a mischievous selfish tramp with delusions of grandeur. A poverty-stricken figure inhabiting a ramshackle squat, Freddie's conquest of hardship is the engine of all the comedy, and is not without pathos – he plumps up a brick for his pillow, and sleeps in a bath that pushes into the wall like a fold-out bed.

At the height of his fame Skelton was cast in *Those Magnificent Men in their Flying Machines*, along with some of the finest comic character actors of the age, including Robert Morley, Tony Hancock, Benny Hill, Terry-Thomas, and Eric Sykes. In true Buster Keaton fashion it was the vehicles themselves that became the true stars of the picture. Complete with stunts reminiscent of Harold Lloyd and romance reminiscent of Chaplin, *Those Magnificent Men* was essentially a 1920s film writ large and shot in spectacular technicolour, and was part of a short-lived but key strand of comic moviemaking that included Blake Edwards' *The Great Race* (1965) and *Monte Carlo or Bust* (1969).

Blake Edwards, whose career with Peter Sellers we will cover in Chapter 16, had already made *The Pink Panther* (1963) and *A Shot in the Dark* (1964) when he fixed his ambitions on producing 'the greatest comedy ever.' The grandson of silent film director J Gordon Edwards, Blake stuffed *The Great Race* with all the tropes of the madcap capers of 1920s comedies, including what was billed by the promoters as the 'greatest pie fight ever.' Starring Jack Lemmon, Tony Curtis and Natalie Wood, Edwards dedicated his film to Laurel & Hardy, the pie-fight in particular having been inspired by *Battle of the Century*. Purists say that Laurel & Hardy's pie-fight, while containing rather fewer pies than Edwards', is more finely handled in terms of the pacing and architecture of the scene. But this is carping – *The Great Race* is a fabulous homage to the tropes of visual comedy, and another example of how directors were rediscovering the styles and techniques of the early days of film in order to inject lifeblood into contemporary comedy after thirty years of sound.

In 1969, Ken Annakin and Jack Davies followed up *Those Magnificent Men* with *Monte Carlo or Bust*, (in the US called *Those Magnificent Men in their Jaunty Jalopies*), which reprised the madcap capering, but this time firmly on the ground, in a London-to-Monte-Carlo race. Showcasing the comedy skills of Peter Cook and Dudley Moore, the film is more verbal than its earlier counterpart, but nevertheless contains some stupendous set-pieces of the cars whizzing about the icy French Alps.

*

Comic actor Graham Stark had been playing second banana to many a major comedy star over the years, including Spike Milligan, Tony Hancock and Peter Sellers before he too ventured into the world of the 'sound-effect' comedy in *Simon Simon*, released in 1970. Stark and John Junkin play two hapless accident-prone council maintenance men, the bane of the council depot chief played by magnificently irascible Paul Whitsun-Jones. Written and directed by Stark himself along with Carry On contributor Dave Freeman, *Simon Simon* is one of the most imaginative and accomplished of the 'sound-effect' comedies. It also boasts one of the greatest cast-lists of any British film: clearly Stark was a man respected and liked in the business, for anyone who can attract Michael Caine, Peter Sellers, David Hemmings, Morecambe & Wise, and Bob Monkhouse to a project possesses a verve to be reckoned with.

From the opening shot of *Simon, Simon* it is clear that there is a sharp comic mind at work with a knowledge of the heritage of film comedy – we see Stark's head floating along the top of a tall fence, seconds later to be revealed as seated on a platform atop a crane – a gag of course done before in various forms by Keaton and Etaix but never failing to amuse. The credits themselves are clever jokes on the cast, consisting of shots of various posters plastered about town – 'To Be Sold' – John Junkin, and a cinema poster, 'Play Dirty!' – with Norman Rossington, etc.

Keaton would have relished the comic potential of the huge hydraulic crane that is the star of *Simon, Simon*, with John Junkin and Stark playing two crane-drivers who wreck their elderly crane (by crashing into a railway bridge) expecting the wrath of their council boss Paul Whitsun-Jones, but instead being given a gleaming brand-new machine to play with. Every opportunity for a comic routine is exploited by Stark, as he has the boss order them against the wall as if they're about to be shot by a 'firing squad' – the twist being the reveal of the new crane that becomes the true star of the film.

From this point the film morphs from being a Laurel & Hardy 'buddy workman' comedy in the vein of Eric Sykes' *The Plank* into a Chaplin-style romance. Stark woos a typist (Julia Foster) by bobbing up and down at her office window, then takes her out for a date – on top of the crane. A superbly directed scene follows with Stark fighting off the amorous intervention of the fireman (Norman Rossington) who also has his eye on the sultry typist and who, of course, has his own 'crane' – his fireman's ladder. There ensues an escalating competition between Stark and Rossington to win her affections: one rescues a kitten, the other picks a big flower, the rivalry leading to a 'dogfight' in the air between the two cranes, with even their colleagues on the ground magically acquiring

Two stalwarts of the Silent Renaissance of the 1960s, Peter Sellers and Graham Stark, who spearheaded the 'sound effect' comedy, Sellers on the international stage and Stark in his 1970 short Simon Simon.

military uniforms and rallying round their respective 'leader.' Their differences forgotten when a second secretary falls for the fireman, the two then unite to foil a thief who's robbed the council depot.

Simon, Simon was a successful attempt to inject more plot into the 'sound-effect' comedy than previous examples, and while still typically and Britishly 'broad' – all amorousness, for example, being of the Donald McGill sort rather than the French romantic sort – the film contains sufficient comic ideas to hold its own against the more prolific practitioners of the genre. Just as Peter Sellers' *Running, Jumping and Standing Still Film* introduced this chapter, so Sellers ends it, for he too pops up in *Simon, Simon.* Sellers straddled a decade of vast innovation and experimentation in all fields of comedy: a decade of the rediscovery of the potential of 'silent' film, the building on the advances made by Jacques Tati, the injection of the visual comedy sketch into almost every 'broken' (sketch) comedy show on TV and the invention of the all-visual half-hour or 45-minute film. The finest exponent of the latter was Eric Sykes.

CHAPTER 15

Rhubarb Rhubarb – Eric Sykes and the Spoken Silents

In the 1950s and 60s a pattern can be discerned in the careers of several major comedy stars: after finding stardom and success in the new medium of television, they then exhibited a desire to strip their work back down to the bare essentials of physical clowning. Some earlier comedians were purely physical clowns to begin with – Norman Wisdom and Jerry Lewis – but the new crop of post-war comics like Benny Hill, Peter Sellers, Marty Feldman, Ronnie Barker and (later) Rowan Atkinson, found fame first as verbal comedians then reinvented themselves as visual comics. It is somewhat akin to Picasso saying 'it takes a lifetime to learn how to paint like a child.' They appeared to be seeking to release their inner visual comedian, and manifested this by returning to the tropes, personas and styles of the silent greats as a basis for their own creative expansion. One such performer – who was the chief exponent of the new genre of the 'visual featurette', a thirty/forty-five minute comedy film with no dialogue but with sound – was Eric Sykes.

Eric Sykes' forays into visual comedy were altogether richer, subtler and more cultured than Benny Hill's, possessing as he did an acuity for gags whose reach was far wider than toilet humour or leering at women. In a sense Sykes was Benny Hill grown up. While Hill was childish and smirking, Sykes drew inspiration from a bigger arsenal of comic tropes, including in his films a colourful range of characters that extended across the whole spectrum of the British class system – the Workman, the Toff, the Aspiring Middle-Class Man.

Sykes' career is of particular interest in the history of comedy in that it straddles a period of profound cultural and technological change: he saw the decline and death of variety, the rise of radio, the eclipsing of radio by TV, and the reinvention of a new genre of visual comedy – and at each twist in the story Sykes worked at the cutting edge.

At the dawning of the 60s, the origins and training-grounds for comedians were changing. Variety was dying, radio and TV had become the dominant entertainment media, and audiences no longer looked for their stars in the twice-nightly bills of provincial theatres but on their

Bush radios and their Radio Rentals TV sets. A new generation of comics was being spawned whose acts had not been formed over years touring the halls, but in the troop concerts that had blossomed in the Second World War. It was an altogether more spontaneous, more anarchic humour – Variety artistes, after all, could eke out a single act for decades, but the consuming power of radio and TV ate up new material and demanded of the writer-performer an unceasing creativity.

An allied consequence of the triumph of the new media was the emergence of what can be described as a wholly new profession: the comedy writer. Pre-war radio comedy was largely variety performers reproducing their acts for a vast listening audience; post-1945 a new breed of comic appeared that required a new breed of cohort – the scriptwriter. Frank Muir & Denis Norden, Ray Galton & Alan Simpson, Dick Hills & Sid Green, Spike Milligan, John Antrobus et al – a new army of literary humourists were first germinated, then nourished by the expansion of the wonderful new platform of the wireless. They became a highly paid and highly celebrated cadre of creators whose names eventually were placed above the show's title (at least, in Galton & Simpson's case). They founded whole new genres of humour from surreal stream-of-consciousness in the case of Milligan, to socially realistic comic drama in the case of Galton & Simpson.

And it was as one of this new breed that Eric Sykes first established himself, as what became known as a 'comedians' labourer' for stars like Frankie Howerd, Max Bygraves and Tony Hancock, then as a TV star in his own right, with a prime-time BBC1 sitcom spanning nearly two decades from 1960 to 1979. A lifelong fan of Laurel & Hardy, Sykes specialised in writing visual routines in pantomimes such as the long-running smash hit *Mother Goose* at the Palladium in 1954, the BBC's *Pantomania* in 1955 in which he performed with Hattie Jacques, *Val Parnell's Saturday Spectacular* in 1957 starring Peter Sellers, Hattie Jacques, Deryck Guyler and Spike Milligan, and *Large as Life* with Harry Secombe. This was all vital training for his future in visual comedy – indeed, a routine he wrote and performed with Max Bygraves for *Mother Goose* was so popular the producers of NBC's *Ed Sullivan Show* got wind of it and whisked them over to New York to perform it on the same bill as Bob Hope and Bing Crosby.

By 1961 Sykes was better known as a writer than performer, but his break as an artiste came when Head of BBC Comedy Tom Sloan – the force behind such classic comic hits of the early 60s as *Hancock's Half Hour* and *Steptoe and Son* – commissioned a pilot script for a Sykes show.

Pioneers of the British 'sound effect' comedy, Eric Sykes and Tommy Cooper proving that the spirit of Laurel & Hardy is alive and well in The Plank *(1967).*

Sykes' first starring vehicle was a simple sitcom with a twist – instead of a husband and wife scenario, he and his old chum Hattie Jacques – with whom he'd been working since the early 50s from *Educating Archie* onwards – were to be brother and sister, and 'not only brother and sister, but twins,' said Sykes to the press. 'And what's more, identical twins.' The pilot had not been written by Sykes but by his protégé from Associated London Scripts, Johnny Speight. With Speight about to launch his own smash hit *Till Death Us Do Part*, however, Sykes took over writing duties on his own show, and soon the sitcom built into a ratings winner.

From the outset *Sykes And a...* had a deftness and lightness that marked it out from other sitcoms of its time: it wasn't crazy or farcical like *The Army Game* or *Bootsie & Snudge*, nor melancholic like Hancock or darkly dramatic like *Steptoe and Son.* The individuality of *Sykes And a...* lay in its presentation of gentle, easy tableaux – whimsical excursions into everyday life. There was no delving into social problems, no sense of the claustrophobia of Steptoe or the political realities of Alf Garnett: Sykes stripped his comedy back to a clownish base – getting a toe stuck in a bath, running a bus like a passenger jet, carrying a plank around: one might say that the world of 24 Sebastapol Terrace had a touch of the *Beano* about it. With Deryck Guyler as a bumbling copper and Richard Wattis as a snooty neighbour, this was an Andy Capp version of Britain with no emotional or political axe to grind.

The overriding component of the series, however, that ensured its international success, was the strong element of the visual. 'To me a visual laugh is worth three pages of dialogue,' said Sykes in his biography *If I Don't Write It, Nobody Else Will.* 'Two visual gags and you're well on the way to fame and fortune.'

Many of the most memorable episodes of his long-running TV series involved a physical predicament. In one show he and his sister found themselves handcuffed together, performing a classic mime sequence as they try to eat dinner: the tug and pull of each other's arms as they both attempt to take mouthfuls is an hilarious routine whose deftness disguises meticulous rehearsal.

Sykes' judgement that 'a visual gag is worth three pages of dialogue' was acute – the show was a huge hit for the BBC across the world, including Australia, Indonesia, and Egypt: in fact, on August 24 1962 Tom Sloan wrote excitedly to Sykes that the episode *Sykes and a Bath* had won a prize at the Alexandria Film Festival, leading to a '£100 rise for his next series.' And when in 1964 he wrote *Sykes and a Plank,* he unwittingly was sowing the seeds for the flowering, three years later, of the first silent British comedy feature film for three decades.

*

Intended first as a vehicle for Peter Sellers, with whom Sykes had a series of lunches at which Sellers' excitement mounted exponentially (indeed, so excited was Sellers to 'have fun in a silent movie' as Sykes put it, that within three weeks he had secured the finance from Bernard Delfont and booked the film crew and location) *The Plank* began filming on August 9 1967 and contained a veritable 'who's who' of British comedy. But not Sellers. The former Goon had 'had a better offer' – having been lured by Hollywood to star in the ill-fated *Casino Royale* directed by John Huston – and others. Enter Tommy Cooper, who was cast as his replacement.

In his autobiography Sykes offers an insightful glimpse into the *modus operandi* of making a purely visual film. For a start, he says he didn't write a script, stating that he was '... simply writing with the camera.' This is an echo of Mack Sennett's boast that he and his film crew would just 'turn up' at a location and start shooting off the cuff. Neither Sykes nor Sennett were being quite truthful, for Sennett – and indeed also Chaplin and Laurel & Hardy – all worked to specific pre-written scenarios and left huge archives of scripted treatments.

Besides, Sykes was already well known as a great mental preparer. His colleagues at Associated London Scripts testify to experiencing periodic anxieties as a script deadline would loom and Sykes would be nowhere to be seen. He'd be on the golf course, and while his secretary

Beryl Vertue waited anxiously back in the office for a script, Sykes would to all appearances be lazing around playing nine holes.

But of course he was doing no such thing. On his return he would sit at a typewriter, type non-stop for a couple of hours, and deliver a completed script to Beryl well within the deadline.

He'd been writing the entire script in his head. Unlike Galton & Simpson who would sit for hours in front of their typewriter staring ahead and sculpting and chiselling each line of dialogue until it was satisfactory before committing it to paper, Sykes' way of working was to dream up entire half-hours while ostensibly lording it on the golf course.

There is no reason, then, to believe that he did anything differently with the script of *The Plank*. Indeed, not only was the story based on an old episode of his TV sitcom but he had also spent long hours with Peter Sellers discussing gags and scenarios. With Arthur Wooster, the lighting cameraman, he was materialising scenarios and routines not only formulated in his mind prior to shooting but also nourished by two decades of writing and watching the visual routines of the masters.

The shape and substance of *The Plank* follows that familiar classic configuration of silent film – entropy. Almost all Laurel & Hardy's pictures, and many of Keaton's, adhere to that law of decay, the descent from order to chaos. Whether consciously or unconsciously, Sykes' first all-visual feature depicts, in chronicling the journey of an inanimate object in its journey from timber-yard to building site, the utter chaos that the plank leaves in its wake.

Although possessing a very British style, in unpacking *The Plank* one can detect a treasure-house of international influence. The opening shot of the vast towers of planks in the timber yard bears a striking resemblance to the post-titles shot in Jacques Tati's *Playtime*, even to the point of Sykes' use of dramatic music to establish the import of the objects.

As in many Laurel & Hardy shorts, Cooper and Sykes are workmen, and not only workmen but builders, characters with a long tradition as comic protagonists. One of Laurel & Hardy's greatest silents was *The Finishing Touch* (1928), in which two builders have to construct a house in complete silence as it's right next door to a hospital; Buster Keaton's first solo picture, *One Week*, had him attempting to build a home in seven days.

Another Tati-esque element employed by Sykes is his use of the placid observer. Tati would often place an onlooker on the edge of or at the back of frame: not only to highlight the comedy but also to punch home and magnify its truthfulness – look, the gag is actually happening in the real world and hasn't merely been made up for the cinema or television viewer. So when a milkman arrives to deliver a bottle to Cooper and Sykes through a window in the unfinished building, he stands and watches as the two comics struggle to get the window open. The window is opened but of course there is no pane. Having handed the milk through the empty frame the milkman remains to observe the topper: Cooper hands the milk to Sykes, then shivers because of the 'open' window. He closes it.

An ingenious use of shadows as the source of a mistaken-identity sight-gag sees an angled floorboard making the sign of the cross on the wall: on entering the room Sykes sees what appears to be a genuflecting Cooper (actually kneeling to complete his work on the floorboards), and respectfully removes his cap to humble himself before the crucifix.

The house is complete! – except for one single plank, which our intrepid heroes set out to acquire. Once in the outside world, the vast gallery of supporting characters, each with their own little plot, come into their own: Jimmy Edwards, Roy Castle, Barbara Windsor and Jim Dale.

And funny sequences abound: a memorable one is when Sykes performs a bull-fighting routine in the middle of the street, only with racing bikes instead of bulls; a lovely touch is a woman in curlers at an upstairs window to whom Sykes blows a kiss after his display of matador skills. At one point a racing bike whizzes up a ramp and flies into the back of an open lorry. There's a beat, and the cyclist appears from the cockpit of the truck carrying an utterly crumpled machine. Another finely built routine has the plank backed up to, and unwittingly inserted through, the window of saloon bar. A suitably burly man inside places his glass on the end of it, the plank is pulled out, the beer falls in a window-cleaner's bucket, the window cleaner holds up the empty glass – and naturally the man in the pub thinks window-cleaner has drunk it. Sykes could have ended the gag there, but instead ingeniously inserts a well-timed lingering pause, and the window-cleaner is hauled sharply and cartoonishly through the window into the pub.

Jimmy Edwards stamps his bumbling copper act with an individuality all his own, hitting the ground running by cocking a leg suggestively (and unwittingly of course) against a lamp-post as he attempts to mount his bike. Sykes places Roy Castle on a plank strapped to a car and demonstrates his awareness of silent comic heritage by having him glide across the frame blank-faced, just as Buster Keaton would have done. Jim Dale as a short-sighted decorator sets up a nice routine in which Tommy Cooper gets covered in red paint. Of course it's mistaken for blood and immediately attracts a gathering crowd, who think he's been injured. At first repulsing their ministrations, Cooper begins to enjoy it, thanking them for the tea and the cigarette, leading to the comic climax of the routine when the onlookers realise it's just paint. Without the camera leaving Cooper's prostrate position, we see the tea taken away, the fag whipped out of his mouth – even the rolled-up jacket is whisked out from under his head.

It's a sequence that proves Cooper's skill as a mime. Because of Cooper's insecurity at the start of filming, Sykes had to constantly reassure him that he was being funny. Indeed, at a lunch before filming began, at which all the film crew were present, Cooper suddenly got up and lay down on the floor. 'What are you doing?' asked Sykes. 'I just thought I'd do something visual,' Cooper replied. (quoted in Sykes, ibid).

Sykes may not have written a complete script beforehand, but the shape of *The Plank* clearly demonstrates forethought: from the outset he established a shape for his films that he would stick to for the next twenty years. A main plot would be surrounded by several minor stories of escalating gags and predicaments. Sight gags would not exist in isolation but possess consequences; like a snooker ball being gently nudged across the green baize and ricocheting into others, characters would be introduced then interact, creating repercussions. This was gleaned from Tati, the seeds of whose principle of 'democratic comedy' had been sown in *Monsieur Hulot's Holiday* and bore fruit in *Playtime* (released in 1967 before *The Plank*) where Hulot was relegated to merely one of the cast and the story was an interweaving of several threads.

Sykes and Cooper are the principals, but the supporting comics are no mere garnish: Roy Castle has an escalating routine in which, after having been propelled into the back of a rubbish lorry, he has to cross town smelling unpleasantly of refuse. This predicament could almost have been the basis of an entire film, but in *The Plank* Sykes is content to drop back to it four or five times, each scenario more heightened than the previous one, culminating in the final chaotic confrontation in a police station, in which everyone we've met throughout the film ends up shouting their complaints at a laconic tea-drinking Stratford Johns.

At bottom *The Plank* is a caper, but for all its broad British humour the film is deceptively sophisticated. The architecture is finely constructed and serves one major purpose, that of gradually increasing tempo: as the piece progresses, the pace increases exponentially and the scenes correspondingly shorten. The interlacing of four or five plots, all building to a culminating point, reveals a depth of knowledge of the techniques of Tati, Keaton, Chaplin and Laurel & Hardy – and for Sykes, of course, one couldn't choose finer mentors.

*

The success of *The Plank* led to a follow-up in 1969, *Rhubarb*. Once again Sykes uses his familiar repertory cast of players – Kenneth Connor, Hattie Jacques, Graham Stark et al – but this is where a slight confusion descends, for Sykes remade each of his visual comedies for Thames TV as slightly shorter 30-minute specials in the 1980s: and in the second version of *Rhubarb* (re-titled *Rhubarb Rhubarb*, clearly to hammer home the meaning of the actor's expression for 'background mumbling') the cast included Bob Todd, Charlie Drake, a wonderfully half-cut Bill Fraser whose pair of binoculars are a secret whisky flask, and Hattie Jacques, who sadly died between the filming and release. These second versions were largely superior to their first outings.

Thames TV's backing of Sykes' visual comedies was no mere whimsy but symptomatic of a deliberate movement: in 1980 the channel broadcast the ground-breaking 13-part documentary series 'Hollywood' chronicling the era of silent cinema, produced by Kevin Brownlow and David Gill, and the success of that series led to the sponsoring of Thames Silents, a project that restored and screened major films from the silent era in cinemas and on TV, and also *Unknown Chaplin* (1983), *Buster Keaton: A Hard Act to Follow* (1987), and *The Third Genius* on Harold Lloyd (1989). Sykes' silent specials were clearly part of this renaissance, and Thames had such confidence in their popularity that they continued to commission him for ten years.

Rhubarb Rhubarb has a somewhat mystical tone, using some surreal sight-gags reminiscent of Buster Keaton. Once again the central premise of the story is simplicity itself – a chief inspector plays a vicar at golf. The inspector (Sykes) cheats, using bumbling bobby Jimmy Edwards to clandestinely assist him, and the vicar in turn uses God. Cheating gags, and divine intervention gags – the script writes itself.

Once again Sykes hits the ground running with a deftly directed opening sequence: having smashed his own office window with a wayward golf ball, he diverts blame onto a boy he summons in from the street, producing a brick. After a perfectly timed comic beat, the boy fishes into his pocket and produces the guilty golf ball.

In a lengthier role than he was usually cast in by Benny Hill, a delightfully sozzled Bob Todd presents us with his comedy vicar, slipping out of his church mid-sermon and joining Sykes on the course for a pre-arranged match. At first bamboozled by his opponent's trickery – mainly consisting of Jimmy Edwards either hiding Todd's ball or giving his chief inspector the advantage by plucking his ball from the rough and dropping it on the green (there is a wonderful piece of whimsy when he pops the enemy's ball into a hole in a tree only for it to be ejected seconds later by a squirrel rubbing his bruised head) – the browbeaten cleric resorts to his own machinations by appealing to God for help.

His prayers are answered, in the form of a series of innovative special effect gags: a divine wind curves his ball onto the green; his club emerges from the bag of its own accord; the Creator even makes a shed move right in front of Sykes just as he's about to tee off. And the miracles become more impressive: a tree does a nifty sidestep; Todd walks Christ-like across a lake; and in an animated graphic particularly novel for its time the ball makes divine progress from hole to hole adorned with angels' wings and accompanied by a choir, while the policeman's ball careers into the rough to the strains of a siren.

These surreal touches elevate *Rhubarb Rhubarb* above mere slapstick.

*

It's Your Move followed in 1982. This, once again, was a remake from an earlier work, a cinema-released short made in 1969. Much of the cast were reunited to make what is perhaps Sykes' finest all-visual piece. The plot builds perfectly, each strand gently set up then colliding later with the others. Sykes and Cooper head up a small group of bumbling removal men and are introduced to the viewer by flying out of the back of their van on a bed that then rolls unfeasibly about half a mile along the road, in spectacular Keaton fashion. Jimmy Edwards joyfully reprises his bumbling copper, who in his opening routine gets his bike caught on the removal van and blusteringly commandeers a car to chase after it. The chauffeur he dragoons is Brian Murphy, whose pursuit of the removal van lasts the entire film, long after the vehicle's parked up. Meanwhile, newlyweds Richard Briers and Sylvia Syms turn their car sharply into the driveway of their lovely new home only to run up a mountain of sand, and we are afforded tantalising glimpses of nosey neighbour Bernard Cribbins as he mows his lawn and peers inquisitively over his fence …

In this masterly fashion Sykes quickly sets up his gallery of British grotesques, giving each character their own opening gag, and leaving us to sit back and watch them dance.

Are Laurel & Hardy consciously alluded to by the addition of a 'cuckoo' in the opening music? It seems likely. There are certainly plenty of gags reminiscent of the boys: Briers attempting to carry his bride across the threshold only for the front door to slam shut on her head echoes Hardy's treatment of his fiancée in *Our Wife*, and the central relationship itself between Sykes and Tommy Cooper reminds one of Laurel & Hardy in Sykes' assertion of his status in insisting on entering a doorway first.

Sykes specialises in gags that have consequences: each slapstick element, while funny in itself, has a future, supplying forward momentum to the comedy. the bride's bump on the head doesn't occur in a vacuum – it leads to her hat being ripped off, then her dress torn, which in turn sets up her quest throughout the movie to find a place to change, away from the prying eyes of the brown-coated removal men. Whose attitude towards her, incidentally, is (unlike Benny Hill) verging on the demure; they are respectful and un-leering. Indeed, when they do catch sight of the scantily clad bride, they politely pull their caps down over their eyes.

Once again this is a 'spoken silent,' the only intelligible words in the whole film being uttered by a parrot, whose repeated screeches of 'I'm sorry darling!' embarrass its owner – the henpecked Richard Briers – who promptly throws a curtain over its cage.

Each gag also has a prior subtle set-up, with Sykes not afraid of joke-less shots; for example we glimpse Bernard Cribbins innocently and uneventfully mowing his lawn, but it is far from gratuitous, for a moment later Tommy Cooper tosses a doorknocker over the fence, and we hear a cry from the now invisible and concussed Cribbins – who then ploughs his lawnmower through his garden fence. By setting Cribbins up in the previous shot, he has quickly become planted in our minds as a nosey neighbour – which magnifies the pay-off by colouring in our imaginations as we hear the off-screen comic sound effects.

Having straddled the two golden ages of 1950s radio and 1960s TV sitcom, writer and comedian Eric Sykes was determined to reinvent visual comedy for a mainstream UK audience. Having made The Plank *and further dialogue-free films for the cinema, he brought his warm, broad silent comedy to Thames TV in a series of slapstick shows including* It's Your Move *(1982), demonstrating that the sight-gag had a renewed place in contemporary comedy. Here the removal man (Tommy Cooper) enjoys a break by playing a spot of pool in the front garden while his fellow worker plays the piano.*

There are many beautiful character moments in *It's Your Move*, the personalities of Cooper and Sykes having seemingly deepened since *The Plank*. The removal team have left a big brass bed in the front garden, and Cooper is tempted to climb on for a bounce. He is ordered into the house by Sykes, but then Sykes climbs on himself and launches into his own childish bouncing, watched by copper Jimmy Edwards from a distance. Sykes' somersaults get more and more elaborate until in long-shot he (actually his stand-in) is flying through the air like a circus acrobat. In another scene, having shifted the bed, Cooper sneaks a quick lie-down. Boss Sykes clocks him, and rings the iron bedstead so it clangs like a boxing bell and Cooper leaps up sharply, adopting a pugilist's stance.

Other memorable gags include the removal men carrying a grandfather clock on their shoulders sedately through the garden gate: Brian Murphy, the running chauffeur, stops momentarily on the pavement, doffing his hat and bowing his head respectfully, mistaking it for a coffin. Sylvia Syms pushes a big cupboard in front of her bedroom door so she can get changed in peace: Tommy Cooper then emerges magically from inside it, places an item in the room, then disappears Narnia-like into the wardrobe again.

There are also some Laurel-inspired moments: a light-bulb becomes magically illuminated in Sykes' hand after he's received an electric shock, a piano-lid levitates … Indeed, there is a touch of *The Music Box* about the entire piece, for at one point there is a snooker table and piano on the front lawn and the removal men, stopping for lunch, turn the garden into some kind of leisure club, playing snooker and having a sing-song at the Joanna, which is highly reminiscent of the dancing-during-the-clear-up-routine in the 1932 picture. Further Laurel & Hardy tropes are paid homage to in the closing scenes, with a 'mutual destruction' routine between roadsweeper Andrew Sachs and Irene Handl, who has crashed her car into Sach's street-cleaning equipment. Methodically and intently Sachs tips the contents of his bin into Handl's car, who then responds equally methodically by lifting Sachs and dropping him into his own bin.

*

There was a hiatus of six years before Sykes produced his next half-hour silent for Thames, this time tackling the misadventures of a firm of incompetent undertakers in *Mr H is Late*. Once again Sykes recognised that in visual comedy it is one simple physical event that constitutes the plot, and the quest he chose for this picture is the attempt to carry a coffin containing a dead body from the upper floor of a tower block to the hearse parked at the pavement below. One should say ostensibly parked, for one of the running gags is the funeral vehicle being continually moved along by Jimmy Edwards, who has departed from his run of bumbling coppers to play a bumbling traffic warden. With a plethora of sub-plots that are neatly set-up, pursued and interwoven, *Mr H is Late* contains all the familiar tropes of a Sykes silent but with added elements of the bizarre, perhaps as a result of the presence in the film of Spike Milligan – the ex-Goon playing an old soldier living in a decrepit caravan with no roof.

Sykes cast his net slightly wider for his supporting characters, using a selection of the current crop of comedy stars including Mike Yarwood, Freddie Starr and *Hi-de-Hi*'s Paul Shane, in addition to his old stalwarts Edwards, Henry McGee and Bob Todd. Yarwood has a nice cameo 'mistaken sign' gag when he places his 'Out of Order' sign on the lift instead of the WC, leading the undertakers to troop up fifteen flights.

Clearly the shadow of Oliver Hardy has not left Sykes' psyche for he reprises the beloved 'let me go first' routine twice, once in disembarking the hearse and second in climbing the stairs, his presumptuous cohort this time played by Freddie Starr. Starr's mime in the film is accomplished – he has a sublime sequence in which following the decrepit Bob Todd's physical exhaustion at having to carry the coffin, he slyly attempts to measure his partner up.

The traffic warden slaps tickets on everything in sight, from a piano to a road-sweeper, while Paul Shane has a bizarre gag where – in his efforts to spy on an attractive woman – (yes, the Benny Hill influence and the pressures of the age were plainly being brought to bear on Sykes) he magically slides the peephole further down his front door so he can get a better look.

Sykes' commitment to the kind of 'democratic comedy' pioneered by Tati was unwavering, with all the minor characters given equal weight: even John Alderton pops up as a flustered vicar waiting for the undertakers, giving Sykes a chance for another magical gag when a parishioner pulls at his surplice and makes the sound of a bell ringing.

Mr H is Late was another success but as the 1980s came to a close, so too did Sykes' silents. His sitcom for the BBC had ended in 1980 after the death of Hattie Jacques and his final all-visual effort came in 1993 with the bizarre international co-production *The Big Freeze*. Made for a Finnish broadcaster, who supplied Sykes with a director with whom Sykes did not get on, the end result is a hybrid of bawdy comedy and sight-gags that largely don't come off. With Spike Milligan turning in his Hitler character and Sir John Mills popping up as the resident of an old folks' home, it is a curiosity lacking the inspiration of his former movies, and

Sykes, pioneer of a whole new comic genre in the 1960s – the half-hour 'spoken silent' – in his final silent short for Thames, Mr H is Late *(1988) once again demonstrated his commitment to the kind of 'democratic comedy' pioneered by Tati in* Playtime *– that is, an ensemble cast with no weight placed on a single protagonist. Once again the plot centres on one simple physical challenge – this time transporting a coffin from the upper floors of a tower-block – and with cohorts such as Spike Milligan, Jimmy Edwards, Henry McGee, Bob Todd and – above – a young Freddie Star, the film weaves several character narratives together with deceptive cleverness.*

one suspects that Sykes, though physically present, was mentally absent and wishing the whole thing over. There is certainly no onscreen rapport with his cohort Bob Hoskins, who sadly shows no flair for pantomime. With a plot that resembles a fusion of Chaplin's *Gold Rush* and one of Laurel & Hardy's tradesmen shorts, an old folks' home in the middle of the snowy wastes of Finland forms the backdrop for a thin mixture of comic business and surrealism. There are a few gems hidden amongst the dross – an attempt to fix a frozen pipe turns into a percussion routine performed with a wrench; a cold wind blows through the home and turns a stream of tea being poured from a teapot horizontal (a homage to Tati's gag in *M Hulot*); the thawing out of a rigid Hoskins after falling into a barrelful of icy water (a homage to Laurel in *Below Zero*) – but these are exceptions. In short, *The Big Freeze* is not a befitting swansong to Sykes' career as a visual comedian.

So he should be remembered for his inspired re-invention of the visual short – first in his BBC sitcom where several episodes were virtually wordless, then secondly in his Thames silents, in which Sykes relocates his gawky, sympathetic everyman to a landscape of soundless confrontation and struggle, transforming the everyday tropes of 70s British life – marriage, moving home, death – into bright, energetic and inventive comic tableaus. His silent persona was an extension and purification of his sitcom character: in realising that more and more of his plots hinged on simple physical events, he took the logical step and abandoned dialogue altogether, entering the more abstract terrain of wordless slapstick. In this, he approached the greatness of Keaton and Laurel.

CHAPTER 16

Chameleon Boy: Peter Sellers

A day-old infant is carried onstage at the Kings Theatre Southsea by Dickie Henderson Sr, who'd once screen-tested for Hal Roach as the plump partner to a certain Stan Laurel. Thus Sellers' connection with the Golden Age of silent clowns was forged – quite literally on the day of his birth.

Not simply fanciful osmosis – as a regular act at the Kings Theatre in Southsea, the seaside town where the Sellers family lived, Henderson would have boasted in his cups of his (short-lived) silent movie career. And as Sellers grew up he lapped up Laurel's movies, absorbing his style and stillness until the influence became explicit in his late, great performance as Chauncey Gardner. In that film the magic of Laurel's Holy Fool is stark when Gardner steps out onto water – and walks effortlessly across it. All his life, it seems, Sellers was waiting to play Stan Laurel. 'Laurel and Hardy are my two favourite comedians,' he would later say in interviews, 'the two funniest men who ever lived.'

But it was a long – and occasionally troublesome – journey to that last, great performance.

The dark and complex contours of Seller's psyche have been explored and chronicled by a number of authors – my sole purpose is to examine how Sellers became a prime mover in that great revival of visual comedy in the 1960s. Like Sykes and, later, Ronnie Barker, Sellers' comic roots were nurtured by a love of the old silent comedians, but because Sellers possessed perhaps a greater ambition than both, not only did he make an all-visual feature film – Blake Edwards' *The Party* in 1968 – but in his invention of Inspector Clouseau created the greatest visual cinematic clown since Norman Wisdom's 'gump.'

Some see Sellers' career as a Rake's Progress descent from early brilliance into steady decline. This is a distortion, for even after his towering Oscar-nominated performance in *Dr Strangelove* in 1964 he went on to make three, four or even five cinematic masterpieces – *The Party, There's a Girl in my Soup, The Pink Panther Strikes Again, and Being There.*

Seller's comic journey is akin to that of both Jerry Lewis and Sykes; the achievement of success in one field or genre – in Sellers' case that of international character actor, the 'man of many faces' – whose real ulterior aim was to distil his comic talents into a purely visual essence. In other words, he was a verbal comic actor in search of a purely visual identity. As his power and influence in the film industry grew and he was able to make more choices in the roles he played, he edged towards fulfilling his ambition: along the way his acting style matured, becoming less mannered and showy, and his presence and energy became more contained.

For someone who first established himself as the BBC's 'voice-man' alongside such stalwarts as Tommy Handley, Maurice Denham and Ted Ray, this was quite a transition. He first made a big splash in the early 50s, the era when radio performers and writers were at the top of the entertainment tree: an act could win a lucrative national variety tour as top-of-the-bill off the back of a successful wireless comedy series. An age when an entertainer could become a household name and never actually be seen.

But Sellers wanted to be seen. George Harrison, in a 1995 BBC documentary *The Peter Sellers Story*, said of him, 'Peter could have stayed in the world of steam radio, settled there. But it's clear he was aiming for more. Like the Beatles, we knew he was going to make the whole journey.'

That journey began with the Goon-show spin-off *Down Among the Z Men* (1952) and the now little-known *Orders are Orders* made in the same year, acting alongside his old RAF pal Tony Hancock. There followed a stream of sprightly, delightfully liberal Ealing (or Ealing-style) films including *The Ladykillers* (1955), *The Naked Truth* (1957) and *Up the Creek* (1958). The following year was particularly rich with Sellers making *The Battle of the Sexes*, *The Mouse that Roared* and *I'm Alright Jack*, in which latter film his portrayal of communist shop steward Fred Kite established him firmly as an international star. One is tempted to name 1959 as his golden year were it not that 1963 saw him appear in both *The Pink Panther* and *Dr Strangelove*, two films that would cement his reputation as *the* great comic actor of the decade.

*

This was indeed the blossoming of an extraordinarily uncommon talent: in ten years Sellers had risen from being a vocal comedian to Oscar-nominated international star. To present to the world, within twelve months, not only one of the finest cinematic performances of the century in his portrayal of three characters – the President, RAF Group Captain, and the eponymous Strangelove – but also create one of the great visual comic characters of the sound era, is an achievement difficult to match.

Where did Clouseau spring from? What was his provenance? Once again the vast shadow of Tati must be acknowledged, and for more than the mackintosh and worn by both Hulot and Clouseau. The kinship between Tati and Clouseau is stark, their relationship overtly acknowledged by Sellers himself: 'I was ready to lie down and die for Tati,' he said. Sellers made the pilgrimage to Paris for an audience with his idol, but the encounter was tinged with disenchantment: Sellers afterwards complained to his friend and Goon-show musician Max Geldray that 'All (Tati) did was talk about his comic theories, and how great he was!' (quoted in The Life and Death of Peter Sellers by Roger Lewis). (Possible translation: 'He didn't talk about me – in fact, I doubt he'd seen any of my films!') At the time Tati was perhaps the world's most renowned film comedian: to him, Sellers must have simply seemed to be a keen British fan of whom he had faintly heard and the purpose of whose pilgrimage was to seek advice from an elder statesman. What was Tati meant to do but to talk comic theories?

Despite the lack of rapport on a personal level, Sellers worshipped Tati's art, and set out to emulate it. The erectness of Clouseau, the formality of his posture, the transformation of his body into an expression of the strict ceremonial of his profession – all these ingredients are pure Tati and owe perhaps just as much to François, the postman of *Jour de Fête*, than to Hulot.

Both François and Clouseau are men whose uniforms have taken then over, their weaknesses banished by the opportunity to wear a costume. With relief they don the apparel of their work in the morning, and are thus ready to face a hostile world: their uniform is the alchemist's fabled Magic Cloak, protecting them from almost certain disintegration, from a world that constantly rejects them and in which they singularly fail to operate successfully. In François' case, his dignity as a public servant is mocked in the very first scene of *Jour de Fête* by a group of children – he doesn't even command the respect of infants. Likewise Clouseau is established instantly as a loser struggling to appear as normal. He falls, he prods himself in the eye with his own baton, he slips, he steps on his own violin: every inanimate object is his enemy. Yet throughout this battling to appear as an adult he maintains a stiff stoical, invincible self-belief, the outward expression of which is his detective's uniform.

After stealing The Pink Panther *(1963) from the rest of the cast, the following year Sellers' Inspector Clouseau is rewarded with his own solo vehicle,* A Shot in the Dark *(1964).*

In the history of silent film, of course, there is a rich tradition of comic policemen: it is, indeed, an archetype whose genealogy can be traced back to the Shakespeare's Constable, or the wooden bobby in Punch and Judy. Mack Sennett founded an entire studio on the antics of a gang of incompetent coppers. Ford Sterling and his fellow Keystones were, however, little more than bumbling clownish buffoons. Chaplin deepened their social reality by depicting them as forces of a hostile social order, the enemy of the vagrant, the victim, the downtrodden. We never *like* Chaplin's policemen.

Sellers' creation is far more nuanced. From his first appearance as a supporting character in the farcical thriller *The Pink Panther* in 1963, the character of the bumbling detective, striving to maintain dignity whilst begetting chaos wherever he goes, hits the ground running and immediately begets a franchise. Remarkably for a visual clown character, Clouseau sprang fully formed into being; he doesn't evolve over the series – his very first gag contains the template for his entire identity. A spinning globe, a mental wandering, a placing of the hand on the still-rotating world, a plunging to the floor: from the very first time we see Inspector Clouseau on screen in 1963, to the last shot fifteen years later in 1978's *Revenge of the Pink Panther*, the character is complete.

The films are replete with classic slapstick – indeed, Spike Milligan observed that 'The Pink Panthers were based on classic silents; they were expensive Hal Roach movies.' (quoted in Lewis, ibid).

This wasn't Sellers' first foray into visual comedy; his avant-garde experiment with *The Running, Jumping and Standing Still Film* has been examined in a previous chapter. In *The Pink Panther*, however, the jokes are far more traditional: we see Clouseau collapse on top of a recumbent David Niven as he's stretchered off the ski-slopes; he stands too near a rotating fan and gets his jacket caught up in the blades; he sits on the edge of a swimming pool and, his eyes following an attractive woman as she approaches the pool to dive in, leans further and further back until he topples neatly into the water; he attempts a bout of gymnastics on a handrail, only to plummet down a flight of stairs; his hand is wedged in the spinning globe that is his inanimate nemesis; he gets up from a park bench on a sloping lawn, upending both the bench and Herbert Lom who promptly rolls into a lake; he walks for several moments in a dark room, only realising when he lights a match that he's remained stationary – the room is not a hundred yards long but only seems so because he is on a treadmill.

These are all traditional sight-gags that could have been plucked from any silent comedy from 1910 to 1927. What is unique to Sellers' creation, however, is that Clouseau immediately rebels against the pratfall. Gone is the bewilderment of Keaton, sitting stone-faced and defeated on the ground; gone the weary stoicism of Hardy as he stares deep into the camera in a silent plea for our sympathy: Sellers contrarily dismisses his clumsiness in a trice, bounding to his feet and reassuming his dignified posture – hands clasped behind his back, police uniform crisply ironed, back straight, feet planted firmly on the floor. Not only will he not be defeated by the slapstick, he refuses to even acknowledge it. The world is to blame, not he. This attitude imbues the DNA of Clouseau, and marks the character out as a great icon of pantomime. He is the fulfilment of Jos Houben's dictum that the root of all comedy is the struggle to stay upright – but more than that, Sellers, after falling, pretends he never fell in the first place.

Though the Inspector Clouseau films are not purely visual, they belong firmly in the slapstick tradition and could be appreciated equally well with the sound removed. Sellers' veneration of silent films has been referenced, but this veneration did not simply emanate from him alone: as the grandson of one of the great silent directors, J Gordon Edwards, Blake Edwards was fully aware of his own place in the heritage of sight-gag and sight-routine. The apple never falls far from the tree, and despite making it big with romances and melodramas such as *Breakfast at Tiffany's* and *Days of Wine and Roses*, the genes soon began to make their presence felt. He and Sellers clicked and both *The Pink Panther* (1963) and *Shot in the Dark* (1964) were big hits. It was only a matter of time before the two would seek to collaborate on a solely visual movie. Curiously, however, that opportunity was only to come four years later, when both men's careers were in something of a rut.

*

'Trying to fit in' is perhaps the thematic crystallisation of most silent comedies ever made; here Sellers literally doesn't fit at the dining table in The Party. *More than once Blake Edwards nods to Tati: the entire movie, in fact, descends into chaos like the Royal Garden restaurant sequence of* Playtime, *and the comedic interaction with inanimate objects – memorably the ever unwinding toilet-roll routine – parallels several of Tati's films, especially* Mon Oncle.

The Party, released in 1968, was a revival of sorts for both Edwards and Sellers – after his extraordinary creative blossoming in the first half of the decade Sellers had foundered somewhat and released a few odd pictures in an era when, to be fair, more odd films were made than perhaps at any other time in history. Though not a huge critical or commercial success at the time, *The Party* has accumulated respect and fandom in the ensuing decades and now stands as a sparkling achievement of the post-war Silent Renaissance.

The film had an odd birth. Having initially clicked successfully, Edwards and Sellers had since fallen out over creative differences, vowing never to work with each other ever again after *A Shot in the Dark.* Their collaborative career juddered to an apparent end, with Sellers' individual output wavering somewhat with the legendary turkey *Casino Royale,* (1967). Such was the international success of the two Panther films, however, that it was inevitable that the producers, the Mirisch Corporation, would want more. In a bid to develop the character into a franchise, they greenlit another movie. Both Sellers and Edwards refused to be involved – so Alan Arkin was signed to play Clouseau. A fortnight before production was due to start, however, Sellers rang up Mirisch and insisted he was the only actor in the world able to play the part. Mirisch put the phone down on him. A few weeks later Sellers, clearly bristling and determined more than ever to create a brand new visual character to rival his former creation, patched up any personal animosity he may have had with Edwards and began shooting *The Party*.

The release of Jacques Tati's *Playtime* is, I believe, both crucial to the chronology of *The Party* and its style and tone. Although not distributed in the US until 1973, *Playtime* was given limited showings in Paris in 1967, and the similarity in structure and routines with *The Party* – particularly the Royal Garden Restaurant sequence – is absolute artistic evidence that Edwards saw Tati's film, and drew heavily from it. Enlisting the scripting services of brothers Tom and Frank Waldman – stalwarts of such US sitcoms as *Bewitched* and *I Dream of Jeannie* – Edwards and Sellers set about creating a 'plotless' visual comedy featuring a character as hapless as Clouseau but more gentle and subtle – an Indian film extra called Hrundi Bakshi.

Bakshi owes certain traits to Sellers' earlier Indian doctor character in *The Millionairess*, but is deeper and more nuanced. A shy, well-meaning man without a selfish bone in his body, his benignity approaches innocence, and is a forerunner of the holy fool of *Being There*. As for the film's style, its entire look and feel evokes *Playtime*. The film is neo-realist in style, avers narrative in favour of drift, is picaresque and – despite Bakshi being the protagonist – edges towards the 'democratic' and ensemble comedy that Tati pioneered. Just as in *Playtime* Hulot wanders through a Paris now become alien to him, so the fish-out-of-water Bakshi – an ingenuous soul – is pitched into the phoney world of Hollywood showbiz go-getting. The scenario is simple – after a (somewhat laborious) set-up to establish the incompetence of the protagonist (he inadvertently blows up a building on a location shoot), the credits roll and the film proper begins, with the smiling Sellers, armed with the invitation mistakenly sent to him, arriving at a flash house in Los Angeles.

Sellers' first post-credit scene is pure *Playtime* – just as the first time we see Hulot attempting to manoeuvre himself between parked cars, so too we see Bakshi squeeze his vehicle into a narrow space then struggle to worm his way through to the path. Edwards and Sellers knew that in all the best purely visual films, physical problems are plot; the odder the problem, and the more escalatory, the funnier. *The Party* adheres to that rule, the succession of physical problems beginning with the simple loss of a shoe. Having stepped in mud in the garden outside the house, Sellers at once attempts to wash his shoe in an indoor water-feature so as not to mark the cream-coloured carpeting. His shoe is promptly carried off by the current – and the first fifteen minutes of the film has written itself.

The social problem is the bigger challenge – this is not merely the comedy of a man attempting to recover a shoe from an indoor water-feature, but the embarrassment and awkwardness of being in a crowded room at a Hollywood party with a shoe missing. So at bottom, it is a comedy about status. The guests at the party form a hierarchy of almost feudal rigidity, each having their uniform – the business moguls or corporate elite in their stuffed shirts with their fat cigars; their plump harridan wives or beautiful sinewy trophy dates; and the caterers, drifting about in their tuxedos, carrying trays. This is a movie about class, as Chaplin's were. But there is a third element of the hierarchy – the eccentrics and outsiders. There aren't many of them, perhaps only four, but they form the centre of the story. Apart from Bakshi himself, there is a young French singer played by Claudine Longet; an odd rhinestone cowboy character; and in a fine performance by Steve Franken, an increasingly inebriated waiter. As the film progresses these characters gravitate towards one another and form an alliance of mutual comic understanding against the formal and inhuman structure into which they find themselves. In short, they find themselves in an alien environment, so destroy it. It is the 60s revolution in microcosm.

Of course, this isn't a 'message' film at all – far from it: the slapstick comes thick and fast. In an effort to retrieve his shoe from the indoor pond (a pond incidentally, very similar in design to the water-feature in *Mon Oncle*, right down to the fake white lily-pads that form stepping stones) Sellers propels the shoe high into the air and across the room where it lands in a waiter's tray.

The waiter who has been surreptitiously slugging the drink from glasses rejected by the teetotal Bakshi becomes his sidekick in the gradual unfolding anarchy. Franken's performance was singled out in Roger Egbert's review on the film's release:

> Rivalling Sellers with one of *The Party*'s stand-out performances: Steve Franken as the increasingly inebriated butler, slathering on a layer of slapstick to the proceedings with his incontinent antics. Franken's interaction with his vexed supervisor, his drunken stroll through the shallow indoor pool, his struggle to rescue the roast chicken perched precariously atop a bewigged socialite's bouffant hairdo: all comedy gold.

Using a waiter for a running gag is, of course, another nod to *Playtime*, in which Hulot's waiter keeps ripping his uniform and is relegated to the side-lines of the restaurant, skulking in the shadows in his increasingly shredded outfit. *Playtime* is also echoed in the entire closing third act of *The Party*, in its escalating dancing scene and general growing sense of chaos. A black musician even arrives, just as a French African does in Tati's movie. There is also a young woman who becomes a fourth member of the anarchic clan, taking a shine to Sellers' holy fool just as the young American tourist takes a shine to Hulot.

The unfolding of the physical routines are seamless: problem leads to problem – Bakshi needs to visit the bathroom but is stopped when everyone gathers round the piano to listen to Michele (Claudine Longet) sing. Once in the bathroom the entire contents of the place conspires against him – the cistern doesn't stop flushing, the toilet roll doesn't stop spinning, and Bakshi is forced to flee by climbing out onto a roof terrace, from which he plunges twenty feet into the swimming pool. The stunt allows the relationship between Bakshi and Michele to blossom, for it is she – along with the eccentric cowboy – who fishes him out, followed by a very Stan Laurel-style sequence in which his new friends attempt to get him out of his wet clothes and in so doing send him into paroxysms of ticklish laughter – a tickling scene on a par with the routine in *Way Out West* when the villains are attempting to extract the deeds to the gold mine from Stan's night-shirt.

Unable to get a chair at the dining table, the unassertive Bakshi prefers to pretend to have a chair than ask for one; and spends the entire mealtime crouching. He propels a chicken leg onto a woman's wig: enlisting the help of the now magnificently sozzled waiter, they rescue the food and along with it, the hairpiece. The scene ends with another waiter's head in a huge trifle.

Again, traditional slapstick fare that would not be considered innovative even in 1912: but in the finely-played clowning it is Sellers' demeanour that is his sharpest comic device, his geniality and eagerness to please being the engine of the humour rather than the physical gag itself. From the very beginning when he sits beside a chatting couple to try and join in their conversation and they get up and leave, we become aware of the true interior comedy of this story: it is the gradually emerging division between the stuffy formal characters at the party – the 'phoneys', the bullies, the pretentious trophy-wives – and the free-thinking outsiders, the eccentrics with a spirit of fun. And it is this theme that elevates *The Party* into something more than a string of routines. It is not loosely connected at all, but a finely formulated escalation of anarchy – a structured breaking down of the pretentious social behaviour of Hollywood and a celebration of what might be called pure and genuine human fun.

Once more, this is a direct link to Tati. Just as the final quarter of *Playtime* when the chic Royal Garden Restaurant is slowly transformed into a shambling, anarchic ruin and where a small group of diners even form their own separate restaurant-within-a-restaurant, so too does the Hollywood Party metamorphose from a formal ceremony of status and pecking order and 'phoney-ness' into a glorious mad mess, the neat modernist house even filling with foam to punch home its destruction. This is the Lord of Misrule in action, with reversed roles – the maid ends up dancing wildly in front of the guests rather than serving them, the pickled waiter kisses a beautiful rich woman; joyous Jewish dancing breaks out, replacing the sedate 'cool jazz' of earlier in the evening. And it is no coincidence that an elephant is introduced into the proceedings, the spirit of the Hindu God Ganesh, symbol of prosperity and joy – stumbling through the groovy, wild climax.

By the time the party morning has broken, inhibitions have broken down, and the new generation of free spirits, Bakshi leading them, are triumphant. Bakshi takes Michele home, and will see her again. And like Hulot spluttering off in his makeshift car at the end of his holiday, so too does the lovable Indian drive off up the road, not into the sunset but into the dawn – of the late 60s.

The film was favourably reviewed, and largely seen as a return to form for Sellers. 'Peter Sellers is back at work again,' wrote Roger Ebert, 'and Sellers works. He develops a character and plays it, for better or worse, for the whole movie. No costume changes. No Napoleon suits.'

It is a shame, perhaps, that Sellers did not make another wholly visual film. His ensuing work, including his return to the Panther franchise and his swansong masterpiece *Being There*, contain elements of the slapstick tradition, but Sellers fell back on more orthodox output – if *The Fiendish Plot of Fu Manchu* can be considered orthodox. *The Party* would remain Seller's only foray into a wholly pantomimic film, and despite the films of Tati and the Silent Renaissance of the 50s and 60s, the film industry still exhibited a reluctance to embrace the form as a contemporary genre.

CHAPTER 17

Another Outsider: Marty Feldman

Though Larry Semon runs a close second, rarely in the history of physical clowning has anyone been more facially suited to comedy than Marty Feldman. The askew eyes, the broad angular face, the tatty hair, the shocked expression – here was a face designed by a Komos, god of humour – and its owner was palpably conscious of its vast comedic power.

Yet it wasn't the face Feldman started out with, the famous two eyes with minds of their own being the result of a thyroid problem afflicting him in his early thirties. It was an illness, however, that accelerated his ascendancy as a performer rather than just as a writer – proof if ever there was one of the veracity of the cliché 'if life gives you lemons, make lemonade.'

The cheeky grin, the Harpo-style mugging, the Keaton gait – from Feldman's first major appearance in ATV's *At Last The 1948 Show* in 1967 the public knew that here was a comedian with something special beyond mere patter or acting: here was a visual clown with the potential to become great. After his first solo-starring TV vehicle, *Marty*, aired on the BBC in 1968 the formal post-show reports stated: 'Marty Feldman is a unique comedian – bizarre in both style and appearance and able, by his expression alone, to reduce his audience to helpless laughter … This was visual humour in the fullest sense of the word.'

Born into a middle-class Jewish family in London's East End, it was as a writer that Marty Feldman first established himself, his talents first nourished in the fading world of Variety. Leaving his Aldgate home at the age of sixteen he became, by his own admission, a middle-class homeless bohemian in the boozy neon-lit world of 50s Soho, with one foot in the shadowy world of petty crime. Drifting on the edge of the criminal underworld he worked variously as a fence, a look-out man, a getaway driver, a kitchen porter, a shoemaker, and a trumpet-player in a band. For a year he slept in the empty workman's hut in the middle of Soho Square (it still stands today).

The petty crime was a by-product of the world of Soho at the time and his own state of deprivation: Feldman wasn't a criminal by inclination.

In 1954 Marty Feldman was a homeless Jewish busker living on the streets of Soho. Thirteen years later he was Britain's biggest television comedian, reinventing silent comedy for the flower-power generation.

In fact he described himself as the 'worst getaway driver in London,' constantly being worried that he didn't have a driving licence.

It wasn't comedy but jazz that first tugged at the young man's heart. He busked for a year on the streets of Paris with a group of jazz musicians and on his return to London secured regular gigs at the Blue Spot Nightclub in Soho owned by the notorious Jack Spot, the Capone of London. As he told biographer Robert Ross: 'My generation are transition figures ... between the old-fashioned bohemian, corduroy, bearded, sandals, bare-feet, pipe-smoking generation and the drug pop-culture of today.'

Comedy was his deepest love but the loneliness of stand-up comedy made the young Feldman eschew a solitary life on the road, preferring the company of the music scene. 'The same impulse that makes you a stand-up comic probably makes you a dictator. It's a very lonely way to make a living.' (quoted in Ross, ibid). The trumpet was replaced by a set of drums, but comedy eventually wooed him away from music, and – still only 17 – he joined a variety troupe at the Dreamland Funfair in Margate.

The start of his professional career coincided with the last few years of variety. Television was beginning to deplete live audiences, theatres in every town were becoming drained, and the bottom-of-the-bill entertainers like Feldman were scrabbling over spots at out-of-the-way desolate venues like air bases and out-of-season holiday camps. He joined two down-at-heel musical comics and became one third of 'Morris, Marty and Mitch,' spending four patchy years cutting his teeth in the dying days of music-hall, sharing the bill occasionally with Sandy Powell and Max Wall. The act was inspired by the Ritz Brothers and Harpo and Dr Crock but in his more honest moments Feldman would later describe the act as 'putrid.' The quality of the act was less important than the experience – he was on the road with a trio, and it was on this circuit that he met Spike Milligan, Peter Sellers and the person who was to prove most instrumental in focussing his talents – Barry Took.

His description of Morris, Marty and Mitch as 'putrid' is perhaps harsh, for the trio obtained regular TV bookings and even performed in America and France – from the very start Feldman was developing a comedy style that was international. His heroes were the silent comics of the past, and according to a friend, David Weddle, he would 'watch a Buster Keaton film every day,' keeping 'a portrait (of him) wherever he went, in his office, at home, in his dressing-room, to remind him of his roots.' (quoted in Ross, ibid).

He dipped his toes into the burgeoning medium of TV – a world that hadn't written the rule-book yet. Every Wednesday at Elstree Studios there was a live comedy show, *Fancy Free* produced by Anne Chataway, in which performers could simply turn up and do what they wanted. If you were free on Wednesday afternoons, you popped along and did a sketch. So Feldman and new pals Barry Took and John Law would go along. Marty the TV performer was born.

*

It's one of those curiosities of post-war comedy that the first love of two of its giants – Peter Sellers and Marty Feldman – was silent comedy, yet it was via radio that they first exploded into national consciousness. Just as Sellers had been propelled into the forefront of showbiz in *The Goons*, so too did the struggling, homeless middle-class bohemian from Aldgate find his feet on the wireless writing for shows like *Take It from Here* and *Beyond Our Ken.*

With Barry Took, he formed a writing partnership that was to last until 1974. A successful teaming from the start, over the next ten years it would elevate them into the status of – if not Galton & Simpson – then certainly Muir & Norden. Feldman had initially broken into radio by writing as (one third of the team) on *Educating Archie* for Peter Brough, but when Muir & Norden wanted someone else to write the final series of *Take it from Here* and hired Barry Took, Took insisted that Feldman come and write it with him.

Feldman's career was born. They went on to write *Beyond Our Ken, Round the Horne* and the smash TV hit *Army Game* and its spin-off *Bootsie and Snudge.* The latter sitcom, in which Bill Fraser and Alfie Bass co-starred as soldier and batman now working in a gentleman's club, began displaying innovative and at times surreal elements that played with the genre – looks to camera, dramatised flights of fancy reminiscent of Chaplin, whole episodes set in one room: and this in the early 60s. Clearly here was an original talent already demonstrating a desire to do something different in comedy, even while working in a traditional form.

Feldman wrote thirty-nine TV shows a year for three years, plus two radio shows a week. Sixty cigarettes a day and coffee overdoses fuelled this creative frenzy – and unsurprisingly hospitalised him. Diagnosed with Graves' disease – one of those dramatic illnesses like gout or shingles – the thyroid treatment intended to cure him made his eyes bulge in their sockets, and a visual comedy giant was born.

Arguably Feldman was the first Python, not simply because it was with the proto-Pythons Michael Palin, John Cleese and Graham Chapman that he first began to emerge as a TV performer, but also because of his writing style; the flights-of-fancy, bizarre names and surreal wordplay of *Round the Horne* and his whimsical sitcom series *The Walrus and the Carpenter* broadcast in 1965 were indisputably Python-esque.

The new Oxbridge comics looked up to Feldman – here was a writer who was nearly ten years older than them and had started work in the golden age of the wireless. The seminal *Frost Report* allied Feldman with these young thrusting university turks, but only as writer and script editor (Feldman wrote the iconic class sketch featuring John Cleese, Ronnie Barker and Ronnie Corbett all looking down on each other): he did not join them as a performer until the spin-off series *At Last the 1948 Show* for ATV.

Written by and starring Marty Feldman, John Cleese, Graham Chapman and Tim Brooke-Taylor, *At Last the 1948 Show* was a departure from the satire of *The Frost Report*, preferring surreal whimsy, probably the dominant element of the 60s new wave. Although produced by David Frost, this series was the Oxbridge clowns – plus Feldman – saying 'look, we're more versatile than that'.

Feldman fell in perfectly with university wits Cleese, Chapman, Palin and Jones, Brooke-Taylor and Oddie and it was this homogenous group, plus Peter Cook and Dudley Moore, who were to dominate television comedy for the next ten years. The big gang variously came together, diverged and regrouped, finally dividing in the 60s like some cellular creature into three great series – *The Goodies*, *Monty Python's Flying Circus* … and *Marty*.

Being a low-budget studio-bound series with no location filming, there were restraints on the amount of visual humour in *At Last the 1948 Show*, but sprinkled among the programme spoofs and the proto-Pythonic surreal office sketches were memorable pantomimic flights of fancy. In a send-up of the ballroom dancing show *Come Dancing*, Feldman plays a female dancer who – mid-dance – begins flirting outrageously with her opponent's partner – gliding close, fluttering her eyebrows, even scribbling love-notes on her number-card. Another inspired silent sketch set in a library has a group of policemen attempting to arrest a crook on the run while having to keep utterly quiet: a high point being Feldman stopping mid-fight and consulting a book on self-defence (an echo of a gag in Tati's first short, *Soigne ton Gauche* in which the boxer Roger leafs through an instruction pamphlet between punches). In a brilliant mime, Tim Brooke-Taylor performs another Feldman visual sketch, 'The

Dancing Accountant', demonstrating several mad routines, in that dance-crazed decade, such as the 'reaching for the top shelf' and the 'removing wet swimming trunks'. The team were also not averse to using the kind of camera-trickery being employed by Ernie Kovacs and Benny Hill: in one routine the gang form a dancing line-up and, with clever montaging, suddenly possess high-kicking female stockinged legs.

What is overwhelming in this, his first major TV role, is Feldman's palpable consciousness of the devastating comic power of his face. His early years of stage performing before he settled behind a typewriter for ten years had made him aware that his face was his fortune. His use of reactions is beyond mugging – it's far more subtle: it has a cheekiness, a sense of complicity with the audience, a mutual acknowledgment that he is a comic force whose purpose is to undermine and subvert. His comic persona, in short, is anarchic and akin to that of Harpo.

In one sketch he plays an Arab on a tour of a TV studio during the filming of a romantic costume drama, and inveigles himself into the piece. An unspeaking role, Feldman turns it into a silent *tour de force* worthy of Harpo, sidling up to the woman on the sofa, wiggling his eyebrows suggestively, sandwiching himself between the two lovers, and even dangling his leg over them. Although he fits into the two-hander and three-hander sketches, like Rowan Atkinson in *Not the Nine O'Clock News* there is something that sets him apart from the other comedians as a solo performer: despite how funny Cleese, Brooke-Taylor and Chapman are, it is always Feldman that pulls focus.

The BBC agreed, and it is significant that of all the 1948 team, it was Feldman who was the first to get his own series.

*

When *Marty* aired in 1968, it was an instant smash hit. With a big BBC budget behind him – it was the most expensive comedy series the corporation had yet produced – a great team of fellow writers with Palin and Jones, Brooke-Taylor, John Junkin and Barry Cryer, and a legendary producer in Dennis Main Wilson, this was a show bursting with talent and vitality. It was as if after fifteen years of sitting behind a typewriter churning out comedy for others, Feldman was ready to spring in front of the public and show them what he could do: he shed the old days of variety and *Round the Horne* and the *Army Game* and allowed himself to stretch as a physical performer.

Never has a sleeve-note summed up an artiste so accurately and succinctly: the BBC DVD release of *Marty* states, simply, that it showcases 'a unique comic style that recalls the era of silent slapstick comedy but encapsulates the surreal spirit of 1960s new comedy.'

Feldman was the physical Python. When a compilation of the shows were submitted to the Montreux Comedy Festival (it won the Silver Rose) the jury singled out *Marty* as being something of a cross between Chaplin and Tati. By the second series, Palin remembers that 'Feldman (was) doing more and more of the physical comedy which he enjoying doing. He became very Harpo Marx in those routines. There was a feeling that he didn't like doing lines. He could do them, brilliantly, but I remember Terry and I writing more and more visual items for him.' (quoted in Ross, ibid).

Palin was probably referring to the football sketch in which Feldman plays a Paraguayan who lusts after the Duchess who is shaking their hands in the line-up. Not content with kissing her hand just once, he dodges round the back of the line-up and keeps popping up and grabbing her hand. He smothers her arm with kisses, he follows the Duchess's husband, aping his movements from behind and even hanging his leg on the Duke's hand. All this is pure Harpo.

With *Marty*, speeded-up film and reverse film returned to the screen; and so like Keaton are the style and the tropes that during long sequences in the series the audience might have thought they were watching something made in 1925. Keaton wasn't the only influence, for Feldman also injected a healthy dose of Harold Lloyd thrill

Fuelled by a desire to emulate his idol Keaton for the small screen, Marty Feldman pursued ever-more ambitious stunts with no trick photography: here he hangs off a freight train in Liphook in one of his classic extended sketches, 'The Loneliness of the Long Distance Golfer' from 1969.

comedy into the series. 'A Day in the Life of a Stuntman' has him leaping onto a moving e-type Jaguar, vaulting a garden gate and performing somersaults. In 'The Loneliness of the Long Distance Golfer' (the sketch Feldman said years later was the piece he really wanted to be remembered by), he really pulled the stops out, hanging off the edges of moving trains and dangling from second-storey window-ledges. Just as Lloyd lost three fingers in the pursuit of his art, so Feldman was not immune to injury; Tim Brooke-Taylor remembers him injuring his leg in a dark railway tunnel immediately prior to Dennis Main Wilson shouting 'action!' – and Feldman insisting on carrying on.

Brilliant though many of the verbal sketches are, it is the long visual sequences in *Marty* that are the stand-out ingredients, and indeed are the ones best-remembered today: the 'Night Life of the Chartered Accountant', in which the meek and henpecked husband carries on several love affairs, zooming off to the coast in under a minute, flying off to a tropical island in an equally short time – all the while muttering the excuse that he's putting the cat out or emptying the rubbish. Marty momentarily drops his brow-beaten little man persona and becomes an instant Groucho clad in top hat, tails and cape, meeting his lover in a grand hotel.

In Marty's world, time and space have no meaning, are compacted or stretched: hence the display in a florist's is a vast tropical jungle. In this sketch the bowler-hatted little man is in search of a humble bunch of daffs. He ends up in central Africa. In hindsight Barry Took would say that they were unconsciously tapping into the frustrations and tensions of late-60s Britain: certainly the dominant leitmotif in *Marty* is the anonymous Walter-Mitty-loser liberating his consciousness. Is he *really* driving to the ocean to meet a bikini-clad girl? Or is it in his head?

The lightning coach-tour is another gem, in which a speeded-up coach – driven by a marvellously non-speeded-up lugubrious John Junkin – carries a horde of sightseers to the seaside and back in under two minutes. In this piece Feldman plays his long-coated, eccentric character Mr Glob – a Goon show grotesque come to life, twin brother to Peter Cook's E L Wisty. Another purely silent pageant is 'The Cricketer', (written by Palin and Jones) in which Marty the bowler walks back a hundred miles or more before turning for his run-up. Again, Marty gives us thrill comedy – he crosses an exploding minefield, falls off a cliff. By the time he gets back to the pitch the ball has been rubbed to a tiny red marble and all the other players are bearded ancients or skeletons.

And just as there are shadows of Harpo, Harold Lloyd and Keaton (in the golfing sketch Feldman even puts his hand to his forehead whenever he looks into the distance – a classic Keaton pose), the soul of

Chaplin too imbues the series: in a cod French song Marty nods in homage to Chaplin's gibberish singing waiter in *Modern Times.* And to top off the influences from the silent era there is even a Keystone-Kop-like sketch in which a squadron of black taxi cabs attempt to mow down enemy pedestrians.

A smash hit, *Marty* (and its subsequent incarnations *It's Marty*, and the one-off 45-minute special *Marty Amok*) won two BAFTAs and a Silver Rose of Montreux. A writer and performer on *Amok* was one of Feldman's heroes, the French comedian Robert Dhéry who contributed and co-starred in a couple of his own most famous routines for the show, 'Changing Cubicles' and 'Little Café'.

Visual comedy was back on the map. Eric Sykes' *The Plank* had been released before the airing of *Marty*'s first series and Sykes dashed off an understandably disgruntled letter to producer Dennis Main Wilson after he saw Feldman's 'Bullfighting Policeman' routine, suspecting more than coincidence. Both Main Wilson and Feldman denied having yet seen *The Plank*, and the matter was dropped, but this was an echo of the old days of the silent era when comics would borrow and adapt others' routines and gags for their own work.

*

Now a national comedy star, Feldman reached for wider shores, and made two feature films; the first was a cameo in that hymn to English eccentricity *The Bedsitting Room* by Spike Milligan and John Antrobus, but the second was a self-penned (with Barry Took) satire on the late 60s advertising industry, and was his first starring vehicle.

Every Home Should Have One, released in 1970, although containing some fine visual elements, was something of a red herring. To begin with, Feldman's persona in the movie is not a brow-beaten little man, the kind he specialised in, but a sex-obsessed advertising executive, Teddy Brown. Despite the sluggish narrative, there are some inspired slapstick moments: a merry-go-round Teasmade that attacks Teddy in same way as the food machine rebels in *Modern Times*; careering and skidding along corridors, slamming into doors. A centrepiece is a marvellous Chaplin-like sequence set in a park with Teddy as a Pan statue come to life and dancing off with a troupe of white-robed maidens. Another sequence shot in black and white has Teddy chasing Inga (Julie Ege) round the bedroom in a what-the-butler-saw pastiche.

Feldman was a silent comedian in search of greater vehicles: not yet ready perhaps, or able, to furnish an all-visual feature film like Sellers had with *The Party* or Jerry Lewis with *The Bellboy*, he signed up with ATV to make fourteen hour-long comedy specials, an extraordinarily ambitious move.

*

The Marty Feldman Comedy Machine was produced by Lew Grade, a man who, more than any other producer, was focussed on the international market. With opening titles by Python animator Terry Gilliam, *Comedy Machine* – while not perhaps emulating the original impact of his first series for the BBC – nevertheless contained many superb sequences of visual humour, and was Feldman's calling card for the USA.

While his old gang (Brooke-Taylor, Palin and Jones) from *The 1948 Show* days wrote for the new series, *Comedy Machine* was very much Feldman's solo show as a performer.

The outsider nature of the silent clown is established from the very start, with a cartoon Marty rejected by a factory conveyor belt and chucked out into the garbage. Not so much a collection of sketches as a string of mini-silent movies, they were even titled (as indeed were some of the visual pieces in *Marty*.) Ranging from cartoony and prop-based sequences such as 'The Brave Knight' in which he attempts to reach a fair maiden imprisoned at the top of a tower, to more sophisticated Tati-esque vignettes such as 'The Wheel', (in which the use of sound effects overlaid after filming is very like those of *M Hulot's Holiday* – the squeak of the wheel, the creak of the car), the series was edited down to fourteen half-hours by ABC in America, and established Feldman as an international star – ten years before Benny Hill made it stateside.

The pieces weren't all solo: his old mentor and comic godfather from the 1950s, Spike Milligan, collaborated with him on an extended saga of two rival undertakers, whose competition for business escalates to hysterical dimensions: from 'Buy One Coffin Get One Free' signs in the window to attempting to bump people off in the street. Instead of rescuing a drowning man, Feldman rows out into the middle of the lake in a coffin and knocks him out with a shovel. Another man enters a tall thin outdoor WC, and the funeral directors immediately appear, tipping the narrow shed over to make an instant coffin. Their rivalry builds to an insane climax with Milligan and Feldman chasing each other, clocking each other over the heads with their spades and manically digging grave after grave.

These extended sketches or mini-films were interspersed sparingly with quickies, such as Marty in the bath with a tattoo of a ship on his midriff being torpedoed by submarine commander Bob Todd. With 'Just One More Please' Marty once again restores thrill comedy – so successfully mined ten years later by Michael Crawford in *Some Mothers Do 'Ave Em* – when he plays a press photographer pursuing Bob Todd. The piece allows Feldman to perform stunts of the calibre and style not seen since Keaton or Harold Lloyd: he hangs off the roofs of buses, is hoisted by a crane up the side of a hundred-foot building, and is even suspended from Westminster Bridge, all in order to obtain yet another picture of an increasingly and splendidly befuddled and histrionic Todd.

Although sprinkled with brilliance and innovation – one particular highlight is his percussionist in an orchestra being bothered by a fly and pursuing the offending insect brandishing a gigantic pair of cymbals – several commentators perceived it was in *Comedy Machine* that Feldman subtly began to lose that sheen of English eccentricity that characterised his earlier creativity: the attempt to produce something devoid of cultural references so as to appeal to the international market was apparent.

This was Lew Grade's fault – the instruction to focus on appealing to the US would have come from on high. When the shows were broadcast in the US by ABC, they were cut –wisely – to half-hour programmes, which is what they should have been in the first place. *Marty Feldman's Comedy Machine*, however, won the Golden Rose of Montreux in May 1972, narrowly beating *The Goodies* with their classic 'Kitten Kong'. The win proved controversial, with Oddie accusing him of using the best moments from the whole series of shows and editing them down to half-an-hour. The rules clearly stated that the submission had to be a complete show as originally broadcast, and the subterfuge created ripples amongst his old comedy pals.

The series was not renewed, but it was Feldman's passport to Hollywood. While patchily brilliant, his work in Hollywood is not considered his finest. He delivered excellent performances in Gene Wilder's *Young Frankenstein* (1974) and *The Adventures of Sherlock Holmes' Smarter Brother* (1975) interspersed with oddball creations such as *In God we Trust* (1980) and *Slapstick of Another Kind* (1982) in which Feldman co-starred with Jerry Lewis. Underused in Mel Brooks' *Silent Movie* of 1975, Feldman's swansong – fittingly – was the Python offshoot movie *Yellowbeard*, made in 1983. It was to prove his last appearance in front of the camera, for like Hancock, Ernie Kovacs and indeed Peter Sellers, he would die young – aged only 43, of a heart attack.

It is perhaps apt that the last word be given to his old comedy-writing partner Barry Took, who had virtually discovered Feldman in the early

50s when the young comic was living homeless in Soho. Took summed him up best when he told Ross, Feldman's biographer, that:

> Marty's comedy is full of hidden depths. His understanding of the old, the poor and the ignorant is remarkable. Whether masquerading as a working-class Bishop or as a cloth-capped ballet dancer recently out of prison, Marty's characters epitomise the forlorn hope. Endlessly justifying their actions, angry when questioned, pathetically convinced that they're right all the time, these outrageous pantaloons take us by the scruff of the neck and shake us until we begin dimly to see what a curious, sad, hilarious place the world is.

CHAPTER 18

Ronnie Barker: The Grumble & Grunt Comedies

To look at Ronnie Barker you might think that this mild-mannered, tubby, bespectacled man was a middle-manager from Pinner (indeed, Barker did live Pinner). With softly pleasant voice, pin-striped suit and national health spectacles, he took self-effacement to new levels – and it is one of those delightful quirks of show business that such a modest, genial, *normal* man could rise to become one of the greatest comic character actors of the post-war era.

Barker was not unique in that respect – a similarly good-natured and self-deprecating actor (or so he seemed) was Alec Guinness, whose bland demeanour and blank-canvas face belied a fiery genius for self-transformation. Serendipitously, Guinness was Barker's favourite actor.

Rightly remembered as one of Britain's finest television actors for his role as Norman Stanley Fletcher in *Porridge* and as Arkwright in *Open All Hours*, and for his prime-time sketch show *The Two Ronnies*, Ronnie Barker's range as a verbal comedian was already vast when he, too, turned to silent comedy, becoming one of its most creative champions.

Unlike other comics in this book, Barker's forays into non-dialogue pantomime seem to have been fun interludes between his major works: Sellers, Lewis and indeed Feldman possessed an angst and an ambition that seemed largely absent in Barker – one senses he enjoyed his work far more than they did.

Here was a man who triumphed in both major genres of TV light entertainment – sketch show and sitcom – yet who didn't want his name too many times in the credits, famously submitting material under the pseudonym Gerald Wiley. 'I don't like *produced by Charlie Chaplin, music by Charlie Chaplin, starring Charlie Chaplin,*' he told Bob McCabe in 2004. This reticence to attract attention to himself marks Barker out from many of the subjects of this book: in short, he was an actor, not a comedian, and as such he seemed largely free of the tortured and controlling elements of the comedian's ego.

Barker nevertheless possessed sufficient ambition to write and star in several of the finest examples of that Silent Renaissance that swept into British broadcasting throughout the 60s and beyond. *Futtock's End, The*

Picnic and *By the Sea* were Barker's rich contribution to the canon. Despite his immense success, first in radio sitcom and then in TV sitcom and sketch shows, the ambition to make wholly visual comedy was deep-rooted. As a teenager in middle-class Oxford the young Barker would spend hours with a friend watching Super-8 vintage films of old comedians – 'W.C. Fields, Laurel and Hardy. Fields was so clever with physical business. That's what I liked about him – the things he did with his hat and his stick. There was one film when he kept getting caught up in some bead curtains in the house while having a row with his wife; hed keep walking into this curtains and he was wonderful at getting tangled up.'

Born in Bedford in 1929, Barker had moved to Oxford with his parents when he was four, his father working as a clerk for Shell-Mex in Cowley. Following aborted spells as bank clerk and hospital porter, young Barker threw himself into amateur dramatics mainly to meet girls; became smitten (with both theatre and girls) and launched himself as a professional. Repertory jobs followed in Aylesbury and at the Oxford Playhouse – significantly a season with Clifford Williams' Mime Theatre Company. Barker travelled up to Haverstock Hill in London to start training. 'Mime was absolutely new to me,' he told his biographer, Bob McCabe. '(Clifford) was an ex-dancer with the *Ballet Rambert*, and he knew a lot about mime and he decided to take this company round the country.' Although this brave attempt to take dumb-show to the masses was ultimately doomed – the company were left high and dry in Penzance from where Barker had to walk back to Oxford, sleeping in hedges – the experience was invaluable, and would stand him in good stead when in later years he would write and star in his own dumb-shows.

Success came relatively quickly, and it was in serious roles that he first made his mark; making a splash in the West End in *Mourning Becomes Electra* at the Arts Theatre Club, and *Summertime* at the Apollo with Dirk Bogarde and Geraldine McEwan – a serious beginning for a performer whose versatility and comic bent would soon lead him to become the comic stalwart of the Oxford Playhouse. Snapped up by Christmas pantomime seasons and radio comedy work, he would then focus excusively on comedy (much to the chagrin of director Peter Hall, who would attempt in vain over the years to tempt him back to serious roles). Appearances in *The Floggits* in 1956 with Elsie and Doris Waters, *Crowther's Crowd* with Leslie Crowther, and then a co-starring role in one of the smash-hit wireless sitcoms of the post-war era, *The Navy Lark*, cemented Barker's reputation as a major blossoming force in British comedy. The serious actor was lost to Peter Hall forever – and the variety comedian and sitcom actor was born.

*

In 1964, writer and director Jay Lewis and producer Bob Kellett gathered together a fine repertory company of British comedy character actors, from Bernard Cribbins and Richard Briers to Peter Butterworth and Gerald Campion, to make *A Home of Your Own*, a silent film in the fine tradition of house-construction comedies. The 35-year-old Ronnie Barker was invited to become part of this stellar group. The story of the film, its background, and its place in the Silent Renaissance of the early 60s has been told in another chapter, but as far as Barker's role in the piece is concerned it was both an early demonstration of his physical comedy skills, and an inspiration for his later visual work, planting the seed of his ambition to write and star in a dialogue-free film.

'Occasionally I thought I really must write one of those,' he told Bob McCabe years later. 'There's a lot one can do without any words and I like complicated things. It was a very complicated thing to write. Someone said to me that it must have been very easy because there was no dialogue. But it was the hardest thing to write ... it was a very thick script even though there wasn't a word spoken.'

In *A Home of Your Own* there is a deftness of execution in Barker's performance that has echoes of Oliver Hardy. 'I play the man who was

Only a cameo, but the cavorting labourer in Bob Kellet and Jay Lewis' A Home of Your Own *(1964) gave Ronnie Barker a taste for visual comedy that was to blossom in his own later series of 'Grumble and Grunt Comedies.' Shrewdly Barker used Kellett as director on his first solo dialogue-free work,* Futtock's End *(1970). Here, Barker performs an insane Highland jig of rage as his beloved bed of cement is ruined.*

laying the cement,' he said 'and everyone kept going over it, running over it. I had this great sequence where I suddenly threw everything down and I danced on it.' Barker's outburst in the film is, in fact, majestic – he jumps up and down, performs a ballet routine, even collapses onto the cement and begins swimming in it.

Working on *A Home of Your Own* made Barker want to make a silent film, but he would have to wait another six years before being given the opportunity, and in the intervening years he became a star. Not from *The Two Ronnies* – the first series of which would air in 1971 – but via several portmanteau playhouse series for ITV. In swift succession Barker made *The Ronnie Barker Playhouse* for Associated Rediffusion in 1968, and *Hark at Barker* in 1969: and in 1970 he was given his own silent special, *Futtock's End* – directed by Bob Kellett.

This was not the first appearance of Giles Futtock: Lord Rustless, the peppery, blustering aristocrat – to whom General Futtock is clearly a close relative – made his first appearance in *The Ronnie Barker Playhouse* in 1968, and in the follow-up series was promoted to being the anchor for the show. Barker is explicit as to where he got the inspiration for the character. 'He's Fred Emney,' he explained to Bob McCabe in 2005. 'Rustless doesn't sound like him, but he has that same wonderful character in that he'd sit back and let the world go by and nothing affected him.' Another ingredient goes even further back, to Barker's early days in rep at the Oxford Playhouse, when he played Lord Slingsby-Craddock.

*

Barker always referred to his three silent films (*Futtock's End, The Picnic* and *By the Sea*) as *almost* silent, his grumble and grunt comedies: in them he pared back Tati's use of occasionally intelligible snatches of dialogue and reduced it to language-less ambient sound.

Reading the scripts gives a fascinating insight into the modus operandi of making a dialogue-free movie. Barker's scripts are not just sparse outlines or indications of what might happen in a scene (as with Eric Sykes' films) but are dense, tightly packed novellas, written as a narratives in the third person, each stage direction explicitly outlined. Nothing is left to the imagination or to improvisation. One example, from *Futtock's End*, reads thus:

> Hawk (Michael Hordern the butler) is handing round bread rolls, and drops one from the basket. He looks down, looks round, and furtively kicks it under the table. Under the

table we see six pairs of legs, and the roll shooting in. The chattering begins to swell, and the twelve feet, all shuffling under the table, begin to kick the roll backwards and forwards. After a few journeys up and down the carpet, it is passed along from foot to foot, until suddenly, with an extra strong kick, it flies straight between the legs of Mrs. Brassett, which legs, clad as they are in white stockings, and positioned wide apart, uncannily resemble a set of goalposts. As the roll hits the back of her black net skirt, the chattering is mixed with the sound of a Cup-tie crowd cheering a goal. We see the table from above again, all the guests, including Mrs. Brassett, quite oblivious to what has happened. Giles gets up to carve the roast, as the soup is cleared away.

This is meticulous scripting for a visual gag and the scene on screen is as exactly as he wrote it, with not even the tiniest of changes. Barker's scripts are proof – if proof be needed – that scripting a visual comedy scenario is writing-as-directing, for as a gag depends on timing, so each cutaway has to be built into the script.

Another 'object-switch' routine from Futtock's End *in which a bread roll becomes a football. With bleeding-in commentary and finely choreographed footwork, just when you think the passing of the 'ball' is going to be the culmination of the joke, Ronnie Barker has a woman's legs adopt the shape of a goal – and someone scores with a resounding cheer. The script version of the scene is almost a page long, every single shot and action elaborately described – a huge influence on my own scripting of* Pompidou *with Matt Lucas.*

Interestingly, the script for *Futtock's End* includes several pages of dialogue in its early drafts; clearly Barker wanted to indicate the mental processes of his characters and their interaction – for naturally no dialogue ended up onscreen: indeed, the whole soundtrack including speech was recorded afterwards and edited over the action.

A British Lion release of a Paradine Production – the company formed by David Frost – *Futtock's End* is a joyous *homage* to the Donald McGill saucy postcard. As lusty as Benny Hill, though oddly more lovable, the peregrinations of General Futtock and the inhabitants of his decaying Dorset manor were a throwback to the world of P G Wodehouse, featuring coquettish maids, doddering butlers, idiotic chinless wonders and peppery Colonels. This was Blandings with slapstick. In *Futtock's End*, Barker recalls, 'I wanted to capture that sort of far-off, childhood summer. The feeling you remember of slight weirdness. Although everything was funny in it, there was still a feeling of an unreal little encapsulated world. Which is the same with the others to a degree (*The Picnic* and *By the Sea.*) In *The Picnic* it's an Edwardian picture. It's a situation that's unreal to most people, and that's what I liked about it.' (quoted in McCabe, ibid).

Though securing the services of director Bob Kellett with whom he had worked on *A Home of Your Own*, Barker co-directed all three of his silents. The plot of *Futtock's End* is simplicity itself: a group of people spend a weekend at the country house of retired General Giles Futtock. Like *M Hulot's Holiday* the film is a picaresque sequence of postcards brought to life, stuffed with broad comic types; indeed, the characters don't even have names but are billed as The Twit, The Niece, The Artist, The Aunt, and The Bird, like the grotesque protagonists of a Restoration Comedy. There is a notable cast, including Roger Livesey as the deaf artist Pantaloon character, who despite being in his sixties performs some impressive stunts such as falling backwards out of a car. Further slapstick comes from the redoubtable Michael Hordern as The Butler, for whom Barker originally wrote the script. We first see him spluttering up the driveway of the Manor astride a vintage motorcycle – driving the postman into a hedge and whizzing off out of sight, then immediately answering the front door to the same postman, in a magical gag reminiscent of Tati's postman joke in *Jour de Fête* when he careers into the tavern and appears seconds later at an upstairs balcony.

Slapstick, however, is at a premium, with Barker eschewing pratfalls for more sophisticated gags. And the film is certainly packed with them, cleverly interlaced so as to provide forward momentum: that is, instead of pursuing each gag to its conclusion before moving on, three or more jokes are set up, then alternately cut back to as they develop, thus supplying the picture with the patina of plot. As Barker recalled of writing the script, everyone had their own storyline.

We first see Futtock emerging from his bathroom completely encased in suds. He nonchalantly crosses the room to light his cigar, nods good morning to the butler, then returns to the bathroom. Futtock is Wodehouse's Lord Emsworth in a blissful world of his own, and Barker wisely does not make him a leerer – his butler has that dubious honour, sneaking about the grounds attempting to spy on the female house-guests. Futtock is mild of temperament, drifting through the action benignly oblivious to the shenanigans going on around him. He has an eye for the ladies, but his gaze is not distasteful. He would rather have a cup of tea.

A party of guests arrives for the weekend, and in a sea of mumbling are installed in various bedrooms throughout the labyrinthine manor; indeed, so labyrinthine is Futtock's country seat that he himself gets lost. The party comprises a motley collection of Wodehousian folk from dizzy blonde to lanky upper-class idiot (the typecast Julian Orchard), plus a Japanese visitor who is probably there by accident and who is given a hilarious developing runner: as the hours and days pass, the man descends into a feral state, hiding in undergrowth in the grounds, stealing food from passing tea-trolleys, and sleeping in a laundry cupboard.

A soundtrack from Bob Sharples accompanies the gentle mayhem, Barker using non-diegetic sound brilliantly: the clucking of chickens accompany the kitchen maids and the roly-poly cook, and – as afternoon moves into evening – with the wonderfully dotty under-the-table football match routine with a fallen bread roll, complete with non-diegetic match soundtrack and crowd-cheering. There is a lovely moment when the lively and bubbling chatter suddenly ceases when the entire table dip their spoons in their soup, and heavy silence falls upon the eccentric throng.

Still the gags come thick and fast: The Artist blows bubbles out of his ear trumpet; The Butler secretly eats a hot potato then, finding it too scalding, spits it out in a vase of flowers, creating billowing clouds of steam. Whisky is accidentally poured into the fruit-punch bowl, with The Butler mistakenly assuming the maid has drunk the bottle empty as she staggers off, struggling with a difficult trolley. The entire table becomes gradually and hilariously drunk, bacchanalia once again subverting order and formality.

There follows, of course, a classic morning-after hangover scene, with each breakfast noise painfully magnified. Cereal poured into a bowl sounds like gravel from a dump-truck, Rice Krispies go off like fire-crackers. There is a lovely inconsequential bit of business with The Artist,

Ronnie Barker used the 'misunderstanding' device extensively in his visual comedies of the 70s and 80s – here in Futtock's End *(1970) the butler (Michael Hordern) lifts up an empty bottle of sherry and observes the maid staggering off crookedly towards the door. What the butler doesn't know is that earlier the audience has been privy to seeing the bottle being spilled of its contents; additionally Barker has set up the maid's trolley as having a dodgy wheel – so we now give a knowing laugh at the butler's understandable mistake.*

who becomes terrified by the eye of a trout, intercut with his own eye. A fry-up on a plate forms a malevolent face for Futtock.

For all its gentle English humour, *Futtock's End* is not averse to the surreal: a self-portrait of Van Gogh falls off the wall, causing his hat to drop down over his eyes.

What is very impressive about the film is the relentlessness and fertility of the gags. Even the cutaways and fill-in shots have jokes: the shoe-shine boy has only one appearance but is given a fine gag when counting up the shoes. Finding one too many, he dispenses with the odd shoe down the rubbish-chute – only for The Butler suddenly to appear with the other shoe.

Barker supplied escalating gags for each character: the deaf Artist is happily painting a clump of fir trees in the garden, but – unbeknown to him – the trees are on a gardener's lorry that promptly drives off. Livesey's look up from his canvas and his understandable expression of puzzlement is a picture in itself. This gag is returned to throughout the film – everything The Artist tries to paint is seemingly a temporary feature of the garden that no sooner has he committed it to canvas, instantly vanishes. The obsessive knitter constructs a gigantic white jumper that, when she tries it on, turns the maid into a temporary ghost; later, the same dotty Aunt picks up a croquet ball and pops it onto her lap thinking it's a ball of wool.

An example of Barker's ingenious interlacing of gags – setting them up then cutting away to another set-up – is a simple shot of a ball of wool seen getting progressively closer to a door. We do not know what it signifies, yet instead of pursuing the joke to its conclusion, Barker cuts away to The Artist painting yet another fir-tree. Again he does not develop The Artist's joke but sidesteps from it back to the wool. Back again to the tree, which we now see is being cut down. Back to the wool, which we now see is getting closer and closer to the door of a WC. Then back to The Artist in the garden putting the final touches to his fir-tree, only to look up and see an empty space where it stood. This clever interweaving occurs throughout the film, supplying ingenious forward propulsion.

As its title might suggest, *Futtock's End* is of its time – it contains its requisite share of sex-comedy that today's *weltanschauung* disdains with a knowing shake of the head. In short, there is a predictable amount of male leering. Even the animals leer – a cow performs a double-take when spotting a girl undressing to go for a swim. Futtock himself, however, is not a voyeur: a result, perhaps, of Barker keeping one wise eye on his developing stature as a BBC family entertainer.

As in Sellers' *The Party* there is a dichotomy between the sobriety of the older generation and the gay abandon of the younger: hearing pop music blaring from the kitchens, the gimlet-eyed Butler pauses outside the door. The two servants inside are dancing – and we establish their gyrations. The Butler quickly snaps open the door, and the two dancing servants are suddenly going about their monotonous business, polishing cutlery. He closes the door, and they resume their dancing. There is a neat twist however, as he keeps opening and closing the door, resulting in the guilty parties getting completely mixed up – dancing when the door's open, polishing when it's closed.

The arc of the film follows the arc of nature: we first see *Futtock's End* in early morning as dawn breaks over the lush meadowlands of the estate, and at the end of the picture we say farewell to it as night falls. Each character's subtle escalating story comes naturally to a gentle end: The Twit finds true love, the Japanese visitor finally manages to escape after a weekend of creeping round the manor and grounds as if he's been immured in Colditz – and even Futtock himself finds happiness in the form of The Bird who stays behind with him after seeing her beau, The

Boots (Richard O'Sullivan) betray her by dancing with the maid. They do not fall into each other's arms though, or close the bedroom door with a wink as Benny Hill might have done: Ronnie Barker has them charmingly playing a game of croquet together over the closing credits.

The film was a resounding success with TV viewers. Between the making of *Futtock's End* and its follow-up, *The Picnic*, Barker became a household name. *The Two Ronnies* went into production in 1971, and established both Barker and Corbett as two of the best-loved comic performers on the small screen. But Barker's appetite for making a purely visual comedy had not yet been assuaged, and in 1975 filming began on *The Picnic.* Once again written solely by Barker (under the pseudonyms Dave Huggett and Larry Keith), *The Picnic* features his new co-star, Ronnie Corbett.

*

Stripped back to thirty minutes, *The Picnic* is oddly less pacy than *Futtock's End*, but like the earlier film it hits the ground running with gags: the very opening shot is a cockerel crowing, followed by a gunshot, followed by a milkman delivering bottles of champagne in a crate, which Futtock then pours over his cereal. Once again the film is replete with Barker's favourite type of gag – the misunderstanding joke. This is one of the perennial comic devices for a visual piece, based on supplying information to the audience to which characters in the film are not privy. One can choose whether or not to supply that information to the audience: sometimes Tati supplies, sometimes he doesn't. An example of not supplying it is the kicking joke in *M Hulot's Holiday.* Spotting a stout man bending down and ostensibly spying on a girl through a knot-hole in her beach-hut, an indignant Hulot delivers a swift kick to the offender's backside, only to immediately realise that the man was in fact merely stooping to focus a camera in preparation for a family portrait. Barker more often than not chooses to withhold all information from the characters: at a roadside inn, The Son (Ronnie Corbett) feeds a dog under the table, who then wags his tail suggestively on a girl's leg. Thinking The Son is playing footsie she darts him an admonishing look, while he gives her a surreptitious collaborative shush – meaning, of course, 'don't tell anyone I've fed the dog.' Her indignation is multiplied by misinterpreting the shushing as a plea for complicity.

Further misunderstandings unfold: in the same scene The Naughty Schoolboy character fires a pea-shooter at the rear of a pretty girl; she swivels round to see General Futtock who just happens at that very second to be practising his penny whistle. A little later, back on the road, the motorcycling butler (not Michael Hordern this time) thinks he's collided with someone, so peers over a hedge and spots a couple sprawled in the long grass of a meadow. Immediately assuming they are his victims, he vaults the fence and crawls up to them. They are of course a courting couple, who in turn think he's nothing but a peeping tom. Another misunderstanding occurs when The Son gets out of the car to relieve himself. The owner of the house happens to be watering his garden with a hose, and the occupants of the car gaze wide-eyed as a jet of water soars into the air above the hedgerow like a geyser.

Again Barker interlaces gags rather than presenting them on a plate one after the other: two or three set-ups intercut with each other, then the tags come. A gentle meandering tale unfolds of a simple family day out in the country; Barbara New as the dotty knitting Aunt, Madge Hindle as The Companion, and Julie Crosthwaite as The Girlfriend, the young love interest for The Son who wears a striped blazer and plus-fours.

As with *Futtock's End*, *The Picnic* is circular, the close of the film echoing the opening as night falls across the manor and the annoying cockerel is shot off its perch. In between, *The Picnic* is stuffed full of with seaside postcard gags – a girl slips off her red shorts because they are enraging a bull, only for her to then excite the interest of a young farmer who promptly chases her with the sound effects of a bull groaning; The Son tosses an unwanted kipper into a lake where it is promptly caught by an angler.

Between his second 'silent' film and his third, Barker's stardom and stature was enhanced further with his appearance in the sitcom *Porridge.* There was seemingly no showbiz territory Barker could not conquer. Yet despite being the nation's finest exponent of both sitcom and sketch-show, still he returned to visual comedy as his first love, in 1982 producing arguably his finest work in that genre, *By the Sea.* Once again he cast his now-regular comedy partner, Ronnie Corbett. In a conversation with the author, Corbett expressed his utter admiration for Barker; 'I just learned so much from watching him,' he told me. 'For years I just watched him, and learned. We fell together so well, and it took off.'

*

Barker wanted *By the Sea* to be a feature film. 'It's a harder film than The Picnic and Futtock's End,' Barker recalled. 'Futtock's End was very moody, but this was a harder, glossier version of both of those earlier ones. By the Sea was much longer, it originally ran to an hour and twenty-five

Having mastered both the sketch-show and the sitcom, Ronnie Barker also went on to master the 'sound effect' comedy. Here, with Ronnie Corbett, he advertises his all-visual masterpiece, By the Sea *(1982).*

minutes. I crossed swords with Jimmy Gilbert (the Producer); he cut it to 55 minutes and I said it's just about ok, I suppose. Then he said I think Im going to cut it to 35. I said if you do that I'm out of here. That's murder, Jimmy, that's not cutting, that's murdering it. He left it at 55.' (quoted in McCabe, ibid).

There is much more of a *cinéma-verité* feel to the *By the Sea* than the previous two silents, with languorous opening shots of a seaside town stirring in the morning mist, waves crashing on the shore as in *M Hulot's Holiday*; shop canopies are unrolled, milk delivered. Then suddenly, as with the opening of Tati's film, there is a blunt cut to a noisy steam train entering a station. All modern visual comedy, it would appear, leads back to the Frenchman.

By the Sea was filmed in Bournemouth and used real holidaymakers, but once again the characters Barker pitches into this world are definitely 1930s – unlike everyone else around them, they carry old brown cardboard suitcases, and wear striped blazers and straw boaters. Whereas in *Futtock's End* and *The Picnic* the protagonists lived in a world sealed off from the rest of humanity, those in *By the Sea* are pitched firmly into the real world. Interspersed with the jaunty bonhomie and escapades of Barker's motley collection of comic types are shots of people going about their slow, mundane holiday activities.

Barker's decision to toss his characters into the real world marks them out as misfits, punches up their anachronistic oddness, and deepens the comedy. It is as if they are time-travellers beamed from the 1930s to the present – they even drive a pre-war Bentley, parking it outside the hotel amongst the 1980s Cortinas. The jaunty soundtrack from Ronnie Hazelhurst heightens this contrast, the happy big-band jazz melodies supplying the characters with old-time signature tunes. When we see the comic characters, the film is speeded-up, in imitation of the under-cranked style of the vintage silent: in contrast, the shots of real people and their environment is slow and documentary-like.

Another big discernible difference between *The Picnic* and *By the Sea* is that in the later film Ronnie Corbett is allowed to shine far more brightly. Corbett has a confidence, a swagger and an insouciance that is lacking in the earlier piece – a charisma that probably derives from his intervening rise in fame via his work in *The Two Ronnies.*

From the very start Corbett's character and business as The Son is sharp and defined. He has a beautiful opening routine. Settling into his room, he enjoys the lovely view out of his window, a vista of meadow, beach and seascape – only for it all to vanish seconds later as it is revealed to be an advert on the side of a lorry that starts up and moves off, revealing a grim brick wall. He performs an hilarious routine in the hall while waiting for the bathroom, accidentally breaking the arm of a chair. Not finding anywhere to hide it, his solution is to break off the other arm to make it symmetrical, a solution reminiscent of Hulot snipping away at his sister's vine in *Mon Oncle.*

The 70s and 80s of course were the swansong of the British Seaside Holiday and Barker mines all the tropes of the experience for comic effect: the weirdness of having to get undressed in what to all intents and purposes is a public place; the suggestiveness of the beach-hut; the modesty; the embarrassment. He focusses particularly on the physical change people undergo when they are on the beach: the heightened awareness of one's body that causes one to act. This, of course, was Tati's strength in

M Hulot's Holiday, driving it home with the stylised performance of the athlete character, whose constant stretching exercises and flexing of muscles become more and more exaggerated until he becomes a cartoon of himself.

We are indeed cartoons of ourselves on the beach: aware of this, Barker gets The Son to emerge from his changing-hut like a pocket Charles Atlas in a one-piece leotard. And like the victim in the old Charles Atlas newspaper ads who get sand kicked in their faces, The Son gets a big beach-ball kicked into his face as a running gag throughout the film. Cracking at last, he snatches the ball and jumps up and down on it angrily: cue the menacing approach of the six-foot muscle-man, an encounter that becomes a continuing feud in the picture, with the hapless Son throwing a bucket of water over the top of a windbreak thinking he is surprising a buxom blonde, but in reality drenching his *bête noir*.

Throughout, Barker as The General is once again a serene Lord Emsworth character, happily seated in the sunshine in full suit and waistcoat, reading his paper and getting bombed by seagulls. Delightful misunderstanding gags once more abound: after a couple of shellings by gulls, The General goes off to throw away the soiled section of paper, leaving the untainted sheets on the sand. Cue the kid with the big ice-cream cornet, who promptly spills his huge dollop of Wall's vanilla on his paper. A slow double-take from The General gets a big laugh from the live audience to which the film was shown – whose laughter was recorded for TV broadcast – and a stare up into the sky to try and locate the giant gull, gets another. A classic mosquito-swatting routine gets the Barker treatment in a fine escalating choreography of mutual slapping between him, The Companion (Madge Hindle) and The Girl-Friend (Debbi Blythe). And once again Barker is not averse to peppering his work with the surreal: a slender woman inflates a lilo and in so doing inflates herself: we cut back to her three times as she grows to a large sphere, and on her final puff she blows up. As with Tati's jokes, this is observed not merely by the audience but by a character within the film, which heightens its believability.

Episodic and simple of plot though it may be, *By the Sea* nevertheless adheres to the three-act structure of most orthodox feature films, with the second act opening back at the hotel and the scene set for a comedy dinner. Once again the hotel dining-room, like the beach, is an arena where human beings perform; it is, essence, a theatre where waiters stand like proud soldiers, where diners affect pleasantries with their neighbours: everything that unsettles that lack of authentic, natural behaviour is an engine of comedy. So the maid lets rip an almighty sneeze that blows away all the nicely laid arrangements on the tables – a sign of things to come.

The gags come thick and fast – the pianist finishing with a flourish then immediately swivelling round to tuck into his dinner; the sneezing maid blowing her nose on a lettuce leaf then getting covered in spots of soup, causing the diners to think she has measles. But once again it is Ronnie Corbett as The Son who steals the scene, popping up from behind an unfeasibly gigantic menu to spy on the girl he fancies, creeping round the table.

The third act begins on the pier and once again we are in a seaside holiday of the imagination: 'We had those cut-outs you put your head through,' Barker told biographer Bob McCabe, 'all out of date things. It was of days gone by, it wasn't modern. It could've been any date.' A woman sticks her face through the hole, then after the photograph is taken reveals herself identical to the picture of the massive woman in polka-dotted swimsuit. The Brat runs amok in true *Beano* fashion, giving everyone black eyes with trick paint smeared round the telescopes and the What the Butler Saw machines, and there are several switch-backs to previous gags including The Son at the Rifle Range swivelling his weapon across and blasting the big beach-ball that's been plaguing him since their arrival. On the golf course, The General and The Son lose the ball in long grass and after fruitless hunting agree to drop one. The General duly throws it over his shoulder – and promptly loses that one as well. The Son concusses more pheasants than he gets holes on the green, and wanders back to the clubhouse with a brace of birds.

With a big slapstick finale involving those perennial tropes of farce – the ladder, the open window, the wrong room – *By the Sea* is a cheerful, lusty British flipside to *Hulot*'s melancholy satires: where Tati is subtle, Barker is broad: but his three silent movies nevertheless represent a slice of uninhibited, unashamed English pantomime.

CHAPTER 19

Diehards IV: Visual Comedy on Stage, Film & TV 1970 to present

From 1970 the mainstream TV sketch show came into its own and – like the sitcom – seemed to reach the heights of its powers. *Monty Python's Flying Circus, Morecambe and Wise, The Two Ronnies, Dave Allen At Large, The Dick Emery Show, Russ Abbot's Madhouse, Milligan's 'Q', The Les Dawson Show, The Benny Hill Show, Not the Nine o'Clock News, A Bit of Fry & Laurie, Absolutely, Harry Enfield & Chums, The Fast Show, The League of Gentlemen, Smack the Pony, Big Train, Little Britain* – all broke new ground in their different ways and cemented the 'broken comedy' TV format as the true heir of variety and music hall. Not all these series contained purely visual jokes, but in most the sight-gag was a staple of at least ten minutes in each half-hour episode. The 'visual quickie' became the mainstay and 'in-fill' of most sketch shows, and is the descendant of course of the variety stage 'blackout' sketch or, going further back, the *intermedii* of the sixteenth century.

Such was the verbal wit of the Pythons that their talent as visual clowns is often underrated, yet their shows were replete with slapstick. Indeed, Michael Palin's favourite Python sketch was the 'Fish-Slapping' routine filmed at the lock just outside Teddington Studios, in which he and John Cleese perform an eccentric dance before Cleese whacks Palin with a huge chub, sending Palin plunging into the murky waters of the lock. Terry Jones paid his own tribute to silent clowning in his 'Changing Trousers' sketch (reminiscent of Laurel & Hardy's attempt to swap trousers in *Liberty*) in which he attempts to change right behind a 'What the Butler saw' machine. A couple approach the machine, put a coin in the slot, and marvel at the realism of what they're seeing – until the woman realises what's happening and in true Benny Hill fashion starts beating Jones with a brolly. More famous, of course, is John Cleese's 'Ministry of Silly Walks', which, though flagged with the ubiquitous Pythonic voice-over, is essentially a pantomime, inspired by Max Wall's eccentric dancing.

Another comic grouping spawned by *At Last the 1948 Show* was Tim Brooke-Taylor and Bill Oddie, who together with Graeme Garden,

Rightly lauded for their verbal wit, arguably some of the Pythons' most iconic material was physical: here in the Ministry of Silly Walks from 1970, John Cleese demonstrates an (acknowledged) debt to 'Max Wall & his Independent Legs.'

created the slapstick-rich *The Goodies*, a highly successful and popular series which ran on BBC prime-time between 1970 and 1980, totalling 67 half-hour episodes plus two Christmas Specials. The trio had been solidified on the 1968 BBC2 series *Broaden Your Mind*, a kind of pre-Python encyclopedia of the airwaves – in fact, the working title of *The Goodies* was *Narrow Your Mind*. All the cast were devotees of silent movie comedy, so the tropes and style of 20s films infused the entire project more and more as the years went by. Very often the dialogue in an episode of *The Goodies* was there simply to set up a purely visual plot, all the comic set-pieces being shot in dumb-show and with speeded-up or 'under-cranked' effect, a style rooting the comedies firmly in the classic silent tradition. Riding their modified tandem – a stroke of 'branding' genius that burned into the minds of a generation of comedy-lovers – the bulk of an episode would consist of location filming, with a plethora of big-budget special effects and large-scale clowning in long-shot. In conversation with the author in December 2014, Tim Brooke-Taylor put the success of the series down to '… preparation, preparation, preparation: our pre-production meetings with the art-designers and production designers were almost more important than the writing of the scripts.'

This preparation certainly paid off: the elaborate production values of *The Goodies* remain, to this day, unequalled, and international success came early, the show winning the coveted Silver Rose of Montreux for

In the 1970s The Goodies brought slapstick to prime-time TV. Here in the episode 'The Movies' Bill Oddie takes us back to their roots in silent film.

The Goodies produced some of the most memorable TV visuals of the 1970s, including their famous 'Kitten Kong' episode, winner of the Silver Rose of Montreux in 1972. Tim Brooke-Taylor's old pal from At Last The 1948 Show *won the Gold – Marty Feldman.*

the 1972 episode 'Kitten Kong' in which the key scene of a cat toppling the Post Office Tower in London has become one of the iconic clips of television history. The team won again, for 'The Movies' (1975) in which each Goody makes the film of their choice, Graeme Garden opting for a Western, Brooke-Taylor for an epic, and Oddie for a black and white silent. Oddie's performance as a silent clown is accomplished, complete with manic jumping and observational gags on the techniques of silent film – memorably when he hangs on the window-sill of a tall building, the camera ostensibly looking down from above, followed by Tim Brooke-Taylor struggling past on the vertical wall while grappling with a lion: Oddie stops hanging, stands up to reveal the building is actually horizontal, then tops the gag by sitting down and falling through the open window. The three 'film-makers' lock horns in a final battle sequence that pitches Garden's cowboys against Brooke-Taylor's robed swordsmen and Oddie's pie-wielding Keystone Kops in an 'Anchorman'-like gang-fight. The final ten minutes is a completely dialogue-free litany of sight-gags – Tim Brooke-Taylor firing his broadsword like a rifle, Garden getting shot by his own men and Oddie seeking refuge in 'The Epics' department, only to be clapped round the head by Moses and his two tablets. The *homage* to the silent greats becomes explicit when Oddie releases Chaplin, Keaton and Laurel & Hardy lookalikes into the fray and they reproduce the iconic Keaton scene of the building falling on top of him; this the team did for real, and arguably in a more dangerous manner than Keaton, for all three Goodies are framed by the toppled window and one can see them edging to hit their protective marks.

The Keaton influence doesn't stop there, for the episode escalates into a series of escalating multiple realities as the Goodies play with the comedy of screen/audience in the same way as Buster did in *Sherlock Jr* (1929) when, as a humble projectionist, he enters the movie he's showing. The Goodies similarly watch themselves in a cinema then enter the movie, swapping and re-swapping until the lines of reality are blurred and destroyed. Plot here is forgotten, and the episode ascends into a joyous stream of visual chaos: Garden stands before a screen showing a lorry thundering towards him – he leaps out of the way just in time as the truck crashes through the screen; and in a joke of scale, Bill Oddie (shown in huge close-up) reaches out of the screen and picks up a tiny Tim Brooke-Taylor, and throws him out of shot like a toy.

During this sequence the studio audience bursts into spontaneous applause several times, and rightly so: moreover, the cheering during the end credits is some of the loudest and most prolonged I have ever heard for a TV comedy. They are cheering the Goodies, to be sure, but they are also cheering the special visual effects team of Len Hutton and Peter Day, film editor Ron Pope, and film cameraman John Tiley. *The Goodies* contains some of the best and sharpest comedy filming and editing of the age.Tim Brooke-Taylor told me that he attributes the success of the show to 'extensive pre-planning. Before each episode we would have long meetings with the art department, to convey what we wanted in each sequence, and they would advise us, so when we came shooting it we all knew exactly what we were trying to achieve.'

From its opening titles – that saw Tim Brooke-Taylor falling into a river dressed as an Edwardian nanny – *The Goodies* announced itself unashamedly as unpretentious slapstick, and perhaps for this reason the series has traditionally been compared unfavourably with the more cerebral *Monty Python.* The truth is that the shows, while deriving from the same Oxbridge stable (the Goodies were all Cambridge alumni) are utterly different, two sides of the same coin. It is as if *The Goodies* is Python having a day off. *The Goodies* is a series without angst, and while satirical, its parodies are always celebratory – with Python one can always sense a hint of dark disapproval and judgement in the send-ups. Cleese's genuine anger at the world is discernible in *Python* whereas *The Goodies* were simply loosening their belts and having a laugh. Another great strength of the series of course was the delineation of their characters – the professorial but likeable Garden, the pompous and snobbish Brooke-Taylor, the raffish and untidy Oddie: they seemed a microcosmic comic representation of the England of the 1970s.

*

Morecambe & Wise were, of course, the finest front-of-cloth comics ever to grace a TV screen, and their most memorable achievements are fourfold – the double-act routines at the tops of their shows (which were of course extensions of the front-cloth act that they'd honed since they were fifteen), the spoof 'plays what I wrote' – parodies of theatrical genres ostensibly written by Ernie and usually involving star guest – the song and dance routines, and the extended sketches set in their apartment.

Each episode was essentially structured as a variety bill, the pair functioning as hosts of their own stage spectacular: mid-point through a show, for example, they would even appear in front of a huge pair of stage curtains – Ernie appearing first, to announce the next sequence, then Eric, whose pummelling of the curtain from behind in his attempt to find the gap would be a running gag. During these mid-way front-of-cloth

Just as Chaplin, Keaton, Laurel and Lloyd all borrowed from each other in the 1920s, so too did later comedians: when Morecambe & Wise needed a visual routine for their 1976 Christmas Special, director Ernest Maxin suggested a reprise of Benny Hill's 'making breakfast to music' mime sequence. That Morecambe & Wise's version is far superior is in no doubt – the piece has become one of their best-loved – but it proves that visual comedy is a huge timeless props-and-costume-box into which comedians can dip and share routines and ideas. A verbal sketch could not so easily have been appropriated.

routines there would be much visual horseplay – Eric appearing with a gigantic ventriloquist's dummy, or pretending he was being throttled by his own concealed hand.

Interspersed with this variety fare were many visual sketches dropped in as punctuation; Eric as an orchestral percussionist whose drum was revealed to be a massive basin full of water – and the famous 'Breakfast Stripper' routine. This sketch, in which Eric and Ernie make their breakfast rhythmically to an underscore of David Rose's 'The Stripper', was choreographed and directed by Ernest Maxin. The comics open the fridge to produce a nightclub spotlight, swing a string of sausages around like a silk stocking, and chop up a grapefruit in time to the percussive thump of the trombones. The piece has gone down as one of the pair's most memorable mimes, yet it is not wholly original: Benny Hill had written and broadcast a similar sketch years before in his 1965 BBC series; and though Hill's version is weaker and under-choreographed, the lineage is clear.

*

A master of the visual sketch in the period 1970-80 was Irish comic Dave Allen, who invariably filled the spaces between his laconic, satirical monologues with fast-moving visual routines that complemented the quiet smoothness of the studio sequences. With a regular supporting cast of character actors Michael Sharvell-Martin, Ronnie Brody and Jacqueline Clarke, the lavishly filmed location sequences often continued the themes and tropes of the monologues, and given Allen's obsession with the social and emotional fall-out of his Catholic upbringing, understandably contained lots of gags about the Church. Funerals were a particular favourite: an actor's coffin trundles through the crematorium curtains only to reappear for an encore; a jack-in-a-box pops up out of a priest's chalice; a racing-driver's coffin zooms out of the church at 80mph; a church statue holding a big stone Bible is bothered by a fly and snaps the book shut on the insect; a man run over by a steam-roller is buried in a completely flat coffin. A magnificent set-piece was the 'Funeral Cortège Race' in which two rival funerals attempt to reach the cemetery first. The sketch builds at a perfect pace, and in what escalates to a car chase to rival the film *Bullitt*, the black-coated figures increasingly resemble Keystone Kops as they hurtle along roads and country lanes.

There was a period in British sketch shows where up to a third of the material was purely visual: here Dave Allen abandons ecclesiastical material for a moment to present a group of workers on their way to work – at a sardine canning factory.

With writers ranging from Allen himself to Michael Bentine and Andy Hamilton, the visual sketches weren't confined to religious themes: a short-sighted hunter fires a gun at a hang-glider thinking it's a pheasant; a man walks along a pavement on his way to work and is joined progressively by several others who walk along very close behind each other – the reveal being that they are all employees at a sardine factory; an old woman picks up her dog-litter in her handbag and then has her bag stolen by two crooks whose theft backfires when they reach inside for the contents; a duck hunter in the reeds blows on a duck 'quacking' simulator, only to find he is stalking a female duck-hunter with an identical whistle. Some of the sketches were surreal: in one he plays a zealous traffic warden who pushes an entire pavement more than a foot away from a parked car so he can administer a ticket; and in another he is pasting up a billboard with the warning'Watch Out, there's a Thief About', illustrated with a silhouette of a crook. The silhouette drops down out of the poster and makes of with Allen's vehicle.

*

Russ Abbot is mainly known as a verbal character comic whose broad cartoon-like creations such as Basildon Bond, Barrett Holmes, Julio Doubleglazius and Jimmy McJimmy, were performed like a manic Dick Emery and became immensely popular with viewers. Between 1980 and 1985 his *Russ Abbot's Madhouse* for LWT attracted audiences of millions. Even though *Madhouse* – like much ITV comedy – was studio-bound, there were some memorable and inventive 'silent' routines, such as the 'Trying to Keep Quiet in a Snooker Match' sketch, a deft mime built around Abbot making intrusive noises every time his opponent (Les Dennis) leans down to make a shot. His 'Cooperman' character – a bizarre hybrid of Superman and comedian Tommy Cooper – while not dialogue-free involved many slapstick tags.

The real Tommy Cooper, in addition to being Eric Sykes' stalwart in *The Plank* and *It's Your Move*, had numerous TV series of his own from 1952 to 1980 from *Cooper's Capers* and *Cooperama* to *Cooper at Large*, all for ITV. Tall and gangly like Jacques Tati, Cooper's stage persona was that of a variety entertainer utterly lacking in finesse yet with a desperation to entertain. It is difficult now to appreciate how radical his act was: suffice it to say that in his early days, just after the war, audiences would sometimes walk out of the theatre because he was 'getting the tricks wrong.' In his subversion of the traditional skilled speciality act Cooper was effectively turning a whole genre of performance on its head: just as Tony Hancock's early stand-up routine was an 'incompetent variety entertainer,' so too was Cooper's onstage character an Everyman who appears to have been pushed before an audience, a bewildered last-minute replacement instructed to perform magic tricks. This was, of course, complete artifice, for Cooper was in reality an accomplished magician. But his 'trying and failing' schtick – the same 'trying and failing' trope that imbued the characters of all the great screen comedians from Chaplin to Wisdom – was a stroke of genius, and endeared him to a generation.

In addition to his visual 'front of cloth' routines such as the 'split personality' act where he was half-sailor half-woman, his shows regularly included extended physical sequences, memorably 'Cooper at Sea' where he attempts to perform his act on the tilting set of a rocking ship; and the restaurant sketch where he vents his anger over a rude customer by withdrawing politely into the kitchen then hurling crockery against the wall and smashing things up in an uncontrollable fury – before gathering himself, straightening his uniform and re-entering the dining area with a fixed smile: it is pure dumb-show. Another sketch where Cooper shows his skills as a pure mime has him as a wealthy gambler in a casino on the Riviera. He enters wearing top hat, cape, and carrying a walking stick. He slowly removes these accoutrements, hands them to the cloakroom attendant, and then crosses to the wheel. He is greeted with huge respect by the croupier – he is clearly a famous millionaire. In a masterly slow burn during which the joke is not pre-figured, Cooper loses all his money, then repeats all his actions from the top of the sketch – slowly and deliberately crosses to the cloakroom, dons his hat, cape and stick, and exits. The tension is remarkable. Where is the tag? It is a brave performer and director to then cut outside to a balcony, where see Cooper suddenly break down in anguished tears, howling and crying.

*

One area of TV where clowning was not only still common, but *de rigueur* was, of course, children's television. *Vision On* was a long-running series aimed at deaf children that ran on the BBC from 1964–1976, which by dint of its raison d'être contained rich strands of soundless comedy that appealed, of course, not just to hearing-impaired audiences but to all children. A mixture of art, craft and comedy, a particular favourite was the 'Prof' character, a white-coated lab technician played by David Cleveland, who would attempt various tasks with slapstick consequences, the segments involving some spectacular specials effects using stop-start motion, matting, double-exposure and speeded-up and slow-motion. Sylvester McCoy was another regular, playing Pepe Epep, whose alter ego lived in the mirror. This was avant-garde surrealism of the ilk of Bunuel and Dali – and all on children's TV. In conversation with the author in 2013 while I was recording an audio *Dr Who* episode with him for the production company Big Finish, McCoy looked back on his years at *Vision On* with fondness: 'That visual stuff was great fun to do,' he recalled. 'There was a lot of freedom then in kids' TV, and a lot of experimentation.'

In the era before the proliferation of TV channels, children's shows commanded huge audiences and exerted a power over a generation that will never again be equalled: perhaps the biggest long-running flagship entertainment series on the BBC for young people was *Crackerjack*. Its cast changed over the years with the exception of the comic actor Peter Glaze, foil to such hosts as Eamonn Andrews, Leslie Crowther and Don Maclean. In the Glaze-Maclean era the pair performed in many silent sketches, directed by Alan Bell (who would go on to direct *Last of the Summer Wine*). Their weekly antics in various jobs – as bell-boys, builders, gardeners etc – prefigured the later longest-running children's TV comedy series *Chucklevision*. With music by Ronnie Hazelhurst, these sketches were effectively one-reeler silent comedies sharply written and directed and with a budget that permitted elaborate stunts of the kind not seen since the 1920s – a huge church bell hoisting Maclean 100 feet into the air, a bunch of balloons carrying him airborne, a circus tent collapsing: this was big slapstick stuff interspersed with close-up character gags mainly revolving around the 'incompetent workmen' theme. Maclean was the slightly hoity-toity of the two, with a dash of airs and graces, while Glaze was well-meaning but bumbling. The usual gallery of British authority figures including policemen and council bosses served as their *bêtes noirs* and there were some clever misunderstanding scenarios – such as an old lady thinking Maclean is being savaged by a circus lion when it is a shop-window dummy; gags with twists such as a woman unfazed by Maclean in a horror mask but screaming in terror when he removes it; a man taking the top can of a huge pyramid of soft drinks and bringing the whole lot down; and the window-cleaners who mount a ladder which then sinks into the ground as they climb, leaving them on the same level as when they started. Once again the hand of Tati is observable in some of the gags – Peter Glaze breaks a vicarage window and pretends it is still fine by polishing the empty space, only to reveal the breakage when he reaches in and brings out a flower for the vicar (a nod to the broken glass door of the restaurant in *Playtime).* The sketches were shot in speeded-up motion and although ostensibly set in the contemporary world contained anachronistic figures such as 1920s gangsters, which planted the shorts in a timeless world of the imagination.

Paul and Barry Elliott come from an extended variety family in Rotherham; their father James (stage-name Gene Patton) worked in Ralph Reader's Gang Show during the war with an eighteen-year old Peter Sellers. Paul and Barry had two elder brothers, Jimmy and Brian, who established themselves as pantomime comedians from 1956 onwards, playing Chinese policemen in *Aladdin*, henchmen in *Goldilocks*, and broker's men in *Cinderella:* in short, they were the Arlecchino and Truffaldino of their era, bumbling but well-meaning comical servants undermining the authority of their social superiors. In essence, their younger brothers Paul and Barry, in becoming The Chuckle Brothers on television, were simply continuing these Commedia dell'arte roles – hapless and anarchic employees whose efforts only complicate matters until they end up having to extricate themselves from situations they themselves have created. Winners of BBC TV talent contest *Opportunity Knocks* in 1967 and the ITV equivalent *New Faces* in 1974, the slapstick brothers were given their own children's series, *Chucklehounds*, in 1985. These were 10-minute silent films produced by Martin Hughes and had a very European, abstract look about them, the brothers playing two dogs living in a highly stylised, pictorial world in which they acted out various comic scenarios, such as attempting to construct a tennis court. The mime is clean, crisp and bold, and prefigures their later work in *Chucklevision.* Even in heavy animal costume the relationship between the two characters is established from the outset, with Paul being the 'Oliver Hardy' superior, and Barry being the put-upon and well-meaning Laurel. The use of music in *Chucklehounds* as a substitute for sound effects and dialogue is exemplary – composed and played by Dave Cooke, each movement has its own musical note, each gesture and expression its sound.

In the 1980s & 90s slapstick blossomed on children's TV in the form of Paul & Barry Elliott – aka The Chuckle Brothers – members of a variety dynasty stretching back to the 1930s.

Highly successful, *Chucklehounds* became *Chucklevision* in 1987 and proved one of the longest-running series on television, coming to an end only in 2009 after 292 episodes. By dint of its sheer longevity, the series forms perhaps the largest repository of traditional slapstick in modern television history. *Chucklevision* contains endless variations of physical

Paul and Barry Patton, aka the Chuckle Brothers, were part of a large family of variety comedians, and like Laurel & Hardy adopted the Zanni persona of bumbling servants – comic characters that extend even further back to Roman times and the comedies of Plautus and Terence. Here in 'Et Tu Chuckle' they revert to their ancient comedic roots and play Romano-British slaves.

routines, both fantastical and realistic: in one episode they would be Roman soldiers or courtiers at the palace of Henry VIII, in another they would be pandas in a zoo. With episodes twenty minutes in length, the series more closely resembles the two-reelers of the old days of silent comedy than any other genre; indeed, most of the writers on *Chucklevision* were aficionados of vintage comedy. As a writer on the last three series between 2006-2009, I saw first-hand the expertise of all involved, from the creative pre-production script stage right through to filming. The series was still produced by Martin Hughes, who by being involved in nearly two hundred episodes had seen and filmed almost every possible comical permutation. It is testimony to the vast range of possibilities for visual comedy that new ideas and new ways of making audiences laugh were still being found more than twenty years after the series began. In conversation with the author, Paul and Barry mentioned to me what they thought was the key to their success: 'The live work,' they said. 'You can't substitute working in front of a live audience: you just get to know what's funny. That's why we do two stage shows a year – our own touring show, and pantomime.'

The *modus operandi* of creating a series of *Chucklevision* is worth mentioning here, because I believe that the key to its success lay in the fact that it was made in a similar way to two-reelers in the silent era. Before a series, three or four writers would sit round a table for several days thrashing out storylines, then each individual writer would go off and write several scripts. The writers – chiefly John Sayle, Rory Clark, and myself, together with the producer Martin Hughes and then Jonathan Brown – would in the early stages be gag men and ideas men, throwing notions into the crucible such as 'ski-lift,' 'Japanese restaurant,' 'Draught excluders looking like snakes,' etc. Then scenarios would be concocted surrounding the central comic idea. The essence of Paul and Barry's physical comedy was escalating complication, in which their solution to a particular problem would make it worse: for example, the loss of a coin down the floorboards leading to the house being demolished, or the loss of a lottery ticket resulting in them breaking into someone's house to rescue it from behind a sofa they'd sold to the owner earlier in the week.

Like the '*Crackerjack* Silents,' *Chucklevision* was warm, unpretentious slapstick for children and became a cult series for a generation; in short, those who enjoyed them as children continued to watch them after they'd grown up. The success of the show signified how children's television – first on the BBC then on its own dedicated channel, CBBC – became the only home of slapstick, for during the 90s and 2000s, 'adult' comedy became decidedly darker, more cynical, more intellectual and more reflective. And brilliantly so, with series like *Human Remains, The Office* and *The Thick of It* offering realistic and brooding observations on modern life. With the *Two Ronnies* and *Dave Allen* gone from mainstream TV, and a proliferation of channels dedicated to specific demographics such the 'youth' station BBC Three, audiences in the twenty years between 1995-2015 became more and more fractured. Visual comedy became side-lined as the darker stuff took over, with the notable exception of Rowan Atkinson's *Mr Bean*, whose story is told in the next chapter, and some of the sketch shows outlined below.

*

One physical comedian who enjoyed notable success on children's television was a circus clown called Charlie Cairoli. Cairoli was born in 1910 in Milan to a French circus family; he settled in Blackpool, England, in 1939 and remained there for the rest of his life, his long career spanning the age of transition from live circus to television. A mainstay of the Blackpool Tower circus for more than forty years, he was a star in the age when TV actively sought out circuses as a regular feature of the schedules; indeed, an expected part of Christmas viewing right up to 1980 would be Chipperfield's Circus or a night at the Tower, Blackpool. A circus version of the Chaplin character, complete with exaggerated black moustache and large bowler hat, Cairoli was rewarded with his own long running series on the BBC, *Right Charlie*, ably assisted by the Keaton-influenced Jimmy Buchanan, the 'Fantastic Frozen-Face Phenomenon.' With simple scenarios such as 'decorating a house' or 'the new car,' the value of *Right Charlie* lies in the fact that it has preserved circus clown routines for future generations.

*

Julian Chagrin, son of film composer Francis Chagrin (*The Colditz Story, The Last Holiday*), was a product of the Jacqus Le Coq school of mime and physical theatre (more extensively examined below). After three years in Paris, Chagrin formed his own mime company and became the highlight of the Edinburgh Festival of 1964 with a purely physical show called *Chaganog*. After touring the world for years and excelling onstage, Chagrin found success on TV and in film; Marty Feldman cast him in his series *Comedy Machine*, and in 1985 Chagrin made his own series of ten 'silent' comedies, *The Orchestra*. Produced for Israeli TV, the series was so successful it was bought by Channel 4 in the UK and was a hit, the episode 'The Dance of the Hours' winning the Golden Rose of Montreux. In a series full of hundreds of firecracker visual gags, all filmed and edited to create a fast-paced half hour, Chagrin mined every single comic possibility from an orchestra scenario – from a fat opera singer being punctured by a stage-dagger and flying round the stage, to a cellist supposedly moving a bow rapidly back and forth but in reality shaking talcum powder over an infant; a military orchestra behaving like a unit in battle, with the trombonist firing at the enemy; a South American orchestra gradually taken over by revolutionaries; and a marvellous sequence set inside a prison where both jailers and jailed turn their everyday activities into a musical medley – a prisoner's cheese-grater becomes a percussive instrument, a convict plays xylophone on a fence, and even the warning blasts of a warder's whistle becomes a rhythmic beat for the routine. Another ingenious episode sees the orchestra in a safari park, in which – one by one – the animals join in with the music, culminating in hippos, camels and flamingos singing a resounding chorus of *Toreador*. Chagrin's series fizzed with ideas, possessed something of Milligan in its zany pace and love for outlandish costumes, and is ripe for rediscovery. Chagrin went on to star in a series of what were to became famous TV commercials for R White's Lemonade, playing the 'Secret Lemonade Drinker,' a role which I had the honour to recreate in the 90s when they revived the idea and made six more commercials, co-starring myself with Ronnie Corbett, Frankie Howerd and others.

*

Whereas it is true that visual comedy began, in the 90s, to be side-lined from mainstream TV, in various sketch shows – while not the dominant genre – sight gags and visual sequences would still pop up with welcome regularity. One series that remained loyal to the staple of visual quickies shot on location, punctuating the studio dialogue material, was John Lloyd's *Not the Nine O'Clock News*, primarily a satirical show that sent up politicians and authority figures – in particular the police – but which also contained many whimsical pieces. Rowan Atkinson is the subject of the next chapter, and indeed it was chiefly his visual skills that quickly became apparent. Memorable sketches include Stephen Fry's first sketch as a professional comedy writer, in which a man who has just washed his hands in a public convenience searches in vain for a method of drying them after discovering the mechanical dryer is broken: he knees another man in the groin and dries his hand on the blasts of warm breath. Just as Dave Allen was obsessed with church and funeral sketches, the *Not the Nine O'Clock News* team were enamoured of the comic possibilities of Gent's toilets, perhaps the most memorable sketch being Rowan Atkinson's punk who, clad in leather from head to foot and festooned with dozens of zip-fasteners all over his body, can't find the one that will undo his flies. Other classic mime sequences include the three one-legged men hopping conspiratorially outside a shoe-shop – then making off with a horde of single shoes from the rack; and the simple but hilarious character piece in which Atkinson strolls along the pavement, spots the camera, and is so taken up with it that he walks straight into a lamp-post.

Kenny Everett was a highly successful radio DJ who was rewarded with his own TV sketch show by Thames Television in 1978. Although Everett always conveyed the impression of being a zany person *pretending* to be a comedian, he and his writers concocted some very popular characters that, coupled with innovative use of contemporary video editing techniques and early computer-generated graphics, ensured a run of several years at ITV before the entire team decamped to the BBC in 1981 to make a further five series. Though the series featured broad stereotypical sketch characters such as punk Sid Snot and big-breasted Hollywood starlet Cupid Stunt, visual sketches were interspersed among the gag-driven monologues, memorably the Spiderman sequence, when – perhaps influenced by Rowan Atkinson's punk in *Not the Nine o'Clock News* – the lycra-clad superhero attempts to use a public convenience, and like Atkinson can't find a way into his costume. Another of Everett's regulars was a mime artist in top hat and black leotard who, in probably some of the earliest use of green-screen in TV comedy shows, would usually 'draw' something that subsequently came to life. Though sparkling in its day, one could never help but infer that Everett was merely a member of that unfunniest of species, the 'wacky' DJ, who simply tried too hard to be funny. In my view his performances were lazy and repetitive, his miming dull and basic, and his acting non-existent: his reputation far exceeded his talent.

In the 80s there were two brave attempts at visual 'sitcoms:' *Bradley* for children's ITV in 1989, starring Paul Bradley, the engine of whose comedy was the peradventures he had with the mischievous reflection of himself in a mirror; and an earlier series for Channel 4, *The Optimist*, starring American actor Enn Reitel. This latter, although a British production and written by Rowan Atkinson's old friend Richard Sparks, was shot in the USA (at least the second series was – the first was shot in London and involved the surreal adventures of Reitel at loose in the two big cities.)

Freddie Starr is a comedian whose anarchic antics have led him ultimately to self-parody and the implosion of his act into a drifting indulgence, but his early performances were sparkling reinventions of a 1930s variety pantomimicry in the style of Jerry Lewis – mimings to music and songs that go wrong, speeding up and slowing down, and eccentric dancing inspired by Max Wall. His TV debut on British TV talent show *Opportunity Knocks* and in particular his appearance on the *Royal Variety Show* of 1970 rocketed him to stardom and top billing, not because of any astounding originality but primarily because the kind of physical clowning at which Starr excelled was such a blast of fresh air on mainstream TV.

*

Scots comic actor Gregor Fisher had road-tested his characters Rab C Nesbitt and the anonymous 'Baldy Man' on the sketch show *Naked Video* for five years between 1986 and 1991 before both were rewarded with their own sitcom spin-offs. It would be fair to say that Nesbitt was to prove more enduring, but it was the unspeaking 'Baldy Man' that presented itself as a serious rival to Rowan Atkinson's *Mr Bean.* Thirteen episodes were made (but twelve shown) over two series between 1995 and 1997, principally written by Colin Gilbert and Niall Clark. Stylistically *The Baldy Man* bears more resemblance to Ronnie Barker's visual comedies than to *Mr Bean*, chiefly in its extensive use of ambient gibberish language, although the series emulates *Bean* in that each episode consists of two extended sketches or stories. The comedy originates largely from the central character's utter lack of self-awareness; stout, shortish, and with a ridiculous comb-over, Baldy Man has an inflated view of himself, his abilities and his appearance – which lends him a touch of Hancock. In the opening episode he is on a quest to improve his self-image through fashion and grooming:

In the wake of Mr Bean's success, ITV commissioned two series of The Baldy Man *from Gregor Fisher and writer Philip Differ, who rebooted Ronnie Barker's 'Grumble & Grunt' style of pantomime with Fisher's loveable loser.*

he buys himself a whole new (ridiculous) wardrobe, and covers himself in self-tanning lotion but doesn't quite have enough to finish the job, leaving the dome of his head pale while the rest of his body is golden brown. In 'DIY & The Reunion' Fisher re-treads *The Plank* territory in tackling the comedy of two workmen attempting to refurbish a house, but there are some great new visual gags in the mix, such as the off-screen cry of his colleague who is clearly falling off a ladder while painting a wall – none of which we see, only the route of his fall in a reveal of the twisting path of mauve paint that curls upwards and downwards across the wall; another visual gag is when Baldy Man spends an inordinate amount of time using an electric jigsaw, with much flurry of sawdust – only to reveal that he's merely been trimming his pencil so it can fit behind his ear.

*

In 1994, stand-up comedian Harry Hill, whose rise on the circuit was meteoric owing to his originality (unlike most of his peers of the 'new wave' Hill adopted a costume and a zany persona rather than present himself as himself to the audience which was – and is – the norm), was given his first TV series by BBC 2. Hill was a comedian of the old school, larger than life, a joke-smith in spectacles, ill-fitting suit and platform shoes: here was not so much a Ben Elton, but a Ken Dodd or a Will Hay

One of the finest proponents of modern slapstick is comedian Harry Hill, who after conquering the world of stand-up with his original brand of zany English whimsy made a series of silent shorts for BBC2, Fruit Fancies *(1994) an admixture of high-octane fun and surreal abstract comedy. Having won the hearts of millions as 'Mr. Saturday Night' in* Harry Hill's TV Burp *his first big screen outing –* Harry Hill the Movie *(2014) – was a Fruit Fancy writ large, an extraordinary cavalcade of visual humour peppered with stunts that Buster Keaton would have admired, and proof that Hill is producing work unlike any other British comedian. Here he comes out worse in a dramatic motability scooter race with his ubiquitous Nana, played by Julie Walters.*

or a Max Miller. Whilst founded on jokes and one-liners, his act was visual from the start, and in its first two or three years grew more surreal, with gags becoming interspersed with wild streams of consciousness. One could say that his visual persona constituted a fusion of Harry Worth, Ronnie Corbett and Max Miller, yet the combination proved far greater than its parts: unlike those comedians – and indeed most 'gag' comedians apart from comics like Les Dawson – Hill constructed a 'back-story' for his onstage character, with a 'Nana' and a girlfriend, 'Jean,' and wove his jokes into an expanding fabric of narrative that gradually included a brother, 'Little Alan.'

Intriguingly for a comic of such verbal dexterity and originality, Hill's first foray into TV was a series of silent films. And yet, in truth, it wasn't so unexpected – in the 90s I had supported Hill with an impressionist act quite a few times and on long drives to gigs had learned of his admiration for comics like Laurel & Hardy – like me he knew the routines off by heart.

Harry Hill's Fruit Fancies was a bold return to clever, surreal slapstick, going out on BBC2 at 10.20pm, and bearing more resemblance to the *Telegoons* or *Marty Feldman* than the broader traditions of Eric Sykes and Ronnie Barker. Six ten-minute episodes of *Fruit Fancies* were made in 1994, all shot in black and white, the plots of which were wonderfully bizarre recipes for the kind abstract 'idea' comedy so beloved of Milligan. In one memorable episode the puppet performances of a Punch and Judy man are then mirrored precisely in his own life: he has a hook nose and an aggressive character, and releases his latent violence throughout the coastal town, battering passers-by with his big stick, running people over, throwing babies out of prams. In short, he's a lunatic. He enters a butcher's shop and runs off with a string of sausages. He fights non-stop with his wife Judy, and they engage in a well-shot routine where their battle begins to resemble a kung fu film, as they wield their sticks like samurai swords.

High-octane and zany, *Fruit Fancies* is packed with original visual gags, including a new take on the 'workmen crossing the road with a pane of glass' routine. On his way to the beach, Harry and his family drive their car between two delivery men who 'think' they are carrying a large window – then, after the car skims though the empty space, realise of course that there is nothing there. In another episode he stops at a flower seller hawking buckets of daffodils – in the next scene we see that instead of buying a spray of blooms for his girlfriend, he's bought the bucket. In 'Beached' Harry takes his extended fictional family off to the seaside, including chain-smoking youngster Little Alan (Matt Bradstock), wife (Brenda Gilhooly), and wheelchair-bound Nana, whom they tow behind the car after packing everything but the kitchen sink –which Harry considers taking but then throws offscreen. From the perennial comedy environment of the beach, Hill gleans many original gags and routines, including the loss of his wig which is blown off by the wind and lands in a pile of seaweed; a lengthy search ensues during which Harry tries on various permutations of seaweed as hairpieces.

*

The following year – 1995 – fellow stand-up comedian Jim Tavare made his own series of silent shorts for BBC 2, entitled *Jim Tavare Pictures Presents.* An accomplished musician and actor, Tavare trained at the Royal Academy of Dramatic Art then launched himself as a comic on the circuit in the late 1980s around the same time as Harry Hill, building his successful act round his relationship with his double-bass. His silent film series extended this relationship and the plots mainly concerned the anthropomorphising of the instrument: for example, in one episode, 'Lost Love', his bass carries on a romantic affair with another bass. In contrast with Hill's consciously home-made, ramshackle ambience, Tavare's films were produced and shot in a very polished stylised manner; directed by Ian Emes and produced by Sarah Smith (who later went on to produce *League of Gentlemen*), they were filmed in colour and successfully created their own distinct world – Tavare lives in a bizarre futuristic tower-block not unlike a building out of Terry Gilliam's *Brazil.* Like Hill's *Fruit Fancies, Jim Tavare Pictures Presents* represents an innovative attempt to reinvent

Fifty years after the Three Stooges and Abbott and Costello had stopped hitting each other, Reeves & Mortimer get huge laughs from a mainstream BBC audience in the 1990s by walloping the living daylights out of each other with a frying pan. Post-modern? Comic violence is perennially funny, it appears, whether ironic or not.

the silent short, and formed part of that movement in early 90s comedy of a return to the surreal, a movement spearheaded by two comedians whose work, like Hill's and Tavare's, is still as fresh and funny today as it was more than two decades ago.

Vic Reeves and Bob Mortimer exploded onto TV in 1990 on Channel 4, following cult seasons at the Albany Theatre in south London. Whilst predominantly verbal, their act contains comic imagery that veers between the cartoonish and the gothic, with regular *soupçons* of Lear and Carroll. Their characters are visually outlandish, wearing paper bags for masks and bizarre wigs. Their two series of *Vic Reeves Big Night Out* was a studio-bound parody of a light-entertainment show, while their later series for the BBC, *The Smell of Reeves and Mortimer*, balanced the to-camera whimsy with filmed sketches some of which owed stylistic credit to the French surrealism and Dadaism of the 1920s. For example, two men are trapped inside a car between another car and a petrol pump, and spend minutes attempting to open their doors; and in a parody of TV cookery programme *Masterchef* (a show hosted by eccentric American presenter Loyd Grossman and in which contestants competed against each other to create elaborate dishes) Reeves is hoisted into the air clad in a costume of such grotesquerie that one might be forgiven for thinking he had sprung from the pages of Edgar Allan Poe. Visual exaggeration being a keynote of Reeves & Mortimer comedy, the rather prominent forehead of Grossman is focussed on and enlarged to a gigantic dome. This is a new form of TV parody – television cartooning, a sort of kinetic verison of Gerald Scarfe's savage sketches.

*

A more traditional double-act was found in Rik Mayall & Adrian Edmondson, pioneers of the Alternative Comedy movement of the 1980s, who extended their 'Dangerous Brothers' routine in the 1990s in their long-running series *Bottom.* The series, which features Mayall and Edmonsdson as two no-hopers living in a seedy part of Hammersmith, has been described as 'Beckett with laughs,' (the pair were inspired by a production of *Waiting for Godot* they co-starred in in 1990) and took slapstick violence to levels not seen on screen since *The Three Stooges,* their punch-ups having a realism that increased the frisson. When the gasman calls to read their meter, the pair kill him by beating him to death with frying pans. This is Quentin Tarantino with a laughing studio audience, and the three series broadcast on BBC2 were perhaps the greatest repository of slapstick violence in the period 1970-2015, serving

Another comedy double-act of the 1990s who mined the ancient trope of mutually inflicted violence was Rik Mayall and Adrian Edmondson, whose sitcom Bottom *was replete with increasingly imaginative ways of creating pain: umbrellas in the eye, irons in the face, pincers on the tongue. This was Tom & Jerry meets Samuel Beckett, and their fights made Abbott & Costello's altercations seem veritably angelic.*

to introduce the genre to a generation probably completely unaware of Fatty Arbuckle or the Three Stooges.

*

Both *The Baldy Man* and *Mr Bean* were thirty minutes in duration but cannot accurately be described as sitcoms, the episodes of both series being two or three separate scenes stitched together, rather than a cumulative narrative. The difficulty of making a visual half-hour consisting of one continuous story was a feat still challenging writers and performers – indeed, apart from Eric Sykes and Ronnie Barker, no one had really tried it. So when physical comedian Lee Evans recorded his eponymous series *The World of Lee Evans* in 1995 for Channel 4, he too eschewed a full-length single story, plumping for two fifteen-minute sequences.

Essex-born Evans had developed a predominantly visual act on the 'alternative comedy' circuit since the later 1980s, and despite his originality had by no means been an overnight success. Indeed, I recall some of Lee's early performances at the Comedy Store being met with distinct puzzlement mingled with outright hostility, along with the occasional raucous heckle along the lines of *'can't you speak, mate?'* Evans emerged from a tradition quite distinct from that of the new wave, having cut his teeth on the northern working men's club circuit in the wake of his

Lee Evans' initial incarnation was as a primarily visual 'pantomimist' in the Jerry Lewis and Norman Wisdom mould. Channel 4's The World of Lee Evans, *filmed in 2006, was his last effort at dialogue-free TV comedy, before he focussed exclusively on his career as a largely verbal stadium-comic.*

entertainer father. His act – seen by many punters as starkly new – was in fact a revival of the kind of 'pantomimicry' that Jerry Lewis had been performing on the Borscht Belt way back in the 1930s. He was a variety entertainer of the old school, a little akin to Jim Tavare. Evans would mime to records such as Queen's *Bohemian Rhapsody*; his body would deflate and he'd pump himself up; he'd stalk the stage with his gangly limbs; and to the accompaniment of vocal sound effects would become stuck in a swamp. Inevitably he was compared to Norman Wisdom, and indeed his persona bore some hallmarks of the brow-beaten, put-upon 'little man,' whose comical face expressed wide-eyed bewilderment and an eagerness to please. But his uncontrollable limbs and his wild gesticulation are more like Jerry Lewis: this is a man whose own body is his comic foil, his enemy. Television recognised his originality and he was given his own series of four half-hour shows produced by Granada; bravely (or perhaps shrewdly, noting the success of Rowan Atkinson's *Mr Bean*, Evans chose an all-visual format sprinkled with verbal additions such as radio voice-overs, spoken gramophone records etc.

In addition to the broader slapstick there are some ingenious sequences in *The World of Lee Evans*. In the episode 'One Late Night' Evans prepares a car for delivery to London; not only are his preparations synchronised to a musical soundtrack but are also echoed by another character's movements – a prisoner in a cell (Sean Lock) – with whose actions Evans' pantomime is intercut. It is rhythmic routines and montages such as these that stand out in the series and elevate it from traditional slapstick into something experimental.

Despite being nominated for a BAFTA, only four episodes of *The World of Lee Evans* were filmed, the series coming and going in 1995. Henceforth Evans, regrettably, lessened the visual element of his act and reinvented himself as an orthodox rapid-fire stand-up of the ilk of Max Miller.

*

An intriguing double-act from Australia, Lano & Woodley, first came to public attention when they snatched the Perrier Award from under Harry Hill's nose at the Edinburgh festival in 1994. Formed in 1987, the pair brought physical clowning of the kind that had once been the staple of international cabaret to the new 'alternative comedy' audience. They made a spin-off TV series for Australian Television between 1997 and 1999, but – like their stage act – it became overly reliant on dialogue. Their silent routines in my view were their best work, but they increasingly became few and far between; highlights included their 'Dancing Sleeping Bags' routine, in which the pair join a chorus line of high-kicking dancers clad in sleeping bags. But once again, either through lack of courage or the desire to reach a wider audience, they stuck firmly to cross-talk, and despite several successful stage tours, dissolved the partnership in 2006. Another Australian, solicitor-turned-comedian Shaun Micallef, reinvented Ernie Kovacs' tilted room routine on many occasions in his shows *Full Frontal* and *The Shaun Micallef Programme*, with multiple variations including the drunken husband arriving home, the dinner party host going down to a wine cellar, and the more orthodox 'presenter to camera.' In each case, as with Kovacs' sketches, the entire scene takes place in a completely tilted set, with the camera shooting it as if it is level – a technique that never fails to be effective. The most impressive of these routines is Micallef's tap-dancer over the closing credits of his show, complete with dancing up the wall.

While there has never in the history of television been an all-visual sketch show (as distinct from *Baldy Man* or *Mr Bean* which consist of extended scenes rather than sketches) several TV sketch shows in the 1990s and beyond contained memorable silent items. *Absolutely*, airing on Channel 4 between 1989 and 1993, had in its team a fine physical performer in John Sparkes, whose eccentric dancing to the tune of *Greensleeves* was a memorable visual item in what was predominantly a verbal character show. Perhaps the most innovative sketch show of the 1990s was *The Fast Show*, starring Paul Whitehouse, Charlie Higson et al, and airing on BBC2 between 1994 and 2000. *The Fast Show* has garnered the reputation for stripping back the comedy sketch to its bare essentials, living up to its title by being interfilled with items no more than ten seconds in duration – but this is largely a mis-memory: certainly the show contained more than the usual quota of quickies, but the most memorable sketches – and the funniest – were extended scenes involving regular returning characters, such as 'Ted & Ralph' and 'Swiss Tony', both of which were several minutes' long. Occasional characters such as 'Unlucky Alf' provided intermittent visual comedy, Alf being one of Whitehouse's old codgers who invariably would set off up the street in high spirits on his daily walk, only to have his day ruined by some awful physical disaster such as being electrocuted by a charged doorknob, or spattered with filth from a muck-spreading lorry.

Another series containing memorable visuals was the surreal sketch show *Big Train* from the creators of *Father Ted*, Graham Linehan and Arthur Mathews, a highlight being the fluffy puppet that perambulates along a suburban High Street to the sounds of bossa-nova, and attracts the lascivious attention of many male passers-by, who emit a series of 'phwoars' at the passing marionette in the manner of Robin Askwith ogling a bikini-clad girl in his 1970s *Confessions* films. *League of Gentlemen* (1999-2002) was a masterly character sketch show produced by Sarah Smith and written by and starring Steve Pemberton, Reece Shearsmith and Mark Gatiss, with Jeremy Dyson. Each episode consisted of a day in the life of grisly fantastical northern town Royston Vesey, but interspersed with the extended character scenes were many ingenious sight-gags and runners that would stretch across an entire half hour – such as the young mother pushing her baby's buggy and enlisting the help of a passer-by to lift it up a kerb, a scenario referenced throughout the show with each setting escalating in perilousness and unlikeliness and culminating in a shot of the pair carrying the buggy across a dark swamp-ridden moor. Perhaps the finest sight-gag in the series was a quickie of a large lorry emblazoned with the company name 'Russian Doll Deliveries.' A smaller lorry rolls out of the back of the bigger one, an even smaller one out of the second, and a tiny vehicle out of the third.

*

Smack the Pony was an all-female sketch series that ran on Channel 4 between 1999 and 2002, and contained some spicy visual humour including a 'car-parking' sketch written by Oriane Messina and Fay Rusling, which consists of a locked-off aerial shot of an empty car-park which is then the scene of a lone female driver attempting (and failing) to position her

In the 1990s the visual sketch faded somewhat from the small-screen – an exception being Smack the Pony, *(Channel 4 1999-2003) which contained some memorable dialogue-free material including this 'car-parking' piece.*

vehicle between any of the numerous white lines. The relentless reversing and adjusting was perfectly built and timed to create a cumulative laugh.

*

One of the most successful sitcoms of the 1990s was David Renwick's *One Foot in the Grave*, and contained numerous sight-gags that were often the tags to scenes; the hero, curmudgeonly Victor Meldrew played to perfection by Richard Wilson, ending up in outlandish physical predicaments that were nevertheless believable because of the realism of the writing and the set-ups. For example, in one episode Meldrew finds himself buried up to his neck in the garden with a flowerpot over his head; in another his feet are stuck in blocks of cement; in another a glass tumbler is superglued to his forehead. That Renwick was an admirer of Jacques Tati was evident in the episode entitled 'Rearranging the Dust', in which Meldrew and his wife spend the entire afternoon in a solicitor's waiting-room. In Tati's *Playtime* Hulot waits for a job interview in a stark modernist antechamber of leather seats and clinically white walls, his solitude disturbed by a fellow interviewee who launches into a silent routine of obsessive behaviour – clicking open his briefcase, shuffling papers, freshening his breath, signing documents with a sharp *click!* of a retractable ballpoint, forensically cleaning a speck of mud from the sole of his shoe. Renwick virtually lifts this entire scene action-for-action and gives it to Anthony Sher, who (whether or not he had seen the original) performs it with aplomb.

Another sitcom that made occasional sublime forays into the world of comedy pantomime was the US series *Frasier* – with memorable extended visual sequences such as Niles cooking dinner and Frasier attempting to change his armchair during a psychiatric consulting session. More recently, an entire episode of ex-League of Gentlemen members Steve Pemberton and Reece Shearsmith's series *Inside Number 9* was dialogue-free. The scenario is pure Laurel & Hardy in its simplicity – two crooks break into a posh house and attempt to steal a painting while the owners are home; a clever scenario in which the lead characters of course *mustn't make a noise.*

Although animation is outside the scope of this book, the work of Aardman animation must be mentioned as a major contribution to the genre, given the international reach and Oscar-winning achievements of the five Wallace & Gromit films (four short subjects and one feature-length picture). The adventures of eccentric inventor Wallace and his dog, Gromit, though including delightful dialogue from Wallace – or rather monologue, for his dog is mute – the humour is predominantly visual, and owes much to the classic era of movie slapstick. There is one particular influence that on close inspection is undeniable – and that is the work of Snub Pollard. Pollard was an Australian comedian. As a support for Harold Lloyd at the Hal Roach lot throughout the 1910s, he was given his own series of two-reelers in the 1920s in which he often played an eccentric inventor. In *It's a Gift* (1923) his house is full of crazy inventions, including a tip-up bed that deposits him at his breakfast table on the floor below. As inventor of a 'magnet car,' Pollard simply sits in his vehicle, waits for another larger car to pass him, holds out a giant magnet and is propelled along.

The Wallace & Gromit films are replete with similar wonderful sequences and devices, and introduced a whole new generation of children to the delights of silent comedy. In *The Wrong Trousers* the hand of Keaton can be descried in the climactic model-train chase scene – a scene Buster Keaton would have relished – with Gromit clinging to the front of the locomotive like the great stone-face himself, and rapidly adding sections to the track as the train pelts along. A knowledge of film history imbues the Wallace & Gromit films, which elevates them from mere children's knockabout: horror film tropes are exploited; and sci-fi and even classic films are referenced such as the Powell and Pressburger movie that Park renames *A Matter of Loaf and Death.*

In the realm of film there has perhaps no finer physical performer in the period covered by this chapter than Hong Kong actor, director and producer Jackie Chan. In a career spanning four decades his work

Though only appearing in four short films and, to date, one feature film across almost twenty years, Wallace & Gromit have become the most recognisable and exportable British icons alongside Mr Bean, Harry Potter and James Bond. Mining techniques and gags from the rich history of visual comedy, even the central conceit of Wallace-as-eccentric-inventor owes much to Snub Pollard, whose 'Wacky Professor' series of films in the 1920s made him a household name. Here, both Wallace and Snub Pollard (the latter in It's a Gift *from 1923) wake in the morning and experience a mechanically delivered breakfast.*

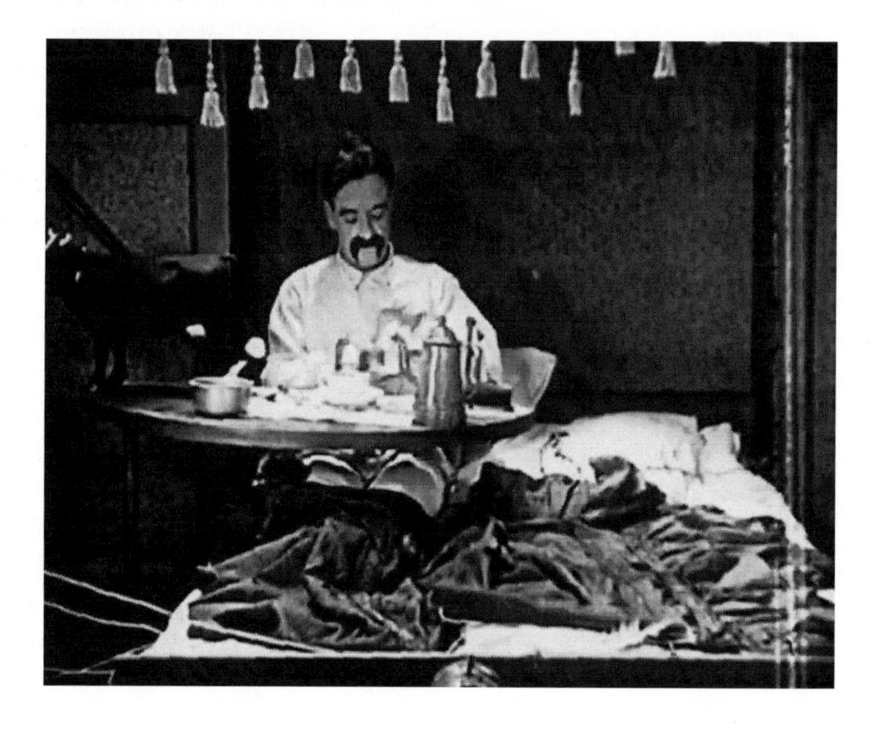

successfully made the transition from pure action movies to a genre he is now perhaps best known for, the action comedy. With a comic timing second to none, his fight sequences in particular owe a huge debt to Chaplin; his characters 'punch up' in that they almost invariably operate from a disadvantaged standpoint, which lends both sympathy and tension to a scene, and his use of the comic slapstick 'tag' in scenes is a trademark. As an acrobat and stuntman he is the modern equivalent to Chaplin and Keaton, and has attained a universality of appeal that has made him a star throughout Asia and the West.

Mel Brooks' *homage* to dialogue-free comedy came with the self-referentially titled *Silent Movie* in 1976. With a cast of comic stalwarts including Gene Wilder, Dom DeLuise, Bernadette Peters and Marty Feldman, (along with cameos from a host of major Hollywood stars of the day), the film is a meta-picture in being a silent film about making a silent film. Packed with sight-gags, there us but a single word spoken throughout the entire movie – 'Non!' uttered with deliberate irony by Marcel Marceau into the telephone as he refuses to take part in Brooks' picture. The film teems with slapstick moments and visual gags including Dom DeLuise performing a Mexican dance on a restaurant table that lowers into the ground beneath his pounding feet; the fizzy drink vending machine that shoots out its products like missiles; the line of a graph that descends off the board and onto the white sofa below. Though most gags in the film are non-linguistic, Brooks was not averse to using intertitles, so that when someone tells his boss that his flies are undone, a caption appears saying *'Whisper whisper whisper,'* the Boss replying 'eh?' and the underling responding with a captioned shout 'YOUR FLIES ARE UNDONE!' Brooks' veneration of silent comedy was rooted in his formative years when he was employed as a scriptwriter for stars such as Jerry Lewis and Sid Caesar – the latter's *Show of Shows* aired on NBC between 1950 and 1954 and contained numerous pantomime sketches (and Brooks cast Caesar as the studio boss in *Silent Movie*).

It has been a bugbear since the advent of the Oscars in the early 1930s that a comedy seldom, if ever, wins Best Picture. For a comedy (of sorts) and, moreover, a silent film, to win in that category in 2012 was, therefore, little short of a miracle. Written and directed by Michel Hazanavicius, *The Artist* tells the story of the career of a silent film star affected by the onset of the talkies. Though one cannot describe *The Artist* as a pure comedy it falls into the same category as many of Chaplin's movies: half-comedy, half-drama. Filmed in the same ratio as the movies of the silent era, and with all the lenses, camera moves and lighting based on films of the 1920s, the film was more drama than comedy, the principal comic highlights deriving from the marvellous rapport between protagonist George Valentin (Jean Dujardin) and his dog – perhaps the most impressive comical use of a dog in a visual comedy since Chaplin's *A Dog's Life* (1918).

Hazanavicius' film has undoubtedly exercised a huge influence on the visual culture of the new century, and demonstrated the potential of silent film to a new generation of film-makers and – perhaps as importantly – commissioners.

*

From 1970 to the present the theatrical tradition of mime comedy underwent a renaissance of sorts. The influence of the French mime schools such as Etienne Decroux's persisted well into the 70s and beyond, and one British disciple of Decroux's corporeal mime who returned to the UK and set up his own school of wordless theatre was Desmond Jones.

The most influential teacher of mime in Britain of the last forty years, Jones had a long and fruitful career as an actor in theatre, TV and comedy with the likes of Peter Cook and the Monty Python team. His mimed Hamlet routine appeared in the first Amnesty International comedy benefit, *Pleasure at Her Majesty's*, and his skill as a physical performer attracted parts in numerous TV series such as *Colditz, The Fenn Street Gang, Doctor in Charge, No Honestly*, and the ITV Norman Wisdom vehicle of 1975-6, *A Little Bit of Wisdom*. In 1979 Jones set up his own school of physical theatre in London. The school lasted from 1979 to 2004, and right from the beginning Jones' aim was to bring the richness of the French tradition to an insular Britain. I met the now-retired Jones at his house in West London in August 2014 and he waxed eloquently about his early days in Paris in the 60s and the profoundly important work he was involved with: 'I studied for two years in Paris with Etienne Decroux and for shorter periods with Jacques Lecoq, so that when I opened my School at the age of 42 I already had a lot under my belt,' he said. 'Although I based my work on Etienne Decroux, I began to forge my own path using everything I knew, all my varied experience, to teach a kind of movement-based theatre that could be used in everything from street theatre to straight theatre.' Jones' influence was wide-ranging: he trained the actors in the films *Greystoke* and *Quest for Fire* and as a major force in bringing styles of performance from the rarefied 'arts theatre' domain into the mainstream, his work is inestimable.

One such company that benefited from the impetus set in motion by Desmond Jones is Théâtre de Complicité. Founded in 1983 by Simon McBurney, Annabel Arden and Marcello Magni, it drew its core inspiration from the school of Jacques Lecoq and achieved rapid popularity. At the 1985 Edinburgh Festival its show *More Bigger Snacks Now* won the Perrier Award for Best Comedy. Further productions achieved more acclaim, including *A Minute Too Late* (1985) and *The Visit* (1989) which won the Olivier Award for Best Actress for Kathryn Hunter.

Individual members of Complicité have gone on to individual careers – Simon McBurney was hired as chief writer for *Mr Bean's Holiday*, and Jos Houben is one of the most acclaimed comic mimes of his generation. In addition to his work with Complicité, Houben was director of the first few shows from physical double act Sean Foley & Hamish McColl, whose The Right Size theatre company flourished between 1988 to 2006, culminating in the two major international stage hits, *The Play What I Wrote* and *Ducktastic*. Houben has starred in his own silent TV comedy series, *Mr Fixit*, for CITV, and more recently has become Professor of Mime at his old school in Paris, Lecoq. His show *The Art of Laughter* is a master-class in physical comedy.

The work of Desmond Jones' School of Mime, of Complicité, and of The Right Size all contributed to the popularising of visual comedy beyond the rarefied realm of the Parisian arts theatres; this was mime invading the mainstream. Indeed, in recent years there has been a crossover from the world of theatrical mime and that of stand-up comedy, a particular champion of this fertilisation being comedian Stewart Lee. Though an intensely intellectual and cerebral stand-up, Lee has always been a student of physical clowning and its tradtions: 'If you look at my first book (*The Perfect Fool*, 2001) or listen to the radio documentaries I made on the history of clowning, you'll see that I am very fond of it,' he told me in July 2014, 'and I've always made extensive reference to Jos Houben's idea that man's basic struggle to stay upright underlines all comedy. And whenever I get asked, for example, to choose picks for the Fringe, I usually flag up Gamrjobat, Derevo, Doctor Brown, etc. I chose Rob Thirtle, the clowning specialist that ENO use for phsyical stuff, to be my assistant director on *Jerry Springer The Opera*.' In answer to my observation (in the introduction to this book) of Lee's criticism of Del Boy's fall in the bar being voted *Britain's Funniest TV Moment*, Lee responds 'Whenever I've been asked about Del Boy falling through the bar, I've always said it is Houben's notion of the struggle to stay upright personified.'

CHAPTER 20

The Alien: Rowan Atkinson

He is that rarest of performers – a genuinely funny mime. Grotesque of face, gangly of limbs, graceful and meticulous of gesture – like Larry Semon, Rowan Atkinson was seemingly lowered into reality from a pre-existing Platonic template for slapstick.

Mime is one thing, *funny* mime is assuredly another: not everyone who dons a leotard and leans against the wind is being funny.

Even Atkinson himself was aware of the unpopular image mime had acquired by the 1970s. At the time he was first starting out as a performer at university, mime – like political theatre – had gained a reputation for what he terms 'worthy of draughty community halls.' The work of Desmond Jones, Jos Houben and Simon McBurney had not yet broken down the barrier of prejudice against the 'silent stage performer,' and even as an established TV success Atkinson would still send up the genre – in *Not the Nine O'Clock News* he played the leotard-wearing leader of silent theatre group *Alternative Car Park* ('My body is my tool.')

But there is mime, and there is mime. To inspire authentic, deep laughter the performer must have funny bones, and these were noticed in Atkinson from a young age. At Oxford, while fellow members of the Revue were staging Python-style fare, the gawky rubber-faced engineering student from Northumberland would be performing pieces of a style and tone not seen since the days of international cabaret in the 1930s. His portrayals of a white-gloved pianist playing the invisible instrument, yawning, checking his watch; a man chasing a spotlight around the stage like a kitten chasing a ball of wool; an orchestral conductor, a drummer, a rock guitarist – all were classic Tati-inspired pieces – but interspersed with these orthodox routines were more experimental Beckettian vignettes, such as the man in pyjamas stumbling around the stage with sticking-up hair, trying without success to give an envelope to the audience.

These early amateur performances blew his fellow performers away, and right from his debut he was identified as a future star; fellow student Doug Lucie described Atkinson's first performance to biographer Bruce Dessau as '... one of the most awesome things I have ever seen ... the others were all doing terribly middle-class stuff about doctors in waiting-rooms, word-play stuff, typical Footlights fare. Then to have someone do something that wasn't wordy, that didn't have a single recognisable word in it … that was an absolute classic.'

Atkinson's fellow student Richard Curtis was equally spellbound, and was soon writing for him, establishing a creative partnership that would last for decades.

It is telling that many of Atkinson's early routines performed at Oxford found their way into his later stage performances, and even into his triumphant revival of silent comedy for the small screen, *Mr Bean.* Many Oxford contemporaries have commented that that they had been witnesses to Mr Bean's routines as students, memorably the changing of the swimming trunks on the beach (with the reveal that the man next to him sitting in a deck chair and wearing dark glasses is in fact blind); the all-over face-shaving routine – and many more.

*

It might be said that Rowan Atkinson has had two careers, spoken and silent. Despite making his first splash as a mime, it was as a verbal comic that he made his first steps towards stardom, initially in radio then in TV sketch shows. Indeed, Atkinson would have to wait ten years before he was able to bring his silent comedy to TV: in the meantime it was confined to the stage in his own West End revues.

In the interim, of course, he became a national star of sketch show and sitcom.

His radio debut was a spoof documentary, *The Atkinson People*, first broadcast in 1979, on BBC Radio 4 and written with Richard Curtis. Thereafter he followed the tried-and-tested route to the ensemble TV sketch show *Not the Nine O'Clock News* and was an instant hit. The show had been a moveable feast, the jigsaw cast at times including Victoria Wood and Chris Langham before producer John Lloyd settled on the team of Mel Smith, Griff Rhys Jones and Pamela Stephenson. While excelling in the series, Atkinson gave the air of being a solo performer slotted into a sketch show, the eccentricity of his performing persona marking him out from the others, who seemed more able to hide in a sketch character. Throughout the series he is larger than life – and was clearly larger than a sketch show. In a nutshell, when performing with others he was a good performer, but on his own, he could be a genius. It was inevitable, then, that he would be given his own starring vehicle, and in 1979 he starred a major new prime-time sitcom, *Blackadder*, written by Richard Curtis and produced by John Lloyd.

Re-lighting the beacon of silent clowning sixty years after the advent of sound, Rowan Atkinson proved the enduring power of visual humour by making Mr Bean the most popular comic character on the planet.

But all the while he was achieving stardom as the snide, amoral Edmund Blackadder in one of the most successful whimsical/historical sitcoms of all time, he was quietly honing his pantomimic skills on stage, in the West End and on Broadway. *The Rowan Atkinson Revue* shows included verbal sketches, but it was the silent routines that were the highlights, and which were laying the foundations for Mr Bean. He and Curtis came up with the 'Cheating at an Exam' sequence that would later become the opening scene of the first Bean episode; but onstage Atkinson was a nine-year old boy sitting a school exam, not a thirty-something nerd at an Adult Education Institute. In another piece Angus Deayton delivered a lecture on 'How to Date', while Atkinson demonstrated the advice through mime and grotesquerie.

In reviewing his stage shows, critics noticed that there seemed to be two types of performer struggling within one Atkinson skin. Was he a verbal wit or a silent clown? The aficionados of course, and old friends from his Oxford days, knew him predominantly as a mime; his success in an orthodox sitcom was partially a red herring. The fact that Atkinson the Mime wasn't yet centre-stage perturbed some people – Benedict Nightingale in *The Times* observed that 'when he spoke he tended to spoil things', and that he 'could have been a master of the silent screen.'. But as Chaplin said, nothing transcends character, and both Atkinson and Curtis knew that a mass-media future for his pantomime depended on the invention of a well-rounded, subtle persona.

As *Blackadder II*, then *Blackadder III*, romped to ever-greater critical and public acclaim, Rowan Atkinson the international silent comedy star became, in effect, unfinished business. He continued to perform mime onstage, honing skills, expanding his repertoire, deepening his character. From a young age Atkinson had acquired the reputation for meticulous, focussed rehearsal – when playing Touchstone in *As You Like It* at Oxford he practised a single walk around a cane 26 times, to get the movement exactly right – so when Richard Eyre cast him in Chekhov's *The Sneeze*, at the Aldwych in 1988, he and Atkinson converted the Russian short story into a masterpiece of finely chiselled dumb-show. Atkinson played a minor bureaucrat, Chervyakov, who finds himself seated behind a bald and dignified minister played by Timothy West. After inadvertently sneezing over the official, Atkinson's efforts at extricating himself from the faux-pas drove the comedy, and stretched his mimetic skills to the limit. Even though the evening contained two other verbal pieces, reviewers singled out the dumb-show as a highlight.

All comedy, they say, is timing, and when the fourth and final series of *Blackadder* was broadcast, the planets of humour aligned and everyone agreed the time was right to develop an all-visual vehicle for its star. Produced by veteran John Howard Davies of *Monty Python* and *Fawlty Towers* fame, and written by Atkinson, Curtis and Ben Elton, the first episode of *Mr Bean* aired on ITV on New Year's Day 1990.

*

Where did Bean come from? From the start Atkinson and Curtis identified him as not of this world – quite literally, as in the opening sequence he is beamed to Earth from outer space. As with every icon of silent comedy, the hero is an outsider, a fish out of water: Mr Bean takes this isolation to another level, in that he literally drops from the sky. Even though the alien motif is clearly a metaphor for otherworldliness, Bean barely occupies the normal world of social reality, living alone in a bedsit and only communicating authentically with toys and inanimate objects. All his interactions with other humans are either selfish or hostile.

Though rarely giving interviews or discussing comedy, Atkinson made a notable exception when he produced a series on comedy for the BBC in 1992: *Funny Business,* in which he wrote and presented the episode on visual comedy. The physical comedian, he said, is an alien: he comes from the other side of the looking glass. In an earlier interview for the *Daily Mirror* in 1991 he had expanded on where Bean came from, virtually confessing that it was him as a child: 'Not only in the sense of his innocence, but also his viciousness ... when things do not go his way.'

This personal exposition of his inner psyche reveals that the creators of Bean had thought long and hard about their protagonist; this was Atkinson the scientist at work, whose approach to comedy was relentlessly forensic. Indeed, he related in another interview that success had not surprised him because it was 'the logical outcome of applied effort' – as if his entire showbiz career had been some kind of school test. Mr Bean as a silent comedy character, therefore, was the result of extensive intellectual pre-planning on the part of its creators, whereas all the vintage silent greats were at pains to emphasise the instinctual origins of their personae.

Bean is a nasty amoral child, ostensibly on an extreme end of the autistic spectrum, who manipulates his way through life without seeking out any human interaction: it's not as if he actively avoids it – he simply demonstrates a complete lack of need for communication. Bean is a gangly Rain Man without, however, showing any signs of being high-functioning.

His neuroses are not completely outside the ken of normal social human beings, however: recognition comedy plays a part. For instance, we identify with him when trying to enter a multi-storey car-park and he can't reach the ticket machine from the driver's seat. When he tries to escape from the same car-park without paying, we want him to succeed: his is the childish semi-criminal urge that we all have and secretly wish we could follow. If Bean can get away with something he will – he is outside Society.

Most of the early episodes were assemblages of three or four scenes or extended sketches, betraying their origins as stage routines. Bean has lunch in the park, goes to the cinema, cheats at an exam, and tries to change his trunks on the beach. The lunch in the park routine, performed as sandwich-eating businessman sits beside him on the bench and observes him in growing puzzlement, is a sublime scene, reminiscent of Stan Laurel but with none of his white magic. Like Laurel, Bean has all sorts of odd items of food stashed away inside his coat, but unlike Laurel there is no surrealism, such as eating a hat or lighting his thumb. Bean rinses a lettuce and shakes it in his sock; slices bread from a loaf; stuns live minnows from a jam-jar and places them carefully inside the sandwich. There are lovely extra touches such as putting the stopper of a hot water bottle in his ear because there's no room on the bench after he's covered it with the detritus of his picnic, and the smashing of peppercorns with the heel of his shoe, pausing, then smashing another one as if it is a live cockroach that's tried to get away.

From the eighth show onwards (Atkinson and Curtis chose to make annual specials rather than a non-stop series) there is more narrative and fewer sketches. The character was allowed to breathe more in an extended plot: instead of small self-contained routines the story began to hold sway, created out of one central situation; so in one episode he goes away for the weekend to a seaside hotel; in another he throws a miserably unsuccessful New Year's Eve Party for two other eccentrics (who at the first opportunity slink out to another party across the hallway); and in another episode he plays a golf game that lasts the entire half-hour.

One of the funniest sight-gags in the series was the final sequence of *Do it Yourself Mr Bean* (1994). It's the morning after his fiasco of his New Year's Eve Party, and the perennially lazy Bean hatches a quick-fire way of decorating his entire flat in one go. He fastens a pot of paint to an indoor firework-bomb, then proceeds to cover with newspaper everything in his apartment that he *doesn't* want painted, even to the extent of wrapping up individual items of fruit.

As he lowers himself behind the kitchen hatchway and prepares to ignite the bomb, one of his guests creeps back into the living-room to fetch his hat. The bomb goes off, the paint is blasted all over the room, Bean emerges from his hiding place – and observes in a marvellously

While the engine of much of the masterly comedy of Mr Bean derived from Atkinson's mime, there were occasional sight-gags that played with image in the style of Tati or Ernie Kovacs. Here Bean has wrapped up his entire room so he can explode a paint-bomb and obtain instant decoration. Post-explosion, he clocks the result of a former party-guest sneaking back to recover his hat.

Tati-esque reveal the silhouette of the man against the wall reaching up to the hat-stand.

In his *Funny Business* documentary, Atkinson breaks down the visual gag into categories: sudden appearances (the reveal); using objects for things other than that for which they have been designed (a sock for a salad-shaker); and using the human body in an unexpected way. Inevitably he mentions Tati, pausing to reflect, 'now there's an artist'.

Tati may have been Atkinson's major influence but it was Marty Feldman to whom he looked for inspiration for show number twelve of the series, *Tee off Mr Bean* (1995) – an episode that opens in a laundrette and finishes on a crazy golf-course. Gags that adhere to Atkinson's list of categories abound in this episode – Bean loads up his washing-machine with odd objects (a lampshade, a doormat and an inflatable toy) all of which emerge from the dryer having shrunk to unfeasibly small sizes, all the polka dots from the lampshade having transferred themselves to the doormat. Sojourning to the Crazy Golf course, he then executes a fine *homage* to Feldman's long-distance golfer routine by pursuing his golf ball all over town; down drains, in a refuse van, into a woman's bag containing eggs. His sociopathy becomes starkly demonstrable in a scene where he smashes the old lady's bag of shopping to smithereens in an effort to locate his ball.

In the following show, *Goodnight Mr Bean,* he is even nastier, blocking the doors of an ambulance with his car, throwing a girl's doll away so he can get ahead of her in the waiting-room queue, grabbing the last vacant seat so an old man has to stand. He then becomes particularly sadistic to an injured woman seated next to him encased in plaster, showing off that he can use his limbs.

If there was any arc in the character of Mr Bean in the five-year life-cycle of his appearances on the small screen (1990-95) it was that this cruel streak became gradually enhanced and exploited more as a source of comedy. In the earlier episodes he was a nerdy alien – in the later episodes, he is a stroppy ten-year-old kid akin to the horrible neighbour in *Toy Story.* In the final (un-transmitted) episode, *Hair by Mr Bean of London,* he pretends to pay to get into a fête, knocks a boys arm playing the buzzing wire game, and generally behaves obnoxiously.

For me, it's his nerdy routines that are the most successful – the bizarre methods concocted to decorate his flat, his neurotic packing in which he cuts everything down to size so that it will all fit in his suitcase, and – one of his finest routines (from *Hair by Mr Bean of London*) when he tries to get past the ticket barrier in a railway station, walking backwards to try and make the ticket collector think he's actually walking forwards, and getting inside a mailbag and crawling along like a caterpillar.
Apart from popping up as Bean on several Comic Relief specials, 1995 was the last TV outing for the character. The series won the Rose d'Or, and sold to 245 territories worldwide, so inevitably movies were in the offing.

*

Bean – the Ultimate Disaster Movie, isn't a wholly visual comedy. It is a dialogue comedy that happens to have Bean in. There are particular challenges involving the transfer of any sitcom character to the feature film, chief of which is that the comedy in a sitcom depends on the character never changing – they exist in a state of absolute stasis and must not ameliorate at all, otherwise the entire comedy vanishes into a black hole – and yet a feature film depends upon a character having an arc, a journey, a learning curve.

The producers of the first Bean movie – Atkinson himself, Richard Curtis and director Mel Smith – solved that dilemma by making the film not so much about Mr Bean himself but the *perception* of Mr Bean via the characters around him. It is their film – it is they who change. The plot incorporates a classic mistaken-identity device (one also happily used by many comedy stalwarts from Will Hay and George Formby to Noman Wisdom). As an incompetent National Gallery warder, he is packed off to the USA to represent the gallery at the unveiling of the portrait of Whistler's Mother. If that part of the plot creaks, then the rest of the movie groans like the ageing hulk of an overused tug-boat. A vastly wealthy American General (are Generals generally multi-millionaires?) played by Burt Reynolds, has bought the painting from the National Gallery, and Bean must speak at the unveiling, for the British have told the Americans that he is the world's leading authority on all things art. Bean is placed with an American family in Los Angeles and wreaks havoc on the house and the marriage, causing a family break-up.

And therein lies the biggest fault-line in this film – the writers and producers called it *Bean: the Ultimate Disaster Movie*, but in so doing are wilfully re-shaping their creation. For Bean was never a disaster-comedy character. He was an oddball who slipped and slid his way through social reality – he was never a Stan Laurel who destroyed things in his path: he never broke furniture, smashed vases, or bumped into people.

That's not to say there aren't some highly amusing elements in the film, one of the most ingenious sequences being Bean pretending to be wheeling a trolley along a narrow corridor (it is actually the Portrait of Whistler's Mother held horizontally and draped in a white tablecloth) and making the sound of the creaking wheels. Ahead of him is someone else wheeling a real trolley. How to get past without giving away that he's nicked a priceless painting? As they approach collision, Bean swiftly diverts the other's gaze upwards, quickly tips the painting vertical – and slips by. Cue the pause of the trolley-pusher, the subtle puzzlement, the double-take. It's a very Marx Brothers moment.

The film was a huge financial success, earning $251 million dollars worldwide from a budget of $18 million. A follow-up beckoned, but there would be a ten-year wait.

*

That the long shadow of Tati should fall across the second movie, *Mr Bean's Holiday*, released in 2007, was perhaps inevitable, given the addition to the creative team of Simon McBurney. Once again the writing team was Atkinson, Richard Curtis and Robin Driscoll, but McBurney, the founder of Théâtre de Complicité, was brought in as story creator and producer, with Steve Bendelack replacing Mel Smith as director. Bendelack (a director whose credits included the hit TV comedy series

All roads lead to Tati, and it is affectionate homage rather than plagiarism that leads Mr Bean's Holiday *(2007) to include bicycle gags akin to Tati's in his 1947 film* Jour de Fête. *Not only does Bean overtake the cycle-racers like François the postman in the earlier film, he also cadges a lift by latching himself onto the back of a lorry.*

League of Gentlemen and *Little Britain*) gave the film a stylish panache and Bean was more at home adrift and footloose in the world rather than crowbarred into the sugary well-trodden confines of an American family. Once again the plot is more about the surrounding characters than the oddball protagonist himself, but *Mr Bean's Holiday* has at least the flavour of a picaresque that worked so well for Tati. Winning a foreign holiday as a prize in a church raffle, Bean sets off across Europe, inadvertently separating a boy from his father, losing his money and belongings, occasionally losing even the boy, hooking up with a young French actress, and after a long cross-country adventure eventually arriving at Cannes to reunite the boy with his father and launch the career of the actress. The arc is therefore Bean's ruining of things – Bean as the engine of catastrophe, then redemptively the solver of the crisis, the healer.

The Bean-Boy relationship that lies at the heart of the film is clearly a nod to *Mon Oncle*, and critics noted more than one direct copying of Tati's gags: in pursuit of a bus-ticket that's been nabbed by a chicken, for example, Bean sets off by bike after a farmer's truck, overtaking a bunch of professional cyclists, just like François in *Jour de Fête* and – like François – hooking himself on to the back of the vehicle.

So yes, there was an invisible and uncredited director on the movie and his name was Tati, but some reviewers – including Ty Burr of the *Boston Globe* – were kind, stating that somewhere, Jacques Tati is smiling. What does not not echo Tati, of course, is the amount of warmth in the film: while there is some emotion in Tati's work (the occasional hints of romance such as the fancy-dress party in *M Hulot's Holiday* where, dressed as a pirate, Hulot dances with the beautiful Martine), sentiment is rationed, the director preferring a cool classical detachment. With *Mr Bean's Holiday* the quotient of feeling is more substantial, and when it isn't blatant in the action it is layered on with Howard Goodall's lush musical score. It is not a comedy score but – not surprisingly for a Richard Curtis film – the soundtrack of a rom-com. And the film climaxes with a typically Curtis ending when, in a beautifully directed piece, Bean – finally glimpsing the goal of his journey, the Mediterranean sea – walks out of the Cannes cinema and across the tops of vehicles that progressively diminish in size, from a juggernaut to a lorry to a truck to a camper-van to a car to a crate – and finally onto the golden sands, where all the characters join him in a heart-melting and smile-inducing chorus of *La Mer*. As if to punch home the fact that the entire film is Atkinson's love-letter to Tati, the closing shot is Bean writing '*FIN*' in the sand with his foot.

Atkinson is no copyist, however: if there is one theme in this book it is that all the great visual comics belong, as it were, to the same family, so similarities of style and trope are inevitable. All visual comics are outsiders, all visual comics are in some ways unworldly, and all visual comics draw on the same cultural reservoir for inspiration. As Atkinson himself said in an interview with talk-show host Michael Parkinson, 'It all just drifted into the subconscious.' Atkinson's biographer Bruce Dessau sums him up very aptly thus:

> Atkinson is a unique talent ... drawing on ancient traditions, often unwittingly. Much has been made of the influence of Jacques Tati and silent comedy on (his) work. But even if his material has a source in this tradition, there is hardly a copyright on it. The idea that any gag is original is unrealistic – if a gag was done in the silent movies it has also probably been done in the theatre since the days of Commedia dell'arte. There are huge similarities between the silent comedy of Ben Turpin, Buster Keaton and Rowan Atkinson. But that is not a case of plagiarism; it is rescuing the art form.

Rescuing the art form indeed. Like Eric Sykes and Ronnie Barker before him, Atkinson had made a series of wholly visual TV shows that proved – by their mainstream success – that pantomime wasn't a form of comedy fit only for retrospectives, but a living, contemporary genre, ripe for reinvention – and not only that, but worthy of worldwide appreciation.

CHAPTER 21

The Human Cartoon: Matt Lucas and **Pompidou**

In the summer of 2010 I was seated in the office of a major television commissioner outlining my plan for a new 'silent' comedy series. 'Silent comedy?' ejaculated the commissioner, 'in the twenty-first century?'

I met his sceptical gaze. I rehearsed the argument that it had been nearly fifteen years since Mr Bean last aired, that there had been a time when most TV comedy sketch series had at least ten minutes of visual comedy in every half-hour episode including *Dave Allen at Large, Marty* and *The Two Ronnies* – as well as the extended visual comedies of Sykes and Barker – and that they had all been on mainstream TV. Moreover, some of the most successful comedies in recent years contained a goodly amount of physical material – Reeves & Mortimer, Harry Hill, *Bottom, Smack the Pony, The Mighty Boosh* and many more. In addition, I concluded, verbal comedy as a genre had made remarkable advances in the last couple of decades – *The Fast Show, The Office, The Royle Family* – yet had visual comedy really progressed that much since Jacques Tati?

After delivering my spiel I sank back in my seat, spent. The head of comedy ruminated, then replied – 'Yes, but Julian, sound was invented in 1927 – *why* don't you want them to speak?'

This is a familiar argument, in response to which I had formulated what I thought was a formidable arsenal of rebuttals, chief of which is that if one removes speech from a script, then the other elements of that comedy will be heightened. Writers have to explore different ways of making people laugh and are forced to become extra-inventive. Because non-dialogue comedy as a genre had been relatively neglected by the mainstream in recent years, then surely that meant there was so much more exciting potential for it?

The head of comedy wasn't convinced. He turned it down. I slunk from his office. I recalled reading something in Michael Caine's memoirs about how he failed numerous auditions in his twenties – and at each rejection, Caine related, a sort of 'click' occurred deep inside his soul, like a gear being changed: far from dispiriting him, each rebuff strengthened his resolve – until one day he was cast in *Zulu*, and his persistence was repaid with stardom. In the following months my project was rejected by three major production companies. My soul did a lot of clicking.

I went back to my job of writing and performing in radio and children's TV and performing an occasional impressionist act in comedy clubs. I'd co-created and written *Scoop* for CBBC, a largely visual show which proved invaluable experience in teaching me precisely what could and could not be filmed, and of course gave me a thorough grounding in story-structure. What I discovered was that while physical humour had faded from mainstream adult TV, it was omnipresent in children's TV. Every episode of (most) young people's programmes contained an abundance of purely physical humour, and moreover, coupled with the length of the series that is usually commissioned for children's television – thirteen episodes per series or more – it is an ideal training ground for anyone attempting to write wholly non-dialogue shows. Working with producers like Martin Hughes and Jonathan Brown, whose knowledge of physical routines is unmatched, any duplication of a gag or idea in a script would be

The author and Matt Lucas on the set of the all-visual 2015 BBC comedy series Pompidou.

immediately spotted, so I found myself forced to create new ideas daily over a period of seven years. Most importantly it made me think visually more or less all the time, and gave me an understanding that the best visual routines contain exactly the same vital ingredients as the best drama – conflict, complication, escalation.

I continued to pitch my own idea of an all-visual series and one Christmas at the annual BBC Comedy Party I bumped into a fellow writer and performer, Paul Putner. Co-star of such shows as *This Morning with Richard Not Judy* and *Little Britain*, Putner was an aficionado of silent comedy, and when I told him I was trying to get a dialogue-free series off the ground he recommended I get in touch with producer Ashley Blaker.

Blaker, a light entertainment producer with a background at BBC Radio, had a reputation for developing original formats, having produced the radio version of *Little Britain* then Matt Lucas' TV series *Rock Profiles*. He immediately saw the potential for the idea, and began championing it with a tenaciousness that is his trademark.

The pitch script landed on the desk of Matt Lucas, an old school friend of Blaker – they had attended Haberdashers Aske at the same time as David Baddiel and Sacha Baron Cohen. Lucas had acquired a reputation as one of the most respected comic performers of his generation: years earlier I came across him when I was performing an impressionist act on the stand-up circuit and he was performing his Sir Bernard Chumley character. I particularly remembered a club in South Hampstead next to the Royal Free Hospital with the salubrious name 'The VD Clinic.' It was an ad hoc club on a Sunday night where new comics would perform in a more or less relaxed atmosphere, try out new material, talk about their ambitions, and chew the fat. It was Harry Hill who had persuaded me to try stand-up, so I went along to the VD Cinic and began developing an act. Vic Reeves, Bob Mortimer and Gerry Sadowitz were regulars. After my third or fourth gig there, a man approached me in the bar. He was bald and smartly dressed, and at first – in the shadows – I thought he was a middle-aged man. He told me how much he'd enjoyed my routine. I gripped his hand in gratitude. As any fledgling comic will tell you, to receive praise and encouragement from anyone when starting out is a fillip worth its weight in gold, and as I observed this intriguing chap – the smooth cheerful oval face, the delightful twinkle in the eyes – I did a mental double-take, for I suddenly realised that he was actually only about nineteen years old. Even at that first meeting I detected in him a steely rod of ambition and determination. He told me he was off to drama school, and when I asked what his aims were he replied, firmly – 'Comedy is my life.'

Indeed it was. It was a phrase I remembered across the years, such was the focus and self-understanding behind it. Lucas went off to Bristol Old Vic Theatre School and on his return to London re-launched his Sir Bernard character onto the comedy stage, including the West End. He was cast in Reeves & Mortimer's hit spoof game-show *Shooting Stars,* and in the ensuing years created a steady flow of TV series with his comedy partner David Walliams, including *Sir Bernard Chumley's Stately Homes,* and *Rock Profiles.* The worldwide smash hit *Little Britain* came in 2003, and the fame of the young man who had been so gracious to a new act a decade earlier in an out-of-the-way comedy club in South Hampstead was assured.

Lucas's performances in *Little Britain* were astonishing: he brought a depth of acting never seen before in a comedy sketch show. This was sketch as theatre, each character possessing a three-dimensionality usually only reserved for a full-length stage-play. The extraordinary success of *Little Britain* was followed up with a to-camera spoof of reality-TV documentaries, *Come Fly With Me* – another innovative series, mining the day-to-day life of a gallery of characters in an airport. Once again, each of Lucas' characters were so rounded they could warrant their own series – the seedy paparazzo, the henpecked husband, the Irish air steward, Precious the plump black coffee-stallholder.

When my all-visual comedy script landed on his desk, Lucas was perhaps at a crossroads in his ambitions: having written and performed in arguably the most successful comedy sketch series since *Monty Python,* like any major artist he was keen to try out something new. He had just set up his own production company, John Stanley Productions, and was beginning to develop projects that he would not only write or perform in, but also make himself.

Our first meeting about the script took place, fittingly, in a room in an old part of BBC Broadcasting House, that wonderful original ocean-liner art deco building in Portland Place now seemingly dominated by the sleek clinical glass and steel twenty-first century extension next door. It was in this building – or rather nearby, in the now-demolished 16 Langham Street – that my comedy career had started, by writing and performing in radio shows in the early 1990s alongside similarly eager young hopefuls as Richard Herring, Stewart Lee, Al Murray, Peter Baynham, Harry Hill and Alistair McGowan; it was here also that *Little Britain* had first been created. Lucas was expansive and enthusiastic about my script and was keen to develop it, but had not yet committed to performing in it. As we chatted we realised we shared a mutual love for the silent greats of the past, and spoke at length of Laurel & Hardy, Chaplin, Tati, Ronnie Barker and Rowan Atkinson – and also how in recent years TV comedy had become so sophisticated, yet at times so dark and cynical, that the notion of a mainstream 'family comedy' had been side-lined. Whereas in years gone by, the likes of Russ Abbott or Ronnie Barker would appeal to an entire family, for a host of reasons (chiefly the proliferation of the number of TV channels) audiences had become fractured, with programme-makers making shows for very precisely targeted viewers, and the 'family comedy show' had all but vanished. In addition, solely visual comedy had not been made for years; despite sight-gags featuring in the top ten *Funniest TV Moments* of all time, no one had attempted a dialogue-free show since 1997. Would it be possible to create a series that not only would be distinct from *Mr Bean*, but would also appeal to a broad range of ages?

It would be risky, but it would be worth a try. By the end of the meeting Lucas had agreed to be in the programme, and I was to co-write the script along with Ashley Blaker, the producer with whom I had developed the show and who had placed it with Lucas.

Over the next few weeks we met in Lucas' London flat in Mayfair and worked on the script. We took it apart, rebuilt it, and took it apart again. The air fizzed with visual ideas. We talked at length of creating an original 'world' for the show, and hit upon something between the colourful 'unreality' of *Mon Oncle* and the timelessness and warmth of Wallace & Gromit. The original script had a 'day in the life of a town' structure, quite reminiscent of Tati in its pursuit of a collection of characters eking out their lives, with progressive complication, comedy consequence and escalating running gags. We agreed that character should be the basis of the comedy, and narrowed it down to being about the people who all lived in the same street. Originally Lucas was intending to play all the characters himself in a kind of Alec Guinness display of versatility, but as the weeks passed and the script progressed we decided that might make the show too sketch-like. So gradually we pared it down, creating a single character around whom the entire comedy would revolve, along with a gallery of minor supporting characters with whom the central figure would come into conflict.

We settled on a perennial, eccentric outsider – the archetype of many silent comedies. Like Chaplin, Keaton, Laurel & Hardy and Tati before him, Lucas' character is a Beckettian clown, a 'gentleman' fallen on hard times in whose drab, mad company we drift as he fills his day confronting the modern world. Lord Pompidou is a poverty-stricken aristocrat who now lives in a caravan in front of his crumbling estate, along with his faithful retainer Hove and trusted hound Marion. These characters are pitched into the real world of survival, but the world of the show would also have an element of the fantastical: thoughts would be animated, characters would swallow birds, a caravan would – Tardis-like – have fifty rooms. We wanted the series to be very different from *Mr Bean* so we aimed to imbue it with a cartoonish style, for however outlandish Bean is, he nevertheless firmly occupies the real world. From the start we also adhered to Chaplin's dictum that 'nothing transcends character' – so tried to make sure gags were not 'grafted on' or 'crowbarred in,' but emanated from Pompidou himself.

After many weeks working on the script, we submitted it to the BBC. At the very most we thought they might commission a pilot programme, or a rewrite, or a further script. I moved on to other projects.

After a few days they rang Matt up. The BBC wanted to commission an entire series of six episodes for BBC1. We were stunned. As far as any of us knew, this was unheard of. Usually a broadcaster will risk making a pilot at most, to minimise loss if the project just can't be made to work.

*

We set to work, and spent a further year writing five more scripts. We were delighted to secure the services of one of the sharpest and successful comedy producers in the country, Charlie Hanson, who guided the series into production in the summer of 2014. I had worked with Charlie for several years on four series of Alistair McGowan's *Big Impression* and as a facilitator of talent he was unmatched.

Pompidou aspires to the tradition of Eric Sykes, Marty Feldman, Norman Wisdom, Ronnie Barker and Rowan Atkinson, but also tries to be its own kind of show. If this book has proved anything, however, it is that all comedy is interconnected and each sight gag possesses a traceable genealogy. So we employed as many templates from the vast aesthetic of visual comedy as we could. We used switch gags (objects behaving like other objects): for example, Pompidou has the ability to make music out of the unlikeliest of things, such as playing a baguette like a flute; the black socks on a rotary washing line resemble musical notes and inspire Pompidou to play a tune on his small Casio keyboard; a pushchair is mistaken for a lawnmower but actually has the ability to cut grass; a chocolate Flake drops into a Sikh's turban and resembles a Wall's 99; a Hell's Angel's long beard falls into the lap of an old lady and melds with the woolly jumper she is knitting; a row of people in the sports section of a department store who block Pompidou's pathway are toppled like skittles when he bowls a ball at them; a tent, blown out of a campsite and along a road, starts behaving like a car to such an extent that it not only stops at traffic lights but signals and turns corners; and in a hospital, the pharmacy is staffed by a jolly old-fashioned sweetshop owner in an apron, who keeps his pills in big glass jars and hands them out to 'customers' in paper bags. There are perspective gags, too, such as Pompidou discovering his lawnmower actually *is* as small as it looks in the distance.

Surrealism, we felt, would supply us with a much-needed contrast with *Mr Bean* and *Futtock's End*, so in *Pompidou* he and his butler go on a budget holiday – inside their own caravan, where they take tourist photographs of their furniture, paddle in the sink, and sleep in a tent erected inside the caravan. Similarly, a shoe-shine machine in a hotel has the effect of grinding people's feet down to fine white powder; and shadows have lives independent of their owners.

Mistaken identity is a valuable engine of visual humour: Pompidou, sunbathing in a park, has a makeshift dog-collar painted on him by a groundsman applying white lines to the edge of a putting green – and from then on is perceived as a vicar. Passing nuns bow respectfully to him, and he's even invited to oversee a wedding – which of course he relishes.

Humans behave like objects: a fat man has a charity badge pinned on him and promptly pops like a balloon; Pompidou accidentally flattens his neighbour with a garden roller, then attempts to post the paper-thin fellow through his letterbox. A man in a hospital waiting-room has a pencil-thin moustache that resembles the hands of the clock right above his head; and as Pompidou stares, the moustache-ends actually start moving in synchronicity with the clock.

The main challenge for us was to construct half-hour storylines, something the writers of *Mr Bean* had chosen to eschew. The key difference between an orthodox verbal sitcom and a visual comedy, of course, is that in the latter a physical event *is* plot: just as Sykes weaves thirty minutes of comedy out of getting his toe stuck in a bath-tap, so we had to create human problems for our central character that would be the launch-pad of the comedy.

As crucibles for stories we mined the perennial Commedia dell'arte tropes of hunger, poverty, and love: there is nothing so funny as the human appetites. So Pompidou is in a constant state of need: he's famished, so tries to catch a bird to eat; he wants to fall in love on Valentine's Day, so to appear younger he dresses up in his teenage gear – platform shoes, flares and ridiculous shoulder-length wig. Each solution to his needs that Pompidou comes up with creates complications that advance the comedy, until the episode, under its own momentum, escalates into chaos – after the climax of which, he's back where he started.

As the creator of some of the greatest comic pantomime onscreen in the last ten years (one need only think of the Lou and Andy routines in *Little Britain* as well as the great visual sketches in that series) Matt Lucas is at the perfect stage to take his place amongst the pantheon of those great international stars. As Shane Allen, Controller of Comedy Commissioning at the BBC said at the time of the series commission, Lucas is one of only '... a handful of performers in the whole world who could pull this off.' Since first germinating our idea, the *zeitgeist* quickly caught up – just a few weeks after an early pitch Armando Iannucci announced that he was planning to make a slapstick picture.

Filming began on *Pompidou* in the summer of 2014. As the trucks rolled in to Wimbledon Studios in south London and began unloading their equipment, we got into costume and waited for the cameras to be set up. A few of us gazed out of a window across the rooftops. Someone mentioned that an old silent film studio had stood only a mile and a half away, towards Crystal Palace. There, a century earlier, long-forgotten performers, with names like John Bunny, Flora Finch and Charles Prince – artistes scarcely-remembered today but stars in their time – had gathered to make a series of *Wiffles* comedies for the growing audience of cinema-goers who would pay a few hard-earned pence to sit in the darkness of a fleapit picture-house and roar with laughter at the silent manic antics of the performers onscreen.

And now, a hundred years later, here we were; another group of people assembling in a similar building not that far from the old silent studio – with the same aim: trying to produce wordless films that would make people laugh. We felt part of a grand tradition.

Things had come full circle. Would it work? It didn't matter. The reward lies in the attempt.

After all, it's only comedy.

ACKNOWLEDGEMENTS

Any attempt to tell the story of a whole comic genre is necessarily a complex historical dance of tracing influence and counter-influence, and as the subject of this book is so vast I have decided to eschew footnotes so as not to interrupt the narrative flow, choosing instead to incorporate all diverting rivulets into the body of the text. The bibliography contains a selection of essential secondary sources for further reading. In addition I must acknowledge the many hundreds of films and TV programmes, theatre programmes and critical reviews which constitute the primary sources for the book. I'd like to thank the staff at the BFI Library and the British Library for being so helpful in tracing items, reviews, articles, films and books.

My thanks also go to all those practitioners, writers and artistes involved in the films, TV series and stage shows whose stories I have told, in particular those I have had conversations or interviews with, including the writers Ray Galton & Alan Simpson, David Nobbs, Peter Baynham, Joel Morris & Jason Hazeley, Ged Parsons, Bill Dare, Rory Clark, Dave Cohen, George Poles, Nico Tatarowicz, Toby Davies; producer Ashley Blaker; researcher Vicky Thomas; actors Liz Fraser, Rufus Jones, Sylvester McCoy and Griff Rhys Jones; comedians Paul Merton, Roy Hudd, Tim Brooke-Taylor, Ronnie Corbett, Paul & Barry Elliott (aka The Chuckle Brothers), Harry Hill, Matt Lucas, Stewart Lee, Alan Francis, Jim Tavare, Mark Hurst, and pioneering mime artist and teacher Desmond Jones.

My thanks also go to TV historians and authors Louis Barfe and Dick Fiddy, and my editor Amanda Field at Chaplin Books.

All the images in this book have been sourced from the public domain. Screen-shots, taken by me, are reproduced for the purposes of critical analysis.

BIBLIOGRAPHY

Adeler, Edwin & Con West, *Remembering Fred Karno: the Life of a Great Showman*, John Long, 1939.

Anobile, Richard J, *The Marx Brothers Scrapbook*, Harper Collins, 1989.

Anthony, Brian & Andy Edmonds, *Smile When the Raindrops Fall: the Story of Charley Chase*, Scarecrow Press, 1998.

Barfe, Louis, *Turned out Nice Again: the Story of British Light Entertainment*, Atlantic Books, 2009.

Barker, Ronnie, *All I Ever Wrote*, Sidgwick & Jackson, 2011.

Barker, Ronnie, *Dancing in the Moonlight: Early Years on the Stage*, Coronet Books, 1994.

Bazin, André, *The Evolution of the Language of the Cinema*, ch. iii, *What is Cinema?* University of California Press; Rev Ed edition, 2004.

Bellos, David, *Jacques Tati, his Life & Art*, Vintage, 2001.

Bergson, Henri, *Le Rire. Essai sur la signification du comique* ('Laughter, an essay on the meaning of the comic') Alcan, 1924.

Berman, Gary, *The Best of the Britcoms: from Fawlty Towers to The Office*, Taylor Publishing, 2011.

Bohn, Thomas W and Richard L Stromgren, *Light and Shadows: A History of Motion Pictures*, Mayfield Publishing, 1975.

Brandreth, Gyles, *The Funniest Man on Earth: the Story of Dan Leno*, Hamish Hamilton, 1977.

Brownlow, Kevin, *The Parade's Gone By*, Secker & Warburg, 1968.

Carpenter, Humphrey, *Spike Milligan*, Hodder, 2011.

Chaffee, Judith, *The Routledge Companion to Commedia dell'arte*, Routledge, 2014.

Chamberlain, Franc, *Jacques Lecoq and the British Theatre*, Routledge, 2001.

Chaplin, Charles, *My Autobiography*, Simon & Schuster, New York, 1964.

Charney M, *Comedy High and Low*, Oxford, Pergamon Press, 1978.

Clayton, Alex, *The Body in Hollywood Slapstick*, MacFarland & Co., 2007.

Dardis, Tom, *Buster Keaton, the Man Who Wouldn't Lie Down*, Unversity of Minnesota Press, 2002.

Decroux, Etienne, *Paroles sur le Mime*, Libraire Théâtrale, 1963.

Dessau, Bruce, *Rowan Atkinson: a Biography*, Gollancz, 2000.

Dessau, Bruce, *Bean There, Done That*, Orion, 1997.

Dickens, Charles, *The Memoirs of Joseph Grimaldi*, Richard Bentley, 1838.

Dondey, Marc, *Jacques Tati*, Ramsay, 1987.

Duval, Gilles & Wemaere Severine, *Integrale Cinéma Restaurée Pierre Etaix*, Capricci Editions, 2013.

Etaix, Pierre & Claude de Calan, *Le Clown et la Savant*, Odile Jacob, 2004.

Frow, Gerald, *Oh Yes It Is: a History of Pantomime*, BBC Books, 1985.
Gilliatt, Penelope, *Jacques Tati*, Woburn Press, 1976.
Harding, James *Jacques Tati: Frame by Frame*, Secker & Warburg, 1984.
Horton, Andrew, *Ernie Kovacs and Early TV Comedy: Nothing in Moderation*, University of Texas Press, 2011.
Keaton, Buster, *My Wonderful World of Slapstick*, De Capo Press, 1988.
Levy, Shawn, *King of Comedy – the Life & Art of Jerry Lewis*, St Martin's Press, 1997.
Lewis, Jerry, *The Total Film-maker*, Random House, 1971.
Lewis, Roger, *The Life & Death of Peter Sellers*, Arrow, 1995.
Lewisohn, Mark, *Funny Peculiar, the True Story of Benny Hill*, Sidgwick & Jackson, 2002.
Lewisohn, Mark, *Radio Times TV Comedy Guide*, BBC, 1998.
Louvish, Simon, *Stan & Ollie, the Roots of Comedy*, Faber & Faber, 2002.
Louvish, Simon, *Monkey Business – the Lives & Legends of the Marx Brothers*, Faber & Faber, 2003.
Maltin, Leonard, *The Great Movie Comedians, from Chaplin to Woody Allen*, Crown Publishers, New York, 1978.
Marx, Harpo, *Harpo Speaks!* Limelight, 2004.
McCabe, Bob & David Jason, *The Authorised Biography of Ronnie Barker*, Andre Deutsch, 2000.
McPherson, Edward, *Buster Keaton – the Tempest in a Flat Hat*, Faber & Faber, 2005.
Meade, Marion, *Cut to the Chase: a Biography of Buster Keaton*, De Capo Press, 1997.
Merton, Paul, *Silent Comedy*, Arrow, 2009.
Montgomery, John, *Comedy Films*, George Allen & Unwin, 1954.
Nepoti, Roberto, *Jacques Tati*, Florence Publications, 1979.
Peacock, Louise, *Slapstick & Comic Performance*, Palgrave MacMillan, 2014.
Peacock, Louise, *Serious Play: Modern Clown Performance*, University of Chicago Press, 2009.
Richards, Jeffrey, *The Golden Age of Pantomime: Slapstick, Spectacle & Subversion in Victorian England*, I B Tauris, 2014.
Rico, Diane, *Kovacsland: a Biography of Ernie Kovacs*, HBJ, 1990.
Robinson, David, *Chaplin, his Life & Art*, Collins, 1985.
Ross, Robert, *Marty Feldman, the Biography of a Comedy Legend*, Titan Books, 2011.
Schilling, B N, *The Comic Spirit*, Wayne State University, 1967.
Scudamore, Pauline, *Spike Milligan, a Biography*, Grafton, 1985.
Skretvedt, Randy, *Laurel and Hardy: the Magic Behind the Movies*, Vintage, 1987.

Sorell, W, *Facets of Comedy*, Grosset & Dunlap, 1972.
Stavacre, Tony, *Slapstick: the Illustrated Story of Knockabout Comedy*, Harper Collins, 1987.
Sykes, Eric, *If I Don't Write it, Nobody Else Will*, Harper, 2006.
Wilmut, Roger, *Kindly Leave the Stage: the Story of Variety 1914-1960*, Methuen, 1985.
Wilmut, Roger, *From Fringe to Flying Circus*, Eyre Methuen, 1980.
Wilmut, Roger, *Didn't you Kill my Mother-in-Law?* Methuen, 1989.
Wisdom, Norman, *Don't Laugh At Me*, Century, 1992.

FILM MAGAZINES & JOURNALS CONSULTED

American Film
Anthologie du Cinéma
Cahiers du Cinéma
Cinema Nuovo
Classic Images
Film Quarterly
Film History
Film International
Filmmaker
Films of the Golden Age
Film Weekly
Journal of British Cinema and Television
Modern Review
Monthly Film Bulletin
MovieMaker
Radio Times
Screening the Past
Sight & Sound
Total Film
TV Times

INDEX OF FILM/TV TITLES

INDEX OF NAMES